Routledge Library Editions

EFFECTS OF MERGERS

ECONOMICS

Routledge Library Editions – Economics

INDUSTRIAL ECONOMICS
In 10 Volumes

I	Monopoly and Restrictive Practices	*Allen*
II	Effects of Mergers	*Cook*
III	Productivity and Economic Incentives	*Davison et al*
IV	An Economic Study of the City of London	*Dunning & Morgan*
V	Industry and the State	*Florence*
VI	The Logic of British and American Industry	*Florence*
VII	The Logic of Industrial Organization	*Florence*
VIII	The British Monopolies Commission	*Rowley*
IX	Studies in Industrial Organization	*Silverman*
X	Mergers and Acquisitions	*Young*

EFFECTS OF MERGERS

Six Studies

P LESLEY COOK

Routledge
Taylor & Francis Group
LONDON AND NEW YORK

First published in 1958

Reprinted in 2003 by
Routledge

2 Park Square, Milton Park, Abingdon, Oxfordshire OX14 4RN

711 Third Avenue, New York, NY 10017

Transferred to Digital Printing 2004

First issued in paperback 2014

Routledge is an imprint of the Taylor & Francis Group, an informa company

British Library Cataloguing in Publication Data
A CIP catalogue record for this book
is available from the British Library

Effects of Mergers

ISBN 978-0-415-31346-9 (hbk)

ISBN 978-0-415-75857-4 (pbk)

Miniset: Industrial Economics

Series: Routledge Library Editions – Economics

CAMBRIDGE STUDIES IN INDUSTRY

EFFECTS OF MERGERS

Six Studies

P. LESLEY COOK

WITH THE COLLABORATION OF

RUTH COHEN

University of Cambridge

Ruskin House

GEORGE ALLEN & UNWIN LTD

MUSEUM STREET LONDON

FIRST PUBLISHED IN 1958

PRINTED IN GREAT BRITAIN
in 10 pt Times Roman by
SIMSON SHAND LTD
LONDON, HERTFORD AND HARLOW

PREFACE

THE preparation and publication of this book has been made possible by a grant under the Conditional Aid Scheme for the use of Counterpart Funds derived from United States Economic Aid. Because of this grant, which enabled Miss Cook to come to Cambridge at this time, we were able to embark on what was originally intended to be a joint production, with both partners writing several case studies and collaborating in the conclusions. I had always expected Miss Cook to complete more case studies than I should myself. As it has turned out, however, I was unable to devote nearly as much time and thought to the study as I had planned. As shown in the Introduction, I have only written one study to Miss Cook's three. These figures, however, give a very exaggerated idea of my contribution to the final product as compared with Miss Cook's. Although the original idea of a book on mergers was mine, it is Miss Cook who evolved and developed most of the general ideas, particularly but not solely in the Introduction and Conclusions, both of which she wrote.

The book, therefore, is infinitely more Miss Cook's than mine. None the less it remains a partnership. We have discussed and argued over each part and usually each paragraph. We have redrafted portions of each other's studies. In the process we hope that each of our prejudices and preconceived ideas on a subject inevitably controversial have been battered down. Responsibility for the final conclusions rests, therefore, both with Miss Cook and myself, with Miss Cook the main contributor.

We should like to record our thanks to Mr George Maxcy and Mr J. E. Vaizey who contributed the Chapters on the motor and brewing industries respectively. They were prepared to give us the benefit of their great knowledge of these two industries in a form which fitted in with the general scheme which Miss Cook had by then evolved.

We should like besides to express our great gratitude to the large number of people who answered our questions, discussed our problems with us, and read and criticized our drafts. They cannot, of course, be held responsible for our findings; and, indeed, we should like to thank them for the way they helped us whether or not they agreed with what we were saying. When so many have helped it is somewhat invidious to single out a few by name.

I should, none the less, like particularly to thank three people who helped me with my study of the soap industry—Mr F. D. Morrell and

Miss K. Oosterveen of Uniliver, and Mr Charles Wilson. Miss Oosterveen provided me with much basic literature and information when I was beginning my study. Mr Morrell read an early draft, corrected many serious misconceptions, threw new light on several important issues, and read and re-read later drafts. My debt to Mr Wilson's *The History of Unilever* will be apparent from the text; but, besides that, I had the enormous benefit of discussions with him.

Newnham College, Cambridge R.L.C.

I wish to record my gratitude to the many people in each of the three industries which I have studied who have given me much help and been lavish with their time and kindness. Industry studies depend very largely upon help from those engaged in the industry and I count myself most fortunate to have received great assistance.

My greatest debt is to Sir Harry Pilkington who not only spent much time telling me of the recent development of the flat-glass industry but also read, corrected and amplified my original draft. I also spent several days at the glass works at St Helens and wish to thank Mr Slade Jones for help and encouragement. My other particular debt is to the work of Dr T. C. Barker who had already written a history of Pilkington Brothers Ltd.

The section on the Calico Printing industry would have been impossible without the generous help of the Calico Printers' Association Ltd. and the Federation of Calico Printers. In this industry a full understanding of the technical and commercial problems is of paramount importance and I am most grateful to the very many people who taught me about the industry. Geoffrey Turnbull's *History of the Calico Printing Industry* proved to be of the greatest value and fully justified the hope of Mr John Turnbull, who edited his brother's book, that the work would be useful to those wishing to study the industry.

My debts to a number of people who are and have been engaged in the cement industry are also very great. There is a good deal of information in this section which has not been made available before and I am indeed grateful to those who have searched their memories and have allowed me to see some of their archives.

Department of Applied Economics P.L.C.
Cambridge

1957

CONTENTS

GENERAL INTRODUCTION

FEW research projects remain unchanged and this is no exception; 'mergers and efficiency' now looks like the first move in an exercise in the free association of ideas. The title suggests examination of the familiar conflict between the increased efficiency arising within the merged firms and the effects of the reduction in competition resulting from the merger. Recognition of this conflict indicates that it would be interesting to examine these changes quantitatively in terms of costs and profits, and that conclusions as to whether or not any merger was in the public interest might be reached by examining the extent to which the cost reductions were passed on to the consumer. With a number of case studies it might then have been possible to formulate generalizations as to the types of industry or types of situation in which mergers tended to give 'good' as opposed to 'bad' results.

This approach was quickly recognized to be quite unrealistic. Mergers are not only the response to a new situation but also it takes a long time for their full effects to be achieved. There are few occasions on which it is useful to compare the situation immediately before the merger with the situation immediately afterwards; such a comparison would only be useful if one could assume not only that in the absence of the merger things would have continued as before, but also that after the merger a new and permanent situation is quickly reached. The first case study undertaken, that of Levers' soap business at home, illustrated clearly the total unreality of any such assumptions.

Attempts to compare the situation before a merger with the situation which developed sometime afterwards are also of little value. Not only is there the complication that even in the absence of the merger the previous situation would have changed, but, in addition, subsequent events cannot be wholly attributed to the merger; further, the temporary, but probably important, effects of the merger cannot be ignored.

As soon as it is recognized that mergers are a reaction to a changing situation the need to consider what might have happened in the absence of mergers becomes apparent. Judgment depends upon comparing the effects of what actually happened with the effects of what might have happened, that is, with hypothetical alternatives. The responsibility of trying to form judgments cannot be shelved and the need to attempt this has played a large part in determining the form of this study of mergers.

The hypothetical alternatives with which actual patterns of development must be compared may be simply the development along existing lines of the previous situation, differing from it to an extent which depends upon the rate of historical change. In many cases, however, the previous situations appear to have been inherently unstable and transitional and one must consider quite different hypothetical alternatives. These alternatives must normally be either the result of definite legal interference, such as the prohibition of mergers, or the result of peculiar historical accidents; one cannot suppose that in any given situation a number of outcomes are possible. Guesses must be made as to how each particular industry would have reacted to alternative stimuli; fortunately only a few of these alternatives are interesting.

Although this work is primarily designed to indicate the role of mergers, the methods and the case studies themselves are well adapted to indicate the role of other forms of structure and organization. In all the industries mergers have been only one among a number of responses to changed situations; in most, some forms of price agreements have been either the actual, or the hypothetical, alternative. In the case of the glass industry mergers have played an insignificant role in the development of the industry and the reasons why an industry of this type, in some ways comparable with the cement industry, should have been so little touched by mergers is in itself of interest as it indicates the conditions which favour that particular alternative development.

The attempt to make judgments as to whether or not particular developments in an industry, in this case mergers, have been in the public interest encounter four major and inherent difficulties. The first is that the construction of alternative hypothetical situations depends upon the assumption that the structure and behaviour of industry is dictated by the circumstances in which it finds itself; in other words, response to incentives must be assumed to be sufficiently systematic and free from unpredictable individual behaviour for one to have some confidence in prediction on this basis. This first difficulty affects the reliability and value of the work but does not affect procedure since no alternative methods are available.

The second difficulty is that the construction of the hypothetical situations depends upon bold individual judgment based upon factors which can neither be measured nor weighted except by such impressions as can be obtained as to 'how the industry works'. Again, this difficulty does not affect procedure as there is no way of avoiding it.

The third difficulty is of a somewhat different order and makes for great complication; it lies in the fact that the results of any situation, either real or hypothetical, are different in the short and in the long period. What has good effects immediately may have bad effects in the long run and vice versa; different effects, lasting for different lengths of time, ought really to be weighed, one against the other. This is generally quite impossible; only if there are one or two features of overriding importance can any judgment be made; in other cases it is not possible to do more than set out the issues involved.

The fourth inherent difficulty relates to the judgment of the effects. Different industrial structures are best suited to different situations; as an industry develops there may be an experimental stage during which it might be good to have many firms competing; this may be followed by a period in which progress can best be made by large firms; after this a stage might follow in which competition would maintain efficiency because it took the form of price competition yet did not involve an undue amount of risk. Changing industries are likely to be best served by changing industrial structures and one can seldom point to a single structure best suited to a particular industry. Largely for this reason attempts to construct an 'ideal structure' for each particular industry had to be abandoned; the construction of an ideal pattern of development is far too hazardous, since it is quite impossible to say that the necessary changes would in fact take place fast enough.

The third and fourth of the difficulties just discussed are usually inextricably mixed in the cases where the more or less permanent solution is inevitable, as, for example, in industries which start with a large number of firms and then become highly concentrated as a result of great economies of scale. In cases of this type the important questions relate both to the speed with which the various industry structures have developed and then been replaced, and to the effects of those structures. Judgment is only possible if the number of alternative patterns of development is limited and reasonable guesses can be made about the timing of the changes in each case.

Enough has now been said to indicate that the study can yield only the broadest, vaguest and most general of conclusions; only the major changes in the structure of industries can be considered and their effects over long periods cannot be assessed with any accuracy. The possible effects of possible or hypothetical alternatives are the only standards by which they can be judged, yet these must be reached by a process of glorified guesswork. We make no apology for this; it is only attempts to answer the right questions that are of any value.

It is the need to be able to study alternatives which has dictated the form of the case studies. In each case it has been necessary to examine the industry in sufficient detail over a number of years (in all cases since before 1900) in order to find out how it has worked and to assess, as far as possible, the major features determining its development. The basic approach is thus historical and descriptive; throughout it has been necessary both to deduce the probable results of known features and to deduce the underlying features from the known results. This two-way reasoning is the only way in which one can discover how an industry works.

There are many unknowns and many, especially those which relate to the characteristics of the industry, are unmeasurable; many actions and reactions must be studied if the number of unknowns is to be reduced sufficiently to allow one to forecast or to contrast the hypothetical alternatives. It is extremely difficult to examine the complicated historical developments, which are the only basis for determining the nature of the industry and its responses, and at the same time make the more detailed theoretical analysis required for the construction of the hypothetical alternatives. For the sake of clarity and in order to distinguish as clearly as possible between fact and fiction, the case studies are almost pure history. Efforts have been made to emphasize the distinction between the underlying and inherent characteristics of the industry and the organizational characteristics which might have been different or which might have been modified by legislative measures. When theoretical conclusions are reached it is necessary to indicate their relevance by restating the characteristics of the situations which have emerged from the historical and descriptive studies. For this reason the theoretical conclusions are mainly brought together at the end of each section.

The number of case studies has been confined to six; limitation to this small number has been necessary because each had to be done in very considerable detail over a long period. There have, however, been many mergers in some of the industries and useful comparisons can be made between the causes and results of the different mergers in a single industry since the number of variables is substantially reduced and the effect of a limited number of differences in the underlying situation can be seen. The small number of case studies has proved sufficient for some quite useful generalizations about the relationships between types of industrial situation and the role of mergers.

The six case studies are: cement, calico printing, soap, glass, motor cars and brewing. In comparison with many other industries, these are fairly homogeneous and well defined. This relative simplicity is convenient for a study of this type since it makes it possible to indicate the effects of dominant features such as high rates of technical progress, particular types of market imperfection, fluctuations in demand, and high capital output ratios. The studies show that when particular features are of different importance in different industries, not only is the outcome very different, but also the judgment as to the net advantages of organizational changes must be different.

The chapters on cement, glass and calico printing have been written by P. L. Cook; each industry is approached in the same sort of way, particular emphasis being placed upon the relationship between the circumstances and the results of reactions to circumstances. Despite the similarity of approach, the chapters look very different because of the attempt to bring out the effects of the most important features in each industry rather than to examine the same questions in each industry.

The chapter on the soap industry has been written by Ruth Cohen; it is concerned with the formation of Levers and concentrates particularly upon the effect of mergers at different periods on the operation of the constituent firms and on the efficiency of a large dominant firm in a multi-product industry.

The chapter on the motor-car industry has been written by George Maxcy. This industry has become highly concentrated, but the high degree of concentration has not to any great extent been the result of mergers despite the undoubted importance of the Austin-Morris merger of 1952. The mergers have mainly been the result of special circumstances; each has to be discussed separately and few generalizations can be made about them. Nevertheless, the chapter provides an interesting study of the role of mergers in a new industry which has expanded rapidly and whose product has been changed and developed continuously.

The chapter on the brewing industry as been written by John Vaizey, who was making a general study of the industry. This chapter is somewhat shorter and less detailed, but it brings out the importance of a number of special characteristics which have played a major part in determining the development of the industry; mergers have been a predominant feature and there have been so many that in this case, more than in any other, generalizations can be made which ignore the effects of outstanding personalities with peculiar individual characteristics.

Having decided to make each case study basically historical there remained the problem of deciding upon a general pattern which would emphasize the characteristics of the industry and the relationships between events and the particular situations in which they took place. The studies of cement, glass and calico printing and, to some extent, the one on the brewing industry all follow the same general pattern. In each case the structure of the industry, the conditions of supply and demand, and the changes taking place in techniques and market conditions are described first. This is followed by examination of the major events which relate primarily to long-term matters. Policies which do not necessarily have permanent impact and which can be reversed are then discussed; on the whole these are the price changes and price agreements which are largely designed to cope with immediate circumstances and are therefore influenced largely by short-term considerations. Finally the new situation is discussed, and the effects of the actual changes and of the possible alternative changes are considered. This process is then repeated for the next period but it is not usually necessary to repeat the fundamental examination of the nature of the industry; as soon as one period has been examined more is known about the relative importance of the factors at work, and although these certainly change over time, information about them is to some extent cumulative.

This arrangement thus has the advantage that throughout the historical survey as much as is known about the underlying situation is given before the events which take place are discussed. This enables attention to be focussed upon the way in which the industry responds to different stimuli; it is upon this basis that the inevitability of events, the possibility of alternative developments, and the response to hypothetical situations must be discussed.

The study of an industry must precede theoretical analysis since this always involves some simplification; the important characteristics must be selected and many others must be ignored. There are many theories because each is based on different assumptions about the world; it is their relevance rather than their logic which is in dispute. In order to bring out the relative importance of different features of the industries studied, it has often proved desirable to isolate three groups of considerations.

The first group deals with the short period considerations which relate to the nature and intensity of competition over periods which are much too short for long period equilibrium to be established. This group includes temporary market imperfections, the kinked demand curve,[1] rapid fluctuations in demand, frequent changes in the price of raw materials and price discrimination such that firms can reduce prices in some markets and for some lines without immediately affecting the prices obtainable in others. This group is useful in relation to

[1] The kinked demand curve occurs when a firm expects its rivals to follow any price reduction it may make but not to follow price increases.

the question of the extent to which the prosperity of firms is affected by what happens in the short period.[1]

The second set of considerations are those related to the process of adjustment to the long period equilibrium. The crucial questions are usually: what is the length of the Marshallian short period and how smoothly is a new long period equilibrium approached?

The third set of considerations relate to the rate and nature of historical change, both on the side of demand and of supply, and the factors which determine how the structure of industry adapts to deal with the problems of change and to promote further development.

The distinctions between these groups of features are by no means clear cut. For example, if the short period imperfections are considerable and the length of the period of adjustment is fairly short the distinction between the first two groups is very blurred. Similarly, if the period of adjustment would be long but the rate of technical change is rapid, the second two groups are inextricably mixed.

Nevertheless, where the distinctions can be drawn, the study of any industry is considerably simplified and comparisons between different situations are made more systematic. The really important point is that firms are faced with choices between different policies but these choices are limited because they are interconnected. When one decision has been made, others follow; thus all policy decisions involve compromises in which some advantages must be sacrificed. In many cases the choice lies between a policy designed to deal with short period matters, one to deal with the establishment of a new equilibrium or one to deal with the problems of change and development. Sometimes all these matters are important and the choice is difficult, but quite frequently one or even two of them can be more or less ignored and then the type of policy required and likely to be pursued is more easily seen.

Recognition of the importance of considering choices between policies which have both advantages and disadvantages shows why it is useless simply to make a list of the reasons why an event took place. Such a list is easily made on the basis of theoretical reasoning; but it is, however, only on the basis of examination of all the relevant circumstances and the general situation that weights can be ascribed, not only to the items on the list, but also to the factors tending to lead to alternative solutions. This is perhaps another aspect of the general point that each real situation is very complicated and theorizing is

[1] Andrews in *Manufacturing Business* considers the influences which tend to give constant prices (given the price of raw materials) in the short period. It is these influences, among others, which are here considered under a broader heading which is not confined to the factors giving rise to constant prices in the short period.

only useful when based on a large number of variables. The simple theories based on few assumptions cannot be applied directly to industrial situations; they must be used to construct a great number of complicated minor theories relating to well-defined situations. Most actual situations are so complicated that one can only refer to a particular industry, draw attention to the most important features and then produce a conclusion which is based upon a mixture of theory and judgment.

The importance of the many variables relating to any situation can only be described and not measured, yet choice of a theoretical framework depends upon which variables are the most important. It is the choice of framework which requires judgment and the theoretical content of any conclusion is usually very small as compared with the judgment content.

Although it would not be appropriate to pursue it at this point, the whole question of the application of theoretical models to actual situations is of considerable interest. The lines of thought which we have used owe much to the existing theories and few are really original. Case studies cannot be shaped by any particular theory; it is necessary to discuss the problems which seem to be important in each industry and to use whichever theory or point of view seems to be the most relevant. There are many features of industry which play a very small part in the general analytical patterns and which tend to be regarded as mere peculiarities. It has been found that many of these peculiarities are of extreme importance and that there are few situations which are not materially affected by one or more of them.

I

THE CEMENT INDUSTRY

1. Introduction

2. The Period Before 1900, and the Formation of the Associated Portland Cement Manufacturers Ltd

3. The Immediate Effects of the Formation of the APCM, 1900–7

4. Price Agreements, 1900–10

5. The Second Combine, 1911

6. 1918–29

7. 1929–34

8. Price Stability, 1934–9

9. 1939–55

10. Conclusions

APPENDIX: HALL AND CO. LTD

CHAPTER 1

Introduction

THE Cement industry is particularly suitable for the study of the relationships between the characteristics of an industry and its structure and organization. The product, if it has not always been homogeneous, can be closely defined, and it is sufficiently homogeneous for measurement by weight to be reliable. The number of firms in the industry has never been very great and relatively few have many outside interests; thus they can both be discussed individually, and grouped meaningfully in ways which make it possible to substantiate generalizations.

Mergers have played a very large part in determining the structure of the industry and the types of competition in it. Unlike the brewing industry, mergers in the cement industry have been rather few in number, but the majority have been of major importance. The four great amalgamations divide the industry into covenient periods for study.

There is first the period up to the formation of Associated Portland Cement Manufacturers Ltd in 1900, this followed by the period between 1900 and 1911 when British Portland Cement Manufacturers Ltd was formed. The third period, 1919–34, covers the time during which the Red Triangle group was formed and then amalgamated with the Associated Portland Cement Manufacturers Ltd; this is followed by the formation of the Alpha group and its amalgamation with APCM and Tunnel in 1938.

The structural development of the industry took place against a background of relatively rapid technical change. This, together with the repercussions due to the changing structure of the industry, which was itself partly due to the technical change, has meant that during the last hundred years the cement industry has rarely been even approximately stable. Change has been more or less continuous and any study of the industry must take full account of the dynamic characteristics; this inevitably complicates the problem of reaching conclusions because it substantially reduces the value of comparisons between situations before and after particular mergers.

EARLY HISTORY OF PORTLAND CEMENT

Joseph Aspdin patented Portland Cement in 1824, but claimed to have been making it since 1811. This new product was an improvement upon the Roman Cement and Medina Cement, both of which were in general use. Aspdin's specifications on the Patent were, however, insufficiently detailed to enable others to use his methods. Further, it is far from clear that he knew exactly what was required. He made no mention of the need to burn the raw materials to the point of incipient fusion, yet it was this feature which was only rediscovered with difficulty by I. C. Johnson in 1847. Aspdin and his son had continued to manufacture Portland cement, but having little chemical or scientific knowledge, they used rule of thumb rather than scientific methods and did not know what were the really important aspects of their process. Further, their methods of manufacture were a very well-guarded secret.

Portland Cement really came to public notice in the late 1840's, and there was public rivalry between Frost's[1] and Aspdin's (William Aspdin and the son of Joseph Aspdin the patentee). There were repeated failures of the Roman Cement which was being extensively used at that time, and tests showed the superiority of Portland Cement. 'In 1850, there were still only four factories where Portland Cement was produced.'[2] Its development was being hindered by the irregularity (in quality) of the output and the competition from Roman Cement.

'After 1851 the number of works on the Medway and Thames increased rapidly and met with more or less success although White's Brand—made by J. Bazley White & Co. at Frost's works at Swanscombe by I. C. Johnson continued to occupy a prominent position.'[3]

'Some measure of the stage of development in the methods of making hydraulic lime and cement can be seen from the fact that in 1852 Portland Cement did not even reach the strength which is obtainable from the ground hydraulic lime of today' (1924).[4]

THE MANUFACTURE OF PORTLAND CEMENT

As in most industries, events in the Portland Cement industry have been to a large extent determined by its technical characteristics and

[1] Frost's works at Swanscombe were bought by J. Bazley White in 1834. I. C. Johnson was the Manager at the time.

[2] A. C. Davis, *A Hundred Years of Portland Cement, 1824–1924*, p. 85.

[3] Ibid., p. 88.

[4] Ibid., p. 113.

the rate of change in methods of manufacture. A very brief outline of the manufacture of Portland Cement and the changes which took place prior to 1914 is thus necessary. The processes can be considered under four heads:

1. Selection of raw materials and quarrying;
2. Mixing and grinding of raw materials;
3. Burning;
4. Grinding of the 'clinker' which is the product of the kiln in which the burning is done.

In the early years there was little knowledge of the scientific reasons for procedures, rule of thumb methods prevailed, and the production of good reliable cement was more important than cost. The chief difficulties lay in the selection of the raw material and in the methods of burning.

The availability of raw material has always been of prime importance to a cement works and the location of the industry and heavy transport costs play a large part in determining the nature of competition. Before 1900 the industry was highly localized on the Thames and Medway, although there were works in Sussex, Cambridgeshire and South Wales and others, mainly fairly small ones, wherever the raw material was available.

Increased scientific knowledge of the exact mixture of raw materials required, combined with improved techniques for grinding the raw material, made manufacture away from the London area more possible; in particular, limestone as well as chalk could be used. Some of these raw materials gave rise to high manufacturing costs but these were offset by the reduced transport cost to the local market.

As quality improved, costs, which had varied considerably between works, became more important. In the mixing and grinding and in the burning there was very great scope for economy; improved methods resulted in substantial saving in labour and fuel. The radical change in the methods of mixing the raw materials was the introduction of wet grinding, which was patented in 1870 by Goreham. Refinements and improvements in layout continued, but there was no further basic change. The drying of slurry[1] became, after that, more closely related to the problem of the type of kiln, for in most cases the slurry came to be dried with heat from the kiln.

The kiln has always been regarded as the central feature of a cement works. This is due partly to the fact that it is the largest single item of capital equipment, but also to the fact that kiln capacity has a definite upper limit whereas in other sections there is normally

[1] The wet mixture which is the raw material of the kiln.

some spare capacity. Further, if maximum output is maintained, there has always been some fuel economy, although of course this has only been of extreme importance since the introduction of the large rotary kiln.

In 1878 an article on the manufacture of cement accepts the bottle kiln as normal equipment.[1] Davis says, however, that in retrospect the last quarter of the nineteenth century is regarded as the 'chamber' kiln era.[2]

The chamber kiln was a more or less natural development of the bottle or dome kiln. The obvious weakness of the latter was that it required to be fed with a dry or nearly dry raw material; the drying required special plant and involved additional manhandling, which caused extra expense. It was, therefore, early realized that a kiln which could combine both drying and calcining (burning) would be a distinct advance on the bottle kiln. 'Johnson's chamber kiln was patented in 1872 and comprised a long horizontal chamber set at right angles to the vertical axis of a bottle kiln, the open dome of the latter being closed in so that the product of combustion and waste heat from the kiln had to pass through a chamber before they could reach the chimney which was attached.'[3] In the chambers the slurry (wet mixture of clay and chalk) was dried. The Batchelor kiln was an improved chamber kiln providing two or even three chambers, one above the other, thus avoiding very long chambers.

The chamber kiln was developed to a high standard of efficiency and such kilns were still being installed as late as 1903. New types were, however, making them obsolete. The first rotary kiln patent was taken out in 1877 by Crampton, but the credit usually goes to Ransome and Stokes who took out patents in 1885 and 1888 respectively.[4]

The first rotary was put in at Arlesley in 1887 and then two others were installed, one at Grays on the Thames and the other at Penarth in South Wales. All were commercial failures. The reasons for the failure were first, the difficulty of obtaining a satisfactory lining; second, the difficulty of maintaining the requisite temperature inside the kiln; third, the frequent formation of large masses of fused or

[1] The bottle kiln is a small upright kiln which is charged with alternate layers of fairly dry, raw material (in the case of cement it was sometimes made into rough blocks) and coke.

[2] Davis. *op. cit.* p. 151.

[3] Ibid., p. 153.

[4] The rotary kiln is a long cylinder, at a slight angle to the horizontal, which is rotated. The slurry is put in at the top end and the heat provided at the bottom end by burning of producer gas or finely ground coal dust which is blown into the burning area. These kilns give a continuous process.

semi-fused clinker in the interior of the burning cylinder which prevented the passage of further supplies of raw material; fourth, the inefficient use of fuel due to the shortness of the cylinder; fifth, the unduly high lime content which was due to the fact that the absence of ash in the fuel employed (producer gas) was not allowed for in the preparation of the raw material; and lastly, the inconvenient quick setting nature of the cement produced.

The list of reasons for failure is helpful. It shows rather clearly that the industry was undeveloped in engineering and scientific knowledge and still lacked real knowledge of the chemistry of cement. Although it is fully recognized that the industry had in general an empirical approach, the failure of the rotary kiln at this date shows that this extended to the most progressive. This industry was among the many, which includes the glass industry, which were hampered by lack of satisfactory refractory materials; any development of refractory materials appears to be an innovation of very wide application.

'The credit for that practical development of the rotary kiln must unreservedly be given to the United States.' Hurry and Seaman took out their major patent in 1896 and others in the years immediately after. 'The practical development of the rotary kiln in Great Britain dates from the year 1900 when the recently-formed company The Associated Portland Cement Manufacturers purchased certain rights from Messrs. Hurry and Seaman and proceeded to build a number of rotary kilns on the Thames.'[1] Other competitive cement manufacturers outside this Company also obtained information from the United States without the purchase of any rights and the year 1900 saw one or two other rotary kilns in course of construction at various places in the country.

A third type of kiln—the shaft kiln—must also be mentioned as it has played a considerable part in determining the nature of competition in the industry, since it was relatively cheap to install. The shaft kiln, of which the Schneider was the most important type in this country, was mainly developed on the continent. The Schneider type does not appear to have been introduced into this country until about 1898.[2] The shaft kiln is a vertical kiln which is fed with raw material and fuel at the top and the clinker when burned is drawn off or taken out by a mechanical grate at the bottom. Thus, like the rotary kiln, it operated continuously and this gave, according to Davis,[3] a saving of some 50 per cent in fuel. The disadvantage of the shaft kiln in this country is due to the fact that the raw material must be dry or nearly

[1] Davis, *op. cit.*, p. 166. [2] Ibid., p. 155.
[3] A. C. Davis, *Portland Cement* (1907), p. 94.

dry in the form of bricks or lumps, and thus it is necessary either to use a 'dry' process for mixing or to have some means of drying the wet slurry. 'Dry' mixing processes depend upon a supply of suitable raw material and upon heavy grinding machinery and even so the mixing is frequently less efficient than that obtained by the wet method.

The early shaft kilns were fed by hand and the clinker removed by hand; this, together with the drying of the slurry, involved high labour costs. However, many improvements to the kiln were made and Davis reported that 'This kiln (the Schneider) has attracted some attention and is installed at three or four factories.'[1] Around 1907 great further improvements were made. Output was increased by the use of forced draughts; mechanical feeds and grates were introduced, and the Schneider kiln became more common. The really important point is that this kiln was very considerably cheaper than the rotary kiln. Its production was about ninety tons a week. The relatively small capital outlay meant that a satisfactory continuous kiln was available to small producers and thus undoubtedly had a great effect in increasing competition in the industry during this period of rapid technical development. Although the kiln was 'satisfactory' some idea of the state of development of the industry in 1907 may be obtained from the following quotation from Davis' *Portland Cement* (1907).

'In whatever class of fixed kiln (as opposed to rotary) it is produced, the clinker is, however, somewhat irregular in quality and contains a good deal of imperfectly-burnt material and unless *this is picked out with great care*, sufficient underburnt material remains to impair the quality of the finished cement to a serious degree.'[2]

In the grinding of clinker, which is an important factor in determining quality, the chief development was the replacement of the mill stones by ball mills and tube or 'Griffin' mills.[3]

Writing in 1924 in *Portland Cement 1824–1924*, Davis describes the economy in labour which was being achieved.

'To one familiar with the older type works nothing is more striking than the appearance of a modern works in which full advantage has

[1] Davis, *Portland Cement* (1907), p. 97.

[2] Ibid., p. 105.

[3] The ball mill consists of a cylinder which is rotated, rather like the kiln, which contains heavy steel balls which fall as the cylinder rotates and so crush the clinker. The Griffin mill is akin to a mechanical pestle and mortar.

Davis, in *Portland Cement* (1907) p. 170 says, 'Until about twelve years ago the clinker grinding was almost invariably done by millstones—indeed in some of the older works in the Thames and Medway district the French buhr stones are still used'.

been taken of mechanical means of transport. Throughout the works there are signs of great activity and yet an almost complete absence of men. At the crushers for raw materials there will be a few; about the fine-grinding plant one or two hands sauntering about with oil-cans; on the platform in front of the rotary kiln a burner, perhaps one to each pair of kilns . . . The whole process of manufacture has been brought very nearly to that ideal state of industry where man is put in his proper place as supervisor and is not used as a sentient machine.'[1]

Thus, during the thirty years 1895 to 1925 the cement industry had changed radically. Almost all the capital equipment had changed fundamentally at least once, and in addition, whereas 'the manufacture of cement was carried on as as an empirical trade, at the present time (1924) it is organized as one of the largest chemical industries and, as all chemical industries must be, is directed by the chemist and the engineer'.[2]

The great changes resulted in substantial cost reductions. The cost at the works by the pre-1900 methods was about 18*s*. per ton under ordinarily favourable conditions. By the modern method, and under similar conditions, the cost up to the World War I was about 13*s*. per ton. These figures are taken as representing fairly enough the difference in cost of the two processes. The reductions in cost were accompanied by increases in the average size of works. Davis speaks of a typical works of fair size pre-1900 as producing about 500 tons a week (i.e. 25,000 tons a year). By 1924 a typical works of fair size produced between 50,000 to 100,000 tons a year.

It is against this background of rapid technical change that the history of the structure of the industry and the role of mergers has to be considered.

[1] p. 223.
[2] Davis, *A Hundred Years of Portland Cement 1824–1924*, p. 206.

CHAPTER 2

The Period Before 1900, and the Formation of the Associated Portland Cement Manufacturers Ltd

THE Thames and Medway area was the home of the cement industry and in this period the firms in this area, of which there were some forty or more by the late 1890's, can be considered without reference to the firms in other parts of the country. The London area accounted for some 90 per cent of the output of the industry and competition from outside was not important.[1]

Between 1850 and the early 1890's, it appears that the efficient production of Portland cement was very profitable. Demand was expanding and the potential market was large as Portland cement was replacing Roman cement, and there was a substantial export market which increased rapidly, being in 1886–90 about one-third of total output. The industry was highly competitive but the variations in efficiency must have been very great, so that when firms got into difficulties they would seldom see hope of recovery and would quickly leave the industry. In addition, most of the weakest firms were rather small. The growth of the industry had been so rapid, that it appears that anyone with knowledge of cement manufacture and some capital could set up a works and it was possible for a manufacturer's son to start a new works rather as a farmer's son buys a new farm. Also, as the demand was high, good managers could quite easily obtain the necessary financial backing. Davis, in *Portland Cement 1824–1924*,

[1] This figure is derived from the fact that twenty-seven were amalgamated into Portland Cement Manufacturers Ltd in 1900. It is known that four substantial firms were not in the amalgamation and, according to H. W. Macrosty *The Trust Movement in British Industry* (*1907*) p. 109 the Associated Company and the four major firms accounted for 89 per cent of the output in the Thames and Medway districts. Thus, as the remaining firms were generally small, it is probable that there were six to a dozen of them. This is born out by the fact that in 1907 there were only sixteen works in the area apart from those of the Associated Company and a few were certainly new.

says: 'It must be remembered that his (the cement manufacturer's) position was one of great security . . .'[1]

Between about 1890 and 1900 the situation changed. The export market shrank as a result of Continental competition and increased production in the United States and, although home demand increased, the capacity increased by very much more. A number of large new works were built such as Martin Earle & Co. Ltd and the Wouldham Cement Company. The story of the latter is told by O'Hagan:[2] S. Pearson & Son had the contract for the Admiralty Harbour at Dover, 'the construction of which was expected to take ten years; they secured for themselves a stone quarry and sought to obtain a binding contract with a responsible firm for the annual supply of the large amount of cement required for the work (30,000 tons per annum) but no manufacturer could be found to risk at a given price to supply such large quantities as would be required, or for so long a period as ten years. Had cement manufacturers been on friendly terms it would have been easy to take the order and divide it amongst two or three firms, but there was no enterprise among the manufacturers, so Pearsons were driven to put up their own cement works . . . Messrs. J. B. White & Co., being the largest cement manufacturers in England, were asked by Pearsons to assist on sharing terms. Some small works on the Thames were purchased with the intention of largely extending them to turn out a great quantity of cement.

'I (O'Hagan) do not understand what the Whites could have been about. . . . When I first interested myself in cement (probably about 1897) . . . Whites and Pearsons were spending large sums of money in increasing the capacity of this Wouldham Cement Works, it being by no means the views of those interested to limit the capacity of the works to the amount of cement required for the Dover Harbour Contract.'[3]

Messrs. J. B. White & Brother were also engaged in 1899 and 1900 in erecting 'new plant with a capacity of 160,000 tons for making cement on the rotary kiln system on royalty'.[4]

Thus, in the 1890's, although competition was becoming serious, the industry was by no means depressed by it. It was, however, in these circumstances that discussion of the possibility of amalgamation began. It must have been clear that competition would become

[1] p. 205.

[2] Mr H. Osborne O'Hagan was a successful company promoter. His colourful autobiography, *Leaves From My Life*, published in 1926, gives much information about the cement industry which is not available elsewhere. Although written in anecdotes, from memory, it is thought to be reliable.

[3] O'Hagan, *Leaves From My Life*, Vol. II, p. 150.

[4] Macrosty, *op. cit.*, p. 108.

increasingly severe as firms became larger and more highly capitalized and the product became more homogeneous.

There appears to have been no serious discussion of the possibility of price agreements. 'The firms in the cement industry had always "kept themselves to themselves" until a few years before the formation of the association when some of them formed an alliance which chiefly dealt with the purchase of fuel.'[1] O'Hagan[2] puts the matter rather more strongly: '. . . cement manufacturers had always shown hostility to each other, and entertained unfounded suspicions of their neighbours'. The secrecy which surrounded methods of manufacture was one of the causes of suspicion. More important, however, was the distrust and hostility which arose as a result of price cutting, price discrimination, and secret price reductions.

Even if price agreements had been discussed seriously it is quite unlikely that they would have been made. New firms were constantly breaking into the market and old ones failing, and quality varied considerably. Further, price discrimination was possible, and was used; it took the forms of freight absorption and of special discounts for particular orders. Although price cutting was serious, it did not have the damaging effects which are found in an industry where the price of the raw material fluctuates; price agreements were not required for the purpose of synchronizing price changes made necessary by changed raw material costs. Thus the short period need was not overwhelming and the rigidity was unacceptable.

As there was severe competition which could not be limited by price agreement, combination appeared to be the main hope. 'The cement industry, being based on the possession of a local monopoly of raw materials seemed well fitted for consolidation but proposals for amalgamation, though often made, met with no favour until the present occasion (the formation of the APCM Ltd, 1900), when negotiations were undertaken by an outside company of promoters whose independent position commanded respect.'[3] The 'outside company' was that of O'Hagan.

O'Hagan became interested in the cement industry in 1896 when he was consulted by a partner of an old-established Medway firm about the possibility of converting the firm into a public company. Nothing came of the negotiations as O'Hagan 'arrived at the conclusion that with the retirement of the principal man who had been running the concern it was unlikely to be more successful in the future than it had been in the past. One of the weaknesses which revealed itself to me in the cement trade was the animosity which existed amongst the various

[1] Macrosty, *op. cit.*, p. 109. [2] *Op. cit.*, p. 41. [3] Macrosty, *op. cit.*, p. 109.

manufacturers, who scarcely knew each other, and this could probably only be removed under a powerful combination'.[1]

The general question of amalgamation was undoubtedly being discussed. In August 1897 a London merchant, whom he met in Norway, told O'Hagan that 'he was on close terms with three or four of the largest manufacturers, and they were contemplating an amalgamation. He said as soon as he got back to London he would bring them to see me, but I heard nothing further of the matter'.[2] In October 1899 O'Hagan was approached by Martin Earle & Co., who owned large new works on the Medway and 'were regarded as interlopers by the older-established manufacturers . . . The directors of Martin Earle & Co. had come to the conclusion that what was wanted to make cement making a more profitable business was close co-operation between the various firms of manufacturers. They had already sounded a few of the smaller firms, who appeared willing to co-operate. They wished to secure my assistance to bring about an amalgamation of some half-dozen of the firms engaged in the trade.' During the discussion the Chairman of Martin Earle said: 'The people whom you are already working with are too old-fashioned, and although now at the top of the tree will not remain there long. You had better come in with us'.[3] O'Hagan then sent a message to the friends of the London merchant he had met in Norway and immediately Mr Bazley White and another member of his firm came to see him. 'These gentlemen informed me that they were engaged in an endeavour to amalgamate the whole of the cement industries of the country; that their firm had given them six months' release from their duties, that they might devote themselves to bringing about a combination. They had interviewed a large number of manufacturers who seemed disposed to consider the proposals, but they found a difficulty in getting any information. . . . I saw that in the hands of these gentlemen with no one to guide them very little progress would be made.'[4] A division of the business was then agreed between O'Hagan and Bazley White and O'Hagan 'formed a small syndicate called the British Incorporators Ltd, which was to purchase all the cement works obtainable and then turn them over to one big concern to be called the Association Portland Cement Manufacturers Ltd.'[5]

Having further investigated the problem of the cement industry, O'Hagan 'came to the conclusion that if we could purchase the whole of the cement works of the kingdom at prices which collectively would amount to no more than ten times the average net profits of the

[1] O'Hagan, *op. cit.*, Vol. II, p. 39.
[2] Ibid., p. 40. [3] Ibid., p. 41. [4] Ibid., p. 41 [5] Ibid., p. 41.

B

previous three years, it would form a good basis for a successful combination'.[1] Before considering the actual capitalization, the floatation and the subsequent history, it is necessary to consider the general conception of an amalgamation and whether it looked at the time as if it would be successful. This is important because it is only on this basis that we can judge whether an amalgamation was more or less inevitable or whether it was the result of historical accident that a few particular individuals decided to combine.

The amalgamation was apparently formed on the basis of two main expectations. The first was that a sufficient number of firms would join for it to be possible to maintain prices at the level of average costs, even when demand fell. The second was that a large powerful firm would be able to take advantage of the rapid technical developments more successfully than small firms, and would, therefore, be efficient enough to be safe from outside competition should it arise. In other words, it was expected that there would be short-term monopoly profits, but that the firm would be fully competitive in the long run.

The potential strength of the combine was made greater by the fact that, despite fluctuations, demand was growing and was expected to continue to grow. Thus it was expected that capacity would have to be increased as well as old plant replaced; and that in a period of high capital expenditure the advantage of the pooling of experiences would be particularly high.[2]

O'Hagan appears to have been confident that the general plan was sound. 'If the combine would be formed, there should be room for very considerable savings and additional profits with all the workers under one management, for hitherto every works had been sealed up so far as other manufacturers were concerned. All works would undoubtedly be found to have introduced economies of manufacture unknown to their rivals. All unnecessary competition could be eliminated, both in buying raw materials and in disposing of the finished product. An amalgamation was a thing of great promise, especially as there appeared to be a revolution coming in the manufacture of Portland cement by the rotary kiln process, which was a costly innovation by reason of the new plant and machinery required, but which produced a higher grade of cement at a lower cost, and which enabled powdered coal to be used as fuel burning instead of the ordinary gas-works coke, which was being put up to prohibitive prices. A

[1] O'Hagan, *op. cit.*, Vol. II, p. 43.

[2] When the company was floated an additional sum (over and above the purchase price) was raised for the purchase of the new rotary plant, stock, raw materials and for working capital (Macrosty, *op. cit.*, p. 109).

large battery of rotary kilns were then being erected by Messrs. J. Bazley White & Co., and there was a prevailing opinion that these would lead to their introduction on a large scale, which would necessitate the expenditure of very large amounts of money which could be best provided by a powerful company.'

Later he said that the manufacturers were 'easily induced . . . to believe that I was engaged in an enterprise which would be the means of putting a profitable trade upon a more permanent basis and avoid loss of prosperity in lean years when production was in excess of the demand, when one firm could play havoc with the remainder'.[1]

According to the prospectus 80 per cent of the cement in the country was produced in the London area. The combine was to include about 85 per cent of the output in that area.

As Macrosty pointed out,[2] the combine was conceived as a local monopoly in the London area. O'Hagan clearly discounted the importance of producers in other areas. 'There were only a few firms who did not come into the combine, and they were chiefly in the Midlands and the North, and as their sales were generally in their own districts, this was not very material; indeed, we did not invite them to join, as it was believed that they would want to come in when the combine was set going. No doubt this would have materialized but for unforeseen circumstances.'[3] This faith that outside firms would join successful combines seems to have been common to a number of those formed in this period. The faith was never justified and appears to have been based partly upon exaggeration of the economies of large-scale technical development and partly upon failure to recognize the strength of the position of the outsider in industries where the large firm cannot force him into agreement either by local price cutting or by exclusive dealing arrangements.

The negotiations with the individual concerns took more than six months, but finally it appeared that only two substantial firms in the London area would be excluded. One was the Wouldham Cement Works, which was jointly owned by J. Bazley White and S. Pearson,[4] the other was Martin Earle & Co. This was a new firm and not prepared to accept a purchase price based on their average profits of three years. O'Hagan was, however, prepared to accept their pledge to work with the combine (this pledge was in fact carried out).[5]

The prospects for the floatation were apparently very satisfactory '. . . as the vendors and their friends were prepared to take so much

[1] O'Hagan, *op. cit.*, Vol. II, pp. 47–8.
[2] Macrosty, *op. cit.*, p. 4. [3] O'Hagan, *op. cit.*, Vol. II, p. 48. [4] See p. 29.
[5] O'Hagan, *op. cit.*, Vol. II, p. 48.

of their purchase moneys in shares it was not considered necessary to go to expense of underwriting the capital'.[1] Macrosty confirms that the industry was fairly confident and says that 'there was a large subscription, particularly from agents, distributors and customers'.[2] In fact, however, the floatation was extremely difficult, and on the second day the money market was in a semi-panic owing to the disasters in Africa and bad news from Pekin. 'Bears' on the Stock Exchange sold and all applications were withdrawn. 'It was apparent we should be short about two-and-a-half million of cash to complete the purchase and provide the working capital required. At that moment I could have returned all the capital subscribed and admitted a failure . . .'[3] A meeting of the vendors was called. 'Various were the opinions expressed, but the general feeling seemed to be that there would never be the like opportunity for coming together, and there was the still stronger feeling that if all parties were back on their own, the competition which had been keen in the past would be even more severe.'[4] It was finally agreed that the vendors, many of whom had taken the bulk of their purchase-moneys in debentures and shares, would find £1,100,000 and O'Hagan would find £1,100,000.

The cause of the comparative failure of the floatation must be in large part ascribed to its unfortunate timing. Had the difficulties been confined to the cement issue O'Hagan would have had very much less difficulty in raising the money for the shares he took himself. Nevertheless, there is, in addition, the question of overcapitalization. In retrospect it is quite plain that the company was much overcapitalized, and it seems probable that this could have been (and perhaps was) realized at the time. The total capital offered for issue was £7,375,000—£2,475,000 in 4½ per cent debentures and £2,450,000 in 5½ per cent cumulative preference shares and £2,450,000 in ordinary shares—the vendors taking one-third of each class. 'The sale price to the association was £6,325,000. . . Against this sum there were land, works, buildings, plant, machinery, etc., valued at £4,522,000 and the difference £1,803,000 or 3·2 years' purchase of the last three years' average gross profits (£561,103) before charging interest, depreciation, etc., stood against goodwill, brands, and trade marks; the gross profits for the last year of account were £658,356. An additional sum of £1,050,000 was required for purchase of the new rotary plant, stock, raw materials, etc., and for working capital.'[5] In other words, in the best recent year the gross profit was less than 10 per cent on the capital

[1] O'Hagan, *op. cit.*, Vol. II, p. 49. [2] Macrosty, *op. cit.*, pp. 109–110.
[3] O'Hagan, *op. cit.*, Vol. II, p. 52. [4] Ibid., p. 52.
[5] Macrosty, *op. cit.*, p. 109.

in an industry in which depreciation and obsolescence were known to be very high. It is clear that the promised 10 per cent on ordinary shares could only be earned so long as the company managed to control the level of prices, if demand continued high or increased, and if outside competition did not increase. Perhaps it was justifiable to hope that the company would be able to exploit its monopoly position for just long enough to renew its plant and become efficient enough to compete at prices equal to the long period costs of production of its more efficient competitors.

The importance of overcapitalization varies with the circumstances. Where the company has no control of prices and does not require further funds, it may be unimportant except to those who lose on their shares; and in so far as these belong to the vendors, this is almost irrelevant. If, however, the company can control prices, there is the question as to whether profits are affected by the capitalization; little can be said on this issue except that there are many cases where 'monopolies' appear to have been content with prices which cover long-term average costs and this is, in general, interpreted as being sufficient to give a 'reasonable' return on capital. Control of prices depends upon the condition of entry into the industry; if this is unrestricted and relatively easy, the price cannot remain above the long-term average costs of new firms for any longer than it takes for new plant to be installed. As entry into the cement industry was very easy, high prices due directly to overcapitalization must be regarded as a temporary phenomenon. The effect of overcapitalization on the availability of further funds may be of great importance. In the case of this cement amalgamation, potential strength lay in the ability to exploit the new developments in manufacturing techniques. This, however, was dependent upon the availability of capital, and as a result of the heavy charges on the debentures and preference shares it was difficult either to raise new capital or to retain profits. Some of the difficulties of the combine can be traced directly to shortage of capital for development and this was partly the result of the overcapitalization.

CHAPTER 3

The Immediate Effects of the Formation of the APCM, 1900–7

THE first effect of the combine was to end the competition in price between the firms. This inevitably caused difficulties and made the combine unpopular; customers not unnaturally resented the fact that they could no longer obtain special treatment. The policy of restricting competition was begun prior to the actual floatation of the company. In the prospectus it was stated that 'an agreement had been entered into with George E. Wragge, on behalf of the principal London Cement merchants which provides, *inter alia*, for all merchants joining them taking their whole requirements of cement from this association for a term of seven years'.[1]

Had these agreements come up against no real snags, the combine would have found sales very much easier. In fact, there were difficulties: 'counsel advised that under the Trades Union Act the agreement would be held to be in restraint of trade, and, therefore, could not be enforced. I (O'Hagan) immediately communicated the advice we had received to Mr Wragge, with a view to meeting and discussing how effect could be given to what we had arranged in a legal and binding manner. Unfortunately, Mr Wragge did not take the matter calmly. He refused to meet me, and said we were trying to wriggle out of a perfectly binding and valid agreement . . .'[2] After some apparently unsatisfactory negotiations Wragge called a meeting of the Builders' Merchants and made a long speech attacking the Associated Company who 'once having got the Builders' Association into their clutches, were now deliberately breaking their agreement with a view to grinding down the merchants and making them pay increased prices for their cement. . . . Finally, he said that there was only one course open, and that was to join together and put up their own

[1] *Financial Times*, November 28, 1901. Mr Wragge was the representative of the London Builders' Merchants' Association (O'Hagan, *op. cit.*, Vol. II, p. 116).
[2] O'Hagan, *op. cit.*, Vol. II, pp. 116–7.

cement works to meet their own requirements. . . .'[1] O'Hagan then addressed the meeting and offered the individual merchants contracts for the next twelve months. 'Some half-a-dozen of the principal merchants went with me to the offices and arranged their contracts, and the next few days we were pretty busy fixing up with the others.'[2]

Macrosty[3] also discusses this matter. He quotes the chairman of the company: 'We are daily impressing upon our customers that the object of this company is not to injure the merchant, or to squeeze out the middleman. We know the advantages of working hand in hand with the distributors, but in return for the hand we hold out to the distributors we ask for a "tied trade".' This agreement antagonized some of the merchants, and when the high price of coke (it increased from 10*s*. to 22*s*. per ton) compelled a revision of cement prices the ill will was increased and some trade lost. The anticipations that the agreement would be profitable were not realized, 'chiefly', said the chairman at the annual meeting, November 27, 1901, 'on account of certain restrictive clauses which, in the changed circumstances, worked against the parties to them, including this company, without conferring on any of us the contemplated advantages of the agreement. There seemed, then, nothing for it but for these agreements to become inoperative.'[4]

A letter to the press from Mr Wragge, of date February 1, 1901, gives a less detached view of the occurrence: 'The agreement was duly sealed and exchanged, and for six months has been acted upon by both the manufacturers and the merchants. At the beginning of January the associated manufacturers gave the merchants notice that they were advised the agreement was not enforceable. The merchants thereupon took the opinion of eminent counsel, and were advised that the agreement was enforceable, and were prepared to enforce it but for the fact that the action would take considerable time and accentuate the present critical and disorganized state of the cement trade in London. Under these circumstances, the merchants under protest agreed to the agreement being cancelled, and have now arranged to supply their customers' requirements from elsewhere.'[5] (There was a plan to build a new works.) Macrosty then says 'Such disputes always favour foreign producers, but in this case the association owned all the best brands'; to illustrate the strength of the company, he again quotes the chairman's speech at the meeting

[1] O'Hagan, *op. cit.*, Vol. II, p. 117. [2] Ibid., p. 119. [3] *Op. cit.*, p. 111.
[4] *Financial Times*, November 28, 1901.
[5] Macrosty, *op. cit.*, pp. 111–112.

in November 1901. 'We are sufficiently powerful to make it clear that where we do not get our products actively handled and distributed by merchants, there we shall organize our own agencies, so as to secure what we have a right to claim—not a monopoly, but our fair proportion of the trade.'[1]

Three circumstances made it particularly difficult for the company to pursue a profitable price policy. The first was the great rise in the price of coke: this was largely due to increased demand, but O'Hagan also suspected that the threat of the introduction of the rotary kiln, which used coal, made coke suppliers concentrate upon profitable export markets.[2] The rise in the price of coke came at an unfortunate time since the combine immediately obtained the reputation of charging high prices. The second difficulty was foreign competition; imports rose from 105,000 tons in 1900 to 221,000 tons in 1901. The competition was mainly from the Germans and the Belgians, but it was the latter which was most troublesome, since they were making 'natural cement', which could be sold at very low prices. 'Natural cement' is cement made by simply burning and grinding a natural product taken from chalk pits; as this contains a varying percentage of clay and lime it is unreliable in quality. 'Natural cement' can only be made in a few places in this country; of these, the Cambridgeshire area has been the most important. O'Hagan says that 'the enormous quantity of this inferior stuff which was not Portland cement coming to England in bags so marked played havoc with the trade.'[3] 'At first, the directors confessed, they were tempted to drive the foreigner out of the market by quoting prices too low for him to undercut, but fear of their shareholders withheld them. The middle course was adopted of letting the foreigner have all the market where cheapness was preferred to quality.'[4]

The third was the fact that the combine did not have a monopoly. 'A further severe blow was caused by the sudden refusal of three firms to fulfill their contract of amalgamation; they represented a production of 140,000 tons on the Thames and Medway, and 50,000 tons on the Tyne. Prolonged negotiations followed by litigation ensued, and the difficulty was not settled for five years . . .'[5] O'Hagan felt very strongly on this matter, for the three firms had even gone so far as to agree to find their share of the extra £1,100,000 which was required. They 'delayed the completion of their assignments to the last and then broke away and declined to carry out their contracts. In one

[1] Macrosty, *op. cit.*, p. 112. [2] O'Hagan, *op. cit.*, Vol. II, p. 58.
[3] O'Hagan, *op. cit.*, Vol. II, p. 59. [4] Macrosty, *op. cit.*, p. 112.
[5] Ibid., p. 110.

case this was after two members of the firm had for two or three months sat upon the board of directors of the associated company, and served on the Works and Finance Committees. Such an extraordinary breach of faith I had never heard of. Of course, actions were commenced . . . and these actions were carried on for some time, causing great bitterness and hostility in which all alike suffered.'[1]

Thus, even in the first year, the combine was only able to control prices to a limited extent, and then only at the cost of reduced sales.

The years between 1900 and 1907 were years of great changes in the cement industry; changes took place both within the APCM and among outside companies, but the behaviour of the latter was much influenced by the existence of the APCM.

Co-operation upon technical matters and the rapid introduction of the rotary kiln were among the objectives of the combine. The first step was to obtain rights to use the Hurry and Seamens rotary kiln processes. This was particularly necessary as J. B. White's, who were installing rotary kilns, had entered into an onerous contract to pay a royalty on all cement made. O'Hagan managed to buy the patent rights for £180,000. The previous owner of the rights took part of the payment in shares. 'As the cement company had no capital with which they could purchase, I (O'Hagan) turned over the patents to them for £180,000 6 per cent certificates of indebtedness payable by instalments in twelve years.'[2] This appeared to give the company the prospect of making very considerable savings. The transaction is of some interest in that it shows once more the shortage of finance. Davis in *A Hundred Years of Portland Cement* says that the practical development of the rotary kiln dates from the time when the APCM bought the patents.[3] During the first five years the company spent £550,000 on additions to plant, buildings and machinery over and above what was spent on repairs and renewals.[4]

Capital was difficult to raise as 'the company's securities stood in the market at a heavy depreciation' and it was impossible for the company to issue any kind of security. 'The only thing to be done was to raise money on certificates of indebtedness, which were just instruments in the shape of a bond which admitted that the company owed the holder the amounts mentioned in the documents, and an undertaking to repay the amount over twelve years with 6 per cent interest by half-yearly instalments. They really formed no security for the

[1] O'Hagan, *op. cit.*, Vol. II, p. 59. [2] Ibid., p. 62.
[3] Davis: *A Hundred Years of Portland Cement 1824–1924*, p. 167.
[4] Macrosty, *op. cit.*, p. 113.

advance, but for some years I financed the company on these certificates, amounting to several hundred thousands of pounds, for I never let the company want for funds with which to carry out the rotary installations.'[1] 'These certificates were difficult to place, owing to their having no security behind them.'[2] O'Hagan then explained that as he had finished raising capital for the purchase he could take some himself; he also placed large amounts among members of his family, friends and certain trust companies.

Although there may have been no alternative to these methods of finance, and they were almost certainly better than starving the company of capital, they nevertheless gave the company a very heavy burden of prior charges and emphasized the extent to which it had been overcapitalized when it was formed.

The actual management of the organization appears to have been relatively successful and the sad experiences of the Calico Printers Association were mainly avoided. The problems were, of course, very much simpler as the product was so much more homogeneous, and individual bargains with customers played a less important part in the day to day prosperity of the business. Further, there had never been any doubt that the combine was to try to take full advantage of co-ordinated sales and production policies. There was a large board of forty ordinary directors, and sixteen managing directors. The managing directors were, however, divided up into a Works Committee, a Sales Committee and a Finance and General Purpose Committee. The organization was discussed in the 1902 and 1903 chairman's speeches and it appears to have been sound and businesslike. After the initial prejudice against the company had worn off, there appears to have been general agreement that it was well organized. For example, on September 24, 1910, the *Economist* described it as 'thoroughly well organized,'[3] and on November 26, 1910, they wrote 'As an industrial undertaking the Associated Cement Company has been a success; it has brought down to the same level the very varying costs of production of the component companies, and it has reduced this level itself by the introduction of the rotary kiln and other improvements. . . .'[4] Further, on October 28, 1911 '. . . we may remember that the company has always been managed by able men, and that after an inauspicious opening, both the financial side and the commercial side have been well and skilfully organized.'[5]

There is little doubt that the combine depended upon efficiency to be derived from economies of scale as well as upon its monopolistic

[1] O'Hagan, *op. cit.*, Vol. II, pp. 70 and 71. [2] Ibid., p. 71.
[3] p. 607. [4] p. 1075. [5] p. 867.

power. The combine included a high proportion of the older, less efficient plants and the range of costs within the combine is said to have been 25 per cent. Reduction of this range and further reduction in the average level of costs was achieved largely by improving and expanding some works and closing others. Comparison between Macrosty's 1900 production figures and the 1907 output figures[1] shows that the APCM expanded very little, if at all, despite very considerable investment.

The output of cement in 1907, given in the Census, was 2,886,000 tons. This compares with an 'approximate weekly tonnage output' of 67,070 tons, i.e. about 3,353,500 tons per annum.[2] According to the prospectus of the APCM 'upwards of 80 per cent of the entire output of Portland cement was produced on the Thames and Medway. . . . The total production of cement on these rivers in 1899 has been estimated at 1,700,000 tons'. The 1900 total was thus about 2,125,000 tons. There were seventy-nine cement companies in 1907 and the APCM had only just over one-third of the output compared with over half in 1900. In the London area outside companies had by 1907 a capacity of about 20,000 tons a week, which means that the APCM had only a little over half the capacity in the area in which they had hoped for a monopoly. Expansion in other parts of the country was equally great, for by 1907 production away from the London area was apparently almost one-third of total output compared with only about a fifth of the smaller total of 1899.

The rapid growth of firms outside the combine cannot be taken as a clear indication that the combine was run inefficiently since they started with much older plant. Nevertheless, it was inefficient as compared with good modern plant, and although this was installed as fast as the shortage of capital would allow, it appears that prices were held at levels which would give an overall profit. In this situation outside firms and new firms had the opportunity for profitable development; not only were the current prices profitable but also the long-term prospects were good since the demand for cement was increasing and the combine was likely in the future to hold prices at levels which would always give a profit to good, efficient equipment.

Not a great deal is known about the expansion of the firms outside the combine. In the London area it appears that many works were

[1] The 'production' of the firms taken over by the APCM was 1,404,569 tons in 1899 (Macrosty, *op. cit.*, p. 108). From this the output of the firms which broke away must be subtracted, leaving about 1,214,600 tons. By 1907 the 'weekly tonnage output' of the APCM is given as 24,000 tons, i.e. approximately 1,200,000 per annum.

[2] Davis, *Portland Cement*, 1907, Appendix III.

simply expanded, for by 1907 eight major works had an output of more than half that of the APCM. There are, however, a number of important and probably fairly typical examples of new firms which illustrate the type of development which took place.

Three new firms, two of which were important, were started by A. C. Davis who was to become one of the chief personalities in the Associated Company. He built a small works at Meldreth soon after 1900. This was very successful, and about a year later he built the Saxon Works near Cambridge. This also was very profitable and within about two years in 1904 he had also put up the Norman Works near the Saxon Works.

The Norman Portland Cement Co. Ltd, was registered in 1903, the chairman being a member of a local firm of builders. 'Formed to acquire sixty-two acres of land near Cambridge and to erect thereon a Portland cement works. Purchase money £9,200 (£4,600 in cash and £4,600 in ordinary shares). The vendors put in a siding and erected and fully equipped a factory capable of an output of 72,500 tons per year (since increased to 110,000 tons) for the sum of £69,000.'[1] As the issued capital was increased from £85,000 to £130,000 in 1906, this may be taken as the date of the expansion of output. The Saxon and Norman works had a combined ouput of 3,100 tons per week by 1907, and together were an extremely important factor in determining the severity of competition, for a very aggressive selling policy was pursued.

The Sussex Portland Cement Company was another of some importance. The company, registered in 1884, had a works at Newhaven, and in 1896 or 1897 bought another works at Shoreham. The Shoreham works had six chamber kilns producing cement at approximately 150 tons per week, and ground the clinker with eight sets of 'flat stones'. The new owners increased the capacity of the works considerably. Between 1898 and 1902 eight more chamber kilns were built and the first ball and tube mills were introduced for cement grinding. In 1902 two rotary kilns were installed. These were supplied by F. L. Smidth (a Danish firm), and were 60 ft. long and 5 ft. in diameter. Two Danes were brought over as kiln burners. At about this time two Schneider kilns amounted to about 600 to 700 tons per week. According to Davis's figures in *Portland Cement*, output in1907 of the whole Sussex Company, including the Newhaven works, was about 90,000 tons per annum.

Another company of some interest is Hall & Co. of Croydon. This company was registered in 1898 as coal, ground lime and cement merchants,

[1] *Stock Exchange Intelligence*, 1909.

having been formed to acquire a company of the same name, for a sum of £95,000. This company, whose chief interests lay in merchanting, opened a new cement works in 1905 and had an output of about 25,000 tons per year in 1907.[1]

B. J. Forder & Co., who already had a brick works, built a cement works during this period. The company had an authorized capital of £280,000. The building of a works by this company may be compared with the entry into cement production of Hall & Co.; each had a special and relatively assured position in the market for building materials. No dividends had been paid on the ordinary shares of B. J. Forder & Co. by 1909.

Many of the firms set up at this time were away from the London area where competition tended to be fiercest. One fairly important one was Greaves, Bull & Lakin at Harbury in Warwickshire; the output in 1907 was 600 tons a week. Another smaller works which was fairly typical was Idens & Brown at Mitcheldean in Gloucestershire. The manager, who left another firm in 1905, erected a new works and in August, 1906, this was just about to come into production, making about 450 tons per week.[2]

Thus the situation in 1907 was very different from that of 1900. The APCM had made great improvements in efficiency, but these had been more or less matched by outside firms. The rotary patents had proved useless; other firms were obtaining the rotary kiln and improvements in the Schneider kiln, in mixing, and in grinding had also been important. The ease with which outside firms obtained technical knowledge was partly due to the fact that pioneering technical developments did not have to be made, but simply imported from the Continent and America. Davis, in *Portland Cement* (1907) wrote 'In fact, so dormant have we been that the impression obtained of our foreign rivals' industrial conditions, so far as cement making is concerned, has been a revelation to us . . . we are actively engaged in putting down modern plant in our obsolete factories with the result that for cost of production combined with quality of product, the British cement manufacturers have nothing to fear from overseas competitors.'[3]

In the new situation in which there were many powerful competitors and numerous small firms, severe competition was almost inevitable,

[1] Appendix I contains an extract from *A Century and a Quarter*, the history of this company.

[2] Certain company records have been made available to me, but exact source references will not be given.

[3] p. 2.

and equally inevitable were efforts to institute price agreements. The nature of competition, which has been discussed briefly[1] made price agreements more difficult to make and still more difficult to maintain. By 1907 the difficulties were in some ways even greater. First, the larger firms were more anxious to maintain output and had larger overheads. Secondly, factory cost was reduced and transport became more important, thus increasing the possibilities of price discrimination by freight absorption. This problem was further magnified by the fact that production was very much less concentrated around London and thus a greater part of the market was subject to this type of discrimination. These features alone would have given rise to severe competition, but, in addition, the feature of large discontinuous orders for specific contracts made regularity of trade relations less important than in many industries. Further, there was the fact that the many new works being erected had to break into the market.

The next chapter is devoted mainly to the history of price agreements between 1900 and 1910, since the efforts to promote them and their comparatively small degree of success played a large part in determining the development of the industry; in particular, their failure was the most important cause of the next major merger.

[1] p. 30.

CHAPTER 4

Price Agreements, 1900–10

THE history of the many attempts between 1900 and 1910 to make price agreements shows clearly the difficulties involved. Every type was tried, from verbal agreements between small numbers of local firms to the detailed organization of national associations. In tracing the history of these agreements it must not be assumed that because none lasted for more than a very short while, they were of no importance and had no appreciable effect. Although it was a period of severe competition, the picture was not one of perfect competition, but rather one of imperfect competition in which there was much price discrimination; some, but by no means all, sales were made at prices equal to marginal costs. General levels of prices fell, but the intensity of competition has to be measured both by the general level and by departures from it, and also, increasingly, by the extent of freight absorption.

The APCM had the greatest interest in maintaining prices, since they were so large that the elasticity of demand for their output was less than the elasticity of demand for the output of smaller firms. Further, they were large enough for their price policy to be the chief factor in determining the prices fixed by the other manufacturers, whether these were equal to the APCM price or undercutting it.

The APCM had hoped to control prices. Agreements to work in unison with the combine were made with Martin Earle & Co. and with the Wouldham Company; the agreement with the former was carried out, but the agreement with the latter subsequently broke down.[1] In the early years the APCM tried to hold prices and accepted some reduction in sales; some of the actual reduction in sales must, however, be attributed to the unpopularity of the combine and suspicion of it. O'Hagan describes the situation: 'But we found the fruits of our work were entirely offset by the competition set up by the three firms who had at the last moment broken away from us, also

[1] O'Hagan, *op. cit.*, Vol. II, p. 48.

from the firms which in the first place we had thought not worth while including in our combine (works largely situate in the North of England and the Midlands) and from newly erected works—competition which was carried out with great bitterness and by our competitors sometimes selling cement below the cost of manufacture in order to take away our customers.'[1] 'I gave much consideration to this state of things, and took a prominent part in negotiating with outside firms to come in on price agreements. But these undertakings and agreements were so frequently broken to the advantage of these outsiders that we reluctantly came to the conclusion that we were better without them. And so matters got worse.'[2] 'It was possible to effect an arrangement with a few of the outside firms as to selling prices with the object of stopping the rot, but the agreements entered into to this end were not enforceable . . . gentlemanly agreements—the passing of the "word of honour", were all that we had to rely upon and they were observed until the manufacturer saw his way to "making a bit" by ignoring them.'[3]

Although prices were almost certainly held at levels above those which would otherwise have ruled, they were not high. 'Several times outside manufacturers would come to us complaining that they were making no profits, and we would enter into working agreements with them; but presently they would break their engagements, saying that the competition of their neighbours made them do so, and it was impossible to enforce such agreements, so we found that by the time we entered into agreements with another set of manufacturers the first lot had broken away.'[4]

The price reductions during this period were in fact quite dramatic, and indicate not only the technical revolution but also the intensity of competition. In 1906 Portland cement could be retailed in London at about 23*s.* per ton as compared with a price of about 40*s.* per ton in 1897. 'In greater detail we have ascertained the average selling prices (delivered from three typical cement works) at a given town in the provinces and find them to be for the five years from 1902 to 1906, inclusive, as follows:

Year	Price Delivered *s. d.*	Reduction on 1902 Prices *s. d.*	Reduction on 1902 Prices Per Cent
1902	31 9	—	—
1903	29 5	2 4	7·35
1904	28 6	3 3	10·25
1905	26 9	5 0	15·8
1906	23 6	8 3	26·0

[1] O'Hagan, *op. cit.*, Vol. II, p. 71. [2] Ibid., p. 72. [3] Ibid., p. 73. [4] Ibid., p. 72.

Official figures furnished by the Commercial Department of the Board of Trade also confirm the above estimate of the reductions of selling prices.'[1]

In the same pamphlet it is stated: 'During this period there has been no invention or improvement in the manufacture of Portland Cement which would account for more than a small proportion of this sum. The rotary kiln, the continuous kiln, the Griffin mill and the ball and tube mills may, perhaps, account for a diminution in cost of manufacture to the extent of say, some 7*s*. per ton on a conservative estimate of the cost of manufacture ten years ago.'[2] (Thus the fall in prices of 17*s*. per ton between 1897 and 1906 was accompanied by a fall in costs of only 7*s*. per ton.)

'A most alarming allowance for unscientific manufacture and other heavy working expenditure would not add 3*s*. per ton to this saving. The relative costs of labour, freight and coal affect the cost price adversely if anything. It is clear then that improved processes of manufacture are not responsible for the present low prices of Portland Cement.'[3]

After considering other reasons for the fall in prices, such as reduced demand, and competition from imports, it is concluded that the low prices are primarily the result of overproduction. Two particularly important points are raised in the discussion. The first relates to the increase in the length of the 'short period' which results from the existence of joint stock companies.

'In ordinary circumstances of commercial trading the absence of profit may be relied upon to have its proper effect in decreasing supply and restoring prices to a profitable basis, but the present method of working joint stock companies at once upsets the theoretical safeguards to prices which may hold in private trading. A limited company, like a railway company, in popular language, may be stated to have neither soul to be saved, nor body to be kicked; absence of profits is no reason for suspension of working. Shareholders may grumble once a year at the loss on trading; capital may be written down, mortgagees may foreclose, but still the works are kept going and fresh capital called upon in the fond hope of better times to come. The effect of this is only to aggravate the position and a private manufacturer who would acknowledge defeat after, say, five years' losses would see in the case of a limited company even ten years' absence of trading profits without disturbing the unloading of cement upon an

[1] A. C. Davis: *Low Prices in the Portland Cement Industry*, privately published, *c. 1907*.

[2] Ibid., p. 2. [3] Ibid., p. 2.

overstocked market, as witness the fact that Portland Cement companies are in existence at this moment while burning their raw materials in the old 'bottle' kilns of 100 years ago.'[1]

The second point of interest relates to the type of competition. Davis discusses the way in which prices fall at some length in terms of a hypothetical example. The general picture is one in which a manufacturer, on examining his costs, finds that additional output can be produced at reduced average cost. The extra output is then made and the manufacturer 'under-bids one of his competitors and gets rid of the extra output'.

'Some other manufacturer now finds that his sales have decreased by 100 tons per week, as no more cement can be sold at 26*s*. 9*d*. than was originally sold at 27*s*. In enquiring into the cause of this failure he speedily finds that his competitor has reduced his price to 26*s*. 9*d*., and as he may now have an accumulated stock of several hundred tons before he sees the necessity of forcing it upon the market he makes a bolder bid for custom and sells his supplies at 26*s*. per ton, thus clearing out his stock.'

'By this time, we may further assume, ten weeks have elapsed, and the total quantity of surplus cement in the hands of the five manufacturers (assumed number affected), amounts to ten times 100 tons, which we may suppose, is evenly distributed among the five makers in quantities of 200 tons each. The customers do not want the surplus and have no use for it at any price.'

'Competition among the makers becomes keener week by week as the accumulation of surplus stock increases until by the end of the year the price of cement is forced down to 21*s*. per ton, as compared with 27*s*. per ton, and each manufacturer still finds himself with an unsold stock which aggregates fifty-two times 100 tons, and averages 1,040 tons each.'[2]

The point of interest and significance in this hypothetical, but nevertheless representative, case, is the great reluctance of the manufacturer to reduce output and the resulting accumulation of stock. This seems to indicate that there was a tendency towards great optimism that trade *might* improve and the stock *might* be disposed of profitably and that a very steady demand was comparatively rare. It is, of course, also a reflection of relatively low marginal costs and falling average costs of production.

At this period it is estimated that a profit of about 4*s*. per ton would have given about 10 per cent return on capital, and that standing charges and profit together equalled about 40 per cent of total

[1] Davis: *Low Prices in the Portland Cement Industry*, p. 4. [2] Ibid.

cost, including profit. These figures are some guide, but do not indicate marginal cost which was very much less than average prime costs, when short periods were being considered.

The seriousness of the competition and the fact that successful agreements would make the trade profitable led to continuous efforts. These met with greater success in 1906. Trade had improved. By the middle of the year it was reported that the market was harder and stocks exhausted and that demand exceeded supply. The export market was particularly active; it has been suggested that this was due largely to the exceptional demand from San Francisco following the earthquake. The APCM were able to increase their prices by 2*s*. a ton at this time.

This period of improved demand gave a new opportunity to make a price agreement, for stocks were low and many manufacturers wished to raise prices. In such conditions most manufacturers will agree to synchronize price increases and they will often promise to continue to observe a price list in the future. (Such agreements are liable to break down as soon as conditions change.)

By July 1906 an Alliance had been established between the principal manufacturers on the Thames and Medway, and suggestions were made for the formation of an Alliance between the Inland Cement Manufacturers.[1]

The reaction towards this attempt was mixed. One small manufacturer wrote: 'This object is, of course, a very laudable one, but so many attempts have been made on similar lines in the past, and all without success, that one is inclined to doubt whether such an agreement can be efficiently worked.' In another letter the same man wrote: 'The difficulties in the way of fixing prices without also fixing maximum outputs for the works allied are so great as to be practically insuperable.'

In October 1906 a scheme was produced which involved an agreed price list, registration of merchants who were eligible for discounts, a fund out of which fines were to be paid by those guilty of a breach of the rules, and another fund, into which firms had to pay if they made more than their registered output, and from which they recovered if they made less. The scheme was recognized as restrictive and it was proposed that the Trustees should live on the Continent.

By early in 1907 the situation was beginning to be confused. On the one hand, manufacturers could write saying 'The result of the working (of the Alliance) up to the present has been very beneficial to many, including ourselves, and the value of the Alliance at the

[1] Letters in company archives.

present time is being proved, as we have been able to induce certain makers to reduce their output and some more favourably situated to release others of their surplus stock rather than start the old system of dumping in their competitors' districts.' On the other hand, there appears to have been a considerable decline in trade which was in part attributed to the hard winter; it was known that stocks were beginning to accumulate and some thought it doubtful whether prices would remain firm. In February efforts were still being made to bring manufacturers into the Alliance, but there was some suspicion that the conditions and rules were so complicated as to be unworkable. It appears that there was considerable 'jockeying' for position and that this was causing increasing distrust.

Although we have no information about the subsequent history of these schemes, it appears that trade declined and although the price lists were not abandoned, there was considerable price cutting.

In August 1907 new efforts were started. An early circular stated: 'It has become common knowledge that for more reasons than one a crisis in the history of the Cement Trade in this country is not far distant and, indeed, is already imminent'. The reasons for the crisis were partly the 'over production' and partly the threat of competition from the new Passau cement which was beginning to be made under patent from basic slag. The urgency of the matter was stressed in the circular. 'I am desirous to make perfectly clear that the matter in question is one which cannot be deferred or remain in abeyance and that unless members elect to avail themselves of the present opportunity it will become an absolute impossibility later on to stem the course of events.' This may have been referring to a possible flood of Passau (or Coloseus, after the inventor) cement, but may equally well have been referring to danger of a return to absolutely unrestricted competition.

Both the experience of the previous years, particularly of 1906, and *a priori* reasoning, show that price agreement was extremely difficult. In *Low Prices in the Portland Cement Industry*[1] the two major points are made very clearly. The first is that minimum prices become maximum prices so that all quotations from members are alike, and non-members, by quoting a slightly lower price, are able to sell their whole output as near as possible to their works. This feature is particularly important when several works are close together in a good raw-material district. The second point is that some members of the trade are unable to obtain orders at the prices quoted by the well-established firms because they have little goodwill, smaller sales organizations

[1] Davis, published privately, *c.* 1907.

and cannot afford to advertise. Because such firms cannot compete at level prices they tend to break away from price agreements. For these reasons the new efforts to organize the industry placed emphasis upon output control.

A meeting was held and sub-committees appointed to deal with (a) Passau Cement and (b) Price and Output Policy.

The most promising scheme was the proposal for a Mutual Association. O'Hagan claims that the idea was his and that it made it possible to work a restriction scheme in accordance with the law.[1] The scheme involved registration of outputs and 'insurance' payments on policies designed to cover variations in output. There were special arrangements for the treatment of additional capacity since the date taken for the calculation of registered tonnage. The scheme, although not used in the cement industry, was subsequently introduced in the milling trade.

O'Hagan said that he was prepared to go ahead so long as he could get 80 per cent of the capacity of the industry into the 'Mutual Association'. In his book, however, he says that he found three major firms who were adamant in their refusal to join. He suspected that they hoped that the scheme would go ahead and that they would either get special terms, or would simply benefit by being outsiders. He felt particularly strongly about two of the firms which were two of the three who had broken away from the APCM just as it was being formed and 'had always been a thorn in our sides'.[2]

The smaller companies who refused to join were in a difficult position. They could remain outside without stopping the whole scheme but, on the other hand, they were in a much more vulnerable position should the Alliance decide to fight against them (by area price cutting). This could be very much more effective against a small than against a large firm.

One of the firms who decided not to join the Alliance backed his decision saying that 'A study of a large number of Balance Sheets of various companies shows me that an Alliance is not very necessary as the price of cement must go up soon without its aid'.

The immediate failure of the scheme was largely due to the determination of three large firms to stay outside. One cannot but realize, however, that the industry was in a condition of such very rapid change that agreement to a comprehensive restrictive scheme was unlikely to last for very long. Few were prepared to commit themselves to any, even semi-permanent, plan, and as firms were changing so much in size and in relative efficiency, it is probable that any agree-

[1] O'Hagan, *op. cit.*, p. 74. [2] Ibid., p. 75.

ment based on shares of the market would have soon been broken.

It was at this stage that the rotary kiln was beginning to be of real importance; the new kilns were larger and more efficient, but not yet so large that an enterprising small firm could not install one. A new rotary installed in 1907 was expected to produce about 500 tons a week, which was the output of what must be regarded as a medium-sized works.

The Alliance failed completely in 1908 as a result of members breaking away, and although it had 'staved off the rot in prices for a year or two', the failure left a legacy of considerable ill feeling.

In the period between the failure of the Alliance to introduce a scheme limiting output early in 1908 and the middle of 1910, competition was intense. O'Hagan wrote: 'But it was so hopeless; it seemed that we were bound to have everything against us.'[1] The profits of the APCM had risen slowly but steadily between 1901 and 1907 from £227,000 to £385,000, but after that they fell each year until 1910, when they were £316,000. No dividend on the ordinary shares was paid but the preference share dividend was paid regularly. Other companies were doing quite as badly, and the large Wouldham Cement Company had also paid no dividend. Martin Earle & Co., which had refused to join the combine, paid no dividend on its ordinary shares in 1904 or from 1907 to 1911; in addition, it paid nothing on its preference shares after 1908. B. J. Forder paid no dividend in 1909 and Hall & Company none in 1907–8, or 1908–9. The Sussex Portland Cement Company, which had paid 15 per cent in 1901 and 1902, only paid 5 per cent in 1907–8. The Saxon and Norman companies, which paid 5 per cent in 1907–8, paid no dividend in 1910–11.

The cause of these difficulties was the very low level of prices which had fallen from about 23*s.* per ton (delivered in the London area) in 1906 to as low as about 17*s.* 6*d.* per ton ex works in some cases by 1910. (This certainly represents a substantial further reduction although the two figures are not directly comparable).

In September 1910 a new effort was made to revive the Inland Cement Makers' Alliance with a view to fixing prices, and it was reported that the Thames and Medway and the North Eastern Cement Makers, respectively, had already made arrangements and that materially improved prices were being obtained. The idea was to institute a price list and to obtain undertakings that the list should be observed; the scheme was to be simple and no penalties were suggested.

Again the scheme appears to have been introduced at a time when stocks were low so that the chances of adherance were greater. The

[1] O'Hagan, *op. cit.*, Vol. II, p. 82.

majority of firms agreed to the new prices, but a few were reluctant since they felt that the whole scheme was bound to fail because of the extreme lack of mutual trust. This appears to have been felt particularly strongly among the makers in East Anglia. There was also the view that the proposed prices were too high and would simply lead to the building up of reserves against the time when the Alliance failed.

Long negotiations were conducted with those who refused to join, but some, including the East Anglian Cement Company, remained adamant. These negotiations turned on such considerations as the actual prices to be charged in different districts, merchants' rebates, the general need for all to belong so that none had the excuse to cut to meet non-members' quotations, and upon the need to make agreements with the Thames and Medway makers, so that they would not use the Midland area as a dumping ground.

It appears that once more an alliance, proposed at a fairly favourable time, did something to raise prices temporarily, but that by and large the more ruthless gained at the expense of the less ruthless.

In this period, despite the low profits, there seems to have been continued faith in the inherent soundness and ultimate prosperity of the cement industry. The APCM were still ploughing back whatever profits they made over and above what was required to pay their large fixed interest charges. Between 1907 and 1910 £465,000 were spent on repairs and renewals. The Rugby company were putting in a new rotary kiln in 1910, and a new large rotary (which was nearly three times as long as the two they put in earlier) was installed in 1911 at the Sussex Portland Cement Company's works at Shoreham. Although rotary kilns had been of considerable importance since 1900, in that they indicated possible benefits, it was with the introduction of the larger improved ones at about this time that their full potentialities began to be realized.

The outlook for the industry in 1910 was uncertain. On the one hand, cement was being used more extensively; in particular, the use of reinforced concrete was developing rapidly. On the other hand, the cement industry was not profitable. Technical development was increasing the optimum size of plants, and, perhaps more important, increasing the minimum practicable scale of production; technical development was also continuing to reduce production costs at such a rate and to such an extent that unprogressive firms could see that they would not last many years unless they made capital expenditure. A related point is that when capital expenditure was made, it almost always increased capacity and thus increased price competition. It is very difficult to see how long this intensively competitive situation would have continued. As firms grew in size and shrank in numbers, the price agreements would have become stronger, but the periods when they failed might well have been characterized by more severe price wars.

Between 1900 and 1911 a rapid rate of change was maintained, the change being brought about as a result of numerous decisions by many individuals. In 1911, however, a small group of people took a major decision; the British Portland Cement Manufacturers Ltd was formed and the pattern of development was suddenly changed.

CHAPTER 5

The Second Combine, 1911

BY 1910 the APCM was clearly gaining ground in the sense that the management had proved itself efficient and the position of the company as a large organization among smaller organizations had been shown, after the initial difficulties, to be fairly satisfactory. In addition, the gains from the maintenance and improvement both of productive efficiency and of the quality of cement were becoming clear. These basic features were not, however, reflected in the values of the shares. The lowest level of the ordinary shares in 1909 was 12*s*. 6*d*. for the £10 ordinary shares. There was some recovery early in 1910 when there was once again hope of agreement between the manufacturers; in January 1910 the price reached £2 6*s*. 3*d*. This improvement soon disappeared, however, and the price fell to around £1 and shares were unsaleable at that figure. In the autumn of 1910 the price of the shares began to rise. In an article in the *Economist* in November 1910, the rise is discussed, but the cause obviously not known. There were many transactions and the price rose; as the price rose, those who had hung on to their shares because they were worth so little, began to sell out, all that were offered were taken up and great numbers were bought at prices up to £4. The purchases were made in the name of bankers and for some time O'Hagan did not know who was purchasing. When more than three-quarters of the ordinary shares had been bought, it was revealed that the buyer was a financial syndicate, headed by Lord St Davids. O'Hagan declared that he was not prepared to co-operate if the syndicate merely wished 'to make use of the company to enable them to resell at a large profit',[1] but that he certainly would if they wished to assist to make the company a success. O'Hagan then reports the company solicitor, Sir Frank Crisp, who had seen Lord St Davids, as saying: 'They have come into the speculation because they have heard of your devotion to the company, of all you have done for it, of your efforts to amalgamate the trade, and your belief that if you have sufficient capital at your

[1] O'Hagan, *op. cit.*, Vol. II, p. 83.

disposal you can bring about a complete combination of the cement makers, which should make their shares worth ten pounds or more.'[1]

Lord St Davids is reported to have said to O'Hagan: . . . 'we have been given to understand that if you were given all the capital you required you were certain you could bring about a complete amalgamation of the cement trade.'[2] O'Hagan appears to have stressed the fact that the outlook was poor unless an amalgamation was achieved.

In a subsequent interview with Lord St Davids and his friends they agreed to find £2 million or more for O'Hagan to go ahead and to try to amalgamate the whole trade. The management of the APCM was not to be changed, but Lord St Davids was to become Chairman in place of F. A. White, and Colonel Stanley and Walter Roche, M.P., were to join the board.

Whereas the entire ordinary capital of the APCM had been valued on the Stock Exchange for £114,000 in 1909, two years later, in October 1911, it was valued at £1,134,000. The *Economist* declared that this change was due to the market's valuation of the new directorate. On the whole, however, they thought that the pessimism of two years previously had been overdone.[3] Thus it appears clear that at this date the proposal for a new combine was not generally known.

The first steps towards the formation of the new combine were the purchases of Trecham, Weeks & Co. (one of the three firms which had broken away on the formation of the APCM), and of the Wouldham Cement Works which belonged to S. Pearson & Sons, the contractors. O'Hagan apparently thought that both these negotiations might prove difficult, but the former agreed to a cash offer and the latter was purchased at what O'Hagan thought to be 'rather a large' price. It appears typical of O'Hagan's negotiations that after Lord Cowdray had accepted £100,000 of the payment in certificates of indebtedness, O'Hagan offered him £95,000 in cash for the £100,000 certificates provided that the price on Pearson contract for cement with the Wouldham Works was increased by 2*s.* per ton. This offer was accepted.[4]

The main negotiations followed the initial purchases of the important works with whom difficulties might be encountered and without which the combine could not be effective. The negotiations were private and confidential, but as there were so many firms an 'Outline of Proposals for the Consolidation of the Cement Trade of the United Kingdom' was circulated. In it there is an estimate of capacity in the

[1] O'Hagan, *op. cit.*, Vol., II, p. 84. [2] Ibid., p. 86.
[3] *Economist*, October 28, 1911.
[4] O'Hagan, *op. cit.*, Vol. II, p. 160.

industry of three million tons per annum, and it was stated that the Associated Company controlled 1,250,000 tons and that it was proposed that the new company should acquire a controlling interest in at least a further 1,250,000 tons. A considerable proportion of the purchase price was to be paid in shares, but the Associated Company was prepared to find the necessary cash both for purchase and for modernization, etc. The negotiations took some time and were continuing throughout the second half of 1911.

A purchase of some importance was that of G. and T. Earle of Hull. The purchase of two smaller works at Hull, Robson's and the Skelsey Cement Works, had already been arranged, but G. & T. Earle was an important company in a strong position. In 1907 Earle's had an output of 2,000 tons a week, compared with 1,450 tons per week, which was the combined output of the other two. The peculiar position of Earle's depended partly upon the fact that from an early stage they had 'set out to disregard costs of manufacture and make a cement slightly superior to that which was made by many of their rivals. They established a brand of cement which commanded a price of a couple of shillings a ton over other brands, and the reputation was a lasting one, for although by the new rotary kiln process the associated company made a cement of a higher grade than that of G. & T. Earle, it was difficult to meet them in competition'. In addition, 'unlike any other concern, they had got into direct touch with their customers by opening agencies all over Yorkshire and Lancashire, so that from the commercial side of their business they held a unique position'.[1]

The works was purchased in 1911. The main reasons for the willingness of the Earle family to sell are of some interest. The development of the rotary kiln had reached the point where it had become obvious that much capital must be spent upon conversion. The main partner was willing to find the money, but the others were unwilling. Thus, in effect, the works was available partly as a result of the major technical developments taking place, and partly as a result of the uncertain prospects for large cement works in a cement industry in which competition was unrestricted.

After Earle's was purchased the two other local companies were merged with it and the three together formed a subsidiary of the new company.

On the whole firms appear to have sold out because, as one manufacturer put it: 'I cannot help feeling that the new amalgamation is one of the few ways by which it is possible to put the trade on a con-

[1] O'Hagan, *op. cit.*, Vol. II, pp. 123–4.

crete footing.'[1] There was, however, considerable personal reluctance to abandon the private companies to the combine. In some cases, the reluctance made such unwilling sellers that they were only prepared to sell at very high prices; in a number of these cases the negotiations dragged on and in some they finally broke down. Some were perhaps induced to sell because they were afraid of the consequences of not joining a combine which covered a very high proportion of the trade. On the other hand, the opposite view was also expressed: 'The building trade has been badly hit and cannot stand the effects of unhealthy inflation of prices through cornering; therefore they at all times support the up-to-date individual maker as against the amalgamation. Why some firms are contemplating the idea of combines, thereby cramping themselves and giving away their old connections is a mystery.'[2] This view appears to have been justified by the subsequent history, for good independent manufacturers were able to compete successfully and were profitable until they became so numerous that intense competition developed again.

There were indeed manufacturers who disliked the clause by which they agreed not to set up new works within a period of ten years. One manufacturer, who was doubtful of the combine, even wrote early in 1912: 'As a matter of fact, the money has been floating which requires only a puff of wind to force me into active participation in the increase of the manufacture of cement in various parts of England . . .'

A public announcement of the formation of the British Portland Cement Manufacturers as a subsidiary of APCM was made in December 1911. The new company had a capital of £3,500,000, and was said to control capacity for about 1,500,000 tons per annum. This compares very favourably with the APCM which had more than twice the capital, but a similar (probably slightly smaller) capacity. The only detailed figures of capacity which are available relate to 1907;[3] these do not give a very accurate picture of the situation in 1911; nevertheless, they are sufficient to indicate the relative sizes of the firms in the industry.

The APCM had a weekly capacity of 24,000 tons in 1907. The BPCM bought thirty-two companies; only twenty-eight of those are given in the 1907 figures but, at that time, they controlled 30,720 tons per week. Thus the constituents of the new big combine controlled a capacity capable of about 55,000 tons per week in 1907. The remainder of the industry had a capacity of approximately 12,350 tons per week. About half their output was produced by ten substantial firms

[1] Private letter. [2] Letter to the *Financial News*, November 8, 1911.
[3] Davis: *Portland Cement* (1907), Appendix III.

with an output of 450 tons per week or over. These ten firms were:

Two large firms at West Hartlepool.
Four firms in Warwickshire.
Two firms in the London Area.
One firm in Somerset.
One firm at Newcastle-on-Tyne.

The other half of the capacity of the independent firms was owned by thirty small firms. Seven of these were in Wales and the South-West of England and eight in East Anglia.

The 1907 figures indicate little opposition to the combine in the London area; less than 2,000 tons per week were in the hands of the five independent firms, one of which was very small indeed.

In 1911 it was estimated that the Associated Group (APCM and BPCM) had control of about 75 per cent of the capacity of the industry. It was not a monopoly and, further, it had no control over new entrants. Both these points had an important bearing on the prospects for the success of the group, and in both respects the outlook was uncertain. The scale of production of an individual firm had increased so much that a new entrant or a major works expansion made a considerable difference to productive capacity. In addition, although there were advantages of large scale organization in relation to technical development and know-how, these were to a great extent neutralized by the fact that Continental methods were at least as good as British methods and the firm of F. L. Smidth was in a position to sell excellent equipment to any firm who would buy it, and to supply technical guidance.

The prospects for price control by the Associated Group depended upon lower average costs making possible low average prices which would discourage outside firms from either entering or expanding. When demand falls the large firm with a high proportion of the market is at a disadvantage because its elasticity of demand is low and it cannot afford to retaliate against the price cutting by the small firm with a high elasticity of demand; the small firm is then likely to be able to work at a higher average level of capacity.

While long-term control of prices made possible by a monopolistic position maintained by high efficiency may have been the general objective, it is possible that the future was conceived in much less optimistic and very different terms. The very strong position obtained in 1911 could have been used to make immediate profits by keeping prices high, and these high prices might then have been maintained at the expense of sales and the capacity of the firm reduced as new outside firms increased in size. This policy might have been possible since the rate of obsolescence and depreciation was high and some works were running out of easily accessible raw materials. In other words, capacity could have been reduced simply by withdrawing capital from the industry, and this would not have involved any loss.

The timing of the formation of the new combine is of some interest. The trade had been badly hit by 1911, but no appreciable volume of capacity had left the industry. Had the efforts to combine the trade been made a year or two earlier, it is quite probable that there would have been another vastly overcapitalized combine. Two overcapitalized units would have had a great incentive to fix prices so that they could pay a reasonable dividend on their ordinary shares; the fact that the BPCM was much less heavily capitalized than the APCM may very well have acted as a check.

It is not at all easy to make a reasonable guess about the price at which the combine could have been formed had it been delayed for a year or two. On the one hand, more of the old plants might have been driven out, although this process was becoming very slow; on the other hand, the installation of relatively large rotary kilns capable of producing up to 60,000 tons a year was going ahead and, therefore, the amount of excess capacity might well have increased. Several small firms had to leave the industry to compensate for the erection of one modern plant at this date. On the whole, it appears that the formation of the combine was well timed from the point of view of its capitalization. Fitzgerald, in *Industrial Combination in England*, even argued that the capitalization was based entirely upon depression profits and that it was somewhat undervalued.[1]

The question as to whether or not the formation of the BPCM was or was not in the public interest is rather easier to answer in general terms than the usual question of this type. The immediate effect on the efficiency of the industry was almost wholly good. The combine was able to reduce the amount of transport costs by confining the sales efforts of individual works to smaller areas and, probably more important, to close the inefficient works which had either high costs or produced poor-quality cement. It is said that after the formation of the combine twenty works on the Thames and Medway were closed immediately. This caused immediate ill feeling and distress, but was nevertheless clearly in the interests of increased efficiency. The value to the company was, however, somewhat diminished by the fact that it caused a deterioration in labour relations and in 1912 there were numerous strikes and 'it is stated that on different occa-

[1] p. 106.

sions the Thames and Medway works were totally closed.'[1] Partly as a result of these difficulties and partly as a result of the poor demand, profits were lower than in 1911 and no dividend was paid on the APCM shares.

The difficulty in maintaining efficiency in imperfectly competitive industries lies largely in the fact that the imperfections protect the existing firms and thus make the elimination of the inefficient slow and reduce the scope for expansion. It thus appears that any change in organization which eliminates the inefficient and reduces the wastes of imperfect competition without at the same time raising prices or controlling new entry is likely to be in the public interest.

The new combine had no control whatever over new entry into the industry. This is demonstrated by the fact that in 1912 two new firms were established. One was the Cliffe works of the Thames Portland Cement Co. This works was built by Broads, the large London company of builders' merchants, and appears to be a clear example of a firm insuring its supplies and taking full advantage of its ensured outlet. The other new firm was British Standard Portland Cement Co., which was associated with E. J. & W. Goldsmith, the barge owners; they were probably afraid that they would lose the cement trade on the Thames.

It is difficult to assess the more short-term effect of the new combine on prices. It was not strong enough to control prices but, by eliminating much of the excess and obsolescent capacity in the hands of outside firms, it reduced substantially the amount of cement which would be put on the market at cut prices. Most of the remaining outside firms could sell their output without either 'special' prices or freight absorption on more than a small fraction. In this situation price leadership was relatively effective.

Trade was moderate in 1911–12, but it was improving and was good in 1913; the APCM paid a 5 per cent dividend (the first) on its ordinary shares. The state of trade was an important factor in determining the effectiveness of the price leadership. Whether prices were higher than they would have been depended largely upon whether the Alliance, which was working fairly effectively in 1910–11, would have continued; and this in turn depended to a large extent upon demand.

It is thus difficult to draw any positive conclusion, for while the new large combine undoubtedly would have prevented competition as severe as that of 1908–10, it is by no means certain that this would have recurred before 1914. It is quite unlikely that the price level set by the Associated Group was any higher than that of the Alliance, and

[1] *Economist*, October 5, 1912.

it is possible that it was lower, since agreement did not have to be obtained.

Since the improvements in efficiency were not offset either by price increases or by restriction of entry, the effects of the new combine in the period 1911–14 appear to have been 'in the public interest'. The more long-term effects must be discussed in the main conclusion after consideration of the subsequent history.

CHAPTER 6

1918–29

THE period between 1911 and 1918 was one of consolidation for the Associated Group. Trade was not good during the war, but prices remained firm. The combine pursued a cautious dividend policy, paying no ordinary dividend and passing the preference dividend in 1917. Immediately after the end of the war both the home and foreign demand for cement rose and there were shortages.

The problem of post-war development and expansion gave rise to differences of opinion on the boards of the Associated Group. Despite opposition, a new scheme of joint management for the APCM and the BPCM was announced.[1] After this time the boards of the two companies remained identical. The only information about the internal conflicts is given by O'Hagan. He found that he had lost his former influence, and after considerable ill feeling he left the Company in about 1921. He speaks of making 'my last dying fight with my colleagues;[2] in this rather confused section it appears that the main conflict arose over the question as to who should control the company. The older directors of the APCM, it seems, were in conflict with those who came from the BPCM companies, but it is not quite clear what policy issues were at stake. It may have been the question of post-war output policy. O'Hagan felt strongly that the post-war boom would be shortlived, but others saw the high demand and thought that it would continue for several years. Proposals were made to prepare for a boom by re-opening old works and largely extending existing works, and O'Hagan wrote: 'After spending enormous sums of money in re-opening closed works and increasing the size of existing works, they waited for the boom which never came, and which everyone should have seen they had no right to expect. The closed works had scarcely been reopened, the additions to existing works had not been completed, when the orders went forward to stop all extensions, for the boom had failed to materialize and the

[1] *Economist*, October 4, 1919.
[2] O'Hagan, *op. cit.*, Vol. II, p. 109.

C

production of cement had to be reduced rather than increased.'[1]

Although the high post-war demand gave rise to difficult long-term policy decisions within the combine, immediate price policy was made fairly simple. Through the initiative of the combine, the old Alliances, the Thames and Medway, the Inland Cement Makers, and the Tyne and Tees were combined to form the Cement Makers' Federation. Plans for this new organization were made in 1918, and it was in being by the time the war ended. The new Federation adopted a fairly simple scheme; it was to negotiate on behalf of the industry, represent the industry, and to effect closer co-operation and control within the industry. Prices and terms were to be agreed on a district basis, but each district, although it was to have the power to raise prices, was not to lower them without consent of the Central Authority. There were no penalties, and no controls over output.

The Federation in this form obtained a membership which covered 90 per cent of the output of the industry. Some attempt was made to curb outsiders by introducing an exclusive trading rebate. While demand was high this had little effect; later it would have influenced the large firms rather than the smaller since the latter often served local markets only.

The Report on Cement and Mortar stated: 'Independent manufacturers numbering approximately fourteen are able, however, in the existing state of the market to sell at high prices.' 'We are informed by several independent manufacturers that they are unable to manufacture profitably at Federation prices and that, although they would like to adopt these prices, they are bound to determine selling prices on costs of production and on that basis the Federation prices are, it is submitted, too low.'[2]

This paragraph is particularly interesting in that it illustrates the fact that the increases in productive efficiency resulting from technical development were resulting in a wide range of efficiency and that the least efficient were getting into a weak position. The Census returns show that the output per man increased from 207 tons per annum in 1907 to 266 tons in 1924; savings in fuel consumption were also of some importance.

On rather rough estimates the industry at this time consisted of the APCM with nine works, the BPCM with sixteen works, about six subsidiaries of the APCM and BPCM, twenty-two other works in the Federation (ten of which were small), and the fourteen (mentioned in Cmd 1091) outside the Federation. In the optimism of the post-war boom some new works were built and many plans were considered.

[1] O'Hagan, *op. cit.*, Vol. II, p. 111. [2] Cmd 1091, 1920.

Lord Cowdray considered the erection, at a cost of about a million pounds, of a large up-to-date cement works on the Thames. He happened to have the site which was suitable, and as he was connected with S. Pearson Ltd, and had made cement at Wouldham works which he had sold to the BPCM, he knew about cement. O'Hagan claims to have persuaded him to abandon his project, partly on the grounds that the boom would not last, and partly on the grounds that it would have been a 'shabby thing' to do, as he had been paid to go out of the business.[1]

Although Lord Cowdray's project was abandoned a number went forward. The Kent Portland Cement Co., a public company with an issued capital of £1,200,000, was acquired, a large works being erected near Greenhithe. The purchase consideration was £450,000, an option over 325,000 shares and the discharge of the vendor company's liabilities which together with its debenture debt of £350,000 amounted to approximately £367,000. The directorate was extremely strong. The nine directors included not only Clarence Hatry and John Cory, but also Sir J. W. Beynon of the Aberthaw and Bristol Channel Portland Cement Co. and of various iron, coal and shipping companies, a director of the London & Rochester Barge Co. Ltd, and three others connected with shipping and finance and coal. This enterprise was a failure, because technical difficulties and miscalculations resulted in so much additional expenditure that the company was unable to complete the buildings and installations. The works were acquired by the APCM in 1922 before cement making had begun.

The Humber Portland Cement Co. was registered in 1917 having been 'formed to acquire a lease of about 434 acres of clay land and 158 acres of chalk land at Melton and Welton Hull, and to construct a Portland Cement Works. The purchase money of £25,000 in fully-paid shares of which 15,000 have been allotted and 10,000 are to be allotted when an output of 100,000 per annum is reached'.[2] The authorized capital was £350,000 and the issued capital £200,000. The authorized capital was increased in 1920 and again in 1921, when it was £500,000. Again the board looked strong. The chairman was R. Lakin of Greaves, Bull and Lakin Ltd (a Portland cement company), and the board included Maxted and Knott, a firm of three or four people connected with coal, engineering and shipping, and G. V. Maxted, a consulting engineer. This company was also a failure, and by 1921 no dividend had been paid and output had not reached 100,000 tons.[3] The failure was largely due to price increases and some

[1] O'Hagan, *op. cit.*, Vol. II, pp. 163–4. [2] Stock Exchange Intelligence.
[3] Stock Exchange Intelligence.

small production delays, both of which increased costs to such an extent that all the available working capital, which had been difficult to raise, was used up. A resolution to wind up was finally passed in July 1924 and the undertaking and assets were sold to G. & T. Earle Ltd, the big Hull subsidiary of the BPCM.[1]

G. V. Maxted played a very important role in the cement industry at this time. His firm, Maxted and Knott, had been engineers to the APCM; when they decided to do their own engineering Maxted determined to continue to make a living building cement works. Apart from F. L. Smidth, the Danish firm, they were the only people with knowledge of modern cement works. Edgar Allens, who became one of the main suppliers of cement making machinery, worked mainly from Maxted and Knott's drawings and obtained their knowledge of the business from them. The building of not only the Humber works but also the Dunstable (see p. 72), and Oxford and Shipton (see pp. 72-3) works may be attributed in large part to the determination of G. V. Maxted.

A third entry into the Portland cement trade immediately after the war was of a very different type. In 1919 the Chinnor Lime Company began to make cement by the old chamber-kiln method. This small-scale business was successful and the firm continued to make cement. A rotary kiln was installed and lit in September, 1928.

A fourth new competitor had also appeared soon after the war.[2] This was the Gillingham Portland Cement Co. Ltd, which was started by an ex-manager of one of the BPCM works. He was under a ten-year bond not to put in a rotary kiln and began with chamber kilns; as soon as the ten years had passed a 200 ft. Edgar Allen rotary kiln was installed. These two examples show that the extreme profitability of cement for the short period after the war was very significant in that it allowed small works to enter cement production and so put them in a position to take advantage of the increased demand of the middle 'twenties.

After 1922 the demand for cement began to expand considerably and by 1924 output was nearly 50 per cent higher than it had been in 1920. One of the results of the favourable outlook was the renewed interest in speculation in the shares of the APCM. The APCM issued an official communique in November 1923: 'My directors have for a long time been aware that considerable purchases of ordinary shares of the company have been made by a financial group with whom we have for some time been in friendly communication, but the total holding of such a group, which has now been disclosed to us,

[1] Stock Exchange Intelligence.

[2] Information on date of actual opening is not available.

can in no sense be described as affording control of our company, even if such had been the object of the group.'[1] This communique, however, soon became out-dated, and in 1924 Mr H. S. Horne was able to march into the board and show that he had control of the company. His purchases had been made over a period; for a time the APCM jobber had been unable to find out who was buying. By 1924, however, Horne had about 1½ to 2 million of the 4½ million £1 ordinary shares. He is said to have paid an average of nearly 25*s.* per share, which, although it looked high in 1924 when the shares fell to about 15*s.*, was not high in terms of the prospects of the company. A. C. Davis of the APCM was saying at the time that the shares would eventually go to about £4. We have been told that Horne purchases were mainly with a view to selling to American interests and that he put up half the money and the (New York) Chase Bank advanced the other half. When control had been secured, four new directors including General Critchley and P. A. M. Nash of Metropolitan Vickers were put on the Board, and P. M. Stewart replaced F. C. Stanley as chairman. Horne's control was, however, shortlived since the American interests, with whom he had no definite agreement, refused to buy and the Chase Bank (of New York) foreclosed and sold all the shares at 12*s.* 6*d.* These were bought by the APCM jobber who put them back on to the market without allowing the price to fall below 15*s.* Horne was bankrupt for the second time in his remarkable career.

The changes which Horne had brought about on the board were not, however, reversed, and the new management set out with vigour to make the APCM and BPCM sound and profitable. Malcolm Stewart's first speech as chairman, in 1925, is of some importance and marks the beginning of a new period. He attacked the past financial management: 'The company started with works which were obsolescent, paid too much for them and then in addition paid £200,000 for rotary kiln patents which afforded no protection against competitors. . . . The overcapitalization must have been obvious but no reconstruction was proposed when such a policy was practicable.' He then explained the need for a conservative dividend policy to reduce the overvaluation of assets. The policy advocated by the board was the improvement of the earning capacity of their assets by the modernization of the two largest works, Bevans and Swanscombe; this was to be done not by patching them up, but by making them second to none. The other important feature of the new policy was a reorganization of the administration of the company. Individual control of sales, production and finance was to re-

[1] *Economist*, November 10, 1923.

place control by committees. In effect these changes meant that the whole organization was to be much more closely integrated. It was at this stage that the Blue Circle trade mark was introduced and the old brand names largely discontinued; only the sales organization of G. & T. Earle, in the north, was retained.

Fitzgerald in *Industrial Combination in England*, published in 1927, evidently regarded the reorganization as long overdue. While saying that the poverty of the combine was chiefly due to the 'prolonged depression in the building trade' he added: 'defective management has, however, been an important contributory factor'.[1] This diagnosis appears to be unjustified and to ignore the difficulties of centralized management in the period before 1914, that is to say, before telephones, cars, good secretarial and accounting staff were readily available; further, it ignores the difficulties involved in altering the management of old private companies in an industry where methods were varied and changing rapidly, and where the product varied sufficiently for brand names to be of great importance. Central control of the sales of a large number of different brands would have been exceedingly difficult. The 'delay' in reorganization of the internal organization of the combine has its parallel in the 'delay' in the reorganization of Lever's soap companies.[2] The wisdom of such 'delay' in some circumstances is demonstrated by the dismal failure of the attempted reorganization in the selling policies of the Calico Printers' Association.[3]

It is perhaps possible that the reorganization should have been made at the end of the war, for by then many of the features which made the post-war conditions different from the pre-war conditions had begun to appear. They did not, however, show clearly until the early 'twenties. Perhaps the most important was the improvement in the quality and reliability of the product. New and much higher British Standard Specifications were introduced in 1915 and again in 1920. This meant that the product of different works were less differentiated. Secondly, the new works were substantially more efficient than the old. In 1929 the *Economist* reported that in the five years ended December 31, 1928, the combine had reduced manufacturing costs by about 37 per cent;[4] the possibility of these reductions in cost must have become apparent by 1924. The economies were partly the result of larger kilns, the new kilns being about 300 ft. compared with less than 200 ft. for the most modern pre-war. By the 1920's however, there were also increasing economies from lay-out

[1] P. Fitzgerald, p. 107. [2] See p. 257. [3] See p. 174.
[4] *Economist*, August 3, 1929.

and mechanical handling, and the point had been reached where the new plants were designed for economy of labour at every stage and were planned for a large flow of production through the works. In 1934 a revised and enlarged edition of *Portland Cement* by A. C. Davis was produced. It is symptomatic of the changed emphasis that there were for the first time chapters on 'Transporting and Elevating' and 'Packing and Despatch'. 'Until 1914 hand filling and hand loading were almost universal.'[1] By 1934 much progress had been made in these departments but 'means of transport of material constitute a large proportion of labour saving appliances and the makers of various types of conveyors and elevators, mechanical and pneumatic, have a wealth of argument which frequently makes decision difficult'.[2]

In this new situation the reorganization of the APCM and BPCM companies was clearly desirable. The new works were run by chemists and engineers and the sales were centrally controlled and nationally advertised under the new Blue Circle trade mark.

The modernization of the APCM went ahead relatively fast. At the Annual General Meeting in April 1926, Malcom Stewart was able to announce that the reconstruction of Bevan's Works was almost complete, that one kiln was already producing, and that he hoped that three would be 'in full swing within two or three months', producing 7,500 tons weekly and, ultimately, he trusted, 10,000 tons weekly. This output replaced an output of 5,000 tons weekly obtained from twelve kilns which were scrapped. In 1927 it was reported that the chamber kilns at the Crown works had been replaced by a rotary kiln, and that the reconstruction of Swanscombe (which involved replacing sixteen rotary kilns by three modern kilns with a capacity of 400,000 tons per annum) had been started. It was also claimed that the assets had been depreciated so that they were no longer overvalued. Further it was stated that 'with the completion of the reconstruction now commenced at Swanscombe works the company will have an annual productive capacity exceeding 1,250,000 tons from efficient rotary kiln plant'. In 1928 the chairman spoke of the 'revolutionized' manufacturing position of the company, and the importance of goodwill of the 'Blue Circle'. By 1929, after an expenditure of £4,500,000, the group had completed the rebuilding programme with the exception of the reconstruction of the Swanscombe Works which was to be ready within a few months. In 1929 the companies were operating twenty rotary kiln works, having closed the smaller and less efficient works.

At this time the capacity of the group was over three million tons

[1] Davis, *Portland Cement* (1934), p. 258. [2] Ibid., p. 26.

per annum out of a total of just over six million tons. It was reported in the *Economist* of August 3, 1929, that the group had increased its manufacturing capacity from two to three million tons in the previous five years. Further, it was pointed out that the company was in a strong financial position having raised only £750,000 fresh capital, spent £4,500,000 and, at the same time, improved the cash position. Dividend policy was extremely conservative.

TABLE I

PROFITS AND DIVIDENDS OF THE ASSOCIATED GROUP

The Associated Portland Cement Manufacturers' Limited

Date	Gross Profit £'000	Proposed Dividend £'000	Dividend % on Ordinary	Additions to Plant £'000
1920	952·5	213·7	10	258
1921	—	—	5	—
1922	657·4	111	5	989·4
1923	582·2	126	Nil[2]	35·4
1924	667	125·6	Nil	117·3
1925	899	198	6	26·7
1926	788	153	4	583·5
1927	901·6	263	8	133·6
1928	634·5	240	8	457·3
1929	936	240	8	240
1930	955	240	8	202·7

British Portland Cement Manufacturers' Limited

Date	Gross Profit £'000[1]	Proposed Dividend £'000	Dividend % on Ordinary	Additions to Plant £'000
1920	558·8	103·7	15	457·8
1921	479·8	69·1	10	486·1
1922	471·8	69·1	10	37
1923	449·4	69·1	10	13·4
1924	479·5	69·1	10	237·3
1925	773	140	15	1,337·5
1926	644·2	105	$12\frac{1}{2}$	[3]
1927	722·3	168	15	137
1928	722·6	168	15	563·6
1929	722	168	15	682·2
1930	732	168	15	181

In the period up to 1929 when the British and Associated Companies were building up a strong, sound position the rest of the industry was also changing rapidly. With the great increase in efficiency which gave a reduction in costs of about 40 per cent, the small firms had become of little importance; but there were by this time a substantial number of new firms and a number of completely modernized firms. The development of these firms must now be examined.

The Kent, Humber, Chinnor and Gillingham Companies which were established before 1921 have already been discussed. New companies and greatly increased capacity continued to appear throughout the 'twenties to such an extent that the industry in 1929 was very far from the almost monopolistic structure of 1919.

In about 1922 the Dreadnought Company was formed with the support of Farrow's Bank; land was acquired at Barrington in Cambridgeshire, and the company began to erect a works. When Farrow's Bank failed, the company went bankrupt and came on to the market. There was some question of its being acquired by the nearby East Anglian Cement Company, but the new undertaking was large and the East Anglian Cement Company disliked the obligations involved in taking over the Barrington Light Railway Company, which is an essential part of the Barrington works. In 1924 the undertaking was acquired by Eastwoods Ltd, a firm of builders' merchants and brick manufacturers, with a new and energetic management and a large sales organization. The works were completed and began to produce in about 1925. The entry of Eastwoods into the cement trade was important, for they were to become a fairly large manufacturer; in addition their vertical organization gave them a marketing strength which made them rather less dependent upon price agreements than most firms and made them an important, and probably permanent, competitor with the combine.

In 1929 Eastwoods acquired the Lewes Portland Cement Lime Co. Ltd, and changed the name to Eastwoods (Lewes) Cement Ltd. Arthur Batchelor, one of the founders of the Lewes Portland Cement & Lime Co. Ltd, which was originally called Glover & Batchelor Ltd, joined the Eastwoods management.

---

[1] The Profit and Loss Accounts of BPCM from 1919 to 1930 inclusive include income from investments in the Gross Profit figure. *Source:* Company Reports.

[2] The figures for 1923–24, years in which no ordinary dividend was paid, show that about £126,000 was required for the interest on debenture and preference shares. This was reduced slightly in subsequent years by repayment of debt.

[3] The value of the assets of the BPCM actually fell in 1926; the large increases in the assets of APCM indicated that there was some transfer of assets from the BPCM to APCM.

In the early 'twenties Albert Batchelor & Co. Ltd. was started by a brother of Arthur Batchelor. This enterprise appears to have been based upon the technical knowledge and commercial connections of the founder. It was a private company and very different from the big public companies. This company was of some importance since it pursued an independent line and generally refused to join any form of price agreement.

In 1925–6 two very important new public companies, the Dunstable Portland Cement Company and the Holborough Cement Company, were established. These companies built works, with capacities of 150,000 and 234,000 tons per annum respectively, and have several features in common. The Dunstable works was put up largely by Maxted and Knott,[1] and Edgar Allen Ltd, the cement machinery makers. The potential strength of the firm clearly lay in the fact that it was an excellent modern works; at this date, as has already been indicated, a good modern works had such an advantage over many of the older works that it was possible to hope that competition in quality and price would be sufficient to make the firm profitable, even though it had no marketing connections. The Holborough works was put up by the same type of people. It was equipped by Metropolitan Vickers and was again a speculative enterprise, largely independent of other cement interests. It seems probable that the promoters of both these works were made to feel more confident by the thought that either the Blue Circle Group would maintain prices or be willing to absorb them, should competition become very severe.

In 1926 Casebourne & Company (1926) Ltd was formed. This was a subsidiary of ICI Ltd, which acquired an old-established cement manufacturer, modernized the works and began to produce cement made from by-products from the heavy chemical works. This firm produced cement which could be sold at very low prices, the output depending upon the amount of the by-product available.

In 1927 a completely new works was built at Kirton Lindsay in Lincolnshire. The Caustic Lime and Macadam Company was registered in 1916, its name was changed to Central Portland Cement Company in 1923, and it became a public company in 1927. As the issued capital was increased in 1927 from £40,000 to £150,000 it appears that a small works was replaced with a small, modern works. The capacity in 1928 was about 50,000 tons per annum.

At about the same time great changes took place in the Oxford & Shipton Cement Co. Ltd. In 1927 it was turned into a public company with an issued capital of £450,000 and a large new works was

[1] See p. 66.

built. The new directors included G. V. Maxted of Maxted and Knott, H. L. Mond of ICI Ltd and a number of others with big financial interests. Although the new company was built up on the basis of an old company its development and form were not like those of the Dunstable and Holborough companies, and a number of the same people were involved.

In 1929 another entirely new works was built. The Ketton Portland Cement Company was formed as a subsidiary of Thomas W. Ward Ltd, of Sheffield, a firm of metal and building materials merchants. The new works with a capacity of 60,000 tons per annum began to produce in the middle of 1929 and the output was marketed by Thomas W. Ward & Co. This company's structure was thus comparable with that of Eastwoods and of similar significance.

The erection of all these new works illustrates two important points. The first is that by this time the making of cement and cement machinery had reached the point where a new works could be ordered and built and a manager engaged to run it. Thus the new firm was at little disadvantage compared with the old-established firm, experience and know-how being of relatively little importance. Second, financial interests could enter the cement industry provided they acquired good plant and were well located; they were less dependent upon the day-to-day running of the business than is usual in other industries.

The history of the cement industry in the 'twenties presents a very clear case of an industry which could be entered rather readily. There was a growing demand, new works were much more efficient than the old, there were constructional engineers and machinery makers who had experience in putting up new works, and no large managerial staff was required. The managerial qualities required for running a going concern were very different from the entrepreneurial qualities required for the establishment of new ones; the managerial and entrepreneural functions had become to a large extent divorced from each other. Prospects for new works remained good so long as there was obsolete capacity in the industry which could be driven out in the event of a decline in demand.

In these circumstances, comparable with those of the pre-1914 period, entrepreneurs were attracted into the industry. However, as the amount of new capacity increased, the opportunities for successful entry into the cement industry shrank rapidly. Two significant events have already been mentioned: in 1929 the Ketton works were started by Thomas W. Ward, and Eastwoods purchased the Lewes Portland Cement and Lime Co. and modernized them. It appears that competition was such that the prospects for vertical organizations had begun to look more attractive and the entry of new independent cement firms was checked.

The prospects of severe competition within the horizontal structure of the industry and the apparent impossibility of the large independent units achieving any degree of stability so long as competition remained almost unrestricted, are perhaps the most important factors which led to the re-entry of Mr H. S. Horne into the cement industry. He was also influenced by his conviction that adequate finance, plus modern management, could increase the earning capacity of old-established firms, especially in an industry which was changing. Mr Horne's theory was 'that financial trusts directed by progressive industrial thinkers and advised by technical and commercial experts could, by acquiring substantial share interests in carefully selected concerns, create industrial units of maximum efficiency.'[1] In this period, Mr Horne put his theories into practice in the cement, wood pulp and newspaper industries.

In 1926 an investment company called British Cement Products and Finance Co. Ltd, was incorporated with a capital of £200,000 to acquire interests in the cement industry; the prospectus disclosed that the company was already engaged in business related to the cement industry.[2] Although this investment company was specifically concerned with cement, two other investment trusts, the Associated Anglo-Atlantic Corporation Ltd, and the Carmelite Trust, were also involved. The finance of the companies was so exceedingly complicated that it is necessary to speak of the Horne Group. In 1926 the Ship Canal Portland Cement Manufacturers Ltd was acquired. This company had works at Ellesmere Port on the Manchester Ship Canal; it was registered in 1911, and its name was changed from Stanlow Works Estate Ltd in 1912. No dividend had been paid by 1925 and in 1924 the paid-up capital had been reduced. The works was fairly isolated from other manufacturers, but had to transport limestone from North Wales.

In the next three years the Horne Group's cement interests were expanded by the acquisition of five more large companies and one small one.

In April 1927, Greaves, Bull and Lakin was floated as a public company; this was an old-established works at Harbury in Warwickshire. The authorized capital was £400,000 and the Ship Canal Portland Cement Manufacturing Co. Ltd took up 400,000 5*s*. shares and obtained an option on further shares at 6*s*. At the end of 1927 the

[1] *Economist*, November 30, 1929.
[2] *Economist*, March, 1927, p. 539.

Horne Group acquired the Dunstable Portland Cement Co. and the Holborough Cement Co.[1] The fourth to be acquired was Smeed and Dean of Sittingbourne. This was a very large transaction, since the firm had a large stock brick works, many acres of fruit trees and a jam factory. The works was an old one and the owner had retained chamber kilns until the early 'twenties, since he was opposed to Sunday work. In the early 'twenties a new rotary plant was installed. The fifth acquisition of a substantial cement works was that of British Standard Portland Cement Ltd. This firm belonged to Goldsmiths who had barge interests on the Thames; the works was one of those built just after the formation of the BPCM in 1911, it had been kept completely up to date at considerable expense and was a good buy.

In addition to the purchase of the five cement works, the Group also acquired a controlling interest in Wiggins & Co. (Hammersmith) Ltd, a firm of builders' merchants. This firm owned a very small cement works, the Rhee Valley Cement Co. at Shepreth, near Cambridge, but it was more important as a merchanting organization, and its acquisition gave the Group an additional market.

There were rumours that the Horne Group was trying to acquire the Thames Portland Cement Co. This would have given them further market outlets, since the company was associated with Broads, a large firm of builders' merchants. The works was built before the war and in the absence of any substantial modernization was becoming out of date.

The Horne Group thus consisted of six large cement works of varying efficiency and one very small works which was of little importance. The works had a combined capacity of approximately 1,000,000 tons. This is rather under one-third of the capacity of the Blue Circle group and about one-sixth of the total capacity of the industry. In July 1921 a merger of the six large firms under one central controlling company was proposed and in August the Ship Canal Portland Cement Manufacturers Ltd was changed into Allied Cement Manufacturers Ltd. This was apparently a financial change rather than a practical administrative one, since the group's products were already sold under the trade name 'Red Triangle'. The Red Triangle and the slogan 'Right Across Britain' had already been extensively advertised, and at the annual general meeting in July 1929, Mr O. J. S. Piper, the chairman of the Ship Canal Co., spoke of the Red Triangle Group.

Before considering the subsequent history of the Red Triangle

[1] See p. 72.

group, it is interesting to examine its position and its prospects in 1929. In 1927 prices were apparently fairly satisfactory, although there was some price cutting which kept the general level low and led to considerable cross hauling. In 1928, however, competition became severe and for five months up to November 1928 'there was a price-cutting war between the Associated group, the Horne group of companies and other independent companies. This was brought to an end in November, when the Horne group and the independents joined the Cement Manufacturers' Federation.'[1] The price arrangements of the period 1919 to 1939 will be discussed at the end of this section, but mention of the price war is necessary for an understanding of the position of the Horne Group.

The *Economist* examined the position of the cement companies in an article on August 3, 1929.[2] On the whole, it appears to have taken a favourable view of the general structure of the Horne Group. It stated that the group united several independent companies with the view of modernizing their equipment and centralizing their distribution and that a new selling organization, Portland Cement Selling and Distribution Co., had been formed. It was thought that the cement trade outlook was encouraging since competition at home was no longer cut-throat. The Chairman of the Ship Canal Company was quoted as stating that the merger of the producing companies should lead to still greater economies, that the group was within measurable distance of disposing of 90 per cent of its combined output of over one million tons, and that the merchanting businesses absorbed (the group having pursued a policy of controlling distributing agencies of builders' materials) were improving their sales and profits. The *Economist* then stated that ' "The Red Triangle" group would certainly seem to be working on the right lines. The operating companies, having paid off their preliminary expenses and survived the rate-cutting war, are now amalgamated in one concern and should gain in many ways as a result. In view, however, of the effect on their balance sheets of the recent struggle (and, one must add, of the policy adopted as regards the distribution of profits) those concerned will probably deem it necessary to submit to the slow process of building up a strong financial position as the best guarantee of future prosperity.' Earlier in the article it was reported that 'this price-cutting was estimated to have cost the "Blue Circle" group about £400,000, but had it gone on longer its effects on the resources of the "Red Triangle" group could scarcely have been contemplated with equanimity'.

[1] *Economist*, March 23, 1929, p. 642. [2] See pp. 230-1.

Even in January 1931, after the bankruptcy of Mr Horne, the new directors of the Red Triangle group thought that the group could be put on a profitable basis if immediate finance could be found to meet pressing liabilities. In a brief note commenting on the failure of the company to secure the necessary finance, the *Economist* stated: 'It would be interesting to know what attitude was adopted by the banks in this matter, seeing that there was some reason to believe that the company, given a solution of its immediate financial difficulties, might ultimately have justified its place in the cement trade in this country.'[1]

A. C. Davis of the Associated Group is reported to have thought that, while the ultimate prospects of the Red Triangle group were favourable and Horne's general ideas sound, his ventures were badly timed. This may have been an *ex-post* judgment based on the fact that the slump occurred just when the group should have been becoming established; on the other hand it may have been based upon the idea that, although some such amalgamation was inevitable, the trade was not at that stage sufficiently concentrated nor the shares of the market of the merged firms sufficiently well established. This is a difficult question, but by 1927 it was probably becoming apparent that it was necessary for the large new firms to have sales organizations to compete with the Associated Group. None of the firms could afford continual price cutting and, therefore, each must have an effective sales organization.

Other opinions indicate that the failure of the Red Triangle Group was due in large part to poor management rather than to unsound structure. At the Annual General Meeting of the APCM in 1930, Malcolm Stewart said that '. . . supreme control should be in the hands of those with practical experience and a record of successful management. . . . Where industry needs reformation it must be reformed from within. . . . There are too many people pulling the strings of industry who have never been through the mill and never gained a practical and technical experience . . .'[2] These remarks appear to have been references to the Red Triangle Group, and while it is difficult to agree that industries must always be reformed from within, Stewart was clearly indicating that the Red Triangle Group was inefficient. Many people have since reported that the internal management was unsound and the technical and commercial direction poor.

All these opinions are of some importance since they all tend to indicate that Horne's Red Triangle Group, although the product of a

[1] *Economist*, January, 17, 1931, p. 129. [2] *Economist*, April 5, 1930, pp. 798–800.

single financier, was not simply a financial speculation. They indicate rather that it was the direct result of the structure of the industry and that its failure was not inevitable. This is emphasized because there is some tendency to regard such short-lived and spectacular enterprises as freaks and to regard the fact that they influenced the course of subsequent development as an indication that that development was, in part, fortuitous.

Having examined the major events of the period 1919–29, it is convenient to summarize the composition of the industry at that time.

The only detailed information about the relative size of firms is given in terms of 'Approximate Annual Capacity' and relates to the year 1928. It is clear that these figures include a considerable amount of obsolete and surplus capacity since the total is 6,288,300 tons per annum, whereas deliveries of cement in that year to the home and export markets were 4,333,000 tons.[1] As some firms had very much more surplus and excess capacity than others their share of 'capacity' is not a measure of their share of the market. Nevertheless a useful picture of the industry is obtained from an analysis of the figures.

The total annual capacity of 6,288,300 tons belonged to thirty-eight companies with sixty-nine works (three of which were thought, by one manufacturer, to be ineffective). Table II opposite shows the way in which the capacity was distributed between companies.

Thus in 1928 the Associated Group had more than half the capacity. This corresponds quite closely to the claim that in 1930 they had 57 per cent of the market. This may be compared with 69 per cent of the market in 1921. The estimate given in the *Economist* in August 1929 that the Blue Circle group had 75 per cent of the trade and a capacity of 4,500,000 tons would appear to be exaggerated.

Having examined the structural changes in the industry in the period up to 1928–9, and the approximate situation in 1928, it is now possible to go back to consider the price agreements and the effectiveness of the Cement Makers' Federation during this period. This is being considered last because, whereas the great changes which took place in the industry appear to have been affected very little by the price agreements, the effectiveness of agreements and the nature of the co-operation between manufacturers was certainly affected by the rate of change in the structure of the industry.

The formation of the Cement Makers' Federation in 1918 and the

[1] *Cement Costs*, report by the Committee appointed by the Minister of Works (fforde Report), HMSO 1947, Appendix V, p. 28.

Table II

The Distribution of Output Between the Companies in 1928

	Works	Capacity Tons per annum	
1. The Associated Group:			
APCM, Ltd ..	8 works	3,648,800	
BPCM, Ltd ..	16 works		
G. & T. Earle (1925), Ltd ..	4 works		
2. Red Triangle Group:			
Ship Canal Portland Cement Manufacturers Ltd ..	6 large works	1,010,000	4,658,800
Holborough Cement Co. Ltd			
Dunstable P. Cement Co. Ltd			
Greaves, Bull & Lakin (Harbury Works), Ltd			
Smeed, Dean & Co. Ltd ..			
British Standard Cement Co.			
Rhee Valley P. C. Co. Ltd ..	1 small works		
3. Five major independent firms:			
Aberthaw & Bristol Channel Portland Cement Co. Ltd	2 works		833,000
Casebourne & Co. (1926) Ltd			
Oxford & Shipton Cement Ltd			
Tunnel Portland Cement Co. Ltd ..			
Eastwoods Cement Ltd			
			5,491,800
4. Ten medium-sized works almost all of which had rotary kilns: (These works were all much the same size —*c* 50,000 tons per annum—and only three of them were near London)			521,000
			6,012,800
5. Twelve small firms: (It is doubtful whether even one of them had a rotary kiln and some were certainly using chamber kilns)			275,500
			6,288,300

institution of price agreements without penalties has already been discussed. The Federation covered about 90 per cent of the industry and only three or four of the more substantial firms remained outside. These price agreements almost certainly led to the maintenance of higher prices than would otherwise have ruled in 1922. Nevertheless, prices were reduced substantially in that year. Between 1922 and 1925 the demand for cement increased substantially and sales rose, on a rough estimate, by about 75 per cent. During this period the Associated Group appears to have acted as price leader. Little information is available about the period, but since the Associated group was both relatively efficient, compared with many of the members of the Federation, and particularly anxious to keep the price agreements in operation, it seems likely that prices were kept down to levels which reduced the incentive to undercut to the minimum compatible with a 'normal' return on new capital. New entrants were breaking into the market and it seems unlikely that the APCM encouraged them to do so by keeping the Federation prices at levels which yielded a more than adequate profit. Certainly in this period prices remained sensitive to changes in cost and changes in shares of the market; prices were again reduced in 1924 despite the big increase in output.

In March 1928 the Chairman of the APCM, at the annual general meeting, said 'cement manufacturers had for many years and to a considerable extent co-operated to secure reasonable trading conditions. . . . No industry called more clearly for the benefits of co-operation than the cement trade . . .'[1] By this time, however, competitive conditions were changing. On the one hand, the older smaller manufacturers were finding the new price levels low. In October 1926, the year of the coal strike, the Cement Manufacturers' Federation announced a new surcharge of 10*s*. per ton in England and Wales which, they said, was necessary on account of the scarcity of fuel and increased freight rates. One small manufacturer found this increase 'very welcome although woefully belated'; it is significant that this firm also suffered a prolonged strike concerning conditions of employment and wages. It appears that at this stage the members of the Federation were co-operating fairly fully, since the company spoke of considerable injury to their goodwill which resulted from the fact that, as a non-member, they were precluded from obtaining from members the supplies of cement which would have enabled them to hold their customers. Further, some members apparently refused to supply some of the more valuable customers unless they signed undertakings not to deal with the non-member firms in the

[1] *Economist*, March, 1928, p. 664.

future. The small firms were also troubled by what the manager described as the 'wild activities of a new firm situated in our immediate competitive area'. He declared that they 'are apparently bent on upsetting the market similarly to another firm in our own immediate vicinity who prior, in about 1912, to their absorption by another company, absolutely demoralized the industry . . .'[1] In November 1926 the same man wrote 'it will ever be, as in the past, our intention as far as we are able, subject to difficulties . . . to assist you (the CMF) in avoiding unnecessary weakening of the market, especially during the critical period through which the trade is passing, and may be still in front of it'. Other correspondence, of the end of 1926, shows that the firm was anxious to harden prices at any opportunity, and was also very concerned that firms should adhere to discount terms, which were of considerable importance since they meant more than 1*s*. a ton in price.

The increased competition gave rise to the suggestion that an Association of Non-Federated Cement Manufacturers should be formed. The initial letter of February 3, 1927, stated 'There is at the present moment a general feeling of uneasiness amongst Cement Manufacturers in regard to selling conditions, which is I think due to the recent increase in the tonnage of non-federated firms and possibly also to the inclination of federated firms to adhere, in face of so much outside competition, less strictly than formerly to the terms of their price schedules.

'The annual tonnage produced by members of the Federation is now probably about 4,000,000 and that produced by non-Federated firms about 1,000,000 with prospects of an early increase.' The letter went on to say that the CMF had undoubtedly done good service to the trade and that as a satisfactory demand might shortly be experienced it was to be hoped that the trade might not find itself too disorganized to take advantage of it. It was suggested that the non-federated members should consider whether they could concern themselves with the stabilization of prices and, if so, whether they should not meet the Federation and see whether it was possible without joining the Federation 'to offer them some support and some inducement to keep their organization operating satisfactorily. . . .'

The response to this letter was almost unanimous and a meeting was held on March 1, 1927. Fourteen manufacturers were represented—six which were new since 1919, the two firms started in 1912 by Broads, the builders' merchants, and by a firm of barge owners respectively, four small firms, and two medium-sized ones, one

[1] Letter.

of which was being much enlarged. Another small firm attended a subsequent meeting at which it was decided to form a Non-Federated Alliance. At a joint meeting with representatives of the Cement Makers' Federation it was declared that all the outsiders had joined the Non-Federated Alliance except one small firm which was considering the matter. This meeting discussed the possibility of agreement concerning terms, discounts and prices. The real obstacle lay in the question of the price concessions which newcomers to the trade demanded because of the difficulties of introducing new brands against the old ones. The question of penalties for non-observance was discussed but some felt that a spirit of co-operation was really required. The suggestion that output should be limited was raised, but it was said that this would require a complex cartel system which would be difficult to operate, especially in the present state of public opinion. 'The conference finally agreed that the crux of the whole question lay in the extent to which price facilities could be granted to those requiring entry into the trade. . . .' In the middle of 1927 eighteen firms belonged to the CMF, eleven to the Non-Federated Association and six to no association at all. These six included the Ship Canal Company and Greaves, Bull and Lakin (the first two members of the Red Triangle Group) and two London firms.

Notes made at a meeting on September 7, 1927, mention the regret that the Red Triangle was not a member of the Non-Federated Association and the hope that they would join. It was understood that the CMF would allow the Non-Federated makers to charge a price of 2*s*. per ton below the Schedule Price, but that they would have to become members of the CMF. Some thought that this should be accepted, but would not join the CMF unless all promised to do so. Other members apparently thought that 2*s*. a ton was not sufficient to outbid the Blue Circle. It was suggested that the agreement should be confined to terms but this was unacceptable, especially to the manufacturers in Kent who were selling mainly in London. There was also some discussion about recent instances of price cutting.

After this effort, the Non-Federated Association lapsed; intermittent price cutting below the schedule prices apparently continued. In the spring of 1928 discussions concerning a new Schedule of Prices were held and probably all members of the trade were invited to attend. One small firm refused on the grounds that they could not agree to the artificial control of selling prices. But they declared that they always adhered to the terms and conditions laid down; in fact, they believed that they had 'out Heroded Herod' in that respect.

In March 1928 the price cutting had become more severe. H. S. Horne, at the Annual General Meeting of the Associated Anglo-

Atlantic Corporation, which had interests in the Red Triangle Group, spoke of the 'unnecessary competition prevailing in the cement industry.'[1] Very soon after this a real price war[2] broke out and lasted for about five months. It was brought to an end when the Horne group and the other major independents joined the CMF.

This period of severe competition was discussed at some length by Malcolm Stewart at the APCM company meeting:

... 'We had at the outset to face a lower but not unsatisfactory average selling price than we had enjoyed the previous year. Unfortunately, this level of prices was not long maintained. The further co-operation advocated in my speech last year was not forthcoming for some time, and we had to face a period of intense competition which continued until the end of October and has left its trail of low-priced contracts to be completed. If co-operation is to be established, opportunities for friendly discussion must be facilitated. These were forthcoming. Ultimately, with the creation of a better understanding all round wiser counsels prevailed, and competitive manufacturers resolved to join the Cement Makers' Federation, the doors of which had always been kept open. Thus was the industry enabled to a considerable extent to stabilize selling prices. There was never any foundation for the statements appearing in the Press that our companies had entered into agreements[3] or made territorial arrangements. Further, it should not be assumed that, on the cessation of price cutting such as was experienced, the situation could immediately revert to the *status quo ante bellum*. Most industries pass through periods of prices warfare, often brought about by overproduction, and the attempt of manufacturers individually to force on to the market more than it can consume. The unrivalled service which we can give, combined with the recognized quality of Blue Circle Portland Cement and Ferrocrete, enables us to hold our own at equal prices. We do not rest on our goodwill; we are always striving to merit it increasingly. But there is a difference in price at which the buyer, often reluctantly, will feel compelled to purchase the cheaper article, and when faced with this situation we are not prepared complacently to see our old-established connections taken away from us by undercutting. Indeed, I would like you as shareholders to know that in such circumstances we deem your true interests to be best protected by the maintenance of our trade connections. We strive to give effect to a policy which will bring a reasonable degree of prosperity to all efficient manufacturers in the industry, but when attacked we are not prepared to sit down and see our trade filched away.'[4]

[1] *Economist*, March 31, 1928, p. 663. [2] See p. 76.

[3] Stewart must have been taking the CMF price agreements for granted and have been referring to other than price agreements.

[4] *Economist*, March 30, 1929, p. 712.

In spite of the price war, the APCM were able, by reducing their costs and increasing their turnover, to increase their net profit by 10 per cent. The Red Triangle Group were, however, reduced to a weak financial position; at the time of Horne's resignation after his bankruptcy the *Economist* declared that the Red Triangle group never recovered from the price-cutting war. Although this price cutting must have weakened the company, and it appears to have been the Red Triangle group which finally called a halt, it is not clear that the difficulties of the company by 1929 were due to this alone. They may well have been the result of inability to compete successfully with the Blue Circle group at level prices. 'During 1929, according to the directors (of the APCM) competition continued to be severe and lower prices were realized.'[1] The severe competition almost certainly involved increased selling effort and in this the older firms would probably be more successful.

The characteristics of the period 1922 to 1928 are the expanding demand, and the building up of new capacity which was very much more efficient and which generally involved large plants, since there were economies of scale. It seems clear that in the absence of price agreements the period would have been one of very severe competition; although the new plants could take advantage of the expanding demand, they inevitably competed locally with existing capacity. Nevertheless, the long-term prospects appear to have been so good that it is not certain that there would have been less investment had competition been more severe; the large works depending upon efficiency and the new plants depending partly upon efficiency and partly on the fact that they had a sales organization, would both have been built. Possibly the risk would have reduced the number of new works; in that case the demand would have been met by greater expansion by existing small works who could expand output quickly with less capital expenditure. All one can say is that the actual situation in which there was limited price competition gave rise to a stability which encouraged the larger type of new enterprise. In view of the economies of scale, this must be regarded as an advantage.

The easiest guess to make is that the existence of the large Associated group, which had already shown that it could survive, if not prosper, was the chief influence in promoting stability. They were efficient enough to give confidence that the stability would remain, and efficient enough to keep prices down to the level where only similarly efficient concerns could compete in the long period, but they had no advantage which enabled them to prevent other firms from sharing the expanding market.

[1] *Economist*, March 1930, p. 716.

Between 1922 and 1927 the market conditions and the technological conditions were such that, despite the expansion of the Associated group, independent firms expanded and increased in number sufficiently to weaken seriously the control of the market by the Associated group and the CMF. By 1927, and in some cases earlier, these new firms had begun to find it so difficult to launch their large new output on to the market that they had had to cut prices in order to get established.

In this situation, with demand increasing and technical change continuing to be important, the possibility of price agreement was remote. With competition severe the future of the newer companies and the medium-sized companies became uncertain. They lacked both the market protection given by an extensive selling organization and the more steady demand which a large firm serving a wide area could achieve.

The formation of a new combine offered the possibility of obtaining both the economies of scale and marketing, and, eventually, some degree of price stability. The Red Triangle group had a successful pattern to copy, for, by this time, the Associated group had shown that it could not only survive but could strengthen its position, if not its share of the market. With two large groups dominating the industry continuous severe competition must have been regarded as unlikely although the immediate future was uncertain.

The formation and establishment of the Red Triangle organization was, in fact, followed by an intense price war. It is not possible to see whether this was inevitable or whether it was due to the personalities involved or the incompetence and desperation of the Red Triangle Group.

The real significance of this enterprise is that in 1929 relatively few differences in conditions might have made it successful. The financial crises, the intensified competition, perhaps internal incompetence, were all either remediable or historically fortuitous. Had it succeeded one might have seen established at this stage a typical oligopolistic industry in which price agreement and competition alternated, but were always accompanied by intense selling competition. The competition would have been between the larger and the smaller combines and the smaller independents, the most important of which would probably have been firms such as Eastwoods with its extensive outlets. The picture of what the industry might have looked like cannot safely be drawn in any detail, but these imaginings do help to put events into perspective. In particular, they help to weight the events between 1929 and 1934, for in 1934 a full price agreement system was established, one which has proved stable and effective with the possible exception of hidden local price cutting.

Further discussion of the question as to which structure of the industry can be regarded as more efficient and more in the public interest is to be left until the whole of the recent history of the industry can be considered.

CHAPTER 7

1929–34

THIS short period from the end of 1929 is one of transition in which events moved extremely fast. The period started with the collapse of the Horne group and ended with the reorganization of the Cement Makers' Federation and the introduction of effective price agreements. During the five years the structure of the industry was altered very considerably, both under the impact of a number of dramatic moves by small groups of individuals, and under the impact of the depressed trading conditions, continued cost reduction and intense price competition. Although by 1934 many changes were still taking place, the whole character of the industry was beginning to take on its modern look; the introduction of the effective price agreements constituted a real landmark; it was in large part a reflection of the changed structure of the industry.

In November 1929 Horne announced that on account of the very serious losses he had sustained owing to the exceptional depreciation which had taken place in his holdings in those companies with which he had been particularly identified, it had become necessary for him to file his petition (of bankruptcy). As the finances of all his companies were hopelessly entangled, it is not possible to discover the extent to which this was due to the cement interests. They were overcapitalized and in some difficulty, but it was the other interests which had sustained the most severe depreciation.

Allied Cement Manufacturers, which had taken over the cement concerns, earned 2·2 per cent for its ordinary shares, but passed the dividend for the year ended March 1930. Financial difficulties were apparent. The company report says that it had been intended, at the time of the merging of the cement interests, to fund the short-term advances; arrangements had been made with British Cement Products and Finance (an associated company), for the underwriting of an issue; this, however, had had to be postponed on account of the financial crisis. At the time of Mr Horne's resignation, changes were made on the board, and in July 1930 more were in prospect.[1] At an

[1] *Economist*, July 26, 1930, p. 189.

extraordinary general meeting on December 23, 1930, a resolution removing all directors including the Chairman, Mr O. J. S. Piper, was carried. The following were elected in their stead:

> Mr Horace Boot, to be Chairman and Managing Director
> Colonel Eastwood
> General Sir P. Maybury
> Sir R. Pretyman Newman.[1]

All except Sir R. Pretyman Newman were directors of Eastwoods Ltd, and Mr H. Boot was managing director of that firm. It is said that a small group who found that they held a small number of shares which gave them control of the company approached Eastwoods. According to the *Daily Express*, April 24, 1931, 'Some of Mr Boot's supporters held the 1*s*. deferred shares of the Allied Cement Co. of a nominal value of £175 which carried equal voting rights with the £1,698,217 of Ordinary capital.' A circular accompanying the notice concerning the meeting (of December 23, 1930), and signed by the secretary on behalf of the board states 'The Directors have no information as to the policy contemplated by the proposed board, but they feel it their duty to draw the attention of the shareholders to the fact that, according to their best information, three of the proposed directors have interests in another and smaller group in the cement trade, which may be difficult and indeed almost impossible to reconcile with the interests of your company.' On January 1, 1931, it was reported in the *Financial Times* 'The new directors now state that they have investigated the financial position and have reluctantly come to the conclusion that there are no available resources or uncharged assets out of which money can be raised to pay the interest (6½ per cent on £587,400 First Mortgage Debenture Stock).' On January 13, 1931, a receiver was appointed as a result of an application by the trustees for the debenture holders, Barclay's Bank Ltd, and the British Maritime Trust. It was on January 17, 1931, that the *Economist* said: 'It would be interesting to know what attitude was adopted by the banks in this matter, seeing that there was some reason to believe that the company, given a solution of its immediate financial difficulties, might ultimately have justified its place in the cement trade . . .'[2] This comment, combined with the view which has since been expressed that it was only the failure to raise adequate finance at short notice which deprived Eastwoods of permanent control of the Red

[1] *Economist*, January 3, 1931, p. 32.
[2] p. 129.

Triangle Group, makes it appear that the short-lived alliance might very easily have become permanent and materially changed the subsequent history of the industry.

During the brief period of control by Eastwoods the Rhee Valley Cement works was closed. This works was obviously of no value to Eastwoods, being close to their large works at Barrington. The Rhee Valley company had not been of any value to the Red Triangle Group. In the Report and Accounts of Wiggins & Co. (Hammersmith) Ltd, for the year ended March 31, 1930, it was said that: 'The working of the Rhee Valley Portland Cement Works shows that, in the present position of the Cement Industry, small works of this nature are at a disadvantage with the other large factories and profits therefore suffer. . . . At present it has not been possible to find a purchaser for the Rhee Valley Portland Cement Works.'

It is worth mentioning at this point that Eastwoods (Lewes) Cement Ltd issued an optimistic first annual report. On December 16, 1930, *The Times* reported that the directors stated that good progress was being made with the development of sales in the southern and south-western counties, where the company was well situated to meet economically the increasing demand for its products. The fact that some time was required for the building up of sales is significant and indicates something of the nature of the competition. Possibly the suspicion expressed concerning the effect of association of the Red Triangle Group with Eastwoods may have been connected with the fact that it would have been difficult to expand the sales of both organizations; Red Triangle shareholders may well have felt that the interests of their firm might be neglected.

The close association between Eastwoods and the Red Triangle Group was short-lived. In April 1931 the receiver, Sir William McLintock, announced that an offer had been made to him for the assets of the company and of its subsidiary operating companies. According to the *Economist*, of August 8, 1931, it was at the time well known that the offer came from the Blue Circle Group. In April 1932 at the Annual General Meeting of the APCM, more information was given.

'The outstanding event of the year was the acquisition of the manufacturing and certain marketing interests of the "Red Triangle" group embraced by the Allied Cement Manufacturers Limited and its subsidiary companies. On several occasions we have been offered shares which, it was stated, would give control. These offers were consistently declined. We had definitely made up our minds that in view of the many knots into which these concerns were tied by an undesirable interlocking of interests, life was not long enough to attempt the task of their unravelling. We were only prepared to become interested if the knots could be cut, and this involved liquidation. The assets of the Allied Company were of varying value; liquidation alone could give complete freedom to fit them advantageously into our own organization.

'The time came when we made the Receiver, Sir William McLintock a definite offer for practically the whole of the assets, provided they were bought in liquidation. This offer was declined; an improved offer, which was made on April 22, was accepted, subject to confirmation of the court. This was given on August 19. I make this statement so as to place the matter in its true perspective. We paid a fair price for the assets and I am satisfied, given fair trading conditions, we shall turn the purchase to advantage.'[1]

Two comments may be made. First, the capitalization was just under £2 per ton, which was actually less than that of the Blue Circle Group and considerably less than that of the works built at about this time. Second, there was little doubt that if the Blue Circle group had not acquired control, other interests would have stepped in.

Although most of the independents had joined the CMF in 1928, after the price war, the Chairman of the APCM said in April 1932 that 'the selling prices realized were reduced by the keen undercutting of the standard prices, which remained in force although they had not been maintained'.[2] He added that the profit margin per ton was approximately one-half of that earned in 1925. However, in September 1932 the Chairman of Eastwoods said that the cement industry had seen a considerable recovery since the absorption of the Red Triangle Group. It was reported that the Associated Group controlled some 70 per cent of the trade after the absorption of the Red Triangle Group of companies.

It seems to have been thought at the time that price cutting would be ended by the new merger but this was not the case. On April 3, 1933, the *Daily Herald* spoke of a new price war raging in the cement industry. The Chairman of Eastwoods spoke of the directors' regret that the co-operative measures envisaged in the last report had not materialized.[3] Then, in March 1934, the Chairman of the APCM 'refused to forecast current prospects in view of the fact that the cement industry had become relatively disorganized and selling prices were low'.[4] In another article, the *Economist* pointed out that 'the exemplary rigidity of the official cement price (46*s*. per ton delivered in the Central London Area) has concealed a fall in the average export price

[1] *Economist*, April 16, 1932, p. 872. [2] *Economist*, April 16, 1932, p. 872.
[3] *Economist*, September, 1933, p. 458.
[4] *Economist*, March 1934, p. 644.

from nearly £2 8*s*. in 1929 to below £1 13*s*. in 1933; a low level of £1 10*s*. was touched in 1933'.[1] It discussed the extensive modernization and stated that outside concerns had shared fully in this modernization, and had used lower costs to improve their turnover by cutting prices. 'In this they have had considerable success . . . They have doubtless enjoyed the advantage which is always open to the outsider of concentrating on the most favourable markets against a combine which must preserve goodwill by giving service in good and bad markets alike. The recent doubling of capacity by Ketton shows that the possibilities of competition are not yet exhausted . . . It is reported in the trade that the very low prices of last year have induced even the most modern and the most aggressive concerns to consider whether agreement might not be preferable to warfare. There is talk of negotiations.'[2] While the official cement price was maintained at 46*s*. per ton Central London delivery, the ruling price in April 1934 over much of the South of England was no more than 38*s*.[3]

During this period of price cutting demand was expanding fast. Total deliveries of cement in the home and export markets were:

	'000 tons
1929	4,628
1930	4,321
1931	4,691
1932	3,958
1933	4,508
1934	5,435
1935	5,793

Source: Cement Costs (fforde Report, 1947), HMSO, *op. cit.*, p. 28.

The relatively slight effects of the depression on the cement industry reflected the excellent long-term prospects; the price cutting was the result not only of the current difficulties in disposing of the output of existing plant, but also of the efforts of firms to strengthen their long period position.

The good long-term prospects were leading to very considerable increases in capacity by the major firms. The Associated Group

[1] *Economist*, March 1937, p. 677. [2] *Economist*, March 31, 1934, p. 709.
[3] *Economist*, April 28, 1934, p. 935.

announced that they were expanding their productive capacity in the London area, Lancashire, Yorkshire, South Wales and Northern Ireland. As mentioned above, the capacity at the new Ketton works was being doubled, and the Tunnel Cement Company was also planning extensions. At this time the Rugby Portland Cement Company came under the management of its present chairman and managing director, Mr Halford Reddish. He took over in 1933 and the company immediately embarked on a period of expansion. The Rugby works was reorganized and output increased, and in 1934 Kaye & Co. Ltd, a small firm near Rugby which was on the verge of liquidation, was acquired and a new works was erected. Although still small in 1934 this firm had become active and was to become very much larger and more important. It was converted into a public company in 1935 and the capital increased from £120,000 to £250,000.

Another new and important figure, A. Y. Gowan, entered the cement industry at this time; he was undoubtedly attracted both by the good long-term prospects and by the very obvious benefits which would accrue to the industry if it could be organized and the price competition brought to an end. Gowan had been engaged in the organization of the cement industry in the United States. It is said that he came over here on holiday, saw the disorganized state of the industry, decided that there were opportunities for profitable reorganization and stayed. Although he was probably concerned to become an efficient manufacturer of cement in this country, it appears that he saw an opportunity for fairly rapid profits to be derived from entering an industry prior to its effective organization; in other words, he looked to speculative profits to be gained from the creation of new organizations, and he himself became an important factor in bringing about the changes.

Gowan first became interested in the Rodmell works, a completely new works in Sussex, with an Edgar Allen plant and a 200 kiln. This company had been started by a combination of scientific[1] and financial interests who had been experimenting with a novel type of equipment with a peculiar vertical kiln. In March 1934 Gowan acquired the Oxford and Shipton Cement Works, changed the name to Alpha Cement Ltd, and increased the share capital from £450,000 to £900,000. A circular letter of July 27, 1933, to shareholders from Viscount Dillon, the Chairman, shows that the company was also contemplating expansion and had decided to install a complete new kiln. In July 1934 it was announced that Alpha Cement Ltd had acquired the share capital of Thames Portland Cement Co. Ltd, that

[1] Girouard and Martin.

arrangements were being made to increase production; a new jetty was to be constructed and the company planned to ship cement to all the coastal ports of England.[1]

Thus, by the middle of 1934 Gowan had amalgamated three large, expanding companies; all were of the type which, in the 'twenties, had tended to cut prices in order to sell their increasing output. He had also acquired control of the Central Portland Cement Company,[2] a medium-sized works in Lincolnshire which had been built by independent interests in 1927. This was formally amalgamated with the Alpha group in 1935. The larger organization had greater incentives to promote co-operation in the industry and Gowan worked in this direction. By the middle of 1934 he had written a book, for circulation within the industry, upon the need for and the advantages of a Cement Association which would promote the use of cement.

The industry in 1934 differed from that of the late 'twenties in that most of the smaller firms had become weak and many had left, or were on the point of leaving, the industry. Those which had not progressed and had not re-equipped could no longer compete. The reduction in costs was a dominant feature of the period 1925–35. In 1935 the costs of the APCM were down to 58 per cent of the cost in 1925. The selling price had fallen to 54 per cent of selling prices realized in 1925.[3] The greater percentage fall in the selling price probably reflects the high profits of 1925 which were made possible by the existence of many less efficient manufacturers. The increase in efficiency is also indicated by the following points from the same source; 'Today every £100 of fixed assets represents 36 tons of annual productive capacity. This compares with 20 tons ten years ago', and further: 'The annual output per man has gone up over 100 per cent, but the number of men employed shows a decrease of only 17 per cent.' In the same period the deliveries of the industry rose from 3,745,000 tons in 1925 to 5,435,000 tons in 1934, increasing each year except in 1932.[4]

These increases in efficiency left a number of firms behind, and by the end of 1934 the composition of the industry had changed considerably as compared with 1928. The trade was now dominated by the Associated Group with about 70 per cent of the capacity of the industry. Beside this there were, as in 1928, five major firms; these now included the new Alpha Group (with four works). There were eight firms which in 1928 had to be described as medium sized, but which, by 1934, should be regarded as small. Three of these were active

[1] *Economist*, July 28, 1934, p. 184. [2] See p. 72.
[3] Chairman's speech reported in *Economist*, April 6, 1935, p. 817.
[4] See p. 91.

and expanding; these were the Ketton, the Rugby and the Chinnor Cement Companies. (Of the eight, only these three remain independent firms today, the other five having been absorbed by larger groups.) The number of firms in this size group only fell by two between 1928 and 1934; the greatest change was in the really small firm category; by 1934 only four out of twelve remained and all these ceased to produce cement within the following two or three years. Thus between 1928 and 1934 the number of units of control had fallen from about twenty-nine to about eighteen. If one disregards the four very small firms in 1934 the change is greater, and it seems probable that this gives a somewhat truer indication of the real difference.

As a result of these changes the large fringe of small firms, which was so difficult to organize, was eliminated. In addition, although there were still variations in efficiency, all were very much closer to the average than they had been previously; any firm, efficiently run, well maintained, and with suitable raw material could hope to compete on costs. Thus the time had passed when a new firm could hope to cut into another firm's market simply by means of price reductions which would not be met.

The intense price cutting of 1933 and the marked improvement in demand made firms anxious to raise prices, but they were frightened to do so unilaterally; this gave rise to renewed efforts to work the price lists. New lists began to be drawn up early in 1934 and by June 1934 it was agreed that the general principle worked satisfactorily. There were suggested prices for all areas but only in some were there proper agreements between the interested makers. Such agreements did not at the time relate to the Midlands and the North.

Throughout 1934 discussions took place about a more comprehensive scheme. A memorandum was issued in February 1934. In June 1934 a meeting was held at which the general principle of a price and quota scheme was accepted. Outstanding points were submitted to a committee which reported in September 1934, and in October the scheme was adopted.

The adoption of the quota scheme marked the end of an era; this was, perhaps, not absolutely clear at the time, but, in fact, price competition between firms has not reappeared. The cement industry became a fairly closely controlled industry; firms, no longer concerned with current pricing problems and the risks of short-period price cutting, concentrated on competition in sales and service, and on the problems of long-term development.

At this point, before turning to the period between 1934 and 1939, it is convenient to consider briefly some of the relationships between the main features of the industry between 1919 and 1934, and the changes in its structure and behaviour. The basic competitive characteristics of the industry had changed relatively little but they were intensified. The product had become more homogeneous, which tended to increase the effectiveness of price competition. Cost of production had fallen with the result that transport costs were more important; this tended to increase the possibility of price discrimination in the form of freight absorption. In addition, the possibility of price discrimination, in the form of special prices and terms for specific large non-repeating orders, had in no way diminished. For these reasons the scope and temptation to cut prices had increased rather than diminished. Changes on the supply side reinforced this: individual works were larger and the importance of continuous working in order to spread overheads was increased. Further, there were no longer the old chamber kiln works which, with relatively high marginal costs, would reduce output when prices fell. The battle was now between the giants who, in the absence of price agreement, could do each other great damage. Many of the features which made the initiation of price cutting tempting were those which made price wars very much more costly to all.

It was the increasing cost of price war, its inevitability in the absence of agreement and the great reduction in the number of firms which were responsible for the agreements of 1934 and which made them both effective and durable.

CHAPTER 8

Price Stability, 1934–9

THE new price and quota scheme came into operation in December 1934. The price lists were largely based on those which were already in operation and about which there were already loose agreements. They were drawn up on the basing point principle, each basing point being surrounded by a number of circles each with a radius five miles greater than the last. In each circle moving out from the basing point, which was either a works or a port, the price was 1*s*. higher. As there was a merchant rebate scheme all merchants were to be registered. Further, in order to detect any price cutting, all forward contracts at low prices were to be registered. Guarantee Funds were also created and any penalties for breaches were to be paid out of those funds; it was hoped that the fact that the funds were already in the hands of the Federation would create confidence that the price lists and terms of sale would be observed. The quota scheme was based upon the percentage of the industry's total deliveries made by each firm; but the council could award additional percentages by reason of special circumstances. A penalty of 7*s*. 6*d*. was levied on all deliveries in excess of the quota, and the same amount was paid to a firm in respect of the quantities by which deliveries fell short of the quota. In the first instance the quota was to operate for one year, 1935, only; it appears that more long-term agreement could not be obtained; it was hoped, however, that experience would lead to its renewal. Further, it was not at this stage considered practicable to try to draw up any definite declaration concerning provisions for changing the quotas.

The scheme was thus limited to what was necessary in the short period and contained considerable incentives for firms to adhere to the price list. Most of 1934 had been spent in obtaining the agreement of the smaller firms and it is clear that, at this stage, confidence in each other was not well established and much of the old suspicion remained. The *Economist* may have exaggerated, but nevertheless, in June 1935[1] it spoke of the arrangements being avowedly of the nature of a truce rather than a treaty, and it suggested, when discussing

[1] p. 1309.

the value of APCM shares, that 'possibly stockholders will not attach undue importance to the existing gentleman's agreement in the light of past experience, for the 30 per cent of home sales is sufficiently large to threaten the price basis if outside companies at any time regard their interest as better served by independence than co-operation. Their quota allocations however appear not ungenerous'.

The introduction of the quota scheme coincided with the time when two small firms ceased production. One of these was the East Anglian Cement Co.; this firm produced about 3,500 tons in 1933 which was only 15 per cent of its nominal capacity. Its costs were high and the introduction of the scheme probably had little effect upon the decision to cease to produce cement. The company continued to produce hydraulic lime and it received small quota payments for a number of years. The Cam Blue Lias Company, which was nearby, also ceased production at about the same time.

At least three companies did not adhere fully to the new arrangements. The first was Casebourne, the ICI subsidiary. This firm said that, as it used a by-product, it could not restrict production: some other agreement had to be made. The second was the Gillingham Portland Cement Company. After some hesitation this company joined the Federation in August 1935. The hesitation was partly due to the fact that, under new management, the company was doing quite well, partly to some fear of the combine, and partly to the possible effects on wage rates. The eventual decision to join the Federation was not regretted. The third company was Albert Batchelor, Ltd; this company had its own particular customers for its output which was not of high quality. The works had two old kilns and an output of less than 50,000 tons per annum. The company was acquired by the Rugby Portland Cement Company[1] in 1936, and then became a member of the Federation.

In the discussion of the condition of the industry in 1934 the reduction in the number of firms was emphasized. The importance of this is underlined, both by the fact that it took so long to obtain agreement, and by the failure to get 100 per cent adherance. The reduction in the number of firms in the industry appears to have been the most important factor making the comprehensive organization of the industry possible. Other factors, such as the elimination of the small firms which were different in kind, and the growth in the size of the more important firms, were significant but probably of secondary importance.

It has sometimes been assumed that when there is one firm of great

[1] See p. 100.

size in an industry, such as the Associated Group, it almost automatically follows that organization of the industry is much simpler and more probable. The grounds for this assumption seem to be particular rather than general. It is true that the large firm usually has the greatest interest in price agreement, because, having a large share of the market, its elasticity of demand will be low. On the other hand, just because it is large and likely to pursue a stable price policy, independent firms may well be loath to lose their freedom to undercut the price leader by a small fraction. For this reason a very large firm may find it extremely difficult to secure the agreement of the smaller firms; prior to 1934, this was generally true in the cement industry. The exceptions to this are to be found in industries where the large firm has some effective weapon which may be used against those which remain outside. In many situations such a weapon is available; it may be related to price discrimination in a particular market, or to exclusive dealing rebates with customers or to patent licensing. In the cement industry there is no such weapon; price discrimination could only be used against the more distant firms, serving small local markets. Exclusive dealing would have relatively little value as such a large proportion of the output is taken for specific projects and in addition the big producers sell only cement and not a range of products. For these reasons it can be seen that the existence of the very large Associated group was probably of significance in bringing about agreement only in so far as it covered a large proportion of the industry and, therefore, tended to reduce the number of firms. Agreement would very likely have been easier to arrange had there been an equal number of firms more similar in size.

The state of trade in the years 1935–7 put little strain upon the agreements, and confidence that firms would abide by their agreements grew. The ten years between 1926 and 1936 saw very great changes in the relationships between firms, but it appears to have been between about 1933 and 1937 that the industry finally became thoroughly oligopolistic, both in spirit and in organization.

The increases in deliveries were really formidable, deliveries to the home and export markets rose by 21 per cent in 1934, 7 per cent in 1935, 15 per cent in 1936 and 9 per cent in 1937. The rather smaller increase in 1935 was largely due to the small increase in exports.

The annual increases in deliveries given in Table III, col. 5 are large in absolute terms; in 1935 the increase was equivalent to the output of two large, modern kilns. The annual average proportion of capacity used was, according to Rostas,[1] generally between three-quarters and

[1]Rostas, *Comparative Productivity in British and American Industry*, p. 113.

TABLE III

Deliveries of Cement—Home and Export

	Home Market 000's tons	Export Market 000's tons	Total 000's tons	Actual Increase 000's tons
1934 ..	4,935	500	5,435	—
1935 ..	5,268	525	5,793	358
1936 ..	6,044	618	6,662	869
1937 ..	6,606	663	7,269	607
1938 ..	6,963	688	7,651	382
1939 ..	7,587	665	8,252	571

Cement Costs, HMSO, 1947 (fforde Report), *op. cit.*, p. 28.

four-fifths of total capacity. (The figures available made more accurate estimates impossible.) Thus the 'spare' capacity is very large in comparison with the annual average increases in demand. When demand rises the available capacity can be used more fully and deliveries can be spread more evenly over the year, and this is what happens except in so far as firms have already built ahead of demand.

The decision to build ahead of demand has to be made on the basis of future expectations about demand, other firms' building plans, and the competitive strength of the firm. During the inter-war period the decision had to be made more than a year before the increased output became available and little or no guidance could be obtained from current output figures. These fluctuated considerably over the year and the seasonal fluctuations were not clearly marked.

Some idea of the irregularity of demand may be gained from the following table which represents the output of about seven-eighths of the industry. The latest figures available apply to 1925.

TABLE IV

Index of Output—Annual Average = 100

	1924	1925		1924	1925
January ..	75·3	85·1	July	107·4	100·1
February ..	87·2	88·3	August	76·8	110·0
March	94·2	109·6	September ..	103·1	100·6
April	102·4	95·6	October ..	123·8	101·5
May	103·5	100·7	November ..	108·1	97·6
June	108·8	110·9	December ..	109·6	99·9

Source: Cement Manufacturers' Federation.

These output figures somewhat underestimate fluctuations in demand since the industry can carry two or three weeks stocks fairly easily.

Although future demand could not be estimated accurately there was, during the 'thirties, the confident expectation that it would increase. Plans for expansion were put into operation, and there was a period of intense activity. The Associated Group returned to a level of expenditure on additions to plant almost as great as that of the 'twenties. One of their most important expansions, that at Swanscombe, was complete by early in 1936. The Annual Reports do not give any indication of the nature or extent of the other expansion, but clearly a number of those announced in December 1934[1] went forward. Nevertheless, it seems likely that if the *Economist's* estimates are accurate the expansion by the Associated Group was insufficient to maintain their share of the trade; they were estimated to have 55 per cent in 1938 as compared with 70 per cent in 1934.

In this period the Rugby Portland Cement Company, hitherto a relatively small company, developed into an important firm in the industry. First, the capacity of the Rugby works was increased so that the two kilns could be used continuously; previously one had been regarded as standby equipment. Secondly, Kaye & Co. was acquired in 1934 and an entirely new works was built beside the old one-kiln works. In 1936, having acquired Albert Batchelor & Co. Ltd, an entirely new works was built at Halling, near Rochester. Finally, in 1938 the Gillingham Portland Cement Company was acquired and closed.

Eastwoods Ltd was another company which continued to expand rapidly. Early in 1936 it was announced that the extensions at Lewes were nearing completion. Then, in November 1936, the Eastwoods Humber Cement Co. was formed. This was an entirely new project which was suggested to Eastwoods who were known to be an expansionist firm, and who were, at that time, selling through their own outlets more cement than they produced. This firm became an associate of Eastwoods who guaranteed the debenture interest until the end of 1938. It was announced that the company would erect a cement works on the River Humber. Production of 75,000 tons per annum from the first unit was expected and this was estimated to yield a profit of £30,000 less fees, interest and administration. The capital issue was £150,000 4½ per cent first mortgage debenture at 101 and 800,000 5*s*. ordinary shares at 5*s*. 9*d*.

The Tunnel Company was also very active; apart from extensive interests abroad both in cement and asbestos, the company was joint

[1] See p. 92.

promoter in 1936, with the Ketton Company, of the Ribblesdale Cement Company which erected a new works. It also had a half share in Cement Ltd, a company formed for making cement in the Irish Free State. The Tunnel Company undertook to provide technical assistance for ten years. Also in 1936 the company raised additional capital of £500,000, most of which was to be used in developing a new cement manufacturing unit. At the Annual General Meeting the chairman said: 'The position today is that we are unable to cope with the demand for our product and we are having to turn away business, particularly in the export market.' He then said that the industry was growing, the increase in cement consumption amounting to about 5 per cent per annum. 'If we are to maintain our relative position in the industry it is essential to increase our manufacturing facilities.'[1]

The increase in capacity by the Chinnor Cement & Lime Co. Ltd must be mentioned for it is of considerable interest. Being small, its development is in some ways comparable with that of the Rugby Company; the company was engaged solely in the manufacture and distribution of cement and lime, and it is the last example in this industry of a small independent firm expanding and holding its own in an industry otherwise composed of large firms or the subsidiaries of large firms. The cement capacity of the firm was 60,000 tons (from one kiln, installed in 1928), and the lime capacity 4,000 tons. In 1936 it was converted into a public company with authorized and issued capital of £200,000; a high proportion was subscribed by the Charterhouse Investment Trust. The issue was to provide for new plant, and a new kiln was put in which came into production in 1937. This second kiln had two advantages; it increased capacity and it reduced the risk of a complete stoppage; both these considerations are said to have influenced the decision. Whichever was the more important, it appears that the firm planned to have adequate capacity to meet peak demand and would, therefore, be working at less than full capacity for a very high proportion of the time. Incidentally, the considerable volume of excess capacity implied by this type of policy indicates one of the disadvantages from which the small firm suffers.

Lastly, there was one completely new entry into the industry. In 1935 members of Power Securities Corporation Ltd promoted the Metropolitan Cement Company. The original promoters and their friends were able to ensure outlets for the cement produced; a fairly large proportion was to be used by the related firms, who were primarily engaged in constructional engineering and transport, and some was to be exported. It appears that there can have been little

[1] *Economist*, June 1936, p. 748.

risk of failure with a market assured. The works was built by Balfour Beatty & Co. Ltd, a subsidiary of Power Securities Corporation Ltd. Henry Pooley, a specialist consultant in cement works, was employed and the plant was obtained from Metropolitan Vickers, one of the directors of Metropolitan Vickers being on the board of the Power Securities Corporation. The works was on the Thames, next door to the West Thurrock works of the Tunnel company, and was built in an old chalk quarry acquired from the Thurrock Chalk and Whiting Co. Ltd; the clay was pumped from about four miles away. In May 1936, while the works were still in the course of construction, the Metropolitan Cement Company was sold to the Alpha group for just over £500,000, the vendors retaining a substantial, but not controlling, interest. The works were completed in the middle of 1937, having been modified slightly by the introduction of some Smidth machinery.

Although this was the only independent promotion during this period, there seems little doubt that if prices had been high or supplies short there would have been others of rather similar pattern. A scheme for building a cement works at Plymouth was 'hawked' about for many years, but no financial backing could be found. Maxted and Knott tried to get backing for this and others in the early 'thirties; just before the war it was being handled by Henry Pooley and might well have gone through had the war not started. After the war[1] a small works was in fact built in Plymouth.

The *Economist*[2] referred to reports that an outside concern was intending to erect factories in Devonshire and Kent, and Lord Wolmer, the independent Chairman of the Cement Makers' Federation, said that the tendency of newcomers to enter the industry was a dangerous development likely to lead to indiscriminate price cutting.[3] On February 11 the *Economist* reported that the plan to erect two new factories, which had caused resentment among the big groups, had been abandoned, and went on to question the reasons. 'Is it because the interests sponsoring the scheme were given to understand that their venture might be unprofitable? In other words have the leaders of the established industry threatened to drive newcomers out of the business by price cutting? Such an explanation would not be at all surprising.' Those in the industry have explained that such an interpretation is misleading; the point being that, if a new works is established, it becomes a basing point and the price in that area is therefore reduced. This applies very particularly to Plymouth since transport costs from the nearest works are very high.

[1] See p. 116. [2] *Economist*, December 3rd and 10th, 1938.
[3] *Economist*, December 3.

This explanation is borne out by the findings of the fforde Committee.[1]

'We directed special attention to the question whether in the past the existence of the quota scheme had operated against the establishment of new businesses in the production of cement. There was some suggestion that in certain localities the view is current that the working of the Cement Makers' Federation has had definitely the result of quashing proposals for the erection of new plants. Of these allegations, we have not succeeded in obtaining first-hand evidence. We believe that in one district a proposal to establish a new cement works died a natural death. In another district there was certainly on foot a proposal for establishing a cement works and the evidence is that those concerned were informed that as a result of the establishment of the new works, the prices in the locality would be reduced. In regard to this particular case, we were assured by the Federation that one of its members was interested in the proposal to the extent of 50 per cent and that the level to which prices in the locality affected were to be reduced was neither more nor less than the level which would have applied under the ordinary working of the price scheme irrespective of the interest by whom the project was sponsored.'

Quite apart from the new capacity which amounted to about 2,250,000 tons per annum, the output of existing plant was in many cases increased considerably; a 200 ft. kiln, of which there were then a lot, would have been rated at six tons an hour in 1930; a few years later, with the addition of various gadgets, they were able to produce up to twelve and in one case no less than sixteen tons per hour. These increases contributed to the amount of excess capacity which developed despite the increased demand.

The elimination of 'obsolete and uneconomic' plants during the five years before the war amounted to about 125,000 tons per annum.[2] This took a number of forms. Three very small firms in the Cambridge area ceased production. The East Anglian Cement Company and the Cam Blue Lias Company both ceased to produce cement, although the former continued to make hydraulic lime. These companies, unable to compete with the prices based upon modern production methods, were quite willing to accept payment under the quota scheme. Robert Stephenson & Co., a very small firm, closed in the early 'thirties; the land was bought by the Associated group and the plant and machinery dismantled. The goodwill of the Warren

[1] *Cement Costs*, 1947, *op. cit.*, p. 20.

[2] Annual General Meeting of the Rugby Portland Cement Co. Ltd, reported in the *Economist* April 29, 1944, p. 581.

Cement Company of Hartlepool was acquired jointly by the Associated group, Tunnel and Rugby Companies, in about 1938. This fairly small works which depended upon raw materials from the Thames could no longer compete successfully, but the goodwill was a definite asset and, if this had not been sold, the company might have struggled on for a little longer.

In 1936 Albert Batchelor & Co. was acquired by the Rugby Co. and the existing works was only kept going until the big new works was complete. Albert Batchelor's works had two small kilns and an assortment of plant and although the rated capacity was 50,000 tons per annum, output was less. The quality was not high and Albert Batchelor had always refused to join any price agreements. He had his own particular customers for his small output. Such a works could not continue indefinitely without drastic reorganization and rebuilding, and something had to be done if gradual decline was to be avoided. The Rugby company claim that, by buying an existing works, they obtained a share of the local market and that the works was well situated for the export market. While the Halling works was being built the Rugby Co. was developing a market for the output; a standing arrangement was made with the Gillingham Portland Cement Co. whereby the Rugby purchased all their surplus output.

This contract was the first association between the Rugby and Gillingham companies, but much happened between 1937 and 1939 when the Rugby company finally acquired the Gillingham company.

The history of the Gillingham company is of particular interest in that it was the last successful small, independent on the Thames. From the time of the installation of the rotary kiln (a 200 ft. Edgar Allen) in the late 'twenties until 1933 it lost money, but in 1933 trade improved and profits were made. The works were small but satisfactory and the output of the kiln was increased very considerably. Throughout the period the owners, who took little part in the management of the business and had little faith in its future, were trying to dispose of it. The kiln was shut from December 1, 1935, to the end of February 1936 because stocks were high and sales low; despite this profits were satisfactory. In November 1936 the agreement was made with the Rugby company whereby all surplus output was sold to them at cost price. This enabled the works to run to full capacity while selling their quota in the best market; inter-member sales were not included in the quota. As a result of this contract a satisfactory profit was made.

At the end of 1935 and in 1936 an association of merchants discussed the possibility of taking over the works in order to break the price ring. They thought that prices were high and that at least one large merchant was getting preferential terms. In the end nothing came of the negotiations; this appears to have been partly due to the fact that they had thought that the gains would be greater than appeared likely on closer investigation.

In 1937 an offer for the company was received from the Amalgamated Roadstone Corporation and the directors accepted a price of something under £100,000. The Amalgamated Roadstone did not use cement but supplied crushed granite to several large concrete product manufacturers. The acquisition of a cement firm was mainly a financial move but it was related to a scheme, which never materialized, to link Amalgamated Roadstone with three of the concrete product manufacturers. Gatty Salt, the managing director of Amalgamated Roadstone, had also contemplated the possibility of amalgamating the Gillingham works with the project for building a cement works at Plymouth.

After the Gillingham firm was bought by Amalgamated Roadstone the agreement with the Rugby company was brought to an end, but as no other outlets were developed this reduced profits considerably. In 1939 the Rugby Company offered £130,000 for the company and Amalgamated Roadstone accepted this willingly, having made a profit of about £35,000 in less than two years. During this period it was suggested that the Gillingham company might be amalgamated with the Aberthaw company. However, the latter was not making good profits and the scheme was dropped. Had this happened the Gillingham works would almost certainly have remained open. The Rugby Company kept the works running for a few months only and then, just after the war began, the business was transferred to the new Halling works, the land sold and some of the machinery moved to Rugby.

The purchase of the Gillingham company made it possible for the Rugby Company to expand sales from the new works at Halling. Some have attributed the merger almost entirely to the quota scheme which was reintroduced in 1938. Mr Reddish of the Rugby company maintains, however, that the value of the quota played little part in the negotiations. It may well be that a market was needed and that the penalty payments to the CMF, which would have been incurred if the Gillingham work had not been acquired, were regarded as being of secondary importance; they cannot have been negligible. In so far as the quota scheme was regarded as temporary the value of the quota was less than its discounted value.

During the period 1934–9 there was one other major change in the structure of the industry. In 1938 the Alpha group, controlled by A. Y. Gowan, was acquired jointly by the APCM and Tunnel. At the

Annual General meeting in April 1938, the chairman of APCM said, 'An important feature of this acquisition is that it is jointly entered into by ourselves and the Tunnel Portland Cement Co. Ltd, who take up 26 per cent of the Alpha ordinary shares and issue us in consideration, therefore, 231,660 Tunnel Company non-voting "B" ordinary shares of 10*s*. each fully paid. However, the transaction rests on a much broader basis than that of a joint ownership of the equity in the Alpha company. The Tunnel, the Alpha and our companies are entering into a working agreement for a term of years which provides for the co-ordination and for the closest co-operation of sales policies.

'The purchase was completed on March 24, and Sir Arthur Marshall and Mr Gowan are being elected directors of this company and the British Portland Cement Manufacturers Ltd; Mr Gowan will shortly be appointed an *ex officio* member of the managing directors' committee of both companies.'[1] It was estimated at the time that the Associated Group controlled about 55 per cent of the industry, Alpha some 15 per cent and Tunnel some 12·5 per cent.[2] (These figures are rough estimates only and the three probably had nearer 80 per cent than 85 per cent of the industry.) The Alpha company at this time had five works (Oxford and Shipton, Rodmell, Thames, Metropolitan and Central (Lincolnshire).)

Some of the reasons for this merger are obvious, but it is impossible to assess the importance of each and difficult to know whether the list is exhaustive. Much though the method of simply listing causes is to be deplored, no more can be done in this instance and the following points are offered for consideration.

Gowan, an American who had already played some part in the reorganization of the American industry, may well have been prepared to sell out. He has sometimes been regarded as being primarily a speculator and he may have decided that the industry was 'ripe' for organization and seen that profits could be made by entering a competitive industry and then selling his share in an industry free from the risks of price competition. This view is not, however, borne out by the fact that Gowan became a managing director with special duties in the APCM and although far from indispensable played an active role for a short time. The merger was primarily designed to obtain the advantages of closer co-operation; and it is clear that considerable advantages were expected. All three firms were competing in markets in and around London and were engaged in the export market. This competition would have increased when the

[1] *Economist*, April 2, 1938, p. 54.
[2] *Economist*, January 1, 1938, p. 30–31.

Metropolitan works was complete and this may well have been the immediate cause of the amalgamation.

Before the competitive aspect can be discussed fully, it is necessary to turn from the events which may be regarded as being primarily influenced by long-period considerations to the course of the day-to-day competition in prices and selling.

The price agreements and the quota system were put into full operation at the end of 1934, the quota agreements being for one year in the first instance. As has been pointed out, they were put to no great strain as the demand was increasing fast, and in addition most of the weak firms ceased to be of any importance. The really small firms dropped out, finding the new price structure too low for them. During the years 1934 to 1936 it appears that mutual confidence developed to the point where the firms became satisfied with each other's assurances that prices were being maintained. This is a development of the greatest importance, for it is when an industry has reached this degree of oligopoly that it becomes impossible to conceive of a return to full price competition. Even in an industry in which price cutting is liable to be tempting, organization becomes quite easy. The real sign that this degree of mutual confidence had been achieved was the suspension of the quota at the end of 1937. This action was not the result of price cutting and it did not give rise to price cutting. It is not publicly known whether the quota was suspended because it was thought unnecessary or whether it was impossible to reach agreement; it may well have been the latter since the new capacity which had been installed may have made alterations in the quota necessary. It should perhaps be mentioned that although the quota was suspended, the guarantee fund was maintained; this was the fund out of which fines were to be paid by any firm found to be price cutting. The quota was reintroduced in 1939.

The prices during the period after 1934 gave rise to considerable comment; this arose largely because they were frankly administered prices which were not influenced by temporary changes in demand. In fixing a price for the industry as a whole it was assumed, almost certainly correctly, that the short period elasticity of demand was extremely low.

Prices rose by about 2*s*. per ton when price agreements were made in 1934; this brought the actual London delivered price to 40*s*. per ton, 4*s*. less than the old list price. The price was reduced to 39*s*. at the end of 1935, and it remained unchanged until December 1937 when it was raised by 3*s*. per ton to 42*s*. In June 1939 a reduction of 1*s*. was made.

These prices show a negative correlation with profits and with output, and it is clear that they were not determined by inter-firm competition. The 1934 prices were the outcome of the negotiations to bring all firms into the agreement and were probably as high as they could reasonably be in view of the low prices ruling previously. The reduction in 1935 was made possible by the high level of demand and was influenced by the desire to discourage new entry. Between 1935 and 1937 wages and coal prices rose substantially, but no change was made in the price of cement until as late as December 1937. In July 1938 the chairman of Eastwoods stated that, 'The long overdue adjustment in selling prices was delayed until December 1937 in circumstances entirely out of our control.' It thus appears that margins were low. Eastwoods Cement Ltd had profits carried to the balance sheet of £27,363 for the year 1937–8 compared with over £37,000 for the previous year. In general, however, satisfactory profits were earned because of the high output. The delay in the price increase may, in the absence of any other evidence, be linked with the suspension of the quota in 1937 since the reduction in profit margins reduced the incentive to increase sales by energetic selling and freight absorption.

The reduction in price by 1*s.* per ton in June 1939, when demand was expanding again, shows clearly that prices were administered so as to stabilize profits. The *Economist* reported, however: 'Actually it now appears that the producers are unlikely to lose over the new prices, for a good deal of the reduction will be borne by the merchants in the shape of smaller margins and discounts.'[1] In other words, it is suggested that the price reduction was associated with the increased strength of the cement makers *vis-à-vis* the merchants, which was the outcome of the new agreement on quota and prices signed in April 1939.

Under the price and quota scheme, which continued up to the end of 1937, sales competition between the firms was directed towards obtaining a share of the expanding market. This was clearly important since the quota was renewable annually and there was always the possibility that the scheme would be discontinued, as indeed it was, at the end of 1937. In 1938, in the absence of the quota, list prices were kept fairly low. Home demand fell off slightly towards the end of the year; Lord Wolmer stated that the industry was working at only 60 per cent of capacity and that the rate of operations might be expected to fall to 50 per cent in 1939.[2] The price agreements were adhered to, but competition in selling became increasingly severe during 1938.

The chief feature of this competition was energetic selling which gave rise to considerable cross-haulage and the resulting waste of

[1] June 24, 1939, p. 734. [2] *Economist*, December 10, 1938.

increased transport costs; orders were taken wherever they could be obtained and as transport costs are normally some 25 to 30 per cent of total cost, the scope for waste in this direction is very great. It has been argued that the basing point system which is the basis of the price lists tends to reduce the wastes of cross-haulage since beyond a certain distance the price, being determined by the distance from another production centre, falls. This is true, but the marginal costs of production are so low compared with total costs that it was still worth going a long way into other price districts.

Another form of competition was in quality. This was not of great importance since in most uses the quality of cement used is based upon British Standard Specifications. Nevertheless, some firms could obtain a few more orders by grinding particularly fine, and advertising the fact to their customers. The Federation discouraged this form of competition.

It has sometimes been suggested that energetic selling was on occasion accompanied by various disguised forms of price shading,[1] but on the whole this probably amounted to relatively little. It seems more likely that competition in selling took the form of offering merchants and other customers a very high level of service in the form of frequent and rapid delivery—a degree of service for which some did not pay fully and which encouraged customers to give little or no thought to the convenience of the producer.

Thus the day-to-day competition involved wastes in cross-haulage and selling effort. The possibility of reducing these must be given as one of the major causes of the APCM–Alpha-Tunnel agreement.

The Chairman of the APCM spoke of the problem in March 1939. 'A high degree of efficiency has been procured in respect of production, but for some time there have been weaknesses which have been a matter of common knowledge with regard to distribution and selling of Portland Cement. The liaison between our group of companies and the Tunnel Company made some twelve months ago is working well. It has contributed to the possibility of making more orderly the somewhat chaotic selling conditions. What is now sought is the provision of a similar plan to benefit the industry, as a whole, and as opportunity affords, the consumer.'[2]

In February 1939 the *Economist*, speaking of plans to close the ranks of the industry by the revival of the quota scheme, said, 'But, whereas the old scheme was based on cash payment for under-production and penalties for over-production, the scheme now apparently

[1] Merchants selling a variety of goods had the greatest scope for the various forms of price shading.

[2] *Economist*, April 1, 1939, p. 53.

under discussion would involve the distribution of orders to each unit of the industry by a central organization, the share of individual concerns to be based on the volume of orders secured in the preceding twelve months. The prospects of a fall in consumption, and the possibility of a new bout of price-cutting, recently forecast by Lord Wolmer, chairman of the Cement Makers' Federation, have obviously encouraged the industry to strengthen its position.'[1]

Although a comprehensive cartel system would certainly have eliminated some waste it would have been rigid and firms would have lost much of their independence in long-term matters of growth and expansion. Such a scheme did not receive support and new agreements, reviving the quota in its old form, were signed in April 1939.

Although the system of agreements on prices and deliveries had the support of the industry, it was not a final solution; it was a temporary solution designed to meet immediate problems. The industry had become an oligopoly and would never, except for short and very exceptional periods, be without agreements of some sort; those agreements were, however, likely to undergo continuous modification. 'Referring to the quota scheme, the chairman of Eastwoods said that they had long advocated it, provided a satisfactory forward policy could be evolved, coupled with suitable safeguards for the smaller makers. The alternative would again have been over-production and all the evils of price confusion, should any recession in sales . . .'[2] This statement summarizes the situation admirably, and indicates clearly that the industry, while wishing to remain organized, would only do so under a scheme which allowed for change. The industry had not become a rigid cartel as is sometimes suggested, and any inflexible scheme was bound to break down from time to time and be replaced.

The willingness of the members of the Federation to co-operate depended to some extent upon their fear of the alternative, and to some extent upon the degree of mutual trust which had developed. The central organization was, on the outbreak of war, sufficiently strong and influential to draw up and present to the Government a system for wartime control.

CONCLUSION, 1934–9

THE period between 1934 and 1939 was dominated by the existence of effective price agreements. These had become possible for the first time. The most important reason was the reduction in the number of firms, but it was also due to the fact that there were by this time a

[1] *Economist*, February 11, 1939, p. 313. [2] *Economist*, July 15, 1939, p. 140.

number of substantial firms rather than one large group surrounded by a number of smaller firms. These changes in the structure of the industry had been accompanied by changes in the relative importance of different aspects of efficiency. Methods of production were more standard and economies of scale especially on the marketing side had become more important.

In the new situation entry into the industry became rare and was only contemplated by large organizations. Entry was now the result of particular market opportunities and financial considerations rather than a regular result of bigger profit margins. It is rather important to emphasize the fact that these historical changes had reduced the incentive to enter the industry, for otherwise it is tempting to attribute the absence of new entry after 1934 largely to the possibility of effective exclusive dealing rebates and other discriminatory price policies being operated by the Cement Makers' Federation. This form of argument would be indicated since, taken by itself, a price agreement reduces the risk of entry into an industry by making it clear that a small reduction in price will secure full-capacity working.

The price agreements almost certainly tended to retard the elimination of the inefficient. This might have been of considerable importance in time but the process of elimination is very slow. Prime costs and fixed expenses must become very high before a firm withdraws altogether from its local market. On the whole it appears that elimination of the unprogressive and inefficient has always depended upon technical progress rather than upon short period price competition which is unrelated to long-period average costs. During the period 1934 to 1939 the number of inefficient firms was small; those producing in 1934 had been able to meet both the new lower price levels after 1929, and the intense competition of the period of almost stationary demand.

The effects of the price and quota agreements upon the extent to which mergers took place in the period is uncertain. The mergers were of three types and each must be considered separately. First, there was the acquisition of what was little more than the goodwill of a number of small or very inefficient firms; it is possible that these acquisitions were accelerated somewhat, since the larger firms liked to ensure that the scheme would not be undermined by new interests entering the industry. Secondly, and rather different in kind, were the mergers which involved the acquisition of the small to medium-sized businesses which, being without ambition to expand or to maintain their independence, were prepared to sell to the larger firms which could obtain managerial, commercial and financial economies of scale. It is difficult to see any close connection between these acquisitions and the existence of price stability and the quota scheme. Although the incentive to acquire was increased, the incentive to remain in business was also increased; perhaps the former was slightly more affected than the latter since the acquiring firm was buying a method of easy expansion, whereas the selling firm was usually selling a business whose more distant future was, under existing management, unpromising.

Mergers of large firms constitute a third type. How far such mergers are connected with the existence of price agreements is uncertain. It seems doubtful whether the fear of intense price competition is an important cause since in this type of situation price wars would be rare. It seems more plausible to suggest that such mergers result from the desire to limit the wastes of the competition, particularly in sales and freight absorption, which tend to occur in an imperfect market in which price competition is limited; further conjecture would be dangerous.

The extent to which the price agreements resulted in higher average prices is uncertain, since they resulted in a very different pattern of prices. The prices were frankly 'administered', but were on the whole designed to give 'normal' profits. Prices were reduced when demand was high in 1937 and were increased slightly when demand fell. It is not at all clear whether this unpopular policy could have been continued; it was designed to meet temporary rather than permanent changes in demand. Substantial profits were earned when demand was high and it is probable that profits during the short period 1934–9 were above 'normal'.

Perhaps prices would have been lower in the absence of agreements, but it is possible that low prices in 1934–5 might have discouraged investment and caused higher prices in 1937–8. This is, however, a matter of pure conjecture; very small differences in expectations can have a big effect on the level of investment and the expectation of price control in the relatively near future might have given rise to investment during a period when current prices were unprofitable.

A second field of uncertainty lies in the possible effects on prices of adjustment to prolonged price competition. If each firm found it necessary to strengthen the imperfections of the market and to increase sales efforts, costs would have risen. It is possible that, in the absence of price agreements, the price would have been practically as high, but the profit margin smaller. In addition, there would probably have been considerable price discrimination. In 1933 the list price was 46*s*. per ton, but a price of 38*s*. per ton was said to be common in the south of England; it would be interesting to know the volume of business done at 46*s*. Price discrimination in a fluctuating trade tends to increase selling costs and to reduce the connection between profitability and 'efficiency'. As a result a higher average price is required to yield 'normal' profits.

Consideration of the possible effects of the price agreements and quota agreements, as operated between 1934 and 1939, shows that they were rather small and by no means certain. Part of the uncertainty concerning the effects is due to the fact that in this period people did not really know whether co-operation was temporary or whether the new situation was to be the normal thing. For this reason, it is not possible to deduce whether they were operating in such a way as to maximize their profits in the situations which actually developed, or whether they were operating on the basis of expectations which proved to be unfounded.

Whether the industry would have continued to be fully organized by the Cement Makers' Federation had there been no war appears to depend largely upon the rate of change. In a relatively stable situation the system would almost certainly have worked well, but if a new period of great technical or commercial change had appeared, it would perhaps have been difficult to operate, since the system had no provisions, apart from hard bargaining, for alterations in the share of the market. The quota payments would also have had to be large if great wastes in selling and cross-haulage were to be avoided. A genuine selling cartel, as was suggested, might well have emerged.

CHAPTER 9

1939–55

THE cement industry was well organized in 1939 and wartime control and planning of the industry was done jointly by the Government and the industry. The normal economic forces were in abeyance but some firms went into the war on the tide of an expansionist wave, whereas others were more or less stationary. In 1942 Mr Miller of Eastwoods was speaking of plans for post-war expansion. In the same year the APCM acquired the Barnstone Cement Co. Ltd, a small works in Nottinghamshire. In 1944 both the Rugby Co. and the Tunnel Co. announced that plans for expansion were ready, and the APCM spoke of the urgent need for considerable capital expenditure, especially upon major maintenance and renewal.

It was estimated in 1941 in the Ministry of Works report[1] that the industry could produce about 7·5 million tons with the existing labour force; this is approximately equal to the actual output of 1938 (7·7 million tons). It was thought that with an adequate labour force the output might be 9 to 10 million tons.

After the war demand rose rapidly both at home and abroad and there were definite shortages, especially in 1949, 1950 and 1951. These shortages were due not only to the high demand but also to great delays in getting machinery and plant. Licensing of capital projects has been blamed for delays but this was, of course, partly the reflection of the pressure of demand upon the investment goods industries. By 1949 new plant was beginning to come into operation and output reached 9·2 million tons.

The post-war situation was peculiar in a number of ways. First, although demand was high and was expected to continue to grow, there was some uncertainty, due to a belief that a post-war slump was inevitable. Secondly, prices in the home market were controlled and were low in relation to the capital costs of new plant. This resulted in a

[1] Report of the Committee on Cement Production. Ministry of Works and Buildings, 1941. Cmd 6282.

situation in which completely new works did not yield an adequate return, and new investment had to be made on the basis of the very favourable, but possibly somewhat uncertain, long-term prospects. Finally, there was the threat of nationalization which did to some extent influence the Associated Group, making them more anxious to diversify and more willing to allow their share of the market to shrink.

These factors influenced different firms in different ways. The Associated Group built a large new works at Shoreham, and rebuilt and did major renewals at many of their works; they did not, however, retain their share of the expanding market. The Tunnel and Rugby companies both expanded substantially. The proportional expansion of the latter far exceeded that of any other company. Total deliveries from all works in the United Kingdom rose by 64 per cent between 1938 and 1955; over the same period the Rugby companies' deliveries rose by 276 per cent. Some of this is to be accounted for by pre-war expansion but nevertheless it shows a really dramatic change in the importance of a company which was only of medium-size by 1938. Both the two medium-sized companies with merchanting associations, Eastwoods, the larger, and Ketton (which had a 50 per cent share in the Ribblesdale Cement Co), expanded considerably; two large new kilns have been installed at Eastwoods' Barrington works and two at Ketton and one at Ribblesdale. All the five groups mentioned so far expanded at the earliest opportunity and most have continued to do so.

In these conditions of expansion and optimism two of the smaller units in the industry were absorbed by large companies. In 1945 the Rugby Cement Co. acquired Charles Nelson and Co. Ltd, an old firm near their works at Stockton; this firm was in a weak state and the works in a poor condition. After the war the Associated Portland Cement Co. acquired the small, old-established firm of Mason's Portland Cement Co. Ltd, with a works at Claydon in Suffolk. These two minor mergers are in part a reflection of the uncertain long-term prospects for small firms but they also illustrate what happens when management lacks efficiency or drive in an industry in which there is technical progress.

There are two cement firms which did not expand at the first opportunity. The first is the Aberthaw and Bristol Channel Portland Cement Company Ltd with two works in Glamorgan; the Aberthaw works has three large kilns and the Rhoose works two kilns. This is then a substantial firm which has the further advantage of a relatively sheltered market, their nearest competitor being the small APCM works at Penarth. The firm did not retain its share of the market in the 'thirties and has not expanded since the war; now (1956), however, it is planning to install a fourth kiln at Aberthaw.

The other firm which did not join in the race for expansion immediately after the war was the Chinnor Cement Co. This is now the smallest cement firm in the industry; it has one works with a large and a small kiln. The large kiln was installed in 1936 and the continued existence of this small firm in the cement industry may be attributed to this enterprise. The firm has now placed orders for a third kiln. The relatively late plans for expansion by these small companies are an indication of the estimation of the risk involved in making so large an investment at high capital cost at a time when the price of the product largely reflected the costs of the equipment installed when costs were very much lower.

The five big groups and these two smaller firms constitute the core of the cement industry. There are, in addition, however, seven other organizations: first, the three works associated with the chemical industry; secondly, the group of three Scottish iron and steel firms who make cement from basic slag and have a joint selling organization, and finally the new works at Plymouth, belonging to the Amalgamated Limestone Corporation. These subsidiaries of large organizations now form the fringe of the industry and have replaced the small independent firm; the change which began with the making of cement from basic slag, and continued with the entry of ICI into the cement industry in 1926, has now gone a long way, and only two small firms now remain.

ICI entered the cement industry in 1926 and has continued to make cement, using a by-product from its chemical manufacture. In 1955 it was announced that it had a new plant being constructed at Billingham which would soon come into production with an annual capacity of about 70,000 tons per annum. The second chemical interest in the cement industry is new. Marchon Products Ltd has a new subsidiary, Solway Chemicals Ltd, which has built a large sulphuric-acid plant and a raw material for cement is produced as a by-product. A cement kiln has been installed by Edgar Allen Ltd and the cement output will be produced as a finished product, not as cement clinker as at first planned. An output of about 90,000 tons per annum is expected. One of the most interesting features is that the Solway Company are not attempting to market the cement, but have made a long-term agreement, to run for several seven-year periods, by which the APCM have guaranteed to dispose of the whole of the cement production. The third chemical interest is the United Sulphuric Acid Corporation which is jointly owned by Fisons, Distillers and APCM. The firm has a large sulphuric acid plant at Widnes which came into production in 1955. The cement clinker which is produced is sold to the APCM who have a clinker grinding and packing plant at Widnes. It was estimated that output would be about 132,000 tons per annum.

The one new entry into the industry since 1939, apart from these special cases, is the Amalgamated Limestone Corporation, a subsidiary of the Amalgamated Roadstone Corporation. A limestone quarry at Plymouth was acquired and it was then decided to experiment with some new methods of burning clinker. Plant was acquired and, although the new system failed, a German shaft kiln was finally installed and production started on a small scale. A small works in a distant part of the market presents difficult questions of price policy to the Cement Makers' Federation since the local works, despite higher costs, can take a proportion of the market and force all other suppliers to take the brunt of fluctuations in demand. In this particular case the marketing of the small output has been undertaken by the Cement Marketing Company of the Associated Group.

Despite the interesting new entries into the cement industry the bulk of the great expansion in output has come from the big five, and, as has been mentioned, a greater proportional increase in the output of the four outside the Associated group had reduced its share to about 67 per cent by 1952, a share which may well have fallen still further by now.

After war-time control was removed in 1950, the quota scheme was not renewed. Competition in sales has not reappeared, as there remains a strong sellers market. Policy is mainly concerned with expansion, but the high prices of capital equipment and uncertainty have not yet allowed any over-expansion and surplus capacity to appear. The friendly relations within the Cement Makers' Federation allow for discussion but it would not seem that there have yet been issues which would cause conflict of interests.

There was one interesting change in the structure of the control of the industry in the post-war period. In 1949 it was stated by Mr Jenson, the chairman of the Tunnel Portland Cement Co., that they had sold their share in Alpha Cement to the Associated Company.

'From 1938 until early this year, your company held 26 per cent of the Ordinary capital of Alpha Cement Limited, and the Associated Portland Cement Manufacturers Limited held the remaining 74 per cent. The joint interest worked satisfactorily on partnership lines until last year when it became clear that the Associated Company proposed to exercise fully its majority powers, with little regard to the view of your company, and to cease co-operation on the previous lines. Your Board decided that, in this situation, it would be better to bring this joint interest to an end, although our share in the productive resources of Alpha has been a useful supplement to your company's own production. Eventually it was agreed that Associated would purchase your company's holding of Alpha stock, and, at the same time, they undertook to dispose of the stock in your company which was issued to them when the Alpha stock was acquired. These transactions were duly carried out in the earlier part of this year.'[1] The full reasons for this were not made public but it can be assumed that the market conditions had reduced the short-term advantage of reducing sales competition.

These brief notes upon the post-war events are no more than a general indication of the main trends. Much of what happened is to be explained as the response of the industry to new circumstances but, at the same time, the fundamental changes which had been taking place before the war continued. The present result is a modern industry which is controlled by few firms and in which short-term price competition has been eliminated. The co-operation in the industry is such that not only does price war seem unlikely, but so also does any other form of mutually damaging competition. One of the dangers of discussing the recent period lies in the fact that it is difficult not to assume that the present industry, a mature modern oligopoly, is the final form. This could be unjustified if the industry were exposed to more difficult conditions and were unable because of new legislation to resort to any formal agreements relating to price and output.

Economist, September 17, 1949, p. 640–1.

CHAPTER 10

Conclusions

IN the preceding chapters the underlying and the immediate causes of the mergers, and the short-term results, have been considered. In this section the long-term results and the effects of possible alternatives are discussed and tentative conclusions are drawn about the way in which the public interest has been affected.

The most important determinants of events in an industry are the persistent characteristics of that industry. In the cement industry there are, on the demand side, the natural imperfections of competition; these are now due largely to transport costs, but before about 1900 to 1907 quality differences were as important, the product being less homogeneous and the industry more highly concentrated. The imperfections of the market due to high transport costs and to the possibility of discriminating between customers of different types and orders of different sizes, give rise to immense scope for price discrimination. On the supply side, the chief features are the importance of fixed expenses in relation to average total cost, the durability of fixed equipment, the existence of surplus capacity associated with seasonal demand, obsolete capacity due to the high rate of technical progress, and optimism concerning both future demand and the virtues of new equipment.

These general features, when found together in a multi-firm industry, give rise to circumstances in which, in the absence of any agreements, there is intense competition. This intense competition occasionally allows high profits, but in general the average is low. Further, on account of the imperfections or of the durability of the fixed equipment, the rate of elimination of capacity is low; on the other hand, technical progress gives rise to considerable increases in capacity which are unrelated to specific increases in demand. For these reasons, although a competitive equilibrium in which normal profits were earned would be found in a Marshallian static equilibrium, it is seldom approached in the dynamic situation.

As a result of these conditions in the cement industry, the energies of firms, both individually and collectively, are bent towards the reduction of competition and the resulting reduction of risk and uncertainty. Before 1900 even temporary price agreement was impossible. Firms in the cement industry were changing rapidly, many were expanding fast, and the variations in efficiency were very large. In industries in which raw material prices fluctuate the desire to synchronize price changes sometimes makes price agreement possible despite otherwise unfavourable conditions. This feature was, however, absent from the cement industry. In intensely competitive conditions, in which there was no hope of satisfactory price agreements, the APCM was formed.

Prices were immediately raised; at first the APCM had some monopoly power; subsequently, their existence made it somewhat easier to reach temporary agreement on prices. The full objectives of the promotion were, however, not realized; the APCM comprised many inefficient firms, was short of capital, and was thus unable to maintain a monopoly which could only be based on technical superiority. The severe competition and the failure between 1907 and 1910 of price agreements were the prime causes of the formation of the BPCM in 1911. The circumstances were very similar to those of 1900, but the industry was very much larger and it had already been proved that the APCM was a fairly satisfactory form of organization. It is very doubtful whether the BPCM could have been formed if the APCM had not already existed; further, the BPCM was a safer and more profitable promotion if done in conjunction with the APCM, since the profits of the promotion were partly to be found in the increased profitability of the APCM. Thus the formation of the BPCM appears to have been a special development dependent upon the appearance of particularly determined individuals who took advantage of a situation created by the formation of the rather unprofitable APCM. Of all the mergers in the industry this appears to have been the most fortuitous and there was only one form which it could take; it was very much what the APCM was meant to be.

Had the BPCM not been formed, the 1920s would probably have been more like the pre-1914 period, and the APCM would have become a relatively weak influence. With the high rate of technical change and the increased demand, new firms would have continued to appear, but not perhaps in such large numbers as they did under the protection of the large Associated Group, which was bound to try to maintain prices at a 'normal' level, since it had so high a proportion of the market.

A number of instances of semi-vertical organizations have been mentioned, of which four are perhaps the most significant—the two set up in 1912 and Eastwoods and Ketton. These semi-vertical organizations have two advantages. First, there are savings in sales effort, and secondly, possibly more important, they have assured outlets which are less vulnerable to discriminatory price cutting. It seems likely that organizations of this type would have played a larger part had there been the intense competition which would probably have occurred if the BPCM had not been formed.

The mergers forming the Horne group and those forming the Alpha group appear to have been brought about for very similar reasons. Two possible ones are of interest. First, the mergers may have been caused by a desire to secure the profits likely to be obtained when competition in the industry was reduced. This view depends partly upon the assumption that a substantial firm would be able to reach agreement with the Associated group, and that, after agreement, the two would be able to maintain adequate control of the industry. As the industry was tending to become more homogeneous, the rate of technical development slowing down and the size of individual works increasing, the view might have been taken that competition was bound to be reduced by some means in the relatively near future. Nevertheless, the existence of the large Associated group must be regarded as one of the factors leading to the formation of these two groups. By 1927–8, the Associated group was in a strong financial position, its organization had been proved and it was clearly a permanent feature of the industry. By 1933 it was even stronger, having acquired the Horne companies in 1931 at prices which were probably below replacement cost.

A second possible reason for both the Horne and Alpha mergers may have been the growing need for a marketing organization. The economics of scale in marketing, which are to be found partly in the advantages of a widespread sales organization, could best be obtained by merging. The similarities between the two organizations are so striking that their development can be attributed more to the circumstances than to the appearance on the scene of the two particular individuals. The similarities were great but there were two differences which proved to be of crucial importance. The Horne group was ill-timed and mismanaged and it failed, whereas the Alpha group, different in both these respects, was extremely successful.

At the end of 1934, after the formation of the Alpha group, it was possible for the first time to reach price agreements made effective by quota arrangements. The industry had become relatively compact, and by 1936, after further concentration, it had acquired most of the characteristics of the classic type of oligopoly. The action of each group affected the others to such an extent that full price competition had become extremely unlikely. The experiences of 1938, when the quota was suspended, show that the quota was not even a necessary condition of price agreement. Long period competition for larger shares of the market remained, however, and this was intense. The importance of the long period competition is indicated by the marked differential expansion of the firms. The absence of short-period price competition resulted in higher costs of selling and cross haulage. It appears that the agreements between Associated and Tunnel for the joint control of Alpha were in large part a direct result of the competition. As these three groups controlled about 80 per cent of the industry, the costs of competition in selling and cross haulage were substantially reduced.

The other result of this competition was the re-introduction of the quota in April 1939. Although highly concentrated, the industry still required formal agreement to mitigate short-term competition, and as a result of this, long-term competition was largely confined to attempts to increase sales, hard bargaining over quotas, and cost reduction to meet possible lower price levels. The war was followed by the great expansion of demand and the apparently willing abolition in 1950 of the quota system on the recommendation of the fforde Committee. It now appears that the industry is so compact and so willing to adhere to price agreements that a quota system is unnecessary. It is quite probable that even if the price lists became mere recommendations, they would be followed.

It now seems so natural that the cement industry should be highly oligopolistic that there is some temptation to make the implicit assumption that the events since 1900 have been tending towards that goal and that the present structure was not only inevitable but is also final. These ideas must now be examined explicitly.

In the absence of the large amalgamations, enterprising firms would probably have expanded by acquiring others and by growth. This would have given rise to an industry with a greater number of fairly large firms, but not necessarily to domination by a giant firm. The industry would have consisted of organizations such as the Horne and Alpha groups and the Rugby and Tunnel companies. Once the numbers had been reduced, the organization of agreements would, in all probability, have been easier rather than more difficult, since there would have been one firm which would have been able or prepared to hold prices stable over a large proportion of the market in the absence of agreement. Such a situation is unlikely to have been reached any earlier than 1934, since it was largely dependent upon the rate at which technical progress reduced costs and drove out the smaller units. This would have proceeded less quickly in the absence of the great concentration which took place within the Associated group.

The difficulties of the Cement Makers' Federation after 1934, and in particular the expenses of the competition in sales which developed, indicate that, had the industry consisted of a fair number of substantial firms, a very tight cartel organization might have been formed. This was first made unlikely by the existence of the large Associated-Alpha group and then the war eliminated the need for such arrangements.

Judgment as to whether the structure of an industry has been in the public interest depends largely upon the level of prices over a large number of years if there is unemployment. If, however, there is full employment, the economy of real resources becomes important and increased efficiency is in the public interest so long as there are not counterbalancing disadvantages in the form of high prices.

In the pre-war period prices were the prime consideration. Average prices in the cement industry were almost certainly higher than they would have been if the works *which were in existence at any given date* had competed fully. The only possible exception to this conclusion is the period of very high demand in 1920–1. However, when considering prices over a considerable length of time, one cannot assume the structure and capacity of the industry as given, and it becomes necessary to examine the probable effects of prices and organization in the previous period upon the cost structure and capacity of the industry in subsequent periods, This is particularly important in an industry in which there has been substantial technical change and increases in demand.

The average costs of the combine have almost certainly fallen faster than the costs of the constituent firms would have fallen, and the inefficient have been eliminated more quickly because the closing of works depended upon their efficiency and was not delayed by the market imperfections. Further, a large combine could ensure that its major new works produced at a high level of capacity by reducing the output of less efficient works. The efficiency of the combine was also greater than the efficiency of many independent ones would have been, because it did not have to keep reserve capacity and reserve plant to meet peak demand at each works. Further, although the selling organization was large and there was competition between the sales staff, the selling and transport costs were probably lower than they would have been had there been a large number of firms in competition with each other. Thus within the combine the cost structure was lower than the cost structure of a large number of competing firms would have been.

The existence of the combine has tended to keep prices more stable than they would otherwise have been. This, combined with the considerable technical progress and the generally expanding demand, has led to very favourable conditions of new entry for large new works. It is new works with high, fixed expenses which tend to suffer particularly severely when price competition is severe because they cannot reduce output without incurring heavy losses. Although, with fluctuating prices, the average profits over a number of years of the newer firm may well be higher than those of the older firm, the new firm is risking the possibility of crippling losses in the early years. Thus, in other terms, the incentive to invest in new equipment is increased by stable prices because this reduces a type of risk which is liable to be greater for the newer firm than for the older. Thus, when prices fluctuate severely, new firms are less likely to appear and old firms, with low overheads but high costs, tend to remain in existence hoping for another period of good trade.

Although the existence of the combine appears to have increased the efficiency of the plant in the industry it has, by maintaining prices, tended to encourage excess capacity and has caused some plant to be scrapped unnecessarily early. The importance of this cannot be estimated because the market is so imperfect that competitive elimination is extremely slow and much excess capacity would have existed so long as technical change encouraged the building of new works.

The effects of the combine on the selling costs of the independent firms are extremely difficult to assess. In so far as prices were maintained at higher levels there was greater incentive to increase sales by energetic selling and freight absorption. On the other hand the agreed CMF prices were fixed on the basing point system which discourages cross freighting; the most severe competition takes place in the areas where the rings radiating from two basing points cut.

The price structure has an important bearing upon the amount of price discrimination, and this in turn affects costs. This issue is complicated by the variation in the durability of the market imperfections which make price discrimination possible.

If demand remained stable for long enough (or if the temporary market imperfections were sufficiently short-lived) for a short period equilibrium to be reached, price discrimination would only result in waste of real resources due to the fact that the consumer was not supplied by the firm with lowest marginal costs. The extent of the waste would depend mainly upon the extent to which firms maintained prices in their local markets in which they had monopolistic positions. The higher costs would have no effect upon the consumer but would be borne by the firms themselves. In this case price discrimination does little harm and has a definite advantage in promoting change; in an imperfect market it enables the more efficient to expand without incurring temporary losses while obtaining a larger share of the market. If this were the whole story, it could be said that price discrimination and competitive waste of cross haulage were no disadvantage to the consumer. The difficulty lies in the fact that the need to sell varies as demand varies; the fluctuations are fairly rapid, yet it is not very easy to obtain new orders from new customers either at short notice or intermittently, and there is thus a considerable tendency for firms to maintain whatever connections they may make. This is done at some expense during periods of better trade and may be regarded as a sort of insurance policy; also, it is easier to expand sales in an area or type of market where some are already being made. The result of this, which tends to become cumulative over the years, is that high distribution costs become embedded in the average price structure of an industry like the cement industry where there are possibilities of freight absorption, some market imperfections and a fluctuating demand.

It is extremely difficult to draw conclusions from these general considerations. The existence of the combine and the price agreements, which at least until the mid-'thirties have been largely attributed to it, tended to increase efficiency while maintaining profits. In the absence of the combine price would probably have been lower compared with costs, but costs might have been higher. They would certainly have been higher if multi-firm competition had continued in so imperfectly competitive a market; but this structure would almost certainly have been unstable. Had an oligopolistic industry with, say, twenty to thirty substantial firms, developed, it is likely that a highly restrictive cartel with the usual disadvantages would have been established. Had such a cartel been illegal severe competition would probably have led either to major mergers and the emergence of the present type of structure, or to a great increase in vertical organization which would have increased market imperfections and given some protection from short-term price competition.

Against these alternatives the actual structure appears to have been relatively favourable. A large firm has every incentive to increase its own efficiency and it reduces the wastes of imperfect competition. In this industry it has no long-term monopoly power and its very existence tends to bring in new and efficient firms. The period over which the structure of the industry gave rise to cartel organization was short compared with most industries, and now the industry is so concentrated that 'gentlemen's agreements' are sufficient to eliminate severe competition; these, in general, are less rigid than formal agreements and, correspondingly, they are less likely to inhibit long-term adjustment. The short period price changes of perfect competition naturally do not occur, and prices are not equal to marginal costs; this, however, affects profits during periods of lower demand rather than output, since the demand for cement is very inelastic in the short period. The real point at issue is whether the possible somewhat higher profits are offset by the probability of considerably lower costs. Examination of the industry has indicated that this is probably the case.

The general conclusion of this study must be that, despite the disadvantages which have from time to time resulted from the structure and organization of the industry, there were no practical and, what is more, no theoretical courses of development which would have yielded substantial advantages.

APPENDIX

HALL AND CO. LTD

Extracts from *A Century and a Quarter* by C. G. Dobson, published for private circulation by Hall and Co. Ltd, Victoria Wharf, Croydon, Surrey, 1951.

The Directors' Report presented at the 1903 Annual General Meeting mentions a further increase of £4,145 in the net profit, and contains the first public intimation of the Board's decision to build a cement works.

In the freehold land at Beddington from which gravel is being removed, a valuable bed of clay has been uncovered. Both the chalk and clay have been carefully tested and found suitable for making cement, of which the Company sells very large quantities at its various depots.

The Directors have, therefore, after careful consideration, decided to erect works for the manufacture of cement by the most approved and up-to-date methods, in the confident hope that they will prove a valuable addition to the earning power of the Company.

The decision to build a cement works was not due entirely to the discovery of that bed of clay under the Beddington gravel. The idea had been germinating in Mr Joe's mind ever since he had joined the firm, and it was probably in his father's mind long before that. It was at first intended that the works should be at Coulsdon, where we had chalk, but not the other essential constituents of cement-making clay. This scheme had to be abandoned because in 1898, after a long correspondence, our Coulsdon landlord refused permission to build the works. But the idea persisted.

In July 1903 Mr Harry went to the United States 'to examine and report on the Rotary Kilns . . . now in use for making cement in America'. Works were also visited on the Continent and in Sweden to ensure that ours should be the most efficient in England.

Even after the statement made in June 1903, Mr Harry and Mr Joe were not satisfied that Beddington was the ideal site for the Works. At a Board Meeting on December 29 it was agreed that the Works should be built at Ewell, but this decision was rescinded in January 1904. The Board reverted to the Beddington scheme, and plans were made for building to start as quickly as possible. We cannot tell in detail of the alternating periods of hope and disappointment that attended the building of the works. Progress was far too slow for Mr Harry and Mr Joe: the latter in particular found the delays irksome, and early in 1905 went to Dessau with Mr Maxted, the Consulting Engineer, to see Mr Polysius, the designer, and offered him a bonus of £500 to complete his contract by a certain date. The Ferbeck Construction Company were also in trouble with Mr Joe about delays in the erection of the two chimneys.

Our records do not, in the main, justify the strictures of the two Managing Directors on the men and firms concerned. Rather do they suggest that this girding at the slowness of erection was due to the impatience of Mr Joe to see the accomplishment of an idea that had been germinating in his mind for at least twenty years. His co-directors did not share his enthusiasm, and were thankful when the works were at last sold.

The date when the first cement was made at Beddington is not recorded, but it was between July 1 and October 1, 1905. The Chief Chemist was Mr G. Edon Brown, a fearless critic when he thought the Board's policy unwise.

In October 1905 a handbook entitled *A New Industry in Surrey* was printed by the company and widely circulated. . . . Here are some extracts from the text:

> THE WORKS AND THE WORKMEN
>
> The building of these works employed many hundreds of labouring men during the winter of 1904 and 1905. On starting the manufacture of cement, however, the bricklayer and his mate were superseded by the more highly trained mechanic. During the fixing and starting of the machinery it was necessary to employ German mechanics as these alone understood its proper management. It was very interesting to note in this connection the extraordinary adaptability of the English mechanic and even of the labourer, who not only learned to operate the various machines, but quickly superseded the German workman in all departments, so that now it is almost impossible to hear the German language spoken about the works. . . .
>
> The installation, which has just been completed, is unique in many respects, and for up-to-date design, size, and the minute attention which has been paid to every detail conducive to efficiency and economy, is unsurpassed in this country. If at any time it is found expedient to enlarge the works, this can be accomplished at comparatively small cost, as the whole has been designed with this end in view.
>
> The works are very compact, and have been arranged in a most systematic manner, the raw material coming in at one side and leaving as the finished product at the other. During this journey the material is not touched by hand until it is deposited as finished cement in the store.

The works had been designed for an output of 30,000 tons per annum, but in the first year it produced only 18,000 tons and thereafter about 24,000 tons. The failure to achieve the estimated output was due to lack of knowledge of rotary kilns on the part of most of those concerned. This type of kiln was not new to England, but we had not access to English works and the Board had to rely on information from other countries. There was in those days little inclination among manufacturers of building materials to exchange information. Our Board sternly discouraged visits by outsiders to Beddington, but a Board minute of October 18, 1905, tells us that 'a letter was written to Mr Percy Stewart agreeing to his looking over the Cement Works, after the usual agreements had been signed'. Sir Percy

Stewart later became President of both the Associated Portland Cement Manufacturers Ltd and the British Portland Cement Manufacturers Ltd.

The chalk for the cement works had to be taken from Coulsdon, and the demand kept the chalk quarry busy for many years. In the first seven months after September 1905, for example, 9,000 tons of cement were made, and for this over 13,000 tons of chalk had to be sent by rail from Coulsdon.

The rest of the story of Beddington Works is soon told. In some years the works made a profit, but there was usually a loss. As time went on it became clear to the Directors that they would do wisely to become cement merchants again instead of manufacturers. Late in 1911 conversations were started with the Directors of the British Portland Cement Manufacturers Ltd, and arrangements for the sale to that company, were completed in February 1912. The transfer was effected in June of the same year.

The idea of our adventure into cement making was not ill-conceived, nor were the works an unmitigated failure. It is probable that Mr Joe allowed himself to be over-influenced by his enthusiasm for a long-cherished idea, but there was much to justify his hopes of success.The decision to build was made at a time when foreign cement was coming into England in impressive quantities. At the 1905 Annual General Meeting Mr Joe said:

> Many people wonder whether we shall be able to dispose of this cement and keep the works going. Well, I think if I give you a few figures of the amount of cement imported into the United Kingdom you will consider there is room for the output of our works. The total imports are: For the year 1902, 240,893 tons; for 1903, 261,077 tons; and for the year 1904, 272,961 tons. Into London alone, right into the heart of the cement industry, the imports were: in 1902, 14,025 tons; in 1903, 18,026 tons; and in 1904, 27,905 tons. By these figures you will see there is a steady increase, and that the imports to London alone have almost doubled in three years. The prices of cement, I believe, are lower than they have ever been; so, if we can make it pay now we ought to be very much better off when trade has improved, and as we have adopted the most up-to-date machinery now in use by our foreign competitors, we have every confidence in being able successfully to compete with them.

This forecast was over optimistic. Soon after we went into production the building trade ran into a period of depression from which it had not fully recovered when war broke out in 1914. Cement prices remained low in the London area, partly, it must be agreed, because of the existence of Beddington Works.

The Board minutes and correspondence on the cement works are voluminous, and reading them through today, and recalling all that has happened since 1912, we are left with no doubt as to the wisdom of the Board's decision to sell out. By 1910 cement was occupying far too much of the Board's time, particularly Mr Joe's.

It may have been imprudent—it was certainly courageous—to try to enter the cement-making industry, but whatever view we may take there can be nothing but commendation for all those, on both sides, who arranged the sale. The negotiations were friendly from first to last, and the agreement between the British Portland Cement Manufacturers Ltd and Hall and Co., Croydon Ltd, effectually restored any goodwill that may have been lost through our building the works. Over the years the goodwill between the Company and the cement makers has grown, and is greater today than at any time in the past.

II

THE CALICO PRINTING INDUSTRY

CHAPTER 1

Introduction

THE calico printing industry has proved one of the most illuminating of these studies since it has changed very much less than most of the industries studied and much that was true of the period before 1900 remained true throughout the inter-war period. There has thus been a long period in which to assess the role of the merger; and as a result this study gives an opportunity to consider in some detail the effects of a large firm in an industry in which there are also a number of other firms of varying size. This structure has existed in a number of the other industries, particularly cement and soap, but only in this case have the processes remained comparatively unchanged for a long time; they are complicated and are discussed at some length in Chapter 2. The one merger of importance took place in 1900 and since then the industry has been dominated by the Calico Printers' Association Ltd.

In the introduction it was stressed that one could not assume that any situation would remain unchanged and, therefore, we had to compare the effects of what actually happened with the possible effects of what might have happened. In this industry it appears that the alternative development was more akin to a continuation of the previous situation than it was in the others; the problem of deducing alternatives is, therefore, somewhat simpler.

Another feature which makes this an admirable case study for this purpose is the fact that the three 'groups of considerations', those relating to the short period competition, the establishment of long-period equilibrium, and the historical trend[1] can be fairly clearly distinguished. The process of adjustment of the size of the industry to new levels of demand is seen in a clearer form than in many other industries since it is less affected by historical change; such change was relatively unimportant, and could frequently be ignored. But more important, the short period competition dominates the day-to-day prosperity of firms; it relates to seasons, fashion and particular orders

[1] See p. 17.

and thus deals largely with transitory features which seldom last for more than a year. By contrast, the elimination of firms from the industry takes many years as firms are highly capitalized and the equipment durable. It is failure in short-period affairs which normally defeats firms, and adjustment is more often the result of repeated short-period failures or successes than the result of inferior major decisions.

In the calico printing industry the related features of price discrimination, heterogeneity of product and numerous dissimilar multi-product firms are of great importance. These characteristics are found in many industries but in few do they play so large a part in determining what happens. They are characteristics which are usually regarded as peculiarities; this study shows that, when they are associated with changes in both the volume and direction of demand, they suggest somewhat unorthodox conclusions.

The history of the calico printing industry has been divided into three periods. The first is the period between about 1880 and 1899 during which an intensely competitive situation developed. The persistent characteristics of short-period competition are discussed at length in this section. The second is the period 1900 to 1914 during which the immediate results of the merger of 1900 were seen. The third is the period 1918 to 1954 in which the industry had to adjust to reduced export trade; in this section both the process of adjustment and the establishment of fully organized price agreements are examined.

CHAPTER 2

Before the Merger, 1850–1900

IT is necessary to consider the history of the industry from about 1850 to bring out the fact that the situation just prior to the merger was new. The last half of the nineteenth century was a period of rapid change in the calico printing industry and the merger cannot be understood except as a response to a rather new situation, one which appeared after about 1880 and was characterized by intensified competition.

One of the most important technical changes in the calico printing industry has been the introduction of the roller printing machines which have largely replaced block printing. The printing machines were introduced in 1785 but although there were 435 machines and about 8,200 block tables by 1840,[1] the machines at that time worked alongside the block tables rather than superceded them. The replacement largely took place after 1850. In 1845 there were 5,337 block printers in Lancashire. By 1888 there were 429 (distributed over only twenty shops), and by 1912 there were 423. 'From these figures for Lancashire for different years it would seem practical to deduce that by the former date—1888—the replacing of tables by machines was comparatively complete.'[2]

This marks an important turning point. Until the 1880's the machine printers were intra-marginal and if demand declined, even temporarily, it was the block printers rather than the machine printers who suffered. As the block printers required little capital and firms contracted or left the industry relatively easily, excess capacity had comparatively little effect on prices. After 1880 competition during periods of slack demand was also intensified by the fact that firms were becoming more substantial. Turnbull says that the number of firms engaged in calico printing had reached its maximum by 1850.[3] The evidence is sketchy, being based upon an examination of the sites of print works in Lancashire and Scotland in 1845 and 1938, which shows that no

[1] *A History of the Calico Printing Industry of Great Britain*, by Geoffrey Turnbull (ed. by John G. Turnbull), 1951, p. 423.
[2] Ibid., p. 89. [3] Ibid., p. 111.

further extensions have taken place and that the majority of those working today were already well established in 1845; the conclusion, however, is probably correct. Not only were some firms expanding but also, according to Turnbull, the output per machine probably increased by something like one-third between 1850 and 1880.[1]

The early 1880's were also a turning point in the rate of increase of output. No reliable output figures are available, but Potter estimated that production was about 500 million yards in 1840, and according to the *Manchester Spy* it had risen to between 1,500 and 2,000 million yards by 1889.[2] In other words, output had more than trebled. In the absence of other output figures the exports of 'Printed and Dyed' cottons may be used as an index of output of printed piece goods. The following table shows that exports were nearly trebled between 1850 and 1880, whereas between 1880 and 1900 demand increased slowly and unevenly.

TABLE I

Exports of Printed and Dyed Cotton Piece Goods			*Exports of Printed Piece Goods*		
	m. yds.	£m.		m. yds.	£m.
1850	586	10·5	1889	948	10·9
1860	971	17·0	1890	950	11·2
1865	705	17·0	1891	904	10·8
1870	963	19·0	1892	948	10·8
1875	1,001	19·0	1893	988	11·4
1878	1,067	18·6	1894	982	10·8
1880	1,416	22·0	1895	997	10·5
1885	1,224	17·7	1896	1,073	11·5
1888	1,430	18·4	1897	877	9·5
1889	1,536	19·0	1898	959	9·9
			1899	1,059	10·7
			1900	958	10·6

Source: *Annual Statement of Trade*

Separate figures for printed piece goods are not available before 1889.

Thus the machine printers were faced with a very much more difficult situation after about 1880. They were accustomed to great prosperity, generally increasing demand, and a number of marginal producers, the block printers, who could be driven out when demand was slack. They now found themselves in intense competition with each other for a market which was expanding relatively little.

[1] Turnbull, *op. cit.*, p. 114. [2] Ibid., p. 114.

During this period the technological efficiency of the management was probably the most important factor determining the success of firms. When one firm closed, its premises were taken over by another; this was particularly easy since a considerable amount of the premises and some of the equipment could be rented. Not only were there new people entering the industry but the great variations in efficiency led the more successful to continue to expand whenever opportunity offered. Thus the variations in efficiency and the persistence of the optimism of the earlier period combined to increase capacity even when demand was not increasing and existing capacity had become more difficult to eliminate; the inefficient were eliminated but low prices were experienced by all.

A high proportion of printing has always been done on commission, and at the end of the nineteenth century the proportion was probably at least four-fifths; this included most of the printing for the export trade, as well as much for the home trade. The horizontal structure had great advantages in that it gave the merchant converter and the consumer a wide choice, but it gave rise to the possibility of severe competition. The horizontal structure persisted partly because the expansion of machine printing, a complicated business, took place in a period of great prosperity and many found it profitable to expand horizontally rather than vertically. Further, the capacity of a print works is great and much capital is needed to finance a converting business which would keep substantial print works busy.

The lack of scientific knowledge gave rise to innumerable trade secrets and made 'waistcoat pocket' recipes usual; this, and the importance of the artistic skill of the individual printer, made the range of work which each could undertake successfully relatively limited. As new dyes were invented the degree of specialization tended to increase further, and it was the specialization which gave rise to the major advantages of the horizontal structure. The calico printer was largely dependent upon sales to the merchant converter; these, concentrated in Glasgow and Manchester, were numerous, and they ensured that the market was highly competitive.

Yet the competition remained imperfect, indeed intense, but imperfect competition is a direct result of the characteristics of the industry. These must now be considered in some detail. In spite of the changes in the industry since the 1890's, many of the features which were important then remain important today, although the emphasis is somewhat different. However, as firms are very varied, generalizations which can be made for any one time hold good at later dates, since the change is not great compared with the inherent variety in the industry.

Print works varied in size very considerably at the end of the nineteenth century; this is shown by the range of sizes of the works taken over by the Calico Printers' Association Ltd in 1900. There were forty-six works with an average of eighteen printing machines each, but five had over thirty machines, and thirteen had less than ten. A substantial works would have about twenty-five machines and employ perhaps five hundred people. Today, output per machine is greater and a fairly large works would have about twelve machines and employ three hundred to four hundred people. These facts alone indicate that a print works was generally a large organization with considerable problems of day-to-day management.

In the following section the processes of calico printing are described; and the nature of the more important technical problems is discussed:

(a) The cloth may come to the printer just before it is required for printing, but in many cases the printers are expected to do a considerable warehousing job. (This service is not always given and it is not paid for specifically.)

(b) The design and the variety of colourings or 'ways' in which it is to be printed must be decided. This may be done entirely by the merchant, but the printer may buy some designs, or he may have them drawn in his own atelier. He will hope that the designs he obtains will attract orders.

(c) Rollers must be engraved if the design is a new one. This is an expensive process, particularly if the design has several colours, for each must have a separate roller. The copper roller belongs to the printer and he may have it engraved in his own works or he may have it done on commission. In some types of pattern the engraving may be of crucial importance, but in others 'normal' standards are quite satisfactory.

(d) The main preparatory processes are singeing, washing and bleaching. These processes are similar to those required for any bleaching or dyeing. There are two main divisions to be considered:

(i) Loose cloth cannot be treated as severely as other types. Thus different chemical methods and different machinery is required for different cloths; some may be treated under a certain amount of tension, but others must not be pulled lest they lose their shape. Most cloth can be processed in 'rope' form, but some must be kept in 'open width'. Thus some works have only one set of machinery whereas others may have two or three different sets. Variations of the type of chemical used are easier to make, but where one or two standard methods are used organization is simpler and the rate of output is likely to be higher. Here then is the beginning of the distinction between a mass production and a specialist works. The other important point is that when a works is printing the sort of designs which have white backgrounds (known as 'white grounds') the bleaching has to be of very much higher standard than it does in the works which does heavier all-over patterns or 'dyed grounds'.

(ii) The other preparatory processes apply to a proportion of the cloth only. Some is dyed before printing and the printing may then consist of discharging the original dye and partly replacing it with another colour. This close relationship between dyeing and printing naturally results in firms which engage in both; either the dyeing or the printing may be the subsidiary activity. Another important process is mercerizing. This is a process which is subject to violent fluctuations in demand due to changes in fashion. It is not a complicated process and the cost per yard is low, but standards are difficult to judge, quality varies considerably and 'know-how' is of the greatest importance. At least one firm has a great reputation for the quality of its mercerizing.

(e) The preparation of the dyes is done by the 'colourist' or colour chemist who is one of the most important people in the works. It is his job to decide which colours are to be used. He has to balance the technical, economic and artistic factors; he must decide what dyes and methods are possible, what methods give the 'best' balance between cost and quality and cheapness, and he must decide the exact shade and depth of colour. In some branches this is exceedingly important and there is very little margin between good, indifferent and poor colouring. Further, there is considerable difference in the type of colour interpretation required in the high-class dress trade compared with the furnishing trade; thus, a firm with a colourist who is good in one field cannot be certain of success in another.

(f) The actual printing is usually regarded as the main process. Firstly, the machine itself is the largest single piece of equipment, and the printers who have one or even two assistants are the most highly paid workmen. Secondly, in a works where there are printing machines capable of doing a different number of colours, the work has to be planned through the machines rather carefully. Thirdly, the output of the machines varies unpredictably; the time taken to set up and fit rollers may vary very considerably; a pattern may come right quickly or it may take a long time. Depending on the type of work and the length of runs, a printing machine may print anything from 50 to 60 per cent of its time down to 25 per cent of its time, or even less. Lastly, and this is particularly important where there are many new designs, it is at the printing machine that great losses due to bad work may be incurred.

Although a printing machine can do a number of types of cloth the versatility of any particular machine is limited in three ways. Firstly, it may be of narrow width and only capable of taking cloth 48 in. wide; secondly, while some machines print only one or two colours, they may be designed to do as many as twelve or fourteen; thirdly, small detailed patterns requiring few colours cannot be done as efficiently on large machines, and large patterns cannot be done on small machines. Beyond the normal ranges, there are the really specialized machines which will do the very large patterns required for sarries and table cloths, the surface printing machines which are used mainly for various furnishing fabrics and the 'duplex' machine for printing both sides of the cloth simultaneously.

(g) The development and fixation of colours by steaming, ageing or chemical treatment is the next process; it is an extremely important one and faults may occur at this stage. Different types of dye each require different treatment; some firms use a limited range of dye-stuffs, others do not specialize. If a new type of dye is used considerable cost may be incurred in carrying out trials and there is the risk of spoilt or inferior work.

(h) The washing and soaping to remove loose colour involves the handling difficulties already mentioned in relation to the preparation of the cloth.

(i) The final finishing of cloth varies from simple calendering to 'crimping' and the 'raising' of winceyette. The importance of finishes has grown appreciably; there are now various types of crease resist, anti-shrink and permanent glaze finishes, which provide yet another field of specialization.

Apart from the equipment for the actual processing of the cloth, larger firms usually have a power plant, a large boiler, plant for dealing with effluent, and plant for water purification. Not all make their own electricity, but as a great deal of steam is required, it can be made relatively cheaply in the larger works. Effluent presents a problem which was made more serious by the 1948 Rivers Act; few substantial works have the right to use the common sewer. Water is extremely important as a substantial works may use as much as a small town; the need for plant for water purification varies with the supply and the standard of work to be done.

Both the degree of specialization and the extent to which firms can change from one type of printing to another are very important in determining the extent to which firms are in competition with each other. The description of the various processes indicates that the range of work done by a firm can vary very considerably; the actual degree of specialization is very much greater because of the numerous difficulties involved in undertaking unfamiliar work.

Those in the industry are constantly emphasizing the point that calico printing is an art. This has great relevance to the question of specialization because it means that nothing new can be tackled with any certainty of success; it may, for instance, be a long time before a works which has been doing bold, heavy patterns reaches a similar high standard in small neat, patterns. Any new pattern involves some risk and large changes are difficult; except during periods of very high demand the standards are extremely high and quite small points of quality and interpretation of design are crucial.

It is extremely difficult to give a clear picture of the extent to which firms can change from one type of work to another; a change may be possible but inefficient, it may take a long time, it may involve considerable risk, it may involve much re-equipment. When a works is equipped for a limited range of work some additions to the range may be made with relatively little additional machinery; if, however, a change must be made from narrow cloth (up to 48 in.), to wide cloth (up to 72 in.), extensive re-equipment will be necessary. Even more radical re-equipment is necessary if a works is changed from doing heavy cottons to light fragile fabrics.

Changes in emphasis may alter the character of a works and a distinction must be drawn between a works which is simple and concentrates upon the efficient mass production of relatively few styles and a works with a much wider range of equipment which is set up to undertake a wide range of work and to tackle new difficulties. The complicated works usually has heavy overheads, both in special equipment and in extra staff. These works are frequently mainly concerned in the fashion trade and are prepared to undertake the printing of new and special fabrics and to do the relatively short runs associated with the high fashion trade. Although such a works can do any type of printing it cannot make a profit at the prices which are sufficient for the more simple works with lower overheads. If the simple works tries to extend its range it may have great difficulty in detecting the source of faults and may find that its routine is disturbed and all work slowed down.

Another distinction which is semi-technical is that made between a 'clean' works and a 'dirty' works. A works which handled heavy colours which tend to make a mess such as indigo blue and alazarine red would not willingly do clean work such as white grounds. There is the danger that the 'nips' of machines or, perhaps, the trucks might get dirty and mark the clean work. If dirty and clean work is to be done side by side very great care must be taken and some risk is involved. The difficulties of trying to do dirty and clean work together are somewhat the same as those of trying to do heavy strong cloth together with delicate cloth, for the employees must treat each job upon its merits rather than handle it by a routine method; this causes difficulties and risks and puts strain upon the supervisor. People tend either to cause faults, or to do it all so carefully that the tougher stuff is handled more slowly than necessary. Small differences in efficiency over numerous processes have a large cumulative effect.

Specialization is affected by market as well as by technical considerations and the range of work done by printers is often designed to meet the requirements of particular markets; when co-operation between printer and merchant has been established, the printer has a good chance of getting further orders from that merchant.

The groups into which the trade is divided by the Federation for the purposes of price fixing give some indication of the relationships between the technical and commercial categories. There were originally nine groups: cotton dress fabrics, shirtings and pyjamas, furnishing styles, winceyettes, dipped indigos, West African native styles, handkerchiefs tablecloths and flags, kangas and sarries, and wool and union fabrics. Two new categories, rayon dress fabrics and plastic sheetings were added when they became necessary. Both the cotton and the rayon dress fabrics categories covered an extremely broad range of work; although there is much specialization within each of these categories few clear cut distinctions can be made.

In the period up to 1914 the degree of specialization was greater than it is today; only large firms were engaged in more than two or three styles and many concentrated upon just one or two. The reduction in specialization has been due partly to the decline in the standardized export trade which reduced the importance of standard patterns unaffected by fashion changes. It has also been due to the increased ranges of dyes and the reduced importance of rule of thumb methods which made change difficult.

There are a number of specialized fields in which only a few firms are in competition with each other, yet even here there is potential competition from both existing firms and possible new ones. The more general types of printing are done by almost all firms and here there are numerous competitors even in the short period. Some firms do more than one speciality as well as general work, and it is usually found that, although the level of activity in different firms may vary considerably, a fall in demand in any section very soon makes competition more severe throughout the industry.

The nature of short-period competition and the extent to which price changes are inhibited are determined not only by specialization and product differentiation, but also by the mechanism of the market.

The important market features relate to the risks which the printer must undertake and to the continuity of trading. There are two broad types of business, the indent business and the stock house business.

The indent business is largely associated with the export trade, and, particularly, with the trade in cheap prints for 'native' markets. A definite order is placed for the printing of a quantity of cloth and, since much of it is done to existing patterns which are already engraved, there is no question of terms for repeats being included. The only uncertainty lies in the rate at which the cloth is delivered; sometimes the order is stretched out over a longer period than was at first envisaged. Although new patterns are produced from time to time both by the merchant and by the printer, fashion plays a relatively small part. As the successful patterns are used again and again, the printer is glad to own the rollers, for this ensures that he will get further orders. Most of the orders placed for each pattern are large compared with those of the home and fashion trade, although the average size of orders fell considerably when the Indian and Chinese markets were lost.

The 'stock house' business is the printing done for merchants who hold stocks of cloth and sell to the wholesale and retail drapers and to the clothing trade. Although there are standard patterns which are repeated again and again, the influence of fashion is generally important and the production of new designs and engravings is a major item. The new designs are sometimes obtained by the merchant, but the printer must offer patterns in order to attract trade. The printer also bears the cost of engraving the rollers and he hopes that they will be used a number of times. As in the indent trade, he owns the rollers and thus ensures that he will obtain the repeat orders. When competition is severe, the printer sometimes engraves the rollers before obtaining orders because he may get trade by being able to offer rapid delivery. When there were no price agreements the merchant generally placed orders with the printer for a range of patterns and fixed a single price per yard to cover the whole range and any repeat orders. The initial order is partly used to make up pattern books, and although some is sold, the order is often fairly small. It is largely the number of repeat orders which determines whether or not the printer makes a profit. (The printer must have capacity to deliver repeat orders quickly or he will not obtain the initial order.) The profit also depends upon the items of the range which are repeated; it is usual for the price to be an average price covering the whole range. Thus, if the repeats are all on the expensive patterns done in expensive colourings in small individual orders, the printer suffers a loss; on the other hand, if the price is not too low and the patterns repeated are simple and cheap, he makes a considerable profit. The advantage of this scheme to the merchant is that he can sell the whole of his range at the same price, but will not lose money if it is only the expensive items which are chosen. It can be seen that a hard-pressed printer may be forced to accept a price which will only prove profitable if the repeats are particularly favourable.

It is clear that the indent business was very much less risky for the printer and gave greater continuity. The two types of business are now less clearly defined than they were, as the foreign markets have become less standardized. The indent business is the older type and was much more important up to 1914; practice in the stock house trade has developed from it and is partly a reflection of the extent to which the strong position of the merchant has enabled him to pass on some of his risks to the printer.

From this brief outline of the market mechanism it can be seen that the current work will have been placed with a particular works, or at least destined for that works, for a comparatively long time. If rollers are engraved in March and first printing done in July, they may still be being used in the following January. In the export trade a printer may have a successful pattern and all requirements for that pattern must come to him. The strength of the printer in the short period is based to a large extent on the fact that he has the rollers, and has been accustomed to doing his customer's particular type of work satisfactorily. Thus the printer is able to depend upon a certain amount of trade; his position is, however, vulnerable. If the merchant does not want the cloth because the demand has suddenly fallen, he can usually find fault with it. No cloth is perfect and in times of poor trade jobs and allowances may reach very high levels indeed—over 6 per cent on turnover compared with, say, 2½ to 3 per cent in times of moderate trade and practically nil in times of good trade. Further, although an order may have been placed for a repeat the printer may find that full printing instructions have been delayed, or the cloth not sent, so that the order must be delivered much later than had been expected, and the total amount of work is reduced. More important, however, is that orders may simply be cancelled; merchants place orders in advance, but, if the price falls, they will expect new terms to be arranged. The cancellation of contracts has been so widespread as to be almost common practice. The weakness of the printer *vis-à-vis* his merchant customers lies partly in the fear that the merchant will place future orders with other printers and partly in the fear that the merchant's business will shrink. Although a printer may have as many as a hundred customers on the books he is often heavily dependent upon as few as eight or ten of them. The fate of a printer depends partly, although certainly not wholly, upon the success of his merchant customers; efforts to help them, even by reducing prices, are part of everyday business. It is particularly important that the printer should not accept so many initial orders that he cannot give quick delivery (about four to six weeks) on the repeats. This would involve loss of trade to the merchant and he would probably transfer some of his new orders to another printer.

Although the printer is in a strong position in the very short period, he is in a weak position in the longer period; as a result prices are determined on the basis of expectations over a period of six to twelve months rather than upon immediate conditions. Before considering the way in which major changes in the level of prices come about it is necessary to examine the extent to which price discrimination is possible and the extent to which costs change without there being any commensurate change in prices.

If orders become smaller and the number of repeats fewer the average cost per yard rises but the orders are usually accepted at the same price. The cost per yard also rises if an abnormal number of the repeats are ordered in expensive colourings; even under the Federation Scheme no price variations are given for the different cost of different colours.

Another very important cause of variation in the relationships between the costs and the price is due to the amount of service given. The price does not vary with the amount of service but the valuable customer will get good deliveries, first choice of patterns and other advantages. At times when trade is slack the printer may well go a long way in providing services. He will buy patterns, and even have them engraved, in the hope that he can get orders for these patterns and will then be able to give quick delivery of them. The printer must take *risks* in order to get customers and he must also take risks in order that his customers shall offer a good range, do well, and so provide him with business.

The price will be low in relation to the costs whenever a firm undertakes work for which it was not designed or to which it is unaccustomed. This may take a number of forms; firstly, the work to be done may be simple but the works may have high overheads because it is capable of complicated work; secondly, the only orders obtainable may require special extra machinery; thirdly, the printer may be unaccustomed to the new type of work and there may be considerable risk of a certain amount of unsatisfactory work.

The possibilities of debasing quality offers another method of price discrimination. Thinner or inferior colours may be used, or, despite the danger (or uncertainty) of subsequent shrinking the cloth may be stretched in order that the grey cloth may go further. The extent to which quality (and, therefore, costs) can be reduced at the expense of the merchant is not very clear, although it seems certain that some immediate advantage can often be gained.[1]

The possibilities of price discrimination or its equivalent are thus considerable and varied, and a firm will make a very different profit margin on different orders. This has two important effects. Firstly, competition arises from a large number of firms and the price structure breaks down fairly readily. Secondly, price changes have different effects on different firms; the firm with low marginal costs cannot necessarily drive out its competitors, for work which is important to one firm is marginal to another.

The nature of the industry, particularly the scope for price discrimination and the fluctuations in demand, inevitably gave rise to intense competition. By about 1890 this was becoming obvious to those in the trade; it was realized that although competition had eliminated many firms,[2] others grew and the intense competition remained.

The persistent competition gave rise to a general desire to cooperate and numerous attempts were made. One early attempt, reported by Turnbull[3] was a change in the method of charging; whereas charges had been made per lump (about 120 yards), after 1890 it became customary to charge per yard. This change was partly due to the inconvenience of making charges for lumps, the length of which varied, but it is probable that it was also due to an effort to reduce one method of making hidden price reductions since it removed the incentive to print longer lumps at the old price. Apart from this, efforts to maintain prices were useless over most of the trade. The product varied too much, the processes varied, quality could not be defined and the amount of service given by the printer varied. Further, short-run price cutting frequently paid because,

[1] The final consumer is easier to deceive and the merchant might offer so low a price (in the absence of an agreement) that he knows that he is getting inferior work but thinks that it is worth it. The cheapest will sell both in markets where there is no dependence on quality and in markets where there is complete dependence upon quality. When quality is already debased, extensive advertising of a branded line will have its greatest chance of success. The successful sale of branded lines may raise the quality until there is again general trust in quality; debasement can then begin.again. There is no doubt that there is a self-correcting mechanism, but it works slowly and in cycles.

[2] According to Turnbull (p. 122) there were some twenty-five failures between 1889 and 1892. (There were probably between seventy and ninety firms in the industry at this time.)

[3] Turnbull, *op. cit.*, p. 122.

although firms were multi-product, they were also to some degree specialists. (In Fellner's[1] terminology, joint profits could not be maximized because there was too much conflict about the shares to go to each firm; simple price agreement would have given shares very different from those which actually resulted from the unrestricted competition.)

The extent of the price reductions which had taken place between 1879 and 1892 is illustrated by an example which Turnbull says is typical. 'In 1879 the price of printing one-colour shirtings 140 yards in length was 16*s*. 3*d*. per lump (about 120 yards), in 1892 it was possible to get exactly the same for 5*s*. 6*d*. per lump.'[2]

There was, however, one section of the industry in which attempts at co-operation were successful. This is of great interest for it shows clearly that the underlying characteristics of an industry are the important factors in determining structure. The linings section (which prints the cloth for the linings of coats) formed an Association and produced a price list to which its members were prepared to agree. Linings have comparatively simple stripes and few colours, no particular emphasis is placed on fastness to light or washing, as coats cannot be washed. As the work was fairly standard, not only could the price lists be made precise, but also the competition between the firms was less imperfect so that all price cuts had to be followed and there was a greater natural kink in the demand curve facing the individual firm; in other words, formal agreement merely reinforced tacit agreement. The success of the price lists in the lining's section was also due to the fact that the firms had to have the preparing and finishing equipment; they were, therefore, relatively substantial and were prepared to take a moderately long-term view. There were two new entries in the 1890's; both refused to join the association until after 1900 but, although free to do so, they did not undercut prices. The price lists were more or less successfully maintained in this section right up to the time when the Association was incorporated into the Federation Scheme during the last war.

In the absence of any possibility of co-operation to maintain prices in the main section of the industry other plans were discussed. In 1892 there was the interesting forerunner to the Calico Printers' Association. 'A scheme was put forward for amalgamation of printers by direct purchase.'[3] The idea was to get command of at least 400 machines out of the total of about 1,000; the firms were to work as independent units in matters of day-to-day control. There was an

[1] W. Fellner, *Competition Among the Few*.
[2] Turnbull, *op. cit.*, p. 120. [3] Ibid., p. 123.

extraordinary general meeting in November 1892, when it was reported that the owners of 344 machines had agreed and that valuations were continuing. The scheme, however, fell through; this appears to have been due largely to the fact that 'the terms offered were such as to attract particularly those firms who were not working on a sound footing—this is the only way to look on such a condition as 'If Goodwill be not claimed books need not be submitted.'[1]

The scheme has several features which are suggestive of interesting implications.

Turnbull[2] quotes the savings which were looked for as a result of the elimination of expenses and reduction of costs:

	£
Design and Engraving	33,000
Sampling	40,000
Purchasing Materials	40,000
Better Runs	40,000
Misc.: Warehouse, rentals, etc.	15,000
	£168,000

If one assumes that 400 machines, at £5,000 per machine, would have been acquired, the capital would have been £2,000,000; on this basis the savings which the Syndicate hoped for represented a return of about 8½ per cent. It is interesting that the expected savings all depended upon the reduced costs which were presumably expected to come mainly from reduced competition. This emphasizes the point that despite the severity of price competition non-price competition must have been almost as important. Almost all other proposals for large amalgamations, such as those in soap and cement, depended partly upon increased prices for their expected profits.

This proposed amalgamation consisted of less than half the industry; yet it was apparently hoped that cut-throat competition would be substantially reduced. This optimistic view must have been based on the general idea, which was current at the time, that price cutting was initiated by a few weak firms only, and that a strong firm supported by the majority of others would be able to maintain reasonable prices. This view was expressed in a slightly different context in the *Manchester City News* of September 9, 1899. 'It only requires a dozen or twenty firms to make a stand and most of the rest would probably follow suit. No one likes to continue working at unprofit-

[1] Turnbull, *op. cit.*, p. 123. [2] Ibid., p. 123.

able rates when he knows that others in the same trade are making money. Prices could be raised without resorting to the costly device of an over-capitalized syndicate or amalgamation.' There is an element of truth in this statement for, when demand was fairly high, there were occasions when the problem was to raise prices to levels which could probably have been maintained if they could have been reached. On the other hand, this rather naïve statement ignores the point that, so long as prices are being maintained by some, the gains to be made by others by price cutting are increased. A group of firms cannot hold prices, any more than a single large firm can hold prices, without losing trade. Journalistic cries that sensible behaviour and 'stiffened backs' would solve the problem of low prices were simply misleading; some firms in such a heterogenous industry, especially those firms in difficulties, had too much to gain from initiating price cuts. It may be that the scheme failed partly because people began to realize that a 'strong lead' could not eliminate price cutting.

The fact that the Syndicate was apparently not very interested in the profitability of the firms to be amalgamated now seems surprising, but, at that time, it appears that the success of firms was a function of their management rather than of the quality of the equipment. This view is supported by the fact that firms failed but the works were successfully reopened by other people. Similarly, it now seems surprising that the scheme was devised without giving any thought to the question of redundant capacity; however, the industry was expanding rather than contracting and idle capacity was assumed to be either temporarily idle or badly managed. This point of view is interesting because in fact severe competition in this industry is not a temporary phenomenon which can be attributed to the need to eliminate excess capacity.

Some of those who opposed the Syndicate did so on the grounds that it was introduced by company promoters who knew little of the industry and were merely looking for an immediate profit. This view is supported by the fact that the Syndicate did not accept any liability for its work.

After the failure of this proposed amalgamation severe competition continued and, as price agreements were found impossible, the view that something must be done grew. It was apparent that severe competition would be a persistent feature of the industry if the multi-firm horizontal structure without price agreements was retained. The industry was not shrinking and, although some firms failed, new ones were still entering, and growing, in some sections. The *Manchester City News* commented on September 9, 1899—'The great majority of the firms are well employed and engaged ahead. We hear few complaints about quantity but a great many about price.' This sort of statement seems to have been applicable to much of the time during the period 1890–1900. It emphasizes the fact that one of the important aspects of price cutting is the extreme difficulty of raising prices again in an industry in which future merchant/printer relationships give rise to 'unmeasurable preferences' yet the threat by a merchant to place his orders elsewhere must be taken seriously.

Many firms, especially the larger ones, were anxious for agreement but it was recognized that this was impossible unless all joined and that the most that could be hoped for was agreements which would prove temporary; these, however valuable to the trade as a whole, involve considerable unfairness since those who break away first usually gain at the expense of the remainder.

An increase in the amount of vertical integration offered little scope in the industry at this time because so large a proportion of sales were to distant foreign markets. Even if a few firms had been able to develop in such a way as to reduce the impact of price fluctuations, there were still the problems of fluctuations in the demand in particular markets and for particular styles. In a period of intense competition it would have been extremely difficult to establish a large and strong vertical organization with few natural advantages. The development of firms suited to stand the intensely competitive situation would probably have taken a long time since the change required was great.

With all other methods of escape from intense competition blocked, the Calico Printing industry turned to amalgamation. This was the period of trusts; the development of the stock exchange, the success of J. & P. Coats Ltd in sewing cotton, and the confidence in large organizations, which was common at this time, made large amalgamations appear feasible. Increased education, the development of book keeping and the introduction of the typewriter made their administration possible. In 1899, just prior to the formation of the Calico Printers' Association, three firms engaged in Turkey Red printing in Scotland were merged to form the United Turkey Red Co. Ltd; a further firm was added in 1900. This combine 'was almost a complete monopoly, for although other printers did a little Turkey Red work, they were unable to compete on a price basis. Moreover, the quality of the product was unassailable and there was a tremendous amount of goodwill attached to each of the old-established firms.'[1] This minor amalgamation was quickly followed by the combination of a large proportion of the rest of the industry.

[1] Turnbull, *op. cit.*, p. 325.

CHAPTER 3

The Formation of the Calico Printers' Association Ltd, 1899

AFTER long negotiations the Calico Printers' Association Ltd was formed in November 1899. Mr Ernest Crewdson, of Messrs Jones, Crewdson and Youatt, the firm of accountants who carried out the valuations, was the actual promoter of the amalgamation, but he had the support of most of the important members of the trade. The combine was very different from that which could have been achieved in 1892, when the suggestion for an amalgamation was first put forward; it now attracted the leading firms and covered 85 per cent of the capacity of the industry.

The forty-six printing firms in the combine had 830 printing machines out of an estimated total of 1,000. There were fourteen large firms with over twenty machines each, and several of them, for example Gartside & Co. Ltd and Edmund Potter & Co. Ltd, had important cloth manufacturing sections. The thirteen merchanting firms which were acquired included such major firms as Hoyles Prints Ltd and Gemmel & Harter. Among the smaller firms there were fourteen with less than ten printing machines. In addition to the printing and merchanting activities, the combine acquired 6,656 power looms, 277,264 cotton spindles and a quantity of hemming machines and packing equipment.[1]

Although the amalgamation was basically horizontal, it was by no means an amalgamation of similar firms run on similar lines; the problems facing each were different and the difficulty of running and co-ordinating the concern proved very great. Each firm was accustomed to intense competition; what was now required was co-operation within the organization, but continued competition with the firms remaining outside.

The only large firms which did not join the combine were the

[1] The Prospectus of the Calico Printers' Association. Turnbull, *op. cit.*, Appendix 6.

United Turkey Red Co. Ltd[1] and F. Steiner & Co. Ltd. These firms were rather similar. Both were public companies and they had capitals of £1,500,000 and £925,000 respectively; both had large merchanting sections and concentrated upon the 'shipping' (i.e. export) market, especially the Indian market.

Most of the other firms which remained outside the combine were either in the 'linings' trade or in the furnishing trade; both these sections had peculiar characteristics and competition was not as intense as in the other parts of the trade.

The 'linings' trade which was relatively prosperous, has already been discussed.[2] It is thought that the promoters of the Calico Printers' Association had no intention of including the linings section, and only did so when firms were anxious to join the combine or when they were partly engaged in other types of work.

A number of firms in the furnishing trade refused to join the combine; this part of the trade was mainly a luxury trade as there was little mass market in furnishing fabrics. Design and quality were of such importance that the market was very imperfect; this gave each firm some protection against intense short-period price competition and they had less need to seek the protection of a combine. Turnbull[3] said that the cretonne printers, as a result of new and successful types of design, were able to avoid the depression which occurred in other sections of the printing trade in the years following 1890. The firm of Turnbull & Stockdale was able to expand considerably in the 1890's and as the Turnbull family was large and the firm successful they wished to remain independent.

The Calico Printers' Association Ltd thus included most of the trade, the important exceptions being the two existing public companies, the firms in the linings section and a few firms in the furnishing trade. The issued capital of the new combine was £8,200,000[4] and the assets acquired were:

	£
Properties, plant, machinery, etc.	4,750,233
Book debts guaranteed by the vendors and stock in trade amounting to	895,587
Copper and other rollers	894,716
	£6,540,536

[1] See p. 150. [2] See Ch. 2, p. 147.
[3] *Op. cit.*, p. 167. [4] The prospectus of the CPA.

The average profits earned by the individual concerns in the combine over a period of five years, which for most cases was a period between 1893 and 1898, was estimated to be £455,826; £100,000 was thought to be a suitable sum to deduct for depreciation and it was estimated that there would, therefore, be a net profit of £355,826, if profits continued as before. This would have given a return of only about 4·4 per cent on total capital and this is certainly not very high in view of the fact that there were over three million pounds of 4 per cent Perpetual First Mortgage debenture stock. The return on the ordinary shares would have been just over 4½ per cent.

Despite the low yield on the basis of past earnings the prospects of the Association were obviously thought to be good. The issue was practically twice subscribed and the ordinary shares rose until they had, for a short time, a premium of five to six shillings per £1 share. It is clear that the vendors had considerable faith in the companies' prospects for they took £2,661,836 in part payment and bought a further third of the shares; only £3,200,000 had to be raised in the capital market.[1]

The grounds for optimism were set out in the prospectus:

'Though some of the firms included in this Association have been and are earning large profits, the results of the trade generally for the past few years have been of an unsatisfactory nature, attributable chiefly to internal competition and cutting of prices. The directors believe that amalgamation of interests and definite community of action promise the following advantages:

1. The avoidance of undue or excessive competition and of the selling of goods below cost.
2. Large economies to be effected by the centralization of buying and finance and the concentration of production.
3. The prevention of overlapping upon the part of the firms constituting the Association.

'In the past there has been an immense waste in sampling, engraving and pattern distribution. This can be greatly reduced without detriment, and it is evident that large economies must ensue.'

It is difficult to assess the extent to which these claims were justified. It is doubtful whether the price cutting and excessive competition could be eliminated simply by telling the firms not to indulge in price cutting. While the firms retained independence and individuality it was difficult to reduce the competition on which business behaviour had been based. A co-ordinated price policy was bound to lead to considerable changes in the relative prosperity of the firms. It is clear

[1] *Manchester City News*, September 22, 1900.

from the prospectus that the gains from combination were expected to go much further than this, and that they depended upon a successful centralized policy. If the wastes of pattern making, engraving and sampling were to be reduced, a general policy had to be laid down and the freedom of the individual manager limited. Considerable centralization was also necessary if the economies of bulk buying were to be realized.

Even more drastic limitation of the independence of individual firms was a necessary condition for the concentration of production. In this field there was considerable scope for economies since within the Association there were certainly firms which were relatively inefficient. In any industry where efficiency has many aspects it is possible to achieve economies by concentration as better use can be made of the good qualities available. There was also some idle capacity and, therefore, some works could be closed and others worked more fully. The hope that economies might be achieved by 'preventing overlapping' can only be interpreted as indicating that there were thought to be advantages in greater specialization. This is highly probable since there were two incentives making for diversification; firstly, firms were frightened to remain dependent upon one or two types of trade only and secondly, when a particular market contracted, or was partly lost, firms usually turned to other lines. The reduction of overlapping involves even closer centralized supervision than the concentration of production since each salesman is likely to take whatever orders he can get.

There were good grounds for claiming that considerable advantages could be achieved by amalgamation, but it is also clear that if they were to be achieved the organization and management must be drastically modified.

According to the Prospectus the long-term security of the Association was thought to rest primarily upon economies of scale; in addition to the economies in production, efficiency was thought likely to be higher because the skill of many could be combined. Perhaps more important was the confidence that the combine would benefit first from technical progress. 'The magnitude of the operations will practically ensure to them the first offer of all new inventions and discoveries relative to the trade, and also the best productions of the designer and engraver.'[1] It is interesting that there was no mention of the possibility of research; at this stage developments were made by individuals. There had been considerable competition for new methods and dyes, much emphasis upon trade secrets and many

[1] Prospectus.

efforts to steal them. Firms who obtained new discoveries were able to grow and prosper at the expense of others despite in many cases relative inefficiency in many aspects of the business.

The expectation that the large business could be more efficient than the small because it could have specialized central management seems to have been the natural result of the managerial difficulties experienced by some small firms which had expanded. It was known that there were very great variations in each particular aspect of efficiency and it was apparently assumed that an efficient central management could raise all branches to the same high level. It was easy for those with faith that the theoretical advantages of large-scale organization could be realized to think that the prospects for the Association were good.

Looking back on the early history of the Association it appears that, if the proposed co-ordination of policy, and the reorganization of management which was a necessary condition, could have been achieved quickly, while the Association still had the semi-monopolistic position derived from its large share of the trade, the subsequent history would have been very different. In actual fact, the failure to take advantage of the situation immediately following the formation of the Association was decisive. Although mistakes were made, the problems were extremely difficult. The crux of the difficulties lay in the problem of determining the correct price and sales policy for a large firm in competition with small firms. This is a general problem which occurs in many industries, and it is the specific features of the particular industry which determine whether or not a large firm can be successful.

Quite apart from the inherent nature of the calico printing industry, the organization of the Association was not in any way suitable for the pursuit of a co-ordinated policy. The Association started with 128 directors, eight of whom were managing directors, and the majority of the remainder had some managerial function in their original firm. This structure, which was probably a condition of the formation of the combine, was undoubtedly partly responsible for some of the early difficulties. It is also some indication, however, of the fact that many of the vendors were quite unaware of what membership of the combine would involve.

CHAPTER 4

The Early Years of the Association 1900–2

THE main purpose of the Association was to raise prices and reduce price cutting. In order to pursue this policy quickly and effectively price lists had to be issued to the salesmen. Co-operation was not sufficiently developed to give the individual salesmen general policy directives and thus the system introduced was comparatively rigid.

The increases in prices which were issued to the salesmen in the form of current minimum prices caused immediate complaints and outcry. A letter in the *Manchester City News* on February 3, 1900, scarcely two months after the formation of the Association, spoke of a 25 per cent increase in price and maintained that 'soon outsiders will be so fully engaged that they cannot accept all orders' and suggested that some trade would be lost to foreign competitors. On March 3, 1900, the same paper said that the CPA was apparently losing no time in making itself unpopular among buyers, and gave a long diatribe against the newly published conditions of sale and allowances. It was supported by a letter which prophesied 'disappointments for the shareholders and disaster for the trade'.

There were some, however, who supported the new regulations. A 'Calico Printer not in the Combine'[1] attacked the unscrupulous buyer and thought that 'it was high time to stop this barefaced plundering' (in relation to jobs and allowances).

It is clear that the company lost a considerable amount of trade by enforcing its prices and conditions. As early as April 21, 1900, a letter to the *Manchester City News* said that 'combines can be but temporarily successful, inducing, as they have done, competition not only from abroad but at home. In a few years a state will arise when they will have to hold their own as heretofore'. It was reported in September 1900[2] that the Association had put all the concerns on 'the same dead level as to printing prices' thus giving no discretion to the

[1] *Manchester City News*, March 17, 1900.
[2] Ibid., September 22, 1900.

salesmen concerning reductions for particular customers, and no price differential between firms offering less service and those offering more. The unpopularity of the combine was not altogether due to its price policy; a letter to the *Manchester City News* on June 30 said: 'it is being freely predicted that part of the CPA policy was to be the wiping out of all intermediaries.' The writer, a convertor, was not, however, alarmed; he went on to say that 'the absurd competition was such that only the buyers who squeezed things to the furthest point could get business at all'. Although some thought that the combine was behaving reasonably, it was, on the whole, unpopular. It has nearly always been said that the combine had to quote a slightly lower, rather than an equal, price to obtain or keep an order; in other words, if all else was equal, orders tended to go to independents.

The difficulties of the Association were also partly due to the fact that exports in 1900 fell by about 1,000 million yards and were 10 per cent less than in 1899. The Association was particularly heavily engaged in the export trade and, therefore, suffered more than proportionately. The loss of trade was the main cause of a policy of concentration. It was not, however, the only cause. According to a letter to the *Manchester City News* of January 12, 1901, at the time of the floatation there were a total of 1,175 machines in the industry of which 805 were in the combine. (This figure is probably somewhat inaccurate as, according to the Prospectus, the combine had 830); the letter continues 'I think the total number actually employed in the production of all printed textiles in Great Britain during the last five years did not exceed 850. I have good reasons for believing this to be about accurate and should say that a fairly large proportion of the machines standing idle were in the works now taken over.' Although it is difficult to rely upon these estimates it appears probable that the general picture is not misleading; the Prospectus claimed 85 per cent of the capacity of the industry but in 1901 the CPA only had just under half of the trade.[1]

One of the works acquired by the CPA was closed when it was acquired, another never worked and was closed in September 1900. During 1900 six other works were closed; between them they contained sixty-seven machines; some had as many as fifteen to twenty machines each.[2] Most of the works which were closed in the early years were those which were in rented premises, thus the size or other features of those closed give no indication of policy.

The policy of closing works and concentrating production con-

[1] See Table II, Ch. 6. [2] Information from the Calico Printers' Association Ltd.

tinued throughout 1901 when ten works with a total of 108 machines were closed; thus in two years eighteen works containing over 175 machines had been closed.[1] At the Annual General meeting in 1902 the Chairman said that the total capital in the closed works was estimated at £561,000, but some machinery had been transferred and some buildings let. This drastic closing of works is indicative of several features.

The first point is that a number of unprofitable and even useless firms were acquired. A rumour is still current that a number of old machines were bought and put into a building and sold to the Association. The value of the closed works is not known but it appears likely that some of the general overcapitalization can be traced to this source.

The second point is that the rapid and determined elimination of redundant works was the outcome of determined management in a field in which the central management was effective, as well as the result of the very apparent economies to be obtained. Indeed, the closing of so many is further indication that, although competition was severe prior to the formation of the Association, it had failed to eliminate redundant capacity. The concentration of production was one of the economies which were expected when the prospectus was drawn up.

It is plain that the closing of works resulted in economies but it also had other less tangible effects. It caused great uneasiness among the staff because it involved sacking a number of people; the feeling of insecurity made many employees dislike the Association and it thus became even more unpopular. Further, it increased the tendency of the individual managers to compete within the Association and thus made it more difficult for the Association to pursue a co-ordinated policy.

The difficulties of the Association are reflected in its financial results and in the value of the shares. The £1 shares rose to 25*s*. and 26*s*. soon after they were issued but by September 1900 they were down to 14*s*. The unrest was such that in October 1900 the directors issued a circular explaining the fall in share prices. They claimed that the fall was due primarily to enforced sales by weak holders, dear money, and the general economic stagnation.

They expressed confidence in the future and made four points. The first was that although the trade with India and China was unsatisfactory it was not of fundamental importance; this point was disputed by the Editor of the *Manchester City News*. The second

[1] Information from the Calico Printers' Association Ltd.

point was that the high prices of raw materials were temporary. The fact that this point was made indicates that it had proved impossible to pass the increased costs on to the merchants. The third point was that some firms were making good profits and, although mistakes had been made and reorganization was difficult, there had not yet been time to put the unprofitable ones on a satisfactory footing. The final point was that the profits at June 1900 had been better than those for the separate concerns in the previous year. While no doubt true, this point was somewhat misleading since the increased profits were largely a reflection of the increased prices, and the loss of trade which was resulting from the increased prices was not mentioned. In December 1900 the CPA showed a profit of £334,000 and kept a surplus of £100,000 in hand. The profit in April 1901 was the equivalent of 4 per cent on the ordinary shares. This was better than the Editor of the *Manchester City News* had expected but he declared that 2½ per cent allowance for depreciation (£219,000) was inadequate.

By August 1901 the shares had fallen to 7*s*. 6*d*., and in March 1902 the balance sheet of the year ending December 1901 was published. This showed that the balance had fallen from £144,367 to £38,525 after debenture interest had been paid. Considerable losses had been made on stocks which had to be written down, and the spinning and weaving sections, which were depressed, had made losses. The shares were down to 6*s*. 6*d*. As it became obvious that the concern was over-capitalized in relation to current levels of trade, both the vendors and Ernest Crewdson, the main promoter, were attacked; these attacks coincided with the development of antagonism against all company promoters.

Crewdson had received £160,940 out of which he was to pay the expenses of the promotion. This large sum represented 2 per cent of the issued capital and, although he clearly made a large profit, he did not take more than was usual for that type of work; in the cases of smaller floatations the promoter quite frequently took as much as 10 per cent, to cover expenses and underwriting risks.

The second annual general meeting, held in March 1902, was crowded and lively, and there was much criticism of the directors. One of the most vocal and fully reported critics was a Mr Forbes who argued that the branch managers should 'manage their own businesses as heretofore'. This was apparently the general tenor of the criticism, and Forbes had enthusiastic support. The opposite view was held by some; on March 22, 1902, a letter from H. G. Pasley, published in the *Manchester City News*, maintained that the floatation was not a swindle but a mistake shared by vendors and outside shareholders alike, 'a mistake made by the almost universal belief in monopoly'.

He pointed out that the management of combines had always been one of their chief difficulties, and suggested that perhaps an administrator from some organization, such as the railways, should be employed. Further, he said that Forbes was simply suggesting that there should be no central management, and that if this was the proper course no association was necessary.

A week later an Adjourned Meeting was held which appears to have been dominated by an excellent speech by L. B. Lee, one of the managing directors. The main points from his speech were:

1. That the directors received no pay (this surprised the meeting);
2. That £39,134 had been spent on reconstructing warehouses and the concentration, which had thus been made possible, had resulted in a saving of £11,000 a year. (This had been a subject of exaggeration and criticism);
3. That 'the real troubles of management were due to the fact that responsibility and control were in different hands. The Managing Directors had no power to enforce orders and some people not only did not carry them out but discussed them with customers';
4. That the closing of works had certainly paid;
5. That Mr Forbes' suggestions about management were obviously impossible, and that the central management had not interfered when works were being run on good lines.

Finally, Lee stated that he was the largest shareholder and that he had not sold any shares. He suggested that a committee be appointed to examine the difficulties between the vendors (mainly directors) and the eight managing directors.

Forbes spoke again but received a very much less enthusiastic reception. Lee's speech was endorsed by a Glasgow man who was representing £150,000 worth of shares. He said that he was attending the meeting only because of the alarm caused by Forbes' remarks at the previous meeting; he declared that 'what the Association wanted was a dictator'.

The Report of the Committee of Reconstruction appeared in 1902. It not only gives a clear picture of the difficulties of the Association, but is also of great interest in relation to the general problem of the administration of combines in this period.

Report of the Committee of Reconstruction to the Shareholders of the Calico Printers' Association Limited[1]

Para. 1. The adjourned general meeting of shareholders on March 24 last decided to appoint a committee which should:

'(i) Investigate the difficulties which had arisen between the vendors and the managing directors, as well as the system of management in the past.

(ii) Draw up a scheme for the future management of the Association on lines likely to be successful.'

Para. 2. 'It was agreed that the committee should be composed of an equal number of directors and of non-vendor shareholders.'

The six directors appointed came from six of the big firms in the Association and included Mr L. B. Lee.

The non-vendor shareholders appointed to the committee were:

'(i) Hollins, Frank, of Messrs Horrockses, Crewdson & Co. Ltd.

(ii) Mather, Sir William, MP, of Messrs Mather & Platt Ltd.

(iii) Partington, Edward, of Messrs Kellner-Partington Paper Pulp Co. Ltd.

(iv) Philippi, O. E., of Messrs J. & P. Coates Ltd. [who was made Chairman].

(v) 'Stanning, John, of Messrs The Bleachers' Association Ltd.

(vi) Thomson, John, of Messrs Stewart, Thomson & Co.'

Para. 5. 'The investigations of the committee have led to the conclusion that the difficulties which have arisen between the vendors and the managing directors were, generally speaking, the unavoidable outcome of adequate provision not having been made for conducting the affairs of the Association on sound lines, and that the want of success and absence of satisfactory profit are also, to a considerable extent, attributable to the same cause.'

Para. 6. 'When the Association was formed, suitable arrangements should have been made for working the business as one, and for increasing the efficiency and earning power of the numerous concerns of which it is composed. To accomplish this a central authority, having complete and effective control of all the business belonging to the Association, was indispensable, but it should have been constituted on lines enabling it to secure the confidence and loyal support of the directors and branch managers. It was not so constituted, and the best efforts of successive chairmen and managing directors have on that account been more or less paralysed. If their duties and sphere of influence had been defined and restricted, they would probably have met with less opposition. Many of the branches were, for a variety of reasons, disinclined to carry out their instructions. Some

---

[1] Passages in quotation marks are direct quotations, and the others are summaries of the 'The Report of the Committee of Reconstruction' which is quoted in full in: *A History of the Calico Printing Industry of Great Britain* by Geoffrey Turnbull, pp. 446–458.

of the reasons given were altogether bad, some inadequate; but in other cases the disinclination was justified. It was idle to expect that three or four men, however able, would be recognized by a large body of men, of similar training, and possessing similar knowledge and experience, to be the most competent judges of every question that would arise in connection with some sixty separate businesses. Even if they had been so regarded, it was well known that the time at their disposal was altogether insufficient to enable them to arrive at carefully considered decisions and that this compelled them to depute much of their work to permanent officials. This knowledge could not but increase the resistance, both active and passive, to instructions emanating from the head office. When the managing directors sought the advice of vendor managers, they found that the views of men, whom they were bound to consider equally competent to form an opinion, were in absolute conflict. This resulted, in a great measure, from the latter not being accustomed to take sufficiently into consideration the requirements of the Association as a whole, and from their judging most questions from the standpoint of the business with which they are connected.

Para. 7. 'There can be no doubt of the inherent difficulties of the situation having been aggravated by mistakes made by both sides, more particularly during the first eighteen months, but the want of harmonious co-operation between the board of management and the branch managers resulted chiefly from the absence of a carefully-planned system of administration. There were frequent changes in the board of management, which prevented any continuity of policy; measures, which had been inaugurated and might have produced good results, were abandoned before they could bear fruit.'

SCHEME OF MANAGEMENT

Para. 10. In drawing up a scheme for the management of the Association, provision must be made:

'(i) To secure to the fullest extent possible the many legitimate advantages which can be derived from the combination of a large number of manufacturers.'

'(ii) To counteract the disadvantages which are inseparable from the fundamental changes affecting the individual businesses', and from the transference of many responsibilities to a newly constituted body lacking the specific experience required to deal successfully with entirely new conditions.

(iii) To establish settled relationships within the organization, while providing also for their revision when experience has shown this to be necessary.

I

Para. 11. 'The public was not asked to become interested in an aggegation of sixty-four disconnected businesses which would be worked by the vendors more or less independently of each other and on the same lines as previously. It is, on the contrary, clearly set out in the prospectus that the Association to which the public was asked to subscribe is one concern, consisting of a number of component parts, which would be controlled by a Central Authority, and that the business would be conducted on lines different from those followed in the past, this being necessary in order to secure a better return for the capital employed than has been obtained formerly.'

Para. 12. 'Although it should hardly be necessary to emphasize this point, the committee considers it right to draw special attention to the matter, as it has been stated that some vendor managers resent interference with "their" works, that they claim to be allowed to work "their" business as formerly, and in accordance with their own ideas, as they know its requirements best.'

Para. 13. 'Such unreasonable pretensions cannot be reconciled with the terms of the prospectus and the distinct representation made to the public in order to induce it to subscribe. It was stated that the object of the formation of the Association was to combine the businesses. This implies that as businesses with separate interests they would cease to exist, and that everything affecting them would be made subordinate to the interests of the Association as a corporate body, or in other words, to the interest of the shareholders. It must also be borne in mind that many of the businesses acquired by the Association have been by no means profitable. A certain number have been successful, some even doing a very remunerative business; but the aggregate profits were only sufficient to make a return of about 4 per cent on the share capital of the Company. It is evident beyond doubt that the public subscribed on the strength of the statements contained in the prospectus as to the benefits to be obtained by combining the businesses and by working them differently in future.' Every vendor manager is, therefore, under a personal obligation to further the interests of the Association to the best of his ability.

Paras. 16 and 17. A statistical department at the central office is essential. 'The representatives of three successful combinations have stated that without such help it is impossible to exercise any useful or even intelligent control.'

Statistical information supplied so far has proved very useful. 'It was not to be expected that this work, in many respects new to the officials to whom it was entrusted, would from the first be done in such a perfect manner as to escape criticism.'

Branch managers, who formerly complained of the trouble involved, have now agreed that such statistical information is useful not only to the head office but also to the branches themselves.

II

Para. 18. Where a large number of businesses are combined and sold to the public 'the necessity of meeting outside competition is no longer felt to the same extent, and the incentive to work the business economically in order to obtain an adequate return upon the capital employed is seriously lessened. Too much reliance is placed upon the possibility of obtaining higher prices' but a public company should, in the interests of its shareholders, keep a close check on all expenditure.

Para. 19. 'The opinion has sometimes been expressed that on account of the diversity and complexity of the work, and as success in the calico printing trade depends largely upon "individuality", upon the creative faculty and taste of the leading men, the businesses belonging to the Association cannot with advantage be placed under the control of a central authority, and that perfect freedom of action and absence of control are necessary to their well-being and the indispensable elements of success.'

Para. 20. 'The committee does not share this opinion, and sees no reason to doubt that the business can be worked on the lines of the prospectus without unduly interfering with what is called "individuality", and believes that the advantages which it was stated would accrue from a consolidation of interests can be secured, and would greatly increase the profits.'

Para. 21. 'The Association is in a position to secure additional advantages which the committee considers of special benefit. The best chemical and mechanical science can be employed to a greater extent than in the case of separate concerns, and men of thorough training in practical chemistry, as applied to calico printing, should be engaged on terms sufficiently liberal to attract the most capable. One of the greatest advantages of combination may be shown in improved quality of work all round, by reason of the power of the Association to command the highest skill and knowledge of the newest appliances and processes and the best methods of distribution. The committee recommends that these matters have the immediate and constant attention of the Executive.'

Paras. 22 and 26. 'The new conditions under which the business is carried on render it necessary to prevent indifference and lethargy gaining ground, and suitable means must be devised for giving pecuniary recognition of good work done by individuals.' This, however, could not be on a basis of the profits of the individual branches since (a) different profits were to be expected, and (b) concentration of production and allocation of styles between the various works would alter their relative profitability regardless of the standard of management of the works. Further, changes of this type would meet with opposition if payment was related to profits. Nevertheless, 'it is necessary to introduce in some form the system of "payment by results", and a suitable method of doing so will have to be devised.'

Para. 27. The committee recommends the establishment of a Board of Directors, of not less than six and not more than nine members, an Executive of not less than two and not more than four members, and a small Advisory Committee on the following matters: (a) Works Production; (b) Designs, Styles, etc.; (c) Concentration; (d) Prices; (e) Trading; (f) Cloth Buying; (g) Drugs, Stores, Coal, etc.

Para. 39. 'The co-existence of three different bodies for the purpose of management is unusual, but a careful scrutiny of past and present difficulties leads to the belief that they are necessary, separately, to (*i*) supervise (Board); (*ii*) administer (Executive); and (*iii*) advise (Advisory Committees), whilst co-operating in the general control of the business and directing its policy.'

Paras. 41 to 47. 'All branches must have confidence in the central decisions and this may be achieved by having advisory committees rather than individual specialists. The directors and executives must consider the association as a whole and it is, therefore, "undesirable" that they should be connected with the management of any particular branch or section. The question as to whether the grouping of businesses should be adhered to had better be left for the consideration of a new board.'

Memorandum by William Mather

Referring to paragraph 21 of the report: Sound scientific knowledge and its application is essential to good quality and economic production in Calico Printing.

'The Association of the Calico Printers of Great Britain affords an opportunity, unique in the history of the industry, for the application of the continuous discoveries of scientific research to practical objects in each branch works.'

'To make use of this opportunity I strongly urge that a central department of technical chemistry, applied to calico printing, should at once be established and equipped with necessary appliances for research and experimental work.

'This department would form a "clearing house" for difficulties experienced in any branch works in carrying out complicated processes, and in the introduction of new colours and methods of production.

'It would form the brain of the business, always active and alert to supply the managers of the branches with expert knowledge without interference with the responsibility of such managers in obtaining the best practical results.'

'A combination of many works not only renders such a technical research department relatively inexpensive,' but would afford material for comparison and investigation altogether lacking in a single concern.

'In the absence of such a department I fail to see how this great Association is to be supplied continually, as time goes on, with the requisite men of trained intelligence to conduct its operations on the productive side with that degree of excellence and economy necessary to meet the competition of the highly organized and equipped calico printing works with which I am acquainted in other countries.

'But with such resources as I have ventured to suggest providing the cultured brain to direct the skilful hand of the British workman, it should not be difficult for the Association of British Calico Printers to attain a commanding position for any class of goods in foreign markets, and to supply with profit to themselves a very large portion of the world's demand.'

The report of the Committee of Reconstruction thus gives a clear picture of the acute managerial difficulties. It indicates that because of the problem of administration, combines, such as the Calico Printers' Association, are quite unlikely to realize the possible economies in the years immediately following their formations. It was admitted that the lack of profits was partly due to bad managerial decisions and the failure to carry out some of the better decisions. Paragraph 18 emphasized the lack of incentive to work economically which was due to the possibility of relying upon price increases.

Although the Report emphasizes the new administrative problems it is clear that the committee was fully aware of the inherent difficulties of framing a policy which would make it possible to realize the potential economies of scale. A list of the possible economies, such as that found in the prospectus, is misleading since the full realization of one conflicts with the full realization of others. The most important conflicts related to the price policy. As soon as the Association was formed and began to limit the price cutting by its individual branches, any price cutting by independent firms became extremely effective and was difficult to meet within the overall price policy of the Association. The Association was not organized in a way which enabled it to meet individual price reductions quickly and, as reductions usually had to cover a considerable volume of trade, they could seldom be made without incurring marginal losses. In other words, the branches of the Association had to abide by a common price list and this put them at a great disadvantage *vis-à-vis* independent firms in their struggle to maintain their share of the trade; the combine tended to lose orders whenever independent firms wanted work. Although the difficulties were mainly due to the necessity to work to a uniform price list, some were the result of the problems involved in drawing up the list. It is extremely difficult to fix prices so that they reflect costs accurately, and profit margins tend to vary both between styles and between customers; unless it is watched extremely carefully, there is some danger that a firm will lose profitable orders and retain the less profitable ones.

A rather similar conflict arose when attempts were made to increase the degree of specialization and to reduce the costs of sampling and engraving. As the habits of individual trading were deeply ingrained, and the personal relationships between the merchants and the printers were of the greatest importance, any attempt to make changes which tended to disturb these relationships tended to cause loss of trade to the independent printer. Such losses were liable to be cumulative, since if customers were lost they were difficult to regain without the attraction of special prices.

Most of these policy difficulties have to be faced by all large firms in industries where they have to compete with a number of independent firms. The large firm can only hope to succeed if there are economies of scale. In the case of the Calico Printers' Association, realization of the economies would have involved considerable interference in the day-to-day management of the individual branches, particularly in relation to their trading policy. The failure of the 'marketing scheme', which is discussed later, showed that, even in more favourable circumstances, a centralized attempt to reduce overlapping and increase specialization was unsatisfactory and caused loss of trade.

The size of the combine and the nature of its problems made it absolutely necessary to create a managerial structure which would facilitate close co-operation between the branch managers and the central management. The new managerial structure, devised by the Committee of Reconstruction, was designed to bring about this co-operation and create confidence in the central executive and the directors. The Committee of Reconstruction did not, however, tackle the problem of the exact nature of the compromise between centralization and decentralization which was to be set up: 'The question as to whether the grouping of businesses should be adhered to had better be left to the consideration of the new Board.' (Paragraph 47). It is not surprising that the Committee decided not to tackle this problem as it lay at the root of future policy decisions and depended partly upon the success of the new Board and Executive in gaining the confidence of the rest of the organization, and partly upon such factors as the development of trade, changes in styles, markets, the volume of demand, and the rate of growth of outside competitors. Certainly the general policy was to move towards more rigorous central control and the speed with which this policy could be pursued could not be predicted. The Calico Printers' Association could neither be run as a group of largely independent businesses, with the central management controlling only general price and investment policy, nor could it be run as a single fully-integrated business. The internal development of the firm, right up to the present time, has represented efforts to find the best compromise in changing circumstances.

CHAPTER 5

1902–14

THE reconstruction of the administration of the company was, as far as can be judged, successful. H. W. Macrosty maintained that, 'The greater part of the more satisfactory results must be attributed to improved organization.'[1] No dividend was paid for 1901 or 1902, but in 1903 a dividend of 2½ per cent was possible. A capital reserve fund was created in 1902 and in 1903 £125,000 was added to it, to meet the complaints by the accountants that insufficient had been written off for depreciation. The basic strength of the Association was much increased; Macrosty said that '. . . it must not be concluded that the higher dividend (of Steiner's) is proof of an essentially stronger position. The works in the Association which are actually employed are doubtless as strong as the rival firm, but they have to bear the burden of practically paying the closed works not to compete. That makes the industry more effective and Messrs. Steiner & Co. profit thereby.'[2]

It is clear from the Annual Report of June, 1903, that the Association was indeed overcapitalized; the goodwill stood at £510,292 and had not been written down, and works which had been closed were valued at £675,184.[3] The overcapitalization due to redundant capacity continued; by 1905 about twenty-three works which had contained 258 machines and were valued at £763,000 had been closed. By 1906 five additional print works had been purchased; although some of their capacity was specialized and useful to the Association much of it was either redundant or caused equivalent redundancy in other works. In 1908–9 another small works was closed.

The fact that the CPA was dealing with redundant capacity during a period when trade as a whole was expanding is mainly a reflection of the fact that firms are sufficiently specialized, and the market sufficiently imperfect, for changes in the direction of demand to offer opportunities to some while leaving others redundant. There were not, at this time, many inefficient firms to be driven out since the

[1] H. W. Macrosty: *The Trust Movement in British Industry*, p. 153.
[2] Ibid., p. 154. [3] Ibid., p. 153.

majority had either been eliminated before 1900 or had joined the CPA. Inefficiency takes some time to develop, usually consisting of failure to change rather than absolute deterioration. When there are few palpably inefficient firms, changes in the direction of demand cause particularly intense competition since the excess capacity which develops is eliminated very slowly.

The Association was nevertheless consolidating its position. A further merchanting business, a colliery and a finishing business were acquired; the latter increased capacity in a department which had always been insufficiently equipped. The years 1905 and 1906 were 'print' years; prints were fashionable and sold well, and most firms were prosperous.

The increased strength of the CPA caused some uneasiness in the trade. There was a suggestion that another, rival, combine should be formed.[1] In the document, sent out to those interested, the fear of monopoly was emphasized 'one of the main objects, of course, being to secure economy in working and another to prevent pressure being brought to bear on individual firms by the weight of the larger concerns' and later '. . . the merchants would gladly welcome . . . an alternative source through which they might get their printing done'. On the whole the scheme was expansionist and born of prosperity. A large new works of great efficiency was to be built and was, according to Turnbull, to be 'a body ranking in importance and of a higher efficiency than the Calico Printers' Association'. It was to be confined to job printing and a proportion of the profits above a minimum level were to be paid to the customers. This feature is of great interest for it shows that great efforts were to be made not to antagonize the merchants as the CPA had done. They had been criticized not only for raising prices and trying to make a 'monopoly' profit, but also for trying, if not to eliminate the merchants, at least to compete with them unfairly by favouring their own merchanting sections.

There is another interesting implication in the suggestion of a second large combine. By 1906 the economies of amalgamation were beginning to show and it was beginning to look as if the Association would continue to strengthen its position. This may have been partly due to the fact that the ranges of fast colours and vat dyes were increasing and the techniques of printing becoming more complicated, and, perhaps more important, more scientific.

The scheme for a second combine in calico printing was soon dropped, for trade was bad in 1908 and 1909.[2]

Not only did the decline in trade quickly dispel any fears that the

[1] Turnbull, *op. cit.*, pp. 330–2. [2] See Table II, Ch. 6.

CPA would become too powerful, but also it must have been clear that a second combine would be extremely difficult to establish and finance unless demand was high; the independent firms had already expanded considerably.

Little information is available concerning the other firms in the industry, but they were certainly well employed during the first years of the life of the Association and expanded considerably. They flourished under the price policies of the combine and they were helped by the fact that the Association closed a number of its own works and purchased and closed others. Their rapid and successful expansion between 1900 and 1908 made it obvious that neither the CPA nor any other combine would ever retain a significantly monopolistic position. Merchants were always very ready to give orders to competent independent firms and any steps taken by the CPA to maintain prices or eliminate weak selling benefited the progressive independent firms.

The history of five firms illustrates the types of development which took place outside the Association. The five firms considered are not altogether representative as they are all in existence at the present time; although it is not possible to find out how many firms were in existence before 1914, it seems probable that not more than about a third of them have survived in recognizable form to the present day. A high proportion of those which failed were dependent upon the export trade and failed in the inter-war period.

The five firms to be discussed are, Mark Fletcher and Sons Ltd, John and Henry Bleakley Ltd, Sackville and Swallow Ltd, Turnbull and Stockdale Ltd, and Morton Sundour Fabrics Ltd. This sample illustrates the general point that growing firms usually have some particular speciality and some particular advantage. Sackville and Swallow Ltd is, however, an exception. This firm depended in the main upon sheer efficiency. It was going on a small scale before it became a limited company in 1907. At that date two machines were installed at Pendleton and the company left Pendlebury. After that date, expansion was rapid and by 1914 there were ten machines. In the early years the firm was predominantly engaged in sari styles and voiles for export to the Far East; most of the fabrics were fairly light to handle and correspondingly difficult to print.

Mark Fletcher and Sons Ltd were dyers who, in 1897, purchased a printing machine for the purpose of dyeing book cloth by padding the dye on the cloth; (in effect this involved printing it all over to get a plain dyed effect). This venture proved a failure, but the printing machine was used for printing tailors' linings with stripes. According to Mr Mark Fletcher, junior, a successful and rapidly expanding business developed, which was doubtless aided by the company's experience and capacity in the art of finishing, arising from its long-established experience in the plain dyeing trade. This is an example of expansion outside the Association of a comparatively new trade. The growth of this type of business is part of the explanation for the purchase by the Association of a finishing business. Mark Fletcher and Sons Ltd had three machines by 1910, and, at about this time, entered the newly-established vat colour trade of printed shirtings and pyjamas. Until fast colours were available, shirtings and pyjamas were not printed. It was in this style that the company developed its full strength and made a name for quality second to none. Two more machines, making a total of five, were put in in 1910. In this type of trade, a five-machine works which also does plain dyeing is a substantial works, because the output of the printing machines is large and the preparing and finishing plant represents a large proportion of the capital of the company.

The history of John and Henry Bleakley Ltd is not unlike that of Mark Fletcher and Sons Ltd. The firm originally dyed linings and pocketings mainly for the South American market. In 1905 it joined the Bradford Dyers' Association Ltd. At that time there were no specific 'overlapping' agreements restricting the extent to which the three major associations (the BDA, the CPA and the Bleachers' Association) could engage in each other's main trade, and a printing machine was installed when it became fashionable for linings and pocketings to be printed. By 1910 the printing side had expanded considerably, especially into the new shirtings trade, and the company was a substantial printer.

Turnbull and Stockdale Ltd is an example of another type of development. The firm started in 1881, and by 1900 was well established at the top end of the furnishing trade; both machine and block printing was done and already the firm was selling direct to the retail trade. It did not join the Association partly because it was prosperous (competition was somewhat less severe in the furnishings trade) and partly because a large family of six sons were entering the business. It expanded considerably during the period 1900–14, and became a large, semi-vertical organization with fifteen to twenty machines doing a fairly wide range of work.

Another firm which laid the foundations of successful expansion in this period was Messrs Morton Sundour Fabrics Ltd. In 1904, this firm placed on the market a range of dyed furnishing fabrics[1] which made full use of the new ranges of colours available in fast vat

[1] Turnbull, *op. cit.*, p. 340.

dyes and were guaranteed not to fade; previously, fading had been usual. '. . . they set a very high standard and maintenance of this level, backed by a comprehensive guarantee, caused considerable disturbance in the trade.'[1] The high standards set had much influence on the expansion of the plain dyed and cretonne trade in England. This development came before the Calico Printers' Association had solved their administrative problems adequately to concentrate on development and research. It is, however, the type of opportunity which they could ill afford to miss and one which they probably would not have missed in the later years. Mather's supplement to the report of the Reconstruction Committee is very relevant to this type of change in the industry. It is possible, however, that it would have been difficult for the Association to give comprehensive guarantees without further antagonizing the merchants, who were already afraid that the Association would enlarge its merchanting section at their expense.

The prosperity of 1906 and 1907 was followed by a decline in trade which was particularly sharp in the export market; the CPA immediately found itself in difficulties. Turnbull suggests that the CPA suffered more than the other big combines because of the advance in printing prices in 1907.[2] In 1907 the capital was reorganized and 60 per cent of the ordinary shares were converted into 5 per cent preference shares; no dividend could be paid on the remaining ordinaries either in 1908 or in 1909, although there was some improvement in the later year.

Trade recovered in 1910 and it remained good until the outbreak of war, despite difficulties due to a coal strike in 1912. However, price cutting continued to be a prominent characteristic 'and in 1912 another effort was made to bring the various parties together and establish a Federation for the whole trade.'[3] This proved impossible; the failure may have been partly due to the fact that the Association had been maintaining prices to some extent and was likely to continue to do so.

During the period of relative prosperity the CPA decided to change its commercial methods and 'The Market Scheme' was tried in 1912–13. The scheme was devised to deal with two related problems: firstly, that of gaining the advantages of specialization and continuity of orders in the individual works, and secondly, that of competing energetically with the independent firms without at the same time competing unnecessarily within the Association. The plan was

[1] Turnbull, *op. cit.*, p. 340. [2] Ibid., p. 335.
[3] P. Fitzgerald, *Industrial Combination in England*, Ch. II e, p. 21.

to divorce the selling from the production. The salesmen were to sell whatever they could and the orders were to be sent to head office and distributed between the works. The distribution of orders to the different works was to be done on a fully competitive basis within the Association; thus the Scheme had the additional advantage of maintaining a check on the efficiency of the various works. The Scheme proved a failure and was abandoned by 1914; it is now said that the experiment involved a very considerable loss of trade; the company certainly paid no dividend in 1914. The overriding difficulty was that the close relationship between merchant, salesman and printer is so important that, as soon as it was made less direct, the merchants tended to place their orders with the independent printers who were, by this time, numerous and, in some cases, substantial. This experience showed that the theoretical economies of specialization could not be fully realized, and that any policy must be a compromise between productive efficiency and commercial expediency.

The position of the CPA by 1914 is difficult to assess. It is clear that competition was severe and the industry suffered very considerable fluctuations in profitability. Turnbull thought that the association was holding its position: 'It might be said that this (the low profits) indicated inferior organization but it is not so for by taking the whole industry in the country it would be found that very few companies were able to show a much better return than the CPA and the general level of profits would not average over 3 per cent.'[1] Levy, in *Monopolies, Cartels and Trusts in British Industry* also thought that the CPA had established a strong position. 'On the other hand the Calico Association is now an efficiency combination with which no single firm even of suitable size for economic working could easily vie.'[2] This conclusion is of some interest for it indicates that despite the managerial difficulties the combine was growing in efficiency and was holding its own on this basis. Had the Association established a good research department immediately it was formed, it might have been stronger. However, there was not in this period any major innovation of which only a large firm with great technical resources could take advantage. Had there been such an innovation, the whole picture would have been very different for, while the combine was particularly well adapted to gain from a rapid rate of technical change, it had few advantages if techniques remained stationary. As it was, the combine had to rely upon the expert application of known methods; the central organization helped considerably as techniques became more scientific, but as printing is not an exact science, many day-to-

[1] Turnbull, *op. cit.*, p. 336. [2] Levy, *op. cit.*, p. 258.

day problems had to be solved by the branch managers. The combine appears to have been efficient, but not significantly more efficient than its competitors.

The share of the trade held by the Association changed remarkably little, although its share of the capacity dropped substantially. The prospectus had claimed that the Association would hold 85 per cent of the capacity of the industry, but, by 1910 it is said to have had only 60 per cent of total capacity.[1] The output figures available are those provided by the CPA and given in Appendix 7 of the Monopolies Commission Report. These show that prior to 1914 the Association did about 50 per cent of the trade on average, rather less in years of poor trade and rather more in years of good trade, the highest being 56·9 per cent in 1907. The CPA was in a peculiarly vulnerable position partly because merchants tended to favour independent firms and partly because of the more flexible policy which could be pursued by those firms.

THE SIGNIFICANCE OF THE CALICO PRINTERS' ASSOCIATION IN THE PERIOD UP TO 1914

THE problems of making a judgment about the effects of any particular event have been discussed at some length.[2] It was pointed out that the difficulties lay, firstly, in deciding what might have happened, secondly in determining the effects of the alternative patterns of development and, thirdly in balancing the long- and short-term advantages and disadvantages.

Had the Calico Printers' Association not been formed, it appears likely that intense competition would have continued very much as it had during the 1890's. The competition might have been reduced in a number of ways but it is doubtful whether this would have had appreciable effects over the period up to 1914. The limitations on competition would have taken a number of forms. Firstly, it is probable that there would have been more price agreements such as those of the 'linings' section; most of these agreements would, however, have been somewhat vague and almost certainly temporary, as no other section of the industry was as well defined and homogenous as the 'linings' section. Secondly, there might well have been a few small mergers comparable with the United Turkey Red Co. Ltd in more specialized sections of the industry. Thirdly, some firms might have been able to limit short-period competition by forming closer alli-

[1] The Report on the Process of Calico Printing of the Monopolies and Restrictive Practices Commission, HMSO, 1954, p. 39.

[2] See p. 13.

ances or merging with the major merchanting firms. This development, which was not in fact significant at this time, was not unlikely since vertical organizations are more easily established during times of expanding trade and exports were at their maximum in 1911. In the absence of the CPA non-price competition might have been more expensive, and therefore vertical integration might have been more profitable.

The changes which might have taken place in the absence of the CPA would probably have been gradual. They would have been accompanied by the continuous elimination of inefficient firms. As the smallest would probably have disappeared the average size of firms would have grown; it is, however, doubtful whether such giants as Gartside & Co. of Manchester Ltd, who had seventy-four printing machines in 1900, or Edmund Potter & Co. Ltd with fifty-one machines or Thornliebank Co. Ltd (Glasgow) with forty-five machines would have done more than hold their own, since they grew at a time when size depended upon possible rates of expansion, and large size gave large profits which allowed rapid expansion. They were so large that in more competitive situations they were handicapped by the difficulty of getting orders without initiating severe price cutting, for they tended, like the combine, to be price leaders in their particular sections.

The immediate effect of the formation of the CPA was to change the way in which prices were determined, and to raise them. The increase in prices was not a single all-round increase since those which had been abnormally low were raised more than others; the changes in the terms of sale, such as the allowances for faults, were almost as important and, like the price changes, did not affect all work equally. The general price increases were partly the result of increases in the costs of raw materials which took place in 1900 and 1901. However, in the absence of the CPA, it is unlikely that these increases could have been passed on to the consumer as trade was poor in those years.

In the whole period between about 1903 and 1914 it is unlikely that the average level of prices was higher than it would have been in the absence of the CPA. The combine was in a weak commercial position in the short period and tended to hold a smaller share of the trade whenever demand declined. Further, the existence of a price leader made both entry into the industry and expansion easier. As a result the combine had to fix prices at levels which did not encourage new competition. The fact that it lost little ground indicates that it succeeded in reducing the prices to the level of the long-period average costs plus normal profit of its more efficient competitors.

The balance between the combine and its competitors appears to have been very delicate for the economies of scale were by no means sufficient to allow the combine to expand its share of the market. Research was not done on a large scale, and although the combine probably missed some opportunities it seems unlikely that even a big research programme would have yielded a great deal at that time. It is only when technical change depends upon research and finance that large combines can obtain a commanding position in the absence of great manufacturing economies of scale.

The question as to whether the general level of prices would have been different in the absence of the combine is very difficult to answer. Firstly, it is impossible to judge whether price agreements of some kind, probably of short duration, would have been significant. Secondly, in the absence of a price leader, non-price competition might have been more important and, had this been the case, costs would probably have been higher. On the whole it seems unlikely that average prices would have been lower but they might well have been less stable. The fact that prices never fell to very low levels in this period was not of great importance because there were few really inefficient firms to be eliminated; the majority of them had joined the combine.

So long as there is unemployment, inefficiency is of little importance provided that it is reflected in low profits rather than in high prices. However, if there are a very substantial number of weak firms, the price level may be affected and the waste of resources may be considerable. The CPA raised efficiency considerably, and the increases came about in three ways. Firstly, the average technical efficiency of firms within the Association was, after the initial period of mismanagement, raised substantially; a number of the inefficient works were closed and although some would have left the industry in any case, others might have survived because they had a good designer or a special market; once they were in the combine markets held for these reasons could be served by more efficient works. Secondly, the existence of the combine made it easier to break into the market and to expand because price cutting was more likely to be effective; thus, good, independent works were able to expand. Thirdly, the existence of the combine reduced the importance of non-price competition to some extent.

CHAPTER 6

The Declining Industry, 1918–39

WHEN the war ended in 1918 the calico printing industry consisted of some eighty firms. There was, however, a high degree of concentration; twenty-five firms covered 90 per cent of the industry and the three largest had about 70 per cent of the total trade and a rather larger proportion of the export trade. The Calico Printers' Association had thirty-six works and about 50 per cent of the trade, and F. Steiner Ltd and the United Turkey Red Co. Ltd between them had another 20 per cent.

In 1918–19 the outlook was good and, for a brief period in 1920, trade was excellent. Although the post-war slump was more disastrous for merchants than for printers, the print trade was bad in 1921–2. It revived in 1923–4, but already the decline as compared with pre-1914 was substantial and the whole inter-war period was to be dominated by the falling demand; total trade was halved between 1913 and 1930 and revived very little in the 'thirties.

The great changes were due to the decline in the export markets, exports in 1938 being only 23 per cent of the 1901–13 average. Table II gives exports, total output, and the output and share of trade of the CPA.

This table shows that the export trade, apart from the post-war slump, declined very seriously between 1925 and 1926, increased somewhat in 1927–8 and then fell catastrophically, never to revive. The Far East trade was the first to be affected by foreign competition; exports to China and the Far East[1] fell from an average of 75 million square yards in 1924 and 1925 to 52 million square yards in 1926 and to 46 million square yards in 1927. In the Minutes of Evidence of the Balfour Committee[2] of July 1925, Mr Swallow, the Chairman of the Federation, agreed that British trade was stationary, but was a reduced share of the total trade; he also said that the Japanese had made inroads into the India market. Mr Hirst of the CPA interjected,

[1] Dutch East Indies, Phillipines, Siam and Japan.
[2] *Board of Trade Committee on Industry and Trade, Minutes of Evidence*, p. 1141.

TABLE II

Statistics of CPA—Total Production

Total Yardage Printed by CPA and Proportion of Total Print Trade, 1901–52

Exports of Printed Piece Goods

Date	Total Printed Yardage Delivered by CPA A Million linear yards	B As a proportion (estimated) of the total for the whole trade* per cent	Total for Whole Trade (calculated from columns A and B) Million linear yards	Exports of Printed Piece Goods Million linear yards
1901 ..	549·9	48·5	1133·8	910
1902 ..	612·4	53·9	1136·2	961
1903 ..	640·9	53·7	1193·5	1,028
1904 ..	608·9	49·4	1232·6	1,037
1905 ..	599·3	49·0	1223·1	1,013
1906 ..	658·7	52·7	1249·9	1,087
1907 ..	754·0	56·9	1325·1	1,167
1908 ..	616·3	48·2	1278·6	992
1909 ..	542·2	45·8	1183·8	979
1910 ..	661·1	51·4	1286·2	1,196
1911 ..	742·0	52·3	1418·7	1,241
1912 ..	693·4	48·9	1418·0	1,196
1913 ..	737·8	53·2	1386·8	1,177
1914 ..	671·0	54·4	1233·5	892
1915 ..	444·4	45·2	983·2	674
1916 ..	591·7	59·4	996·1	919
1917 ..	610·8	53·4	1143·8	967
1918 ..	553·4	51·0	1085·1	802
1919 ..	356·8	37·9	941·4	683
1920 ..	544·0	55·3	983·7	885
1921 ..	405·0	45·0	900·0	515
1922 ..	302·6	38·9	777·9	640
1923 ..	393·8	44·1	893·0	751
1924 ..	409·0	43·7	935·9	723
1925 ..	439·7	46·5	945·6	769
1926 ..	398·4	45·5	875·6	584
1927 ..	363·6	44·6	815·2	648
1928 ..	434·9	52·4	830·0	616
1929 ..	368·1	49·2	748·2	543
1930 ..	337·0	48·8	690·6	392
1931 ..	245·0	47·3	518·0	322
1932 ..	266·3	44·1	603·9	452
1933 ..	298·9	43·5	687·1	417

* Accurate comparative figures of yardage for the whole trade are not available. CPA, who supplied the above figures, have made an estimate of total yardage for the years up to 1927 and used the total yardage of Federation members for the succeeding years. They say that the margin of error is unlikely to affect the percentage to a material extent.

Table II—*continued*

Statistics of CPA—Total Production

Total Yardage Printed by CPA and Proportion of Total Print Trade, 1901–52

Exports of Printed Piece Goods

Date	Total Printed Yardage Delivered by CPA A Million linear yards	 B As a proportion (estimated) of the total for the whole trade* per cent	Total for Whole Trade (calculated from columns A and B) Million linear yards	Exports of Printed Piece Goods Million linear yards
1934 ..	292·5	42·4	689·9	442
1935 ..	310·3	43·7	710·1	455
1936 ..	282·8	44·0	642·7	435
1937 ..	308·0	44·9	686·0	454
1938 ..	261·2	42·1	620·4	309
1939 ..	243·0	43·5	558·6	361
1940 ..	290·9	44·0	661·1	283
1941 ..	168·8	40·7	414·7	243
	Including orders passed over by concerns closed under concentration			
1942 ..	153·0	44·4	344·6	140
1943 ..	128·6	51·0	252·2	106
1944 ..	135·2	54·1	249·9	135
1945 ..	135·5	54·1	250·5	136
1946 ..	150·2	53·2	282·3	162
1947 ..	158·1	49·9	316·8	165
1948 ..	207·6	47·8	434·3	277
1949 ..	257·3	48·3	533·1	340
	Excluding orders passed over by concerns closed under concentration			
1942 ..	146·7	42·5	345·2	
1943 ..	97·2	38·5	252·5	
1944 ..	100·7	40·3	249·9	
1945 ..	103·0	41·1	250·6	
1946 ..	121·4	43·0	282·3	
1947 ..	131·3	41·4	317·1	
1948 ..	180·9	41·7	433·8	
1949 ..	233·0	43·7	533·2	
	Concentration arrangements ended			
1950 ..	286·4	47·1	608·1	321
1951 ..	323·8	48·9	662·2	317
1952 ..	265·0	48·9	541·9	240
1953 ..				248
1954 ..				216

Sources: Monopolies Commission Report. Appendix 7.
Annual Trade Statistics.

'Not India, China and Java.' By 1928, Japanese exports to the Far East and East Africa (excluding both India and China) were 62 per cent of UK exports whereas their exports to India were then less than 10 per cent of UK exports. Within the next few years, however, much of the India trade was lost. UK exports to India fell from 176 million linear yards in the year ending March 31, 1928, to 48 million yards in 1938, while Japanese exports rose over the same period from 16 to 102 million linear yards and were restricted to that level by the import quota. Exports to India fell to about the 1937 level in 1931, rose again to above the 1930 level and then fell to the lowest level ever reached in 1938.

Although there was considerable specialization and the Far East trade had a number of individual features, the printers whose trade shrank were normally able to compete in the more standard Indian trade and throughout the 1920's this was intensely competitive. Looking back on the period, it is easy to see that the loss of trade was inevitable, but realization came slowly; in 1926 reports from the Far East which said that competition was hopeless were regarded as fantastic, and few believed that the British industry could no longer compete successfully in the great export markets. The general view was that these were unsettled times and that the trade would come back. This confidence resulted in some delay of the adjustment to the very different conditions of the inter-war period.

Although the decline in the export markets in cheap prints and native styles was the outstanding feature of the 'twenties, changes were also taking place in other parts of the trade. The term 'home trade' is frequently used to include exports to countries such as the Dominions, who take types of print similar to those required by the home market. This trade was increasing in importance and changes in the direction of higher quality, more fashion consciousness and bigger seasonal fluctuations all resulted in greater variety and smaller orders for each type of cloth. Much of this type of business was done by the stock house merchant,[1] who demanded the quotation of an average price per yard over a whole range. As costs varied and the number of repeats was unspecified, this type of contract made it necessary for the printer to undertake considerable risk and to gamble when making quotations. In the more varied fashion-conscious market with seasonal fluctuations, sheer productive efficiency became less important, while flair in colouring and designing, flexibility, and shrewd judgment about prices to be quoted and risks to be taken, became more important. There was also increased competition in

[1] See p. 143.

quality and in service. 'In the Summary of Evidence given by the Federation to the Sub-Committee of Inquiry on the Cotton Trade in November 1929, figures were quoted which indicated that the cost pre-1914–18 war of designs and engravings averaged less than 6*d.* per lump of 120 yards, whereas in 1929 it averaged more than 2*s.* 6*d.* for the same unit of output. There is nothing to indicate that since 1929 there had been any improvement in this respect, rather it would be more reasonable to estimate that this cost had increased to nearer 3*s.* 6*d.* by 1939.'[1]

Further changes in the relative importance of different problems were due to technical developments. Fast dyes, mainly vat dyes, were coming into general use but were not yet available in a wide range of bright colours. These increased the complexity of the technical and managerial problems and also added to marketing problems by presenting a wider choice between fastness and initial attractiveness. The general increase in scientific knowledge and 'know-how' tended to increase competition by reducing the importance of specialities. Major changes in the type of work done could only be undertaken by the more efficient works; the less scientific firms were in a hopeless position, and if they lost their market they had little hope of survival.

The other great technical change which affected the calico printers was the introduction of rayon. Rayon grew rapidly in importance in the 'thirties[2] and the new fibres required different dyes and handling techniques. Both fast dyes and rayon resulted in sufficient change to offer opportunities which only the better firms could use.

These, then, were the major underlying changes in the situation facing the calico printing industry in the inter-war period. From 1918 to 1928 the difficulties were mitigated by the existence of the Federation of Calico Printers and the maintenance of price agreements. The Federation was formed in 1915 as a useful organ of co-operation and to conduct negotiations with the Government. It was concerned with labour problems, supplies of dye-stuffs (most of which had been imported from Germany), and with prices. At the end of the war it

[1] Turnbull, *op. cit.*, p. 367.

[2] The output of printed rayon cloth is not available, but the following table shows the increasing importance of rayon:

Output of Rayon Yarn

	'000 lb.
1912	3,100
1924	22,003
1930	49,975
1934	90,324
1937	154,823

Turnbull, *op. cit.*, p. 373.

was the price agreements which were most important. The Federation then covered firms doing 90 per cent of the trade, and as there are always a number of extreme specialists, this figure implies that for practical purposes almost the whole trade was included.

The immediate post-war years were quite exceptional in that rapidly increasing costs and a fairly high level of demand gave rise to general support for price agreements. 'To a large extent the establishing of the price lists become possible owing to the necessity of having some common means of meeting the rapidly increasing costs of labour and materials caused by the war.'[1] The first price agreements only involved minimum price lists drawn up for the various styles based on what was considered a 'reasonable' charge for the lowest grade of printing which was possible for the particular class. It followed 'that the lists were sufficiently elastic to allow competition to take place freely between firms especially in the better class lines which commanded something higher than the minimum figure. The Federation accepted the word of its members that the figure would be adhered to and no penalties were set out for any member breaking his agreements.'[2]

The fairly loose price agreements were maintained although some modifications were made; for example, inducements were given to the merchant to offer the printer better runs. There were also schemes to offer special prices to meet competition in particular markets. In 1927 a 'Through Ticket Scheme'[3] was negotiated with the Shipping Merchants Committee, and 'this was followed in 1927 and 1928 by 'Specific Cases' schemes. In an effort to revive the Indian trade the Federation granted a great reduction, equal to half the cost, for black discharge on a cheap cloth for India ex contract.'[4]

The existence of a large multi-product combine and a number of other substantial firms, engaged in several types of printing, made it possible to organize some retaliation against price cutting, and the threat of this probably had some effect. 'With one exception, the Federation appear to have taken no special competitive action against outside printers. The exception was the case of a concern which left the Federation in 1922 in order to have a free hand on prices. The Federation instituted an arrangement whereby members interested in the same market as the ex-member could quote specially low prices for work for that market. This arrangement, which continued for nine years from 1922, was supervised by a 'Special Prices Committee'

[1] Turnbull, *op. cit.*, p. 343. [2] Ibid., p. 344.

[3] The 'Through Ticket Scheme' allowed reduced printing prices for cloth clearly destined for a few specific markets in which Japanese competition was particularly severe.

[4] Turnbull, *op. cit.*, p. 344.

which made monthly reports of the business booked. The policy, as put by one member, "was not that they were trying to crush (the ex-member) or yet that they were trying to drive him back into the Federation, but they were trying to prevent the action he took in leaving the Federation from endangering the interests of the Federation". A report of the Special Prices Committee in 1926 says that the effect on the balance sheet of the ex-member "must have been considerable", but the same document speaks of the comparative non-success of the policy in achieving definite results.'[1]

'For the smooth working of the Federation much credit must be given to the Calico Printers' Association.'[2] Turnbull suggests that the CPA was concerned with the welfare of the industry, but their strong support of the Federation can equally be attributed to the fact that, as the largest firm, they had a particular interest in the maintenance of price agreements. The CPA had over thirty works in operation during the period 1919–27 and it would certainly have been extremely difficult to compete successfully with independent firms without incurring losses or losing trade or both.

From about 1928, the price fixing system was showing more and more signs of weakness; meetings were held, but no agreement could be obtained. In 1931 four fairly substantial firms resigned from the Federation in order to get a free hand on pricing. In 1932 the undercutting had increased to such proportion that it could no longer be ignored. 'By the beginning of 1932 the Federation had formally abandoned all price management functions.'[3]

The failure of the price agreements, which began in about 1928 and culminated in their complete abandonment in 1932, cannot be considered surprising. The great scope for non-price competition put the firm who offered little service at a disadvantage compared with those which offered much, and low-cost firms of this type had, therefore, considerable incentive to cut prices. There are, however, two reasons why the price agreements lasted as long as they did. Firstly, all knew that severe competition would be extremely expensive and achieve little in a temporary situation. It was from about 1927 onwards that it began to be realized that the decline in demand was probably permanent. Secondly, the CPA, Steiners and United Turkey Red were large and did not wish price cutting to begin; these firms, particularly the CPA, had been prepared to see their share of the

[1] Report of the Process of Calico Printing of the Monopolies and Restrictive Practices Commission, HMSO, 1954, p. 19, para 46.

[2] Ibid., p. 344.

[3] Monopolies Commission Report, *op. cit.*, p. 20. 'The Lining Printers' Association Prices Continued to be Maintained by that Body.'

trade shrink somewhat and they closed numerous works.[1] They were not, however, large enough or strong enough to do more than delay the breakdown of the agreements in the face of so much redundant capacity.

As firms began to realize that the export market had gone more or less permanently and that new trade and new opportunities were found only in the 'home market', so price and other forms of competition came to be used for the purpose of gaining and establishing new long-period positions. The 'home trade' increased; according to the Federation it varied between 210 and 225 million yards from 1927 to 1932, and then increased to 281 and 266 million yards in 1933 and 1934 respectively. The increase was, however, by no means commensurate with the increased number of merchant houses. The great changes caused considerable upheavals of the old trading relationships. 'Urged by the possibility of building up good and lasting contact with new ranges offering a prospect of expansion in the future, the printers were literally stampeded into an orgy of price cutting.' 'Besides the fall in the price which the calico printer brought upon himself, a further loss, no less real on account of its inability to be computed, was incurred owing to great increase in speciality lines, shorter runs and larger assortments, etc. Moreover, the demands of the market were allowed to press heavily on the printer and in many cases business was obtained, not on the quality of the work, but on time taken for delivery, so that the merchant could get a quick turnover. It became more and more the custom for the merchant to charge the printer with the cost of design, and in some cases even, he had to hold stock 'on call' of the merchants' printed cloth.'[2] While there were some prepared to cut prices in order to obtain future orders, there were others who were simply desperate and were prepared to do anything which would make some contribution towards overheads; they worked on the assumption that there might be hope in the future if they could survive in the present.

According to Turnbull, profits were 'meagre' between 1922 and 1930, representing a return of under 4 per cent on capital.[3] However, in view of the magnitude of the decline in trade and the fact that after 1930 neither the CPA nor Steiners nor United Turkey Red paid any dividends on their ordinary shares, it seems certain that the price agreements were of considerable importance and the maintenance of the price agreements well rewarded.

It is impossible to gauge the fall in prices which occurred after the

[1] See pp. 191–2. [2] Turnbull, *op. cit.*, p. 370–1.
[3] Ibid., p. 348.

breakdown of the price agreements. Turnbull, who was intimately connected with the industry, says, 'to put it at only 10 per cent would appear very conservative and in some cases it was more than 25 per cent'.[1] These rather tentative figures reinforce the general impression that, even though competition is intense, few prices become equal to short-period variable costs.

Before considering the long-term effects of the decline in demand it is useful to examine the cost structure of the industry and the general characteristics of demand, for these played a major part in determining the nature of the adjustments which took place.

Examination of the cost structure, the details of which are given in Appendix I of this section, shows that if 110 is taken as the long period average cost including 10% profit (for a normal output), average variable costs, including the 'fixed expenses' which can only be avoided if the works is closed, are equal to about 94. When the decision to remain in business has been taken, some of the 'fixed expenses' become fixed costs and average variable costs are reduced to about 77. When a period of three to six months is considered, then some of the direct costs must be regarded as fixed, and variable costs are only about 55. Finally, over really short periods, say, six weeks, when a works is temporarily slack, the variable costs are reduced to about 36: i.e. little more than the cost of chemicals (drugs) and dyes (30).

A reduction in prices to a level of 10 to 15 per cent below average total cost (including the 10 per cent profit) can remain for a long time because equipment is extremely durable. If firms could open and close easily, and no price discrimination were possible, prices would seldom fall below this level. However, as was discussed in the earlier section, continuity is important and customers lost are difficult to regain; in other words, there is a large negative user cost because of the future profits which would be foregone as a result of closing temporarily. Over short periods it is worthwhile to take extra orders at prices which are just sufficient to cover very short-run variable costs, that is to say at a level of about one-third of average total cost. If prices fall to these low levels over a wide range of work very large losses are incurred. Although there are intermittent price wars or 'dog fights' these are not frequent and they are generally confined to particular types of work.

The reluctance to initiate severe price cutting and the high incentive to meet such price cutting as does arise in order to keep customers

[1] Turnbull, *op. cit.*, p. 372.

makes it difficult for the better firms to expand and difficult for them to take trade from the less efficient.

In time, the less efficient firm would be driven out by prices below long-period average costs, but as this may take many years the basically more efficient firm which has lost business (perhaps because fashion has changed) may not be able to stand the losses involved in working at low levels of activity for so long. In general the inefficient are only driven out by the more efficient if each happens to suffer rather similar changes in demand, or if the efficient are luckier. The efficient firm who loses trade only replaces it slowly, if at all, when there is excess capacity in the industry; it is largely dependent upon its ability to enter such new and expanding markets as are available.

Thus the cost structure, the length of life of equipment and the importance of continuity of trading give rise to a situation where redundant equipment is eliminated very slowly, and where both the efficient and inefficient firms suffer losses unless they are fortunate.

It is extremely difficult to give the notion of excess capacity any definite meaning in the calico printing industry. It is the practice of the industry to consider that full working on a 45-hour week is capacity working, but as overtime and even night shifts can be worked, very much higher levels of activity are possible. Variations in the level of activity are inevitable because of the fluctuations in demand. Table II shows not only the long-term trend but also that there are annual changes of 10 per cent and more which are not in line with the general trend. Temporary excess capacity is also associated with the seasonal fluctuations in demand which are particularly important in the women's dress trade and, to a lesser extent, in the children's wear trade. Seasonal fluctuations in the dress trade are accentuated by the fact that about four months are required for shipping to Australia, New Zealand, and other distant markets, and, therefore, the busy peaks of Northern and Southern hemispheres practically coincide.[1]

As delivery normally takes from three to six weeks, the fact that orders do not flow in regularly has a considerable effect on delivery

[1] The importance of seasonal fluctuation is indicated by the following table, which shows the fluctuations in the activity of the CPA as a whole, and of one typical works belonging to the CPA.

Monthly Fluctuations in Activity (Av = 100)

	CPA	Typical Individual Works
1934	79–114	47–148
1935	83–122	63–168

dates if a works is running at a fairly high level of activity. As merchants often regard speed of delivery as of prime importance, no works can run at a high level of capacity unless others are doing the same; no firm with unreliable delivery dates will obtain initial orders on which there are likely to be repeat orders. Thus, when trade is poor, there is competition in delivery dates, which makes it impossible for any firm to work to 'normal' levels of activity.

Excess capacity also arises as a result of shifts in the demand from one type of printing to another. These shifts may be large.[1] Changes in fashion and in the direction of demand may take place without significant changes in total demand, but they frequently lead to increased capacity since those capable of dealing with the expanding trade may put in a few extra machines in order to take advantage of the trade. All know that any extra trade must be taken since there is always the possibility that other lines may suddenly fail and that a major decline in orders will reduce the contribution towards overheads. This is particularly important in the case of the more substantial firms.

The inherent tendency of the industry to maintain and develop 'excess capacity' is such that there is always sufficient to cause subnormal profits if the price policy were fully competitive. The combined effect of the tendency of the industry to develop excess capacity and the fact that short-period price competition is largely ineffective made the adjustment to the great decline in demand in the inter-war period both slow and painful.

[1] An outstanding post-war example is the effect of the change in fashion from draping materials to stiffer materials. The following figures indicate the experience of one large crepe specialist:

Percentage of Crepes to Total Output

	No. of Pieces per cent	Value per cent
1951	42	46
1954 (January-June)	7	9

Another example may be given of a firm which specialized in cotton shirtings and pyjamas.

Orders Received for Printing Based on Yardage and Taking 1940 *as* 100

	Cotton Shirtings and Pyjamas	Cotton Over-alls, Dress, etc.	Rayon, Dress and Lingerie	Cotton Linings	Total
1940 ..	57	35	1	7	100
1950 ..	46	27	10		83
1954* ..	16	23	9		48

* Estimated on first six months

Cotton linings, cotton shirtings and pyjamas are a fairly similar type of printing.

Between 1928 and 1939 output fell by nearly 300 million linear yards. This represents very approximately the output of about 200 machines, or, in other terms, the output of about fifteen quite substantial works. The firms which were driven out of the industry in the whole inter-war period did not represent this amount of capacity and much of the adjustment had to be made within the firms which remained in the industry.

Turnbull,[1] gives a list of the firms in 1935. The Federation has a list of all the firms which have been members, and a list of current members and non-members. Apart from these lists, it is necessary to rely on the memory of those in the trade. The information is sketchy, but it does show several fairly important points.

About twenty firms left the trade between 1918 and 1939. In the following list these are arranged in rough chronological order according to the dates at which they left the industry and accompanied by brief notes about the circumstances:

1. Early 1920's. Small.
2. c. 1925. Small firm, which had a fire. Trade fell and it did not rebuild although it had planned to do so.
3. 1925. A small firm bought by Bradford Dyers' Association and amalgamated with their subsidiary, J. B. Bleackley (the owner) wished to leave the trade.
4. 1920's. Lost main business and was indifferently managed. The CPA bought the goodwill and water rights.
5. 1920's. Very small firm.
6. 1920's. Small, poorly managed.
7. 1920's. Irish firm which had a fire and did not rebuild.
8. Slump. Small Irish firm which lost money, although it had a good reputation for some things.
9. Slump. Small Irish firm, not specialized, and lost money.
10. 1928. Sold by owners wishing to get out of industry.
11. 1928. New owner failed during slump.
12. c. 1930. Fairly small firm badly managed. Bought cheaply by United Africa Company, but unsuccessful and sold to United Turkey Red, who closed the works.
13. ? Bought by United Turkey Red and closed.
14. Early 1930's. Small firm, owner quite rich, with other textile interests—equivalent of shutting a branch.
15. 1933/4. Bought by Blue Printers Ltd.
16. ? Small, poorly managed, firm which was glad to be able to sell.
17. 1935/9. Small firm without initiative.
18. 1935/9. Small works which was very run down, as it had hung on as long as possible.

[1] Turnbull, *op. cit.*, p. 427.

19. 1939. Went bankrupt after hanging on for an unbelievably long time with assistance from banks. The works was in a very bad state.

20. 1939/40. A substantial firm which was liquidated. The works was in a poor state and there was some fire damage. The firm had suffered particularly from the decline in the West African trade in 1937. (Some thought that it need not have been liquidated and much resentment was caused by the fact that the machinery was sold very cheaply.)

This rough survey shows that, despite the great reduction in the output of the industry, the elimination of firms (as opposed to branches of the large firms) was comparatively slight. Nine of the firms which left the industry were definitely very small, six were perhaps small to medium-sized, and only two or three were substantial. The most important was No. 20, eliminated in 1939–40. Many of the firms were badly managed and their works were in a poor condition. The evidence shows that firms take a very long time to decline from a reasonable to a poor standard and that they can hang on for so long that final closure often depends upon such factors as the age of the owner and whether he has a family interested or competent to follow him. The exit of firms is not closely related to particular years of bad trade except perhaps in the period 1928–30, and this is another indication of their power to remain in business.

In any industry in which there are small firms some changes are usual, and the entry of new people into the industry is some indication that the turnover of firms in the calico printing industry would normally be relatively high. Two firms were acquired by convertors in 1920 and it must be assumed that these were bought extremely cheaply. In 1933 Blue Printers Ltd bought a works. This was a continental firm which had connections in the South African market and, because of the Ottawa agreements, wished to print in this country. In 1936 another firm was started by people with experience of printing in Germany. British Celanese Ltd began to print in about 1936. The fact that five firms thought it worth while to enter an industry which was already so depressed is partly an indication of the imperfection of the market and the importance of specialities, but it also indicates the extent to which competition had failed to reduce prices.

Although considerable, the adjustment of capacity which resulted from the elimination of firms was relatively small both as compared with the amount of redundant capacity which remained and as compared with the changes which took place within the larger firms. The whole structure of the Calico Printers' Association was altered in the inter-war period. Between 1923 and the end of 1938, nineteen works containing three hundred printing machines were closed and only eleven works with about 230 machines were retained.[1] The main period of concentration was 1927–31, during which years seventeen works were closed and several of them were large. The majority had been engaged in work for the Indian and Far East markets. Nine of these works were in or near Glasgow, but after 1930, when the big new works at Thornliebank was closed, the CPA ceased to print in Scotland.

From 1932 until the outbreak of war the CPA printed at eleven works (three others were retained, but they were sealed and remained unused). Each works was associated with a selling organization and it is clear that the process of concentration made the structure of the firm very much simpler. Each works and sales organization was now relatively specialized and internal competition within the combine was considerably reduced. The concentration had indeed been drastic. In the eleven works which continued to print, only thirteen machines out of about 230 were in place but unused during 1937. These figures indicate that little redundant capacity was retained within the CPA, and that the policy of concentration had been pursued so as to obtain maximum production economies despite the loss of trade which the closing of works always involved. In 1938 the highest number of machines used in any one week fell from 218 to 202, and in 1939 it fell to 174.

Apart from concentration, the CPA modernized and re-equipped much of the remaining plant. This was done continuously in all works, but there were three major projects. Between 1926 and 1928 the large Thornliebank works near Glasgow was completely rebuilt. The idea was to build an excellent new works which would be able to compete successfully in the Indian and Far East markets. However, the seriousness of Japanese competition was underrated and the works was closed in 1930 and never re-opened. Although the works was new, the degree of specialization was such that it was not worth while to transfer other printing to Scotland. (Birkacre, another specialized works, was closed in 1931 despite the fact that it has been described as 'one of the best little works in the trade'.)

The second major project was the rebuilding of an old-established works at Strines. This was started in about 1927 and the new works was designed to do fairly high-quality printing. When the export trade declined, it was able to turn to the home trade.

The third works to be wholly reorganized was Dinting Vale; the works had fifty-three machines in 1900, and although they were pro-

[1] The machines which were retained are not quite comparable with those which were eliminated as they were generally larger and more efficient.

gressively reduced in number, there were still between thirty and forty in 1937. In the course of reconstruction the number of machines was reduced to eleven, but it has been suggested that the works is now capable of producing as much as it ever produced in the past. It is comparatively specialized and is designed for high production of good quality, but relatively simple, styles on cloth up to 48 in. wide which does not require special handling; the average number of pieces per machine per hour is 30 per cent greater than it is at works doing more varied and more complicated work.

These major reorganizations were accompanied by considerable expenditure on the new equipment required for new and specialized types of cloth, particularly rayon filament which requires very careful handling. There are now three main specialist works (Broadbank, Strines and Birchvale).

Whereas the CPA managed to retain its share of the trade, the two other large firms who had specialized almost exclusively in the export markets lost heavily. They both had large merchanting and selling organizations and incurred heavy losses as trade shrank. United Turkey Red still had five works in 1935, but these were reduced to three by 1939 and during the war two more were closed and have not been reopened. The decline of F. Steiner and Co. Ltd was similar; they had five works in the 'twenties but were reduced to one by 1945. Steiner's paid no ordinary dividend between 1928 and 1948, and the arrears on the preference dividend were cancelled; United Turkey Red paid no ordinary dividend from 1930 to 1948, and failed to meet the preference dividend between 1934 and 1946. Since 1953 neither has paid a dividend and Steiner's have now gone into liquidation (1956). Both firms were forced, as trade shrank, to take whatever orders they could get and their two remaining works did a general trade, although Steiner's still concentrated to some extent on the shipping market.

Many of the firms which survived the inter-war period successfully were already engaged in sections of the trade such as shirtings, furnishing fabrics and the West African trade where demand declined little or even increased. The only really expanding trade, however, was the rayon trade. Just as the CPA was able to get a share of this at an early stage, because it had good technical resources, so too did the firm of John and Henry Bleackley, which was a subsidiary of the Bradford Dyers' Association Ltd. This firm was mainly in the shirting trade, but in 1926 it began to turn to synthetics; it was largely re-equipped between 1933 and 1936, and much preparatory and finishing machinery was added; in 1930–31 it successfully entered the crepe trade. This is another trade where methods of handling are of the utmost importance. The Bleachers' Association's subsidiary in the calico printing trade also got into the top quality end of the trade and became largely engaged in the home trade.

A successful switch into different lines has been the exception, and the most important cases have been the works associated with large firms and the CPA in particular. Not more than two or three of the moderate sized firms achieved substantial changes. This is not surprising in view of the depressed state of trade; many assert that a strong firm which is forced to make major changes in its trade will take as much as five years to regain its position in the industry. Most firms make continuous and gradual changes and their structure at any time is largely determined by their past history. Only for the CPA is any substantial degree of long-term planning of individual works at all possible; in this period of declining demand, it was one of the few firms which could plan efficient productive units. In its absence it appears likely that there would have been a larger number of works which simply shrank, diversified, and survived on whatever trade they could get.

The improvement in the relative position of the CPA was, nevertheless, accompanied by financial difficulty. No dividend on the ordinary shares was paid between 1930 and 1946, although funds were available for the quite considerable reorganization and re-equipment. The low profits were attributed almost entirely to the intense and unrestricted competition and the CPA supported all moves towards price agreements.

In 1934 the Federation of Calico Printers set up a State of Trade Committee to see whether any solution could be found to the problems which were besetting the trade. The committee found that rigid price control was out of the question and considered that other methods, such as selling control, were impracticable. 'The report next considered methods of balancing capacity and demand so as to remove the need for price cutting; and it explained that after dismissing the working out of economic forces as too slow and too damaging the Committee had examined two methods, (a) financial amalgamations into one or two combines, and (b) the purchase of surplus machinery by a levy on the trade.'[1]

It is clear that, despite the general wish throughout the 1930's for some reduction in competition, neither price agreement nor combination was possible. Although some printers believed in the effectiveness of a further combine or, what was, perhaps, more probable, amalgamation with the CPA, the outlook of the firms differed too

[1] Monopolies Commission Report, *op. cit.*, p. 21.

much for either to be achieved without great over-capitalization since many were reluctant to join. There was little reason to expect that over-capitalization could be offset by economies of scale and, therefore, only a complete monopoly with power to restrict entry could be sure of success.

CHAPTER 7

1945-54

DURING the war the industry obtained all that it had been asking for before the war. Discussions on the details of a price and quota scheme continued until 1941, but the Federation found it difficult to secure complete agreement. In March 1941, however, the concentration of industry policy was announced and the Federation was able to draw up a scheme embodying a pool and quota and price agreements. This received Government approval and came into force in March 1942; the Government, however, made it clear that while it approved of the arrangements for the concentration of production it was not expressing general approval of the wider aspects of the agreements.

In May 1949 the compensatory agreements were replaced by the Percentage Quantum Agreement. This was very similar to the previous scheme in that it involved a pool and quota system and price lists. In addition, a redundancy scheme received Board of Trade approval and a company called Print Trade Reorganization Ltd was formed.

During a three-month purchasing period, beginning November 1, 1949, six businesses with a total of fifty-five machines were purchased. This was very much below the most conservative estimates of redundant capacity in the industry (the Federation had originally estimated that of some 600 printing machines in the trade about 25 per cent were redundant).[1]

The five firms purchased consisted of two medium-sized firms which had been in a very weak condition in 1939, another medium-sized firm which had decided to concentrate on its other activities, and two small works, one of which was in a very poor condition.

In 1949 there were forty-three firms, thirty-seven of which belonged

[1] Monopolies Commission Report, *op. cit.*, p. 25.

to the Federation.[1] By 1953, although the yardage had shrunk from 648 million yards in 1950 to between 500 and 550 million yards, the industry had changed little; it consisted of fourteen substantial[2] firms (including the CPA) with some 70 per cent of the total trade. All the large firms and twenty-one of the thirty-two smaller firms belonged to the Federation.

Since the war a number of new firms have come into the industry but the amount of printing done by each is small. British Silk Dyers bought Robert Pullar Limited in 1946; these firms had been closely associated for some time. A new vertical organization was formed and acquired two small printworks and a large convertor acquired one. Apart from two or three firms doing complete specialities which do not impinge on the rest of the trade six firms have entered the industry without acquiring existing printworks. Two of these are connected with convertors, one with a dyeing firm, one with a dyer and raiser, one with a vertical organization[3] and one with Tootals Limited. The subsidiary of Tootals, started in 1954, may well become important, but at present all the new printworks are very small.

Few of the new firms have joined the Federation and one or two of them derive substantial benefit from their freedom to compete. The appearance of eight new firms cannot, however, be regarded as a result of the price agreements, since the number is quite comparable

[1] Firms in the industry grouped according to the yardages of printed cloth delivered by each in 1950.

Yardage Category (million yards)	Federation Members	Federation Non-members	Total Yardage (million yards)
1. Over 300	1 (CPA)	—	306·3
2. 21 to 30	2	—	50·0
3. 11 to 20	12	—	189·7
4. 6 to 10	7	—	59·3
5. 1 to 5	11	2	38·3
6. Less than 1	3	5	4·4
	43		648·0

Note: There are three non-member concerns not accounted for by the above table. One of these, whose output figure for 1950 is not available, carries out a small amount of a specialized form of calico printing. The other two began printing after 1950, and would now be comparable with the concerns in category (5) or (6).

Source: Monopolies Commission Report, *op. cit.*, p. 12.

[2] A substantial firm is here defined as one with either more than eight printing machines or a turnover of more than ten million yards.

[3] This firm uses Aridye; this is a type of dye suitable for a limited number of purposes and which is relatively simple to process.

with the number of firms which started, over about the same length of time, in the intensely competitive pre-war situation.

New firms are largely an indication of market imperfections and of how relatively easy it is to start a little printing if one has an assured market for a limited range. Eighty-five per cent of printing is done on commission, and only four of the substantial firms have vertical connections which affect a significant proportion of their trade. The vertical connections of the small firms show a very different picture; of the twenty-one that belong to the Federation, only five appear to be without vertical connections and two of these are highly specialized; the other sixteen are vertically linked in some way and, although they do a proportion of commission printing, they are not wholly dependent upon their power to compete in the open market.

The 1949 Agreements were thus made between firms which were extremely varied and which were subject to slight, but growing, competition from new entrants. The trade, although prosperous at this time, was suffering a slight setback which, because of the great uncertainty about the future, was taken very seriously.

It appears that the agreements were supported by the substantial firms in the industry. The Calico Printers' Association became progressively more in favour of the scheme. The Monopolies Commission reported[1] that during discussions in 1947, a majority of the directors of the CPA agreed that 'a redundancy scheme could be acceptable only if CPA's quota was improved. In April 1948 members of the Federation holding 97·5 per cent of the machines agreed to support a redundancy scheme provided a pool and quota scheme was operated concurrently. Instead of the hoped for increase in its quota CPA decided in January 1949 to accept the apparently certain possibility of a reduction, consequent on the indication given by the Accountant for the Federation of the scaling down which would be required to help to provide quota for new members and to increase quotas for certain dissatisfied members.' There was opposition from one of the directors, but 'the considerations which prevailed with the other directors, as recorded in the minutes, were that: (a) the costs to CPA of the quota and redundancy schemes would be less than that caused by the outbreak of a price war with consequent instability and other troubles in the printing industry; (b) the PQ scheme was an essential buttress to minimum prices; (c) time was needed for the desired expansion of merchanting[2] and the firm establishment of overseas projects, and meanwhile CPA depended on commission printing for in-

[1] Report of the Monopolies Commission, *op. cit.*, p. 41.
[2] This has not occurred.

come. CPA accordingly raised no objection and the schemes were duly ratified. In the event CPA's quota for the first year, 1949–50, although smaller than that held under the concentration agreement, was larger than that discussed and in principle accepted in January 1949, and included allotments made to two businesses acquired by CPA, one during the war and one in 1949.'[1]

The acquisition of J. F. and E. Caulfield Limited by the CPA in 1949 is of some interest. Caulfields, a substantial firm which had been concentrated during the war, had not re-opened but plans had been made and it would probably have started printing if it had not been acquired. The CPA deny that the possibility of acquiring a quota was an important consideration, but, in the event, the quota was of considerable value. Demand was high and the CPA were faced with the decision as to whether they should reinstall machinery in one of their own works, buy Caulfields or allow their proportion of the trade to shrink. Although some were unwilling to expand capacity it was decided to buy Caulfields; this was thought less expensive than recommissioning one of the closed works and also labour was thought to be easier to obtain in that district.

In 1954 the Monopolies Commission Report was published and in a unanimous report it was declared that the Percentage Quantum scheme was against the public interest, but that a price list without sanctions might be maintained. A year later the President of the Board of Trade announced that he accepted the findings of the Commission. The industry most unwillingly agreed to bring the arrangements to an end as they were anxious not to have an Order made against them and they still hoped that if and when a Restrictive Practices Court was set up their case would be reconsidered and a different conclusion reached. The effects of discontinuing the arrangements are not yet apparent. Company reports make no mention of severe price cutting but several firms, mainly those who had considerable African trade, report losses and F. Steiner has now gone into liquidation (August 1956).

With the end of formal agreement the question arises as to whether a situation very like that of the 'thirties will develop. There have been no spectacular changes in the underlying conditions facing the industry, but four are of considerable importance and it appears likely that they will affect both the future conditions of competition and the role of the CPA. First, the conditions in the labour market have changed radically. Trained men can no longer be obtained quickly and in large numbers and, therefore, many must be kept during slack

[1] Report of the Monopolies Commission, *op. cit.*, p. 41.

periods, and a higher proportion of the labour force must be regarded as a fixed cost over temporary situations lasting six months to a year. The first specific evidence of this change is the Printers' Agreement, by which employers guarantee the printers' wages regardless of the amount of work they do. The Calico Printers' Association has found that there have been very big reductions in the correlations between output and numbers employed since 1936–38.

The change in the labour market has made the capacity of the industry less flexible. Idle machinery cannot be started quickly and, therefore, a firm with plant will not find it worthwhile to try to bring it into commission for a short period; further, sudden peaks of demand cannot be met and, therefore, despite redundant plant there is greater possibility of raising prices when demand is good. 'Excess capacity' in the short period now includes idle labour which is very expensive to maintain and puts a very much higher premium on a more regular flow of orders. This might be better obtained by a vertical or semi-vertical organization, or, possibly, by some change in the price structure designed to encourage the merchant to place regular orders with long delivery dates.

The second change which has taken place since the war is the growth in the number and importance of large buyers in the home trade. This has been the result of concentration of the retail trade and the growth of a number of large makers-up in the women's dress trade. These 'valuable' customers already obtain top quality at the minimum price; their value as customers is largely related to the size and regularity of their orders. The appearance of such buyers has had the effect of reducing the amount of trade liable to be subject to short-period intense price cutting; the trade is intensely competitive, but it is competition based on somewhat longer period considerations.

Thirdly, changes in the technical field are of considerable importance; shrink-resist, crease-resist, everglaze and non-iron finishes have been developed and there is now a wide and ever-increasing range of new fabrics made of rayon, nylon and terylene, and of blends of the synthetic with the natural fibres. These developments make works more complicated, additional machinery necessary, and increase both the scientific and technical overheads. (One of the CPA works uses thirty-two bleaching methods compared with eight at a simpler works.) The new developments have not brought the rewards of innovation or monopoly power to the extent that might have been expected; there has been simultaneous development both here and abroad, and the CPA is in competition both with Tootals, who have done much research, and with other firms using systems which are either unpatented or licensed. The CPA's greatest achievement has been Terylene, but this is being developed by ICI and the profits are unrelated to the printing activities.

The increased complication of much of the work has made the control of prices by agreement more difficult because prices have been based on very broad categories. There has been considerable competition in the form of offering special finishes without additional charge. The new situation is beginning to make the price lists obsolete and any new ones will now have to be established without the support of the pool and quota scheme.

Lastly, there has perhaps been a significant change since before the war in the attitude of the industry towards price competition. After sixteen years of price agreements it may have developed the habit of relying on them and be very reluctant to return to severe competition.

Two possible results of the general changes which have taken place since 1939 may be distinguished. The first is the possibility of greater vertical integration, achieved partly by backward integration by those with large outlets and partly by the increased forward integration by the CPA and other large semi-vertical printers. Vertical integration might give greater regularity of work, it would reduce the costs of competing for orders, and it would eliminate losses due to short-period price-cutting. Nevertheless, the chance that such organization will become really important is not high because the output of a normal print works capable of doing more than a narrow range of work is so great that the vertical organization would have to be very large indeed; a trade of about fifteen million yards a year would be necessary, and the capital required and the risk involved would be very great. Further, such firms are very vulnerable to big changes in fashion markets, as is illustrated by the difficulties of United Turkey Red and Steiners in the inter-war period. The Monopolies Commission produced evidence[1] that the CPA intended to increase the proportion of work done on their own cloth; although this may develop to some extent, the firm has to be careful not to antagonize its own merchant customers; further, the amount of capital required and the risks involved in large-scale merchanting are strong deterrents. In the immediate post-war period the risks were slight, but cloth was unobtainable because of the increasing link between merchants and weavers.

The underlying changes combine to increase the importance of the more substantial firm and the type of firm which can gain most from regular trading and stable prices, and which prefers to take a longer period view. Agreements may be becoming easier to reach and, perhaps more important, a situation may be arising in which there may

[1] Report of the Monopolies Commission, *op. cit.*, p. 41.

be adherence to 'recommended prices'. Change in this direction is slow, but already the Calico Printers Association appears to be in a somewhat stronger position, particularly *vis-à-vis* its larger competitors. The printers which are associated with large firms tend to prefer stability and these have grown in importance. There are not only the large printing branches of the Bradford Dyers' Association and the Bleachers' Association, but also a number of smaller firms which include branches or subsidiaries of Wallpaper Manufacturers Ltd, British Celanese, British Silk Dyers, William Hollins (Vyella), Tootals and Courtaulds. The larger vertical organizations are another group of firms which is unlikely to indulge in severe short-period price cutting. The trend is not very clear, but it does appear that there has been a reduction in the number, size and importance of the type of firm which might initiate severe price cutting. The growth of the big orders from the home market buyers has had a somewhat similar effect since these buyers, although anxious for low prices, are interested in stability and continuity.

The serene stability of the industry, with a strong price leader surrounded by firms with little interest in severe short-period price cutting, may be a long way off, but it is possible that it is being approached gradually. In the past, control and agreement was probably the only alternative to intense competition. Now, however, the incentives to cut prices may be falling and the strength of the combine increasing, so that, in the absence of formal agreement, quasi agreement might work for an increasing proportion of the time.

CHAPTER 8

The Role of the Combine

(a) 1919–54

ALTHOUGH there were a number of mergers between 1919 and 1954 not one of them was of any real importance; in most cases little was acquired except copper rollers, goodwill, and a few, usually redundant, machines. It is the effects of the existence of the combine which have to be considered. It continued, throughout the period, to affect both the historical trends and the short-period reactions to new situations.

The previous chapters have been designed to give both the history of events in the period, and to indicate the nature of the industry. In the early section much emphasis was placed upon the short-period features. In the 1919–54 section, the main emphasis has been upon the way in which adjustment in the size of the industry have been made and the factors which have influenced it. In general terms, what was said of the short period in the first chapter remains true of the present day, and, again in general terms, the structure of the industry has changed little, though the industry is very different in detail. The rate of technical change has been slow, but, on the whole, steady, yet the very slowness has meant that the results to be expected from such change are blurred. The great difficulty of analysing the calico printing trade lies in the fact that nothing is clear cut. A print is never perfect; no two prints are quite the same; the same design printed by two printers will look a little different; firms produce a variety of styles and the variety is always different and always changing; printers vary in the amount of service they give; there are gaps of various sizes in the chain of substitutes; some merchants are very closely tied to their printers with bonds of usage, friendship or commercial power, while others are not.

There is competition, but there is also the familiar kinked demand curve, which describes the position of a firm which will gain little trade if it cuts prices because others follow suit, and will lose trade if it raises prices because others do not follow. In the calico printing industry the 'kink' is not well defined because firms are dissimilar and changes in demand affect different parts of the trade differently. The market is too small for much discrimination between customers, but the industry is diverse and consists of enough different markets for there to be considerable discrimination between products.

The competition of the short period is of great importance to the prosperity of an individual firm. Prices do not change readily, but they do change both frequently and considerably; the characteristics of the demand for printing are such that the incentive to cut prices is very strong; in particular there are big and frequent changes in the volume and in the type of demand. Nevertheless, only in very exceptional circumstances do more than a small proportion of prices fall to the level of short-period marginal costs.

The adjustment of the industry to new, long-period demand is immensely complicated since all firms can withstand very considerable changes in demand so long as they are temporary. The industry is not sufficiently standardized for extreme price cutting to result in the rapid elimination of the higher cost firms, nor is it sufficiently specialized for there to be little or no price cutting. When a permanent change in demand occurs, it is seldom clear that it will be permanent, and it is often treated as a temporary one, since temporary changes are much more frequent. Throughout, the industry has sought protection from the rigours of the short-period competition; the fact that this has sometimes involved the slowing down of long-term adjustment has not been regarded as serious by those in the industry, since long-term adjustment has so much less impact upon the industry than the cumulative effect of short-period competition.

The rate of historical change in this industry has been sufficiently slow for its effect upon the structure of the industry to be slight. Technical progress has not been fast enough for those with financial and technical strength to gain more than slight advantages, and commercial and managerial changes have also been slow. Nevertheless, the length of time taken for firms to be eliminated has often been so long that both technical and managerial changes have contributed to the elimination of firms which might have survived in a static industry.

Thus, in the calico printing industry, short-period competition, adjustment, and historical trend are interwoven; although each may be separated for purposes of discussion, the separation is somewhat artificial. There are indeed few clear-cut distinctions, and no particular features are of overriding importance and conclusions are extremely difficult to reach; we can do little more than indicate the general direction in which conclusions may lie.

In the period since 1919 the CPA has both maintained price agreements and promoted efficiency, but the relative importance of these two activities has varied over the period.

The size of the CPA inevitably caused it to affect the average level of prices and it naturally supported the Federation throughout and strove to maintain price agreements. In the years immediately after 1918 all were anxious to increase prices but were reluctant to initiate the increase. The incentive to joint action was thus high and agreement would very likely have been possible in the absence of the CPA. In the 'twenties, however, the existence of the CPA appears to have been crucial. It gave a strong lead in a situation in which many firms were desperate and might have begun to cut prices. Further, it had a high proportion of the declining export market and closed works rather than indulged in price cutting.

It might be argued that the CPA was the price leader and would have maintained prices even in the absence of price agreement. This, however, was not the case in the 'thirties when, in the absence of price agreements, prices were very much lower than they were in the 'twenties.

The maintenance of prices during the 'twenties which must be largely attributed to the CPA gave few incidental long-term advantages which may be set against the immediate disadvantage to the consumer. The industry was declining and permanent changes in the direction of trade were taking place and, as a result, price stability did little to reduce risk and promote specialization. Profits did little to induce useful investment since much of the investment which actually took place was based upon mistaken estimates of future trade and proved useless.

After about 1930 the story is rather different. The price agreements had broken down and the CPA did no more than act as a steadying influence on the prices of certain types of work. The CPA was on the other hand one of the leaders in the field of technical efficiency. Although there is no evidence that it was more efficient than the best of its competitors the very fact that it was so large and set a high standard meant that the average level of efficiency was higher than it would otherwise have been.

The internal efficiency of the CPA was partly achieved by the policy of drastic concentration and the modernization which accompanied it. Such concentration would almost certainly have been impossible if the industry had consisted of a much larger number of independent units; there would have been more works operating at much lower levels of activity.

Greater efficiency was also achieved because the CPA, in common with other larger firms, had the resources to enter the newer branches of the trade such as the printing of rayon. By entering the newer types of trade quickly and setting a high standard, it almost certainly reduced both the premiums which higher-quality work might have earned and the profits which might have been made from successful innovation.

During the 'thirties the CPA might have played the very important role of forming the basis of a new larger combine. Price competition was so severe that many supported this solution. However, in the end no action was taken as new entries and expansion by small outsiders could not have been prevented and the large organization, having no big economies of scale, would have been in a very weak long-term position. Further, had prospects been better, agreement would still have been difficult as the prospects of the different firms were so varied. The abandonment of the project may then be attributed to the moderate rate of historical and technical change; it was sufficient to cause great variations in the efficiency of firms, but insufficient to give rise to large technical economies of scale.

Neither the favourable nor the unfavourable effects of the CPA over the inter-war period were clear cut, and as it appears that they were fairly evenly balanced no conclusions can be drawn.

It is in the post-war period that the effects of the existence of the CPA became more definite. It was solidly behind the agreements, and the introduction of the comprehensive Percentage Quantum scheme which followed the wartime arrangements must be in large part attributed to it. In the absence of the combine there would have been so large a number of so varied firms that agreement would have been, if not impossible, extremely difficult.

It is clear that the Percentage Quantum scheme tended to inhibit adjustment but, on the other hand, such a scheme might, by giving greater security and less incentive to guard against risks, have resulted in greater efficiency and lower prices; further, the agreements by reducing short-period price cutting tended to operate in favour of the larger firm. These points indicate that a scheme which limits short period competition may benefit the types of firm most likely to be efficient. Whether this is the case, and whether such a scheme can be judged to be in the public interest turns upon many points; for example much depends upon the level at which prices are maintained, the rate at which quotas are altered, the amount of change in the size of the industry which is necessary and the rapidity with which unrestricted competition tends to eliminate the inefficient. The Percentage Quantum scheme was not operated for long enough, nor was it regarded as permanent enough, for possible long-term advantages to accrue; all that can be said is that, while it perhaps moderated prices during the post-war boom, it maintained them between 1952 and 1955. Further, the quota payments and the restricted price competition kept in existence a number of firms which might have been eliminated. In other words, whatever the long-run possibilities of such a scheme, this one did not operate in the public interest.

In the post-war period the benefits of large-scale research and scientific experience really began to yield substantial returns. Improved methods, new fabrics, new dyes and, probably of greatest importance, new finishes have been successfully introduced and used. The CPA has been important but by no means the only firm to make innovations. Tootals, Courtaulds, the ICI, the Bradford Dyers, as well as a few of the smaller firms have contributed to the rate of progress; nevertheless it is the CPA which has done so over the widest field.

Thus, over the post-war period, both the restriction of competition and the development of techniques can, to some extent, be attributed to the CPA. Although other firms were also responsible for progress in techniques and efficiency the share of the CPA has certainly been significant, and it is difficult to resist the conclusion that this has been more important than the restriction of competition in an industry where free competition works so very imperfectly.

(b) CONCLUSIONS

THE calico printing industry, in the absence of continuously increasing demand, must inevitably be subject to great uncertainty. Unrestricted competition between numerous firms in such an industry must be extremely uncomfortable. It was this which led to the early combine and, over the last fifty years, this combine has held about half the trade and has dominated the industry.

The extraordinary stability of the proportion of the trade done by the combine appears to have been in large part the incidental result of a balance between the strength of the forces tending to weaken and those tending to fortify the CPA. The CPA might well have become more important with a higher rate of technical progress, but in fact it just maintained its importance despite its rather weak commercial position which made it difficult for it to meet price cutting.

This case is one of the hardest in which to assess the merits of mergers. Both in the period up to 1914 and in the period 1918 to 1954 prices were at times maintained at levels higher than they might have been. This is, however, more true of the early period than the later period. In both periods the existence of the combine led to greater average efficiency.

This view is based upon the assumption that in its absence the industry would have consisted of a large number of firms. The rate of competitive elimination is slow and uncertain, and new chances to enter in specialized fields occur quite frequently. In a declining industry with imperfect competition the size of firm is not determined by long-period decisions, but by the success in maintaining sales; further, this success often depends upon luck and day-to-day commercial skill rather than on efficiency from which the consumer could gain. The CPA increased efficiency because it was able to concentrate and reorganize, and it knew that its position depended upon efficiency and low prices rather than on a series of shrewd commercial manoeuvres. Efficiency is valuable in so far as it is passed on to the consumer in the form of lower prices and higher quality; it is extremely difficult to tell whether, in the absence of the combine, there would have been so many inefficient firms that they would have been 'representative' and, therefore, have played a large part in determining prices.

Progress was certainly made more rapid by the CPA, especially in the period since the late 'twenties. This was important and here the merits of the combine are clear cut. A large firm, which exploited new methods, meant that they spread rapidly and a few abnormal profits were earned.

Despite the uncertainties it appears that on the whole the existence of the CPA has been in the public interest. Had it not been for the high level of unemployment in the inter-war period this conclusion would have been more certain since higher efficiency would have been important even if not entirely passed on to the consumer in the form of lower prices.

APPENDIX

Fixed and Variable Costs in Calico Printing

VARIABLE costs are related to the length of time under consideration and the cost structure. From examination of the cost structure, a number of levels of variable costs may be deduced and these indicate the possible severity of price competition.

The following table shows the main items of cost for a group of eight concerns whose returns relate almost wholly to calico printing. These figures appear to be representative as the variation from year to year is relatively small and they are very similar to equivalent data relating to individual works belonging to the CPA.

Such low levels of prices, as these variable costs indicate, are only relevant to special discriminating prices and not to general levels, but they, nevertheless, have the effect of breaking an existing price structure. These figures are extremely rough, but greater accuracy is of little importance since the time periods taken into consideration are arbitrary; further, expectations are uncertain and *entrepreneurs* seldom know how long a situation will last. The important point which is emphasized by these figures is that future expectations must be the chief guide to policy as very large losses would be incurred if firms pursued a short-period price policy.

The long-period average cost per unit, including normal profit, is equal to the average total direct costs plus the average total indirect costs plus return upon capital employed. In the calico printing industry the capital employed is approximately equal to the annual turnover; that is, capital is turned over once per year; as little industrial investment is made if the expected return is less than 10 per cent, the long-period return on capital in this industry may be taken as 10 per cent of total indirect and direct costs. Thus, if total cost excluding return on capital is equal to 100, then long-period average cost, including normal profit, is equal to about 110.

TABLE III

Cost Structure in Calico Printing

	1937[1] %	1950[1] %
Direct Costs:		
Bleaching materials, dyes and drugs	30·9	31·7
Direct wages	25·8	25·7
Coal, power and water	10·0	10·2
Designs and engraving	6·0	2·4
Transport	1·0	0·7
Sundry materials	2·8	2·9
Outside dyeing and finishing	0·7	3·9
Total direct costs	77·2	77·5
Indirect Costs:		
Non-productive wages	4·1	4·4
Remuneration		
Staff	3·9	3·6
Directors	2·8	3·3
Net annual value of owned premises	1·2	0·6
Rent of leased premises	0·1	0·1
Repairs and maintenance	3·5	4·5
General expenses	3·2	4·1
Depreciation[2]	3·8	1·9
	22·6	22·5
Total cost, excluding return on capital	100	100

Source: Monopolies Commission Report, *op. cit.*, p. 50.

On the basis of these figures the level of variable costs relevant to a number of situations may be examined.

When redundant capacity emerges in the industry it is likely to remain for some time, perhaps as much as ten years, as equipment is extremely durable. Average variable costs over a period of five to ten years would, on the basis of the 1937 figures, be equal to the total cost (excluding return on capital) minus the true fixed costs.

[1] Fiscal year ended December 31 (or nearest date).

[2] Depreciation has been calculated upon wear and tear principles based on cost or estimated cost, and no account has been taken of the enhanced cost of replacing fixed assets. The effect of initial allowances has been eliminated. M. Comm. Report, *op. cit.*, p. 51, para 148.

	Total Cost (Excluding Return on Capital) %
Net annual value of owned premises	1·2
Depreciation	3·8
A proportion of repairs and maintenance (more than 50 per cent)	2·0
	7·0

Thus, over periods of five to ten years, firms will, provided that labour and management costs have been adjusted to any reduction in the level of capacity worked, incur current losses only if prices fall below 93, as compared with 110, which, on this basis, is equal to the long-period average cost. In other words prices up to 10 to 15 per cent below long-period normal prices can continue for five to ten years or even longer.

Over periods of up to two years the only items of the indirect costs (which are 22 per cent of total cost, excluding return on capital) which are avoidable are, firstly, the 7 per cent of total cost which are no part of average variable costs (see above) and secondly, some proportion of directors' salaries and some staff expenses. The indirect costs which must be met are, therefore, equal to about 15 per cent of 'normal' total cost (excluding return on capital). If firms remained in business, despite the fact that prices had dropped to a level which only covered direct costs, the loss in one year would be equal to about 15 per cent of 'normal' total cost; this in turn equals about 15 per cent of capital employed since turnover and capital employed are approximately equal. In two years, losses would be equal to about 30 per cent of capital employed. The possibility of incurring such losses which is the result of the great importance of fixed expenses partly explains the fact that the general level of prices seldom falls to very low levels.

In a temporary situation which may last for only six months very much less adjustment is possible and variable costs, on the basis of 1937 figures, would be only about half the long-period average cost.

	Total Cost (Excluding Return on Capital) 1937 %
Chemicals, dyes and drugs, etc.	31
75 per cent of direct wages	18
Outside dyeing and finishing	2
20 per cent of other direct cost items	4
	55

Over really short periods, for example, a slack period of about six weeks, the variable cost might be as little as 36 per cent of long-period normal costs.

	Total Cost (Excluding Return on Capital)
	%
Drugs and dyes, etc.	31
About 20 per cent of direct wages, 5 per cent of other direct cost	5
	36

III

THE SOAP INDUSTRY

1. Introduction

2. Expansion Without Acquisitions, 1885–1906

3. The Abortive Combine, 1906

4. The Period of Acquisitions, 1906–21

5. The Period of Consolidation and Rationalization, 1921 onwards

6. Conclusions

APPENDIX: NUMBER OF SOAP PRODUCERS IN GREAT BRITAIN AT SELECTED DATES

CHAPTER 1

Introduction

THIS study is concerned with mergers in the home soap industry. This industry has been dominated since the late nineteenth century by the firm which William Lever started in 1885 as a small soap factory in Warrington and which has expanded, partly only by acquisitions and unions, until in 1955 it employed a capital of over £400 million.

Lever Brothers, however, and still more so Unilever, into which it became absorbed (in effect) with the merger in 1929 with the Dutch organization of Margarine Unie NV and Margarine Union Limited, had never, after the middle 1890's, confined itself to soap production in the United Kingdom. Until the first world war, when Lever Brothers began to manufacture margarine, soap in its various forms had been the only important end product.[1] But from the 1890's it had been soap production overseas as well as at home, by 1900 in Australia, Canada, the United States, Germany and Switzerland.[2] From the beginning of the twentieth century, too, Lever Brothers acquired sources of raw materials, mainly, of course, overseas, though never a large proportion of the amount they used, and, during the first world war, ships to carry their raw materials from West Africa. Lever, in 1896, started his own oil and cake mill at Port Sunlight, and produced, as a by-product, cattle cake.[3] After the first world war, not only was there great expansion in existing lines of activity, but also Lever burst into new fields, including buying Mac Fisheries. Some of these side lines were disposed of later. But other lines, particularly of companies selling to the same type of customer as those buying soap and margarine, were acquired towards the end of the second world war and after it ended, notably Batchelors Peas and a firm making frozen frosted foods in the United Kingdom and others overseas. By 1955 soap and other detergents (at home and overseas) represented only 15 per cent of the turnover of Unilever Ltd and NV Groups, and

[1] Glycerine and cattle cake were produced as by-products, the first from 1886 the second from 1896.

[2] Charles Wilson, *The History of Unilever*, Vol. I, p. 98. [3] Ibid., p. 57.

toilet preparations 1 per cent.[1] Developments outside the soap industry in this country will only be referred to here insofar as they directly affected home soap production and policy.

For the purpose of this study four periods can usefully be distinguished, though the dividing dates rarely provide a definite break between one situation or one policy and another.

1. 1885–1906: the date when Lever began soap production at Warrington to that in which he started active discussions to promote a combine in the soap trade. In this period Lever introduced to the trade a better, standardized, hard soap, 'Sunlight', wrapped and advertised, and built up a national market. Only one going concern producing soap in England was acquired, a United States firm, Benjamin Brooke,[2] and that mainly because of its American rather than its British activites.

2. 1906: the year when Lever introduced and then abandoned his idea of a combine. Here we shall be concerned more with what Lever hoped to do and why, which will mean going back a little to earlier years, than with the reasons why the combine did not materialize; these reasons are fully discussed in Mr Charles Wilson's book[3] and are, on the whole, of particular rather than general importance.

3. 1906–21: from the abortive combine to the end of the period of intensive expansion after the war. This period includes the acquisition of the great bulk of the home soap firms ultimately acquired. In the first part of this period, roughly up to the war, the firms acquired were mostly small; the bigger firms were only brought in towards the end of the war, or after it.

4. 1921 to the present day: a period first of consolidation and then of definite integration of sales forces and factories. One firm was bought up fairly early to prevent competition, and several smaller ones brought in, nearly all early in the period; but, on the whole, acquisitions stopped, a fact we must explain. During this period new forms of detergents gained ground rapidly, partly at the expense of hard soap, both wrapped and bar, and new competition developed. Little will be said of the post-war competition with the American firm of Procter and Gamble, since too little information is publicly available.

[1] Unilever, Report and Accounts, 1955, p. 16.
[2] Wilson, *op. cit.*, Vol. I, pp. 56 (and 104). [3] Ibid., Ch. VI.

CHAPTER 2

Expansion Without Acquisitions, 1885–1906

THE first Soap Makers' Directory,[1] published in 1888 (three years after William Lever began manufacturing), listed close on 345 manufacturers of soap in Great Britain, of whom seventy-four were in London, rather over 211 in the rest of England and Wales, and sixty in Scotland. Apparently, no firm before Lever had tried to build up a national market. Generally speaking, these firms produced bar soap for local markets. To safeguard these markets the firms operated a series of conventions, rather loose in their nature, reserving sales in broad zones for the local makers; there were also some private agreements between individual firms to the same end. 'Preserves were respected and poaching was kept to a minimum.'[2] From 1867, also, there existed the Soap Makers' Association, a body whose scope was never easy to define; it was not supposed to fix prices, though it did permit the trade to agree when to alter them, agreements which were rarely, if ever, firmly adhered to.[3] No record exists before 1888 of the changes in the number of firms making soap; but it is probable that in this earlier period, as in later ones, new firms came in and old ones went out; there has never been any effective check on new entry.

The entry of Lever into this trade led to a drastic change in the type of product and the nature of competition in the industry. He began his career in the soap industry in the early 1880's as a salesman of soap manufactured for him by others; in 1885 he acquired his own factory at Warrington and started to manufacture at the beginning of 1886; in 1889 he moved to his new site at Port Sunlight on the Mersey and began a period of rapid expansion.

Lever Brothers started as a partnership between William Lever and his brother James. It became a private company in 1890 and in 1894 a public one, under William Lever's Chairmanship, with his brother, his father, and P. J. Winser as directors. Directors changed, and others were added. But, whatever the formal position, the actual was an autocracy under William Lever. He held from the first a large block of the

[1] See Appendix. [2] Wilson, *op. cit.*, Vol. I, p. 20. [3] Ibid., p. 60.

ordinary capital and ultimately the whole of it. The preference shareholders had, it is true, voting rights, but they left the decisions to Lever.[1]

Lever introduced to the industry what was, in effect, a new, hard soap, of a better quality and soon of a standardized quality. He sold it wrapped in cartons, under the trade mark 'Sunlight' and built up a market which soon became more than a local one by advertising on a national scale and later by prize-gift schemes. He started production in a period when soap sales as a whole were expanding rapidly, partly because of his advertisements aimed at the working-class market where he rightly saw the greatest hopes of expansion, but largely because of rising real wages. Lever not only captured a large part of the new market, but also cut into the market previously held by the older makers of bar soap.

This was a period when the number of firms making soap in Great Britain was sharply reduced. Of the 345 firms recorded in the Soap Makers' Directory in 1888, 153 were no longer so recorded ten years later; but since sixty-five new firms were listed in 1898 as compared with 1888, the total number of firms in 1898 was 257.[2] We cannot, however, attribute this decline in numbers solely to the new competition by Lever's; proportionately, it was greater in Scotland than in England, where Lever's cannot have been so violent a competitor. It was the process of growth and decay in an industry with small-scale production. By 1900 Lever held about a sixth of the sales of soap in the United Kingdom.[3]

By 1900 Lever was producing other soap than 'Sunlight' and the few minor soaps with which he started. He had introduced the carbolic soap, 'Lifebuoy', in 1894, and in 1899 acquired the scouring soap 'Monkey Brand' by buying the American firm Benjamin Brooke. The motives for this purchase were almost certainly to assist in developing Lever's sales in the United States, where Benjamin Brooke mainly operated. The British factory produced only about 2,500 tons yearly of the scourer, compared with Lever's production of around 50,000 tons of soap. This factory was closed, and production transferred to Port Sunlight. (This was Lever Brothers' first acquisition of an outside soap company producing soap in this country, and the only one in the period under consideration. As we shall see later, factories acquired subsequently were not normally closed.) 'Monkey Brand' was followed as a scourer, in 1904, by 'Vim'.

Lever also began in 1899 to manufacture soap flakes, then an en-

[1] Wilson, *op. cit.*, Vol. I, pp. 46–9. [2] See Diagram, p. 273.
[3] Wilson, *op. cit.*, Vol. II, Appendix 10.

tirely new product, first under the name 'Sunlight Flakes', but changed a year later to the much more successful one of 'Lux'. These, new products all of them, were the successes. Less success attended the efforts to cut more directly into the markets of established firms by introducing products designed to compete with the toilet soap made by Pears, Gibbs and Vinolia, and with Hudson's dry soap.[1] In any case hard soap still dominated the trade. With the relatively unimportant soft soap it still accounted, in 1905, for over 90 per cent of Lever's total sales.

Lever had thus broken up the old system of local markets by introducing first one, then several branded products designed not mainly for a limited high-grade market, as were some earlier specialities of other firms, but also for the mass market provided by working-class households. He did not do it without opposition. For, naturally, the old firms had not merely sat down under Lever's invasion of their markets. They also, some quickly, some slowly, began to make branded soaps, to advertise and to provide gifts for soap users. Lever's sales of 'Sunlight' fell off for the first time in 1896; and though they subsequently recovered, the rate of expansion had slowed up. Soap consumption as a whole was also expanding less rapidly now that real wages were no longer rising. And, somewhat surprisingly, if the Soap Makers' Directory is reliable, more firms entered the trade between 1898 and 1906 than left it; ninety-four new names appeared; seventy-five old ones disappeared.[2] A large number of the new quoted their main product as industrial soap, sold probably to manufacturers in their vicinity.

In a sense, therefore, this period up to 1905 really divides, for the purposes of this study, into two. In the first, extending almost to the turn of the century, Lever was expanding his sales satisfactorily by getting first into the field with a new product, 'Sunlight', a wrapped soap, and by breaking into a national market by advertising. He had no need to buy up existing firms to secure new outlets; and in any case both his energies and, possibly, his available finance were occupied. During this period the old agreements between firms went on, though the emphasis was changing from market sharing to price fixing for bar soap; more efforts were made to operate the price agreements in times of difficulty than in times of prosperity. Lever's had become a member of the Soap Makers' Association in 1889, though they by no means always acted with the other firms. Indeed, it was not until the end of the century, in 1898, when the price of

[1] Wilson, *op. cit.*, Vol. I, p. 57. [2] See Diagram, p. 273.

tallow jumped and that of cottonseed rose, that Lever's agreed to raise their prices at the same time as did other firms.

In the second period, it was becoming clear that an entirely new situation had developed. Although the old local markets were breaking down, the soap market had in other ways become more imperfect. Consumers now distinguished between the different brands on offer, and the market of each firm was sustained by advertising. The introduction of advertising, moreover, almost certainly raised the optimum scale of operation for soap firms, by introducing a new overhead cost in the expenses of launching and supporting a brand. None the less, new firms were taking up soap production. There were still openings in local markets, particularly perhaps in the manufacturing areas where firms could build up connections with, for instance, individual textile manufacturers.

Although Lever was trying some products new to the industry and also, less successfully, types of soap new to him but not to others, he was no longer in general taking customers away from these others. In 1905 he probably held about the same share of the United Kingdom soap market, one-sixth, as he had in 1900.[1] In this period Lever was trying to work with the other firms in the Association. For some years, notably after 1901 when prices were fixed for bar soap for each of five regions into which the country was divided, the voluntary agreements worked tolerably well. But they were inherently unstable, since they did not apply to branded soaps. Their existence probably encouraged and hastened the introduction of brands, and a situation where price discrimination appeared profitable. Thus the stage was set for a more drastic reorganization.

During these years William Lever himself was largely preoccupied with raw material problems and with setting up factories overseas. Early in the century he was starting his planting ventures in the South Seas and sending investigators to West Africa; by the turn of the century he had definitely decided to build more factories overseas. But for this, a change in policy might perhaps have come earlier.

[1] Sales by Lever Group in 1905 from Wilson, Vol. I, Appendix 2; estimated total soap consumption in UK in 1905 assumed to be the same as the figure for 1907, given in Wilson, Vol. II, Appendix 10. Figures of total consumption are not available for 1905; Lever's sales had slumped in 1906 and 1907.

CHAPTER 3

The Abortive Combine, 1906

THE actual change in policy came in 1906. For some years before this Lever had become convinced of the advantages to be derived from a combine. He had read a paper at Port Sunlight as early as 1903, explaining his general views.[1] As will be shown presently, he did not believe in either the desirability or the efficacy of price agreements.[2] In 1905, indeed, he resigned his membership of the Soap Makers' Association; he said 'after long experience we have failed to find any benefit in continuing members'.[3] But neither, as will be shown, did he believe in uncontrolled competition.

The drastic rise in the price of raw materials in 1906, of from a third to a half, decided him to try at once to put his ideas of a combine into practice. For he expected the higher prices to persist owing to the expanding demand for his raw materials in the manufacture of margarine and compound lard. Trade, it is true, was good, but not good enough to make this rise in raw material prices other than serious for the soap trade. The Brief for the Plaintiffs, in the libel action shortly to be mentioned, described the position as Lever saw it. After outlining the raw material position the Brief went on to say: 'Having regard to these conditions it was clear in the summer of 1906 that the position was calling for an increase of the price to the retailer, that this must inevitably be followed by a rise in the price of soap to the public, and as the rise in raw materials was unmistakably of a permanent nature and not a mere transient upheaval of prices . . . that some measures must be adopted by the leading soap-makers in conference to allay the fierce competition which had arisen amongst them, to terminate the frenzied competitive advertising which was daily becoming more intolerable, and to arrive at a better understanding which would enable all to live in face of the excessively high prices ruling, whilst at the same time doing justice to the grocer or dealer as retailer, and also to the public as consumer.'[4]

[1] Wilson, *op. cit.*, Vol. I, p. 75. [2] See p. 225. [3] Ibid., p. 69.

[4] Brief for the Plaintiffs in the case between Lever Bros. Ltd, Plaintiffs and the Associated Newspapers Ltd, Defendants in the High Court of Justice, King's Bench Division, 1906–L–No. 2692, p. 19.

In July William Lever took the opportunity of introducing his idea of a combine at a meeting of the leading northern glycerine manufacturers, called by the Glycerine Association. For at this meeting were present the leading soap manufacturers.[1]

It is not proposed here to do more than outline the dramatic events that followed and culminated in the famous libel action.[2] We shall only examine in any detail the advantages Lever's (and other firms) hoped to obtain from the proposed combine, the degree of fusion contemplated and, so far as evidence exists, why particular firms were chosen, or themselves chose, to come in.

In the barest outlines, then, the story is this. In July William Lever put forward his ideas on combines; during August he opened negotiations first with three leading firms and then with others; by the end of the month he hoped the combine was 'an accomplished fact'. In September, because of this, advertising contracts were being reduced or cancelled. Early in October the *Daily Mail* and its associated papers began actively to attack the *Soap Trust*, as they called it, and to advise the public not to buy their soaps. Sales of the firms affected, particularly of Lever's, fell off very seriously indeed, and by the end of November the idea of the combine was dropped; the main firms were no longer prepared to tie their fortunes to those of Lever's. The reputation of Lever's had been seriously damaged, their sales reduced, their shares cut in value. Lever decided to prosecute the *Daily Mail* and other papers for libel. The case opened in July 1907, and in the end the *Daily Mail* settled for £50,000. Including the sums paid by other papers, Lever Brothers received, in total, £91,000, a sum which, large though it was, was much less than the losses Lever later attributed to the affair.[3]

The case, and the Brief prepared for Lever Brothers' Counsel, provide a great deal of evidence on the facts about the abortive combine. It is always difficult to isolate the reasons for any course of action, but here, at least, we have set out in fair detail the advantages Lever offered to the firms that he hoped to combine with, and his own ideas. But, inevitably, we cannot with confidence weigh the importance of the different motives. Those who want to get ideas adopted stress the arguments that they expect will appeal to those they have to convince. In public discussion, again, emphasis is inevitably laid on reasons likely to command public approval.

Lever himself, in his paper on combines read in 1903, had stressed his view that the aim of a combine must be to produce a cheaper

[1] Brief, *op. cit.*, p. 22. [2] See Wilson, *op. cit.*, Vol. I, Ch. VI. [3] Ibid., p. 87.

product rather than to increase profits and bolster up decaying industries.[1] Unless the combine resulted in economies, competition would be bound to emerge.

What sort of economies did he hope to achieve? Here we have his private guess, made in a letter to H. S. Timmis of Gossage's, one of the firms proposing to combine with him; it was put forward highly tentatively:

	£
Advertising, at least	200,000
Increased profit by combined selling, at least £1 per ton ..	250,000
Benefits of combined buying of Soda Ash, Sundry Supplies, Cardboxes, etc.	100,000
Benefits of combined buying of Raw Materials, Oils, Tallows, etc.	
(I cannot put any figure upon this because it is not possible to do so, but it must be an advantage to be able to join in combined buying of these heavy supplies)	
Economies in Agents, Travellers, Travelling Expenses, Branch Offices, management of Salesmen and Selling Expenses generally, at least	100,000
Economies in manufacture by centring certain soaps at certain works, and mutual helpfulness in reducing cost of manufacture, obtained by comparing methods of working, say 5*s*. per ton at least	50,000
Actual economies	£700,000[2]

Advertising comes first on the list, though it does not rank top in money terms. The combine was started at a time of intense competition in advertising and the evidence seems to show that the dominant motive in Lever's mind was to reduce its expense. In the words of the Brief, 'the main economy was to be sought in the cessation of frenzied advertising, particularly in the curtailment of Press advertising, and the control of the giving of prizes for wrappers'.[3] Closely linked with this was the hoped for saving in selling expenses, by reducing the number of agents, travellers, etc. It was intended to set up for the various firms that joined the combine a joint selling and advertising committee.

How much saving Lever hoped to obtain by combined buying is uncertain. The list quoted above, besides including a figure of £100,000

[1] Ibid., p. 75. [2] Brief, p. 56. [3] p. 40.

for miscellaneous items, suggests that he hoped to save something on buying his main raw materials. Probably not much, however, for the Brief says that he 'did not attach any great value to combined buying of raw materials'.[1]

The list puts economies in manufacturing costs at no more than £50,000, only half the figure included for combined buying of the more miscellaneous supplies, and only a sixth of the hoped for economies in advertising and selling. Since the proportion of total selling price represented by manufacturing costs is low, of the order of 10 per cent, perhaps this is not surprising. Moreover, drastic reorganization of production was not, apparently, intended. Certainly the different companies were to keep their identities, and for ten years Lever's were to use their voting power to keep in office the existing Directors of the Companies with which it hoped to unite. It looks as though some specialization was contemplated for different factories, and conceivably a closing down of small or backward companies. Lever, too, clearly hoped for economies in manufacture in some of the firms which he regarded as badly run. Possibly more was hoped for in the long run. The Brief, as no doubt might have been expected, emphasizes rather more than does the letter quoted above the possible economies in manufacture. 'An important object to be gained by the Combine was the centralization and development of chemical research work, and the constant interchange of each firm's experience and knowledge, to elicit the best methods prevailing, for adoption in the Combined firms.'[2] A joint technical committee was contemplated, as well as the joint selling and advertising committee already mentioned. The sort of economies referred to here were, however, ones which would not show themselves at once.

There remains the somewhat mysterious item, the largest single figure in the list, of 'increased profit by combined selling'. This is not, presumably, economies in selling costs, since these are separately itemized. Nor, for the same reason, is it economies in advertising.

The only possibility that remains is an increase relative to manufacturing costs in the average price realized, an increase which could be achieved mathematically either by raising prices for most types of soaps in most markets, or by reducing the extent of price discrimination through the cessation of competition between the firms which it was hoped to combine. And any increase in the price the manufacturer received could be obtained in two ways, either by squeezing retailers' margins or by putting up the price to the consumer.

On these questions the Brief is somewhat ambiguous. Nothing is

[1] Brief, *op. cit.*, p. 40. [2] p. 43.

said about squeezing margins; but a combine would be in a better position to do this than a number of competing firms, each trying to persuade retailers to stock their own product. It is several times stated that the combine was not interested in raising prices, but rather to reduce them. Certainly Lever wished to keep a 3*d.* price for Sunlight soap. It is also stated that in any case there would remain sufficient competition to prevent prices being raised—competition from existing firms at home who did not intend to join the combine, from potential newcomers, and from producers abroad. On the other hand, there is a reference to the existing fixing of prices by the Soap Makers' Association, and why this was ineffective.

'A uniform basis of competition could not be arrived at by merely fixing a uniform selling price, for the reason that some soaps may be advertised while others are not, prizes may be given by one manufacturer for the return of soap wrappers, while other makers' wrappers may not carry any such prizes, bonuses may be given to customers by some makers and not by others, discounts or purchases vary from 2½ per cent allowed by one maker to 7½ per cent allowed by another. Altogether, the Soap Makers' Association, by merely fixing the selling price, could not adequately deal with the conditions existing in 1906, unless in addition to fixing the price some limitation were put upon the inducements offered to the trade and consumers to buy certain brands of soap, which, of course, was impossible so long as each individual concern acted for its own hand alone, independently of its neighbours. It will be obvious (and this was felt by Mr Lever) that the only effective way to deal with this exceptional position would be a working arrangement under which the jealousies between makers would disappear, the frenzied policy of attacking each other's trade should cease, and a broader policy take its place under which the various firms would be able to work together harmoniously, serving their customers and, therefore, the public better, and at the same time opening up much greater possibilities for the development of business at home, and especially in neutral markets abroad.'[1]

This quotation does seem to imply that prices would be agreed by the constituent firms and the agreement made effective; and it is a reasonable assumption that the intention was to prevent short-term price cutting to the retailer and price discrimination and so to raise the average price obtained by the manufacturer in the immediate future. Almost certainly Lever hoped that, if his plans for a combine were successful, the 'normal' price would in future operate over the greater part of the market without fear of cuts for certain types of

[1] Brief, *op. cit.*, p. 27.

soap and for certain periods. As already mentioned,[1] however, Lever believed that, unless a combine reduced costs, competition would be bound to emerge. New entrants could not be prevented. He presumably, therefore, hoped by his plans eventually to reduce the long-term 'normal' price. Competition in techniques he approved of. And he probably felt confident that, protected from the short period frenzied competition he disliked, unhampered by price agreements that gave others a say, even though a small one, on how he ran his business, he could reduce costs and perhaps, in the end, prices. He had confidence in his own abilities; and without doubt he would have been the leader of the associated firms.

On this interpretation Lever's tentative estimates to Timmis of the savings he hoped to achieve by a combine must have represented the short-period savings, to be secured quickly. He saw economies in advertising and selling as certain and rapid; and indeed, as already mentioned, advertising contracts were, in fact, reduced or cancelled when it was hoped that the combine had been arranged, and some specific proposals had been prepared for reducing the number of agents in Scotland. He also felt fairly confident of more secure prices and so included a substantial figure for 'increased profit by combined selling'. But the possible economies in buying and still more in manufacturing were far more hazy, so that he included only such economies as he could see at once and not those he hoped for in the long run.

So much for the reasons for the combine. Next, the firms that it was proposed to bring in. The idea from the first was William Lever's; his first important negotiations were with Watson's (of Leeds), Gossage's (of Widnes), and Crosfield's (of Warrington). These were thus all Northern firms, the largest there apart from Lever; Watson and Gossage had made soap for Lever before he acquired his own factory at Warrington. Like Lever's, they were well situated to produce soap cheaply. Watson, moreover was a powerful personality. These three firms, roughly equal in size so far as the home market was concerned, between them supplied some 22 per cent of soap consumption in the United Kingdom.[2] At this time Lever Brothers (with Benjamin Brooke) provided some 18 per cent. Thus, if these four firms had combined, two-fifths of the United Kingdom market would already have been brought together. And their importance as producers was

[1] See p. 223.

[2] The percentages given here are based on the figures of home sales for 1905 in Wilson and of home consumption in 1907 from his Appendix X, Vol. II. For some firms, figures of sales for 1905 have had to be deduced from figures for later years.

even greater, since Lever's, Crosfields and Gossages between them supplied almost the whole of British soap exports.[1]

But the plan did not stop there. Already, in July, Lever's had closed with an offer to buy Hodgson and Simpson, who were in financial difficulties, and who produced types of bar soap which some of Lever's foreign customers had asked for and which Lever's did not themselves make.[2] In this firm Lever's hoped to achieve economies of as much as £2 per ton.[3] In October, they bought, in their own name but on behalf of the combine, the Vinolia Company, with which they had had negotiations about six years previously, but had failed to come to terms. The owner, wishing to go out of business, had in 1906 been in close negotiation with Ogston and Tennant, one of the firms proposing to enter the combine, who had suggested that he should approach Lever's.[4] Vinolia gave an entry into the market for toilet soap and toilet preparations.

Lever had 'laid it down as a fundamental principle, that his proposal was that all soapmakers were free to join, and that any firm wishing to join could do so irrespective of the size or dimensions of their business'.[5]

The promoters of the combine approached, or were approached by, a number of firms. Negotiations went on successfully with seven fairly small firms, scattered over the country, and supplying between them (together with Hodgson and Simpson and Vinolia) rather over 10 per cent of the market; thus negotiations were, it appeared at one time, complete to unite the supplies of over half the United Kingdom's market.

Negotiations had also taken place with several other firms, notably with Knight's of London. They were unsuccessful with Knight's because Lever considered the firm to be asking too high a valuation as a condition for entering. He thought the same for two other smaller firms that he approached. And he had begun negotiations with three more small firms but not completed them when the idea of the combine was dropped. This group of firms between them supplied perhaps a twentieth of the United Kingdom market.

The proposed combine, then, beginning in the north, was intended to cover the whole country. All firms who wished to come in were to be accepted, provided the terms they asked were thought reasonable. The main soap producers not apparently approached by Lever or Watson, for the approaches were shared between them, were the Co-operative Wholesale Society and Hudson's. The Co-operative Wholesale Society could clearly not participate in an exchange of shares

[1] See p. 236. [2] Brief, p. 39. [3] Ibid., p. 56. [4] Ibid., p. 47. [5] Ibid., p. 40.

with other, differently organized companies. Hudson's had kept out even of the Soap Makers' Association; they made soap products, not soap, out of soap base largely supplied by Gossage's.

In order to amalgamate with the firms mentioned in the previous paragraphs Lever Brothers had proposed to increase their capital (indeed to treble its nominal value) and to exchange their shares for those of their new partners. As already mentioned, the different companies were to keep their identities. No arrangements had been made to appoint to the Boards of these companies directors or representatives of Lever's, but it had been decided that on union taking place two representatives each of Watson's, Gossage's and Crosfield's, and one each of Chr. Thomas' and Cook's, should become directors of Lever Brothers. No doubt Lever himself expected to exercise in the combine that position of leadership which he had assumed in negotiating the arrangements to unite, and desired no more formal control.

CHAPTER 4

The Period of Acquisitions, 1906–21

WITH the breakdown in 1906 of the plans for a combine Lever abandoned the idea of combining in one operation the larger firms in the industry, or even a substantial proportion of them. But he did not give up his idea of uniting them. During the next fifteen years Lever Brothers bought up firms one by one until, in 1921, they controlled something between half and three-fifths of the soap consumed in the United Kingdom. Since, with their associated firms, they dominated the export trade, they controlled a larger share than this of the amount produced in the country, probably about seven-tenths. None the less, a large number of small soap makers still existed outside the combine. The Soap Makers' Directory listed for 1920 about 270 soap firms in Great Britain; at that date Lever's owned fully thirty-three soap firms besides themselves in Great Britain, and had a 50 per cent interest in nine others, all but two in Scotland.

The general circumstances which had led Lever to try to establish a combine in 1906 still prevailed after that date, some of them only up to the war, some after as well.

First, the prices of the main soap-making raw materials continued to rise, slightly until the war and then, with other prices, very drastically indeed until the general break in prices in 1920. Lever expected the shortage of raw materials to continue, because of the increased demand for fats for human consumption, notably in margarine, and was perpetually seeking to safeguard his supplies. Most of his activities in this direction, notably his development of overseas sources of supply and his purchases of companies controlling such sources, fall outside the field of this study, since they were steps towards a vertical combine rather than the horizontal combine in home soap production with which this study is directly concerned.

But the two activities are, of course, clearly related. First, Lever wanted to be sure of the materials for his soap and later his margarine activities and hoped, until the wartime rise in prices made this impossible, to get them cheaply enough to enable him again to reduce the price of Sunlight soap to the 3*d*. from which he had had to raise it in 1906. Although, even before the war, there was no reasonable hope of owning more than a small part of his requirements for raw materials for soap making, he apparently thought that the increase in output that he planned would keep down raw material prices. After the war he needed still more raw materials, both because he acquired more soap companies and because he had entered the margarine business during the war. So far as prices were concerned it is doubtful if he acquired cheaper raw materials by some of his activities.

Secondly, by adding a second and highly important business to his soap and margarine manufacture, he created new demands on the finance and brainpower of Lever Brothers. As will be shown later, this had drastic repercussions on the soap companies after the crash of 1921[1] and later meant that continued expansion of the soap business had to be weighed against alternative lines of development.

Thirdly, the scramble for raw materials to some extent spread conflict between the soap-making firms from the selling to the buying side, and led Lever to embark on several activities in the raw material field, more defensive in their nature, and stimulated by the wish to prevent essential raw materials from being controlled by a monopoly or by rival firms. Within this category come his attempts, beginning in 1911, to secure his supplies of alkali, controlled by Brunner's, and his purchase in 1913 of the Testrup patent for fat hardening and the establishment of its validity against the rival Normann patent, owned by Crosfield's, his rivals in soap making. (Brunner's, as a protection or a weapon against Lever's, bought the Ordinary Capital of both Crosfield's and Gossage's.)[2] Also, to safeguard their supplies at a price they thought reasonable, Lever's met in conference with other European consuming firms to divide up the available supplies of whale oil. A similar motive no doubt actuated Brunner's when they bought the Ordinary Capital of Crosfield's and Gossage's—the motive of securing outlets for their raw materials and acquiring both a protection and a weapon against Lever's incursions into the raw material field. These activities, more fully described in Mr Wilson's book, fall outside the scope of this study, except in so far as they affected, as in several ways they did directly, the acquisition of home soap factories, in this case particularly Crosfield's and Gossage's.[3]

Conflict, or 'frenzied competition', as Lever called it, continued also on the selling side, thus perpetuating this second aspect of the conditions which had led Lever to promote the combine in 1906. Soap consumption as a whole in this country was no longer expanding rapidly, as it had in Lever's first years as a soap manufacturer.

[1] See p. 249. [2] See p. 235. [3] See p. 235.

Between 1907 and 1912 it rose only by 4 per cent. Between 1912 and 1915, it is true, there was a further increase of 5 per cent; but this was a temporary fillip; in 1921 consumption was scarcely higher than it had been in 1915.[1] No really new features appear to have been introduced into the nature of competition in the period between 1906 and the war. Techniques were improving, but not changing rapidly. Hard soap, including the improved wrapped soap which Lever had introduced to the industry, remained the main product. Crosfield's, however, backed by their experience in the chemical industry, were going ahead with flakes and powder which they had introduced earlier, and Lever's, besides selling rather more Lux, began to manufacture a new and improved soap powder, Rinso, which was sold by Hudson, a firm they acquired in 1907.[2] No figures exist of the relative output for the country as a whole of the different types of detergents; but it is unlikely that the percentage represented by flakes and powders rose very much in this period, or that it reached as much as 15 per cent of total soap sales.[3] During the war there were drastic changes in the nature of the market, including a rapid growth in the output of flakes, powders and scourers. The period, however, was peculiar so that it will not be further referred to here.

In the period we are considering the total number of firms recorded in the industry first rose, from 266 in 1906 to 295 in 1914, and then during the war years declined, to 280 in 1920. The whole increase in

[1] Wilson, *op. cit.*, Vol. II, Appendix 10. [2] See p. 233.

[3] The evidence for this statement is as follows. If one adds together the sales by types of Lever, Benjamin Brook, Hudson, Watson and Gossage, for which figures are available, one obtains the following table:

	Percentage of Total Sales				
	1901	1907	1915	1921	1924
Hard and soft soap	82	73	69	54	54
Flakes and powders	16	23	26	38	37
Scourers	2	3	4	7	8
Toilet	—	1	1	1	1
Flakes and powders by these firms as percentage of all soap sales in country	6	8	9	15	14

These latter percentages would give the total percentage of soaps and flakes to total output if no other firms made flakes and powder. In 1924, the total output of flakes and powder, as shown by the table on p. 247, was 85,000 tons, 18 per cent of total soap sales (as compared with 37 per cent for the above four firms), and these firms produced 58,000 tons of soap and flakes, 70 per cent of the total output of soap and flakes. If they also produced 70 per cent in 1907 and 1915, then soap and flakes in these years accounted for between 11 and 13 per cent of total soap sales in both years.

the earlier period came in England outside London; in London numbers fell, owing to a lower rate of entry; in Scotland they scarcely changed.[1] Once again, however, there was a considerable turnover of firms; in 1914 there were ninety-four firms who had not recorded themselves in 1906, and sixty-five names had disappeared; in 1920 there were forty-seven firms recorded not listed in 1914 and sixty-two names no longer appeared. Within the constant total of sales the numerous soap firms continued to compete by advertisement and other means for a larger share for themselves.

Lever Brothers, however, for a time at any rate, competed less actively than before. They kept up the price of Sunlight soap, which they had increased in 1906, until 1909, when they dropped it to its old level. They deliberately cut their advertising costs and their schemes for giving gifts for wrappers and accepted the consequent cut in sales. Partly because of this, partly because of the Press attack aimed at diverting housewives from their products, which led to the libel action, Lever's annual home sales fell by 27 per cent between 1905 and 1907. After that they picked up; but in 1913 Lever's own home sales, excluding those of their associated companies, were still 6 per cent below the 1905 peak, and in 1921 still 1 per cent below.

Not unnaturally, the break up of the combine led to considerable acrimony between Lever's and those of the proposed partners whom Lever thought had treated him badly; these were the large firms. He had found price agreements and the operation of the Soap Makers' Association unsatisfactory before. In this period he would have nothing to do with the Association, though he stated that his firm 'must act "in a friendly way" with the trade'.[2] He did, in fact, co-operate with other firms both on some raw material problems and, as will be shown later, to a limited extent in export markets.

The solution he apparently saw to his difficulties was to buy up individual soap makers. Under the conditions then prevailing this seemed to be the easiest way to expand; and for Lever himself expansion was crucial; business was his life and he wished to extend the field he could control. This meant new outlets. Lever had already found that, unless he had something quite new to offer, as Sunlight soap and Lux had been, the easiest way to enter markets new to him was to acquire firms with established footholds there. In the period we are considering Lever's themselves found no new winners. In addition, if a large part of the industry could be brought under one control, it might still be possible to stop the expensive competition in advertising. Further, in some cases, to bring in a new firm meant

[1] See Diagram, p. 273. [2] Wilson, *op. cit.*, Vol. I, p. 117.

absorbing into the Lever organization an able executive whom Lever wanted to have. Finally, he probably still hoped to make economies in operation; but there is no evidence that this was an important motive.

These general reasons for expansion operated with different force at different periods up to 1921 and as regards different firms. The evidence is far from complete, either as to why Lever's chose particular firms or, still more, why those firms sold out. The price Lever's had to pay is clearly crucial. We do not always know it, or whether a good or bad bargain was secured.

As already mentioned, three firms had been bought before 1907, Benjamin Brooke in 1899 and Hodgson & Simpson and Vinolia in 1906. The years following up to the war were difficult years for Lever's, when the firm could hardly have had the resources for large purchases, particularly in view of their raw material commitments. In those years Lever bought up largely those firms that he could acquire particularly cheaply or easily. Up to 1910, indeed, he secured only one firm, Hudson's, a fairly large one, supplying about 5½ per cent of home soap sales. This was a firm never considered for the combine, a firm which manufactured soap powder out of soap base bought hitherto from Gossage's. It gave him an opening into a market where there were hopes of expansion, to compensate for the declining sales of Sunlight. Lever had tried, rather unsuccessfully, to challenge Hudson's at the turn of the century with a carbolic dry soap.[1] Now he absorbed the firm and, in 1910, used the name to market a new and improved soap powder, 'Rinso', manufactured at Port Sunlight.[2]

His other full acquisitions in the period up to the war were all of them much smaller. Five of them had prepared to join the abortive combine. Three, Christopher Thomas, Cook, and Ogston and Tennant, were medium-sized firms; two, Tyson and Barrington, were rather small firms. Between them they supplied, in 1915, about 6½ per cent of United Kingdom home soap production. Lever had indicated that he was especially anxious to help any of the smaller firms which had been going to enter the combine and which had been hard hit by the difficulties following its breakdown. These firms may have been in difficulties in some ways, but the two for which records of sales are available before Lever acquired them, Christopher Thomas, and Ogston and Tennant, do not seem to have suffered a loss of business, as did Lever's themselves. From Lever's point of view they gave new openings that he wanted, Christopher Thomas in the West,

[1] See p. 219. [2] Wilson, *op. cit.*, Vol. I, pp. 120–1.

Cook in London, Ogston and Tennant in Scotland and Barrington in Ireland. He bought, also, some other small firms, supplying about 2 per cent of the market. Some presented special advantages; thus Hazlehurst's owned the brand 'Sun', which Lever's thought it useful to acquire; and they were owned by the United Alkali Company, supplying a raw material for soap; and United Alkali agreed to go out of soap when they made this sale. The total of acquisitions between 1907 and 1915 accounted for 14 per cent of sales.

According to Mr Wilson, the small firms were willing to enter the combine because of the arrangements on raw materials made by the leading soap and margarine firms.[1] It is true that only a part of the supply of raw material was controlled, and that other soap firms outside the combine and not owning or controlling raw material supplies continued to operate. But only the large firms had access to the fat-hardening patents. The smaller firms, whose knowledge was necessarily imperfect, especially in a time of change and development, may well have feared that the large firms had access to a new source of cheap raw material which would enable them to price other firms out of the market.

Besides these complete purchases Lever's acquired in 1912 and 1913 a substantial but not a controlling interest in two large firms, Watson's of Leeds and John Knight's of London, both manufacturing largely hard soap, and in two small ones, Isdale and McCallum of Paisley, and Richard Wheen's of London. We have no records of why these purchases were made when they were, why Lever did not buy enough to get control, or why the firms were prepared to let Lever's buy even a substantial interest. Watson's dominated the north-eastern market and John Knight's were the most important firm in London, so that Lever would naturally have liked to absorb them, or at least to induce them to work more or less in conjunction with him. John Knight's had asked a very high price for their business when the combine was being considered, which Lever had refused; and 'Lever was inclined to put the blame for the subsequent agitation against the combine squarely on Hope's (the managing Director's) shoulders'.[2] Watson, second only to Lever, had actively promoted the combine, but had subsequently made a settlement with the *Daily Mail* which Lever regarded as dishonourable. The fact that Lever did not obtain complete control may, therefore, be explained either by unwillingness on the part of Knight's and Watson's to give it him, or perhaps by shortage of financial resources on the part of Lever's. Watson's were not fully acquired until 1917, or John

[1] Wilson, *op. cit.*, Vol. I, p. 138. [2] Ibid., p. 78.

Knight until 1920; in this interim period they remained largely independent in policy. Excluding them, Lever Brothers and its associated companies supplied in 1915 just under a third (32 per cent) of the home market; including them, about 44 per cent.

Of the chief combine firms left, Crosfield's and Gossage's between them supplied in 1915 about 14 per cent of the market. Crosfield's, as already mentioned, produced considerable quantities of flakes and powder as well as hard soap; Gossage's concentrated on hard soap. Without controlling them, Lever could not hope to control, though he might dominate, the soap market. Lever's relations with both firms were strained. 'In public speech and in private correspondence with Crosfield, Lever had kept green the memory of how he had been left to bear unaided the expenses of the debacle of 1906.'[1] He had taken from Gossage's their business with Hudson's and won a subsequent lawsuit with them when they started to manufacture a soap powder from their knowledge of Hudson's methods, which were secret but not patented.[2] Neither Lever's financial resources, nor the state of feeling, were good enough to enable him to absorb these firms soon after 1906. And in 1911 Brunner Mond's, with whom Crosfield had long had close relations, bought not only Crosfield's ordinary shares, but also Gossage's.[3] The transaction included an undertaking from Brunner that Crosfield's shares should not be sold to Lever's without Crosfield's knowledge.[4]

This, as already mentioned,[5] was part of a complicated process of manoeuvre and bargaining between Brunner's and Lever's designed, on the one hand, to secure Brunner's sales of alkali to the soap trade and to keep Lever's out of the alkali, and later also the fat hardening trade and, on the other, to safeguard Lever's supplies of raw material, to keep one of their important suppliers out of the soap trade and, also, to secure their general control over home soap factories. The story, fully described in Mr Wilson's book,[6] will not be repeated here. Brunner's were quite prepared to let Lever's have their soap factories and their undertaking not to manufacture soap, in return for Lever's keeping out of alkali and making a satisfactory contract to buy it. But the undertaking to Crosfield stood in the way. In 1913, however, this difficulty was partly surmounted. Lever's placed a large block of their Cumulative Preferred Ordinary shares in the hands of a Trustee in return for a half interest in Crosfield's and Gossage's, and the power of appointing some Directors; Brunner's undertook not to acquire any further interests in the soap trade without the consent

[1] Wilson, *op. cit.*, Vol. I, p. 128. [2] Ibid., p. 121. [3] Ibid., p. 126. [4] Ibid., p. 128. [5] See p. 230. [6] Ibid., Ch. IX.

of Lever's. And arrangements, satisfactory to both parties, were made on raw materials, except on fat hardening, which led to further difficulties shortly.

As soon as the general agreement was made Lever's also sought to make arrangements with Crosfield's and Gossage's to prevent 'cut-throat competition' but not 'healthy rivalry' in the export trade. Lever's, in 1913, controlled about 30 per cent of this trade, Gossage's just under half, and Crosfield's about 16 per cent, or together almost all of it. The idea was to agree on prices, terms and conditions of trade, possibly to divide export markets and to form a joint company for the China trade. Nothing, or at any rate not very much, came of these plans; agreement was too difficult to reach.

There was then a lull, during the war, in Lever's attempts to reach satisfactory arrangements with these firms. During this period his only important acquisition was the remaining block of shares in Watson's, offered to him in 1917. As a condition of the sale Watson undertook not to re-enter the soap trade, but kept the Olympia Oil and Cake Mills Company, a competitor of Lever's in another field, that of oil manufacture.[1] Generally, during the war, Lever tried to keep expenditure in any form to a minimum, since permission to make an issue of capital would have necessitated approval by the Government, which Lever regarded as inspection and interference with his business.[2]

The campaign to control Crosfield's and Gossage's reopened in 1919, when Lever went to law, unsuccessfully, to secure a declaration that his firm were entitled to an equal share with Brunner's in running the two firms. Lever decided that he must secure control, and finally bought the Ordinary Capital in October. At the same time he bought Price's Patent Candle Company and their associate firm D. & W. Gibbs and in 1920 the remaining shares in John Knight's, both at prices very attractive to the sellers.

These purchases, of Crosfield's, Watson's, Gossage's and Knight's, were the important ones. They were no doubt facilitated by Lever's earlier acquisitions of small firms, which strengthened his competitive position and so made the outlook more vulnerable from the point of view of the other large firms.

The purchases of Crosfield's and Gossage's and of John Knight's were discussed, as were those of the Niger Company and of shares in the African and Eastern Trade Corporation, in the *Report on the Soap Industry* of the Sub-Committee of the Standing Committee on

[1] Wilson, *op. cit.*, Vol. I, p. 218. [2] Ibid., p. 217.

Trusts, appointed under the Profiteering Acts of 1919 and 1920.[1]

Lever's paid £4 million for the shares of Crosfield's and Gossage's, which Brunner's had bought in 1911 for £2¼ million and which represented about two-thirds of the Ordinary Capital whose nominal value was £900,000.[2] Lord Leverhulme (as the founder of the firm had now become), in his highly involved evidence to the Sub-Committee, claimed that he got a better bargain for his £4 million than did Brunner's for their £2¼ million, owing partly to profits made in the interval and not paid out in dividends, and partly to the increase in the value of their plant. And indeed, since prices had risen so much during and after the war, the value of the shares must have increased, unless the price rise was regarded as temporary. No real comment on this particular purchase is made in the Sub-Committee's Report.

Not so on John Knight's. Here the Sub-Committee said:

'In February 1920 Lever Bros. acquired a controlling interest in the business of John Knight Ltd. The £1 ordinary shares, which had received a dividend from 1913 to 1917, inclusive, of 8½ per cent, in 1918 of 9½ per cent, and in 1919 (admittedly the most prosperous year ever experienced in the soap trade) of 12½ per cent, were converted by Lever Bros. into preferred ordinary shares with a fixed cumulative preferential dividend of 25 per cent per annum. The £1 deferred shares were purchased by Lever Bros., Ltd, at £13 10*s*. per share; these shares had received dividends equal to about 15 per cent in 1913, 18 per cent from 1914 to 1917, 25 per cent in 1918 and 46½ per cent in 1919. Thus, even if the rate of dividend established in 1919 were maintained, the income of Lever Bros., Ltd, on their outlays would be less than 3½ per cent.'

In recommending the offer of Lever Bros, Ltd, to shareholders, the then chairman of John Knight, Ltd, is reported as having said:

' "Notwithstanding the very strong and satisfactory position of the Company and its prospects, I feel it is my duty to point out to the ordinary shareholders that under our existing constitution it would be very difficult, if not impossible, for us to pay a dividend of 25 per cent on the ordinary shares for the reason that after those shares receive a dividend of 6 per cent the remainder of the profits earned has to be divided equally between the deferred shares and the ordinary shares . . ." He had opposed in the past any combination with Messrs Lever Bros. He had fought them at the time of the formation of the soap trust, and his own personal feeling was, and always had been, that they should maintain their independence.

[1] Cmd. 1126, 1921. [2] Wilson, *op. cit.*, p. 246.

Therefore, he could assure them that if the offer they had received was not of such a tempting nature he would not for one moment have brought it forward but they must look at things as they were. He was afraid they were nearing the peak of high profits and, in his opinion, the shareholders would be well advised to take advantage of what was neither more nor less than a guaranteed 25 per cent.'

Whilst making all due allowances for the fact that the Chairman would naturally endeavour to persuade his shareholders that he had made a good bargain for them, even if this were not the case, we cannot avoid the conclusion that he had clearly done so.[1]

Again Lord Leverhulme had his explanation—high profits; but this time his case is less convincing, since the price he paid was high, even given the level of profits.

Between 1918 and 1921 either Lever's themselves or occasionally one of their associated companies also bought up a number of small firms. We have evidence in some of Lord Leverhulme's letters of the type of consideration taken into account when some of these purchases were made. There was apparently a rough guiding rule on the rate of return to be expected on money spent on buying these small firms, a much more generous rate than could be hoped for on the large purchases already discussed. Thus, when Crosfield's were proposing in 1920 to buy shares in Atkinson's toilet company, Lord Leverhulme in approving the transaction wrote to one of his Directors:

'You will note that the transaction shows our usual margin, namely, double what I call our bait back. Assuming that the money costs us say 8 per cent, the purchase works out approximately at 14 per cent on the purchase money, and this after deducting excess profits, so that it will be on our usual basis.'

Special attention was also paid now, as before, to getting into new markets. Thus, when Gossage's bought the Crown Perfumery Company in 1920, Lord Leverhulme welcomed the idea since the name 'could be used for their toilet preparations. Gossage's had never been a good advertising name'.

The effect of these various purchases of firms large and small was to give Lever, in Mr Wilson's words 'undisputed leadership of the British Soap Industry'[2] with, apart from the Co-operative Wholesale Society 'very few soap makers of any importance outside . . . the Lever Combine'.[3]

According to Mr Wilson's figures, home sales by Lever's and its associated companies represented in 1921 about 55 per cent of total

[1] *Report of the Sub-Committee*, p. 14. [2] *Loc. cit.*, p. 247.
[3] *Report of the Sub-Committee*, p. 17.

United Kingdom consumption. According to the Standing Committee these firms were responsible for at least 70 per cent of British soap output in 1920;[1] this, presumably, includes exports, largely the province of Crosfield's, Lever's and Gossage's, all now part of the Lever family.

The position of Lever's in 1920 is thus described in the *Report of the Sub-Committee*:

'At the present time, there are associated with Lever Bros. Ltd, throughout the world, more than 140 companies in which they hold practically the whole of the ordinary shares . . . Of the 140 companies in which Lever Bros. have pecuniary or other interests, thirty-nine manufacture soap. In thirty-three of those firms Lever Bros. have a direct pecuniary interest; in eighteen they have 100 per cent of the voting power, in thirteen they have 50 per cent or more and in only two have they less than 50 per cent of the voting power. In six others of the thirty-nine soap-making firms, companies controlled by Lever Bros. have a pecuniary interest: in five that interest is a controlling one, and in only one case has the Lever interest less than 50 per cent of the voting power. Thus, in all but three of the thirty-nine soap-making firms in which Lever Bros., Ltd, hold direct or indirect pecuniary interest, they have control. Of the total assets shown in the 1919 balance sheet, amounting to £35,000,000, the sum of £12,700,000 is invested in associated companies and £7,300,000 is due from associated companies making up the total net financial interest in associated companies to £20,000,000. Those thirty-six controlled companies, with Lever Bros., Ltd, make up the group of thirty-seven soap-making companies which we describe as the Lever Combine.'[2]

This was the process of acquisition. It remains to consider its effects, why it was not carried further, and what alternative developments might have been possible. In this Chapter we shall examine the extent to which, up to about 1921, the absorbed soap companies retained their autonomy, and how far they were controlled or helped centrally. We shall also say something about price policy in this period. The next Chapters will consider the development of the industry after 1921, the degree of competition which remained or emerged, and the ultimate integration of the combine.

To what extent, then, was policy or administration unified, up to 1921, as a result of the purchase by Lever's of previously independent companies? Generally, the firms bought up continued with their existing management and their own sales force. Lord Leverhulme, in his evidence to the Sub-Committee of the Standing Committee on

[1] *Report of the Sub-Committee*, p. 16. [2] Ibid., pp. 5–6.

Trusts, emphasized his conviction that each associated company must have its separate salesmen; goodwill could only be maintained by each firm pushing its own line. For by this time there were a number of separate lines, many branded. This did not mean that no economies could be made in the number of salesmen on amalgamation; again according to this evidence, some were achieved. Each firm had its separate trade marks, but sold at the same price as the similar articles sold by Lever's. This, as Lord Leverhulme wrote in 1921 'has always tended to keep third parties out, and we have been able better to hold the field with the mother article surrounded by a group of healthy growing children than would otherwise be the case. I have never known the mother article to suffer in value'.

Rather more surprising was the fact that, by this date, Lord Leverhulme believed that, to keep goodwill, not only separate salesmen, but also separate factories were desirable. In some few cases, mostly early, factories acquired were closed and production transferred to Port Sunlight. As already mentioned, this was done with Benjamin Brooke's factory in 1899; it was also done with Vinolia's factory at Stratford (where the lease was expiring), and Hodgson and Simpson's at Wakefield, making export soap.[1] Further, when Gossage's in 1921 bought the Crown Perfumery Company so as to use its name for advertising toilet preparations, the stock, machinery and plant were transferred to Gossage's factory at Widnes. This decision may well have been made by Gossage's.

For Lord Leverhulme himself, by this time, believed in keeping going the separate factories and even regretted his earlier closings. When asked by the Sub-Committee of the Standing Committee on Trusts whether taking over a firm had never led to the scrapping of its plant he replied: 'Yes, it did! we made that curious mistake when we took over our first business in Yorkshire. We generally keep them going. I do not know why it is, but it is so—it is not only our experience but also in America—round a works rolls a certain atmosphere and a trade grows around. Change the conditions and everything seems to go wrong.'[2] And, in a letter written in 1923, he specifically regretted having closed the factories of Hodgson and Simpson and of Vinolia, saying amongst other things, that 'the figures were always misleading as to what our Manufacturing costs would be at Port Sunlight and what they were at the individual smaller companies'. No doubt a further factor that had to be taken into account was that the firms absorbed had factories in running order, and that new

[1] Wilson, *op. cit.*, p. 121. [2] Typescript of evidence, p. 6.

investment would have been needed at Port Sunlight if much production had been transferred there.

The individual firms continued, then, to operate separately both on production and sales. As Lord Leverhulme wrote in 1921, 'I am encouraging all our Associated Companies in the United Kingdom to compete strongly with Lever Brothers in every line Lever Brothers have got but always, of course, without either frenzied competition in advertising or cut-throat competition on price, competition of efficiency being our aim and desire'. (This appears to be what Leverhulme always meant by good competition.)[1] One of the reasons for keeping this degree of independence may well have been a hope that any one of the firms might produce the next winner and another, perhaps, that Leverhulme feared to leave too great a gap in the chain of substitutes, a gap that some independent firm might enter and fill. Leverhulme, a little later, told the Chairmen of Associated Companies that they should work out and pursue their own policy, even to the point of resignation.

But, clearly, they were expected to consult Lever Brothers, and generally, so far as the large Companies were concerned, Lord Leverhulme himself, on points of major policy. If firms were in a strong financial position, they were permitted and indeed encouraged to look after their own finances. Thus, when Crosfield's were thinking in 1920 of buying shares in Atkinson's Lord Leverhulme told his Directors that 'I much prefer that the Chairman of a Company in the position of Messrs. Crosfield's should—after consultation with myself—deal with matters of this character'. But, as he had said earlier, in 1916, 'where we are responsible for financing, we must control'. Small firms were clearly subject to considerable supervision. Leverhulme would decide when the need seemed to arise what steps he should take.

Control was also exercised over the buying of raw materials. According to Leverhulme's evidence to the Sub-Committee of the Standing Committee on Trusts, no Associated Company was allowed to buy more than a certain amount of raw materials without conferring with Lever's.

Associated Companies could also always get advice and help from Lever Brothers. In the words, again, of Lord Leverhulme's letter of 1923 to the Chairmen of the Associated Companies: 'The position that Lever Brothers desire to occupy with regard to all Associated Companies is one of a sprit of helpfulness, not a spirit of tyranny. If Lever Brothers cannot help the progress and prosperity of an Asso-

[1] See p. 245.

ciated Company, then it seems to me there is no logical reason for Lever Brothers owning the shares in such Company.' And the Associated Companies could, and did, use the central research laboratory, for instance for testing the cause of losses.

It is extremely difficult, especially so long after the event, to assess whether the degree of central control and help that existed did anything much to reduce costs. The Sub-Committee of the Standing Committee on Trusts, reporting at the time, thought not. But it studied the situation too soon, before some changes had been brought about. Its findings on this point were:

'We have endeavoured to learn whether the operations of the combine have resulted in greater efficiency of production. Questions of this nature cannot be authoritatively answered without exhaustive expert examination, but we think we are justified in recording our impression, gathered from the testimony of competent witnesses, that although the acquired companies have the benefit of the advice of Lever Bros.'s experts and of their laboratory, they nevertheless, generally speaking, have continued their individual organizations and have effected little or no economy in any of the items which go to make up the cost of manufacture of soap. The same works are generally continued under the same management, the existing titles and goodwill are maintained, necessitating separate travellers, advertising and distribution. We are aware that particular economies in manufacture and distribution have been made, but generally we have been unable to satisfy ourselves that the saving resulting from the combine has been sufficient to affect materially the cost of production. In the matter of raw materials, representing the larger part of the cost of soap, the concentration of price control in the hands of Lever Bros. has not been accompanied by any arrangement for centralization of purchasing, except that Lever Bros. are consulted before purchases are made by the associated companies. Lever Bros. have a laboratory with highly-skilled experts, upon which, we are told, a sum of £20,000 is spent annually. This is a substantial sum of money, but it does not strike us as very large in proportion to the magnitude of the undertaking. Although it undoubtedly places at the disposal of the associated companies the best technical knowledge available, there does not appear to be any evidence that the *centralization* of research facilities has resulted in any appreciable economies in production. We understand that Lever Bros. have no vital patents and that research has not developed any outstanding process in the soap industry, other than hydrogenation. Some soap makers, however, whom we questioned as to the advantage of the hydrogenation process did not appear to attach any great importance to it.'[1]

[1] p. 13.

It is probably true that when the Sub-Committee reported no substantial economies had come from the union of so much of the industry. Later, however, as we shall show, drastic changes were made.

Quite possibly, also, the Sub-Committee underestimated the effect of union in modifying the practices of the firms concerned. The firms were left under their old management and with their own trade marks. Factories were not closed; it may be that, until the machinery in the factories acquired began to wear out, no real economies could have been obtained by closing them. But this is not clear; machinery was shifted when rationalization actually began in the 1930's. But their production and sales plans did not remain unaffected by union with Lever's, though no drastic change occurred. If one studies the movement of home sales of soap by the different units, it is fairly clear that, after acquisition, most of them lost sales to Lever's in the category of hard soap which Port Sunlight was able to manufacture cheaply. It is possible that production was deliberately shifted from the factories to Port Sunlight, though so many other factors operated that it is impossible to be certain.

In the manufacture of soap flakes and powder, the expanding products, but so far of much less importance than hard soap, production does not seem to have been shifted after acquisition. Since there were few producers and an expanding market, this was to be expected.

So much for economy in production. What about the effect of union on prices? Once more, we have the findings, again critical, of the Sub-Committee of the Standing Committee on Trusts. Since 1914, up to their Report in 1920, the United Kingdom Soap Manufacturers' Association had fixed '. . . directly for non-proprietary and, in our opinion, indirectly for proprietary soaps—the manufacturers' and retail minimum prices for 80 per cent of the soaps sold in the country. . . . There is virtually no competition in price'.[1] Lever's were a member of this Association, as they had not been since 1905 of its predecessor, the Soap Makers' Association. And 'the Lever Combine is responsible for 90 per cent of the output of the . . . Association, and has a majority of representatives on the Council of the Association and on each of its Committees'.[2] It achieved this control by absorbing Watson and the Crosfield group, themselves represented on the Council and the Committees.[3] Thus the process of combination secured control of the price fixing body.

The Sub-Committee concluded:

'The Lever Combine dominates the Association and is in a position substantially to determine the price at which soap shall be sold in this

[1] *Report of the Sub-Committee, op. cit.*, p. 16. [2] Ibid., p. 17. [3] Ibid., p. 6.

country. This power is not seriously affected by the potential competition of independent makers in this country, nor is it, under present conditions at any rate, affected by the possibility of keener foreign competition. The only effective limit on raising of prices is the fear of reducing demand, and this has undoubtedly been operative to prevent full use of the power of the combine. There is nothing, however, to prevent the Lever Combine from maintaining soap prices definitely higher than they would have been had the companies remained unassociated under their own financial control.'[1]

After discussing the basis of price fixing the Sub-Committee went on:

'Since the prices fixed by the Association will usually be such as to afford to the least efficient member of the Association a sufficient profit, the system of price fixing by the Association tends to protect inefficiency and to ensure added prosperity to the efficient; it prevents prices falling as low as they would under a competitive system. The benefit of any economies that may be made by a particular manufacturer is, as a rule, retained wholly by him in place of reaching the consumer.

Lever Bros. have on several occasions acquired companies on such terms as provide for the payment of dividends higher than the acquired companies have hitherto paid or were able to pay even during the period of abnormal war-time profits. Unless, as a result of these acquisitions, Lever Bros. are able to increase the profits by:

(a) expanding the business and/or,

(b) effecting economies in production and/or in distribution—one or both of which they doubtless hope to do—the prices of one or more of the commodities produced or dealt in by the businesses in which Lever Bros. are interested will, if dividends are not to be reduced, have to be maintained at a figure higher than would have been necessary if the companies had not been so acquired. In most of the other businesses of Lever Bros., probably prices could not be arbitrarily maintained, but in the case of the soap trade we have shown that Lever Bros. can maintain prices higher than would have been possible under a competitive system. . . .

We recognize that Lever Bros. Ltd, have had, in the extension of their control, motives other than the mere raising of prices, and the prices have not been raised to the highest possible limit; the Association has always borne in mind the importance of not reducing demand. The price of soap, however, is now definitely higher than it would be if there were real competition of price between the soap makers, and over an average of years has been higher than is necessary to provide reasonable profits.'[2]

[1] *Report of the Sub-Committee*, *op. cit*., p. 17. [2] Ibid., pp. 17–18.

The Sub-Committee, then, were highly critical. Mr Wilson, a much more sympathetic investigator, concludes on this issue of the level of prices. 'On a short view, the Committee were probably right. . . . There is not much doubt that the cost of soap to the public at this time included a contribution towards the cost of keeping afloat a number of other ventures very dear to Leverhulme's heart—particularly his West African projects.'[1] Ultimately, Leverhulme's faith in these projects was proved to be well founded.

There can be no doubt that the combine was intended to prevent 'cut-throat competition in price' between its members. As Lord Leverhulme wrote in 1922, when Erasmic (controlled by Crosfield's) prepared to bring out a solid dentrifice to compete with Gibbs: 'I do feel that the price should be the same and the weight the same . . . I want us all to compete strenuously on everything except price. It is really such poverty of imagination to be only able to compete on price and takes us back into the ruts of the very worst days of the soap trade forty years ago . . .

'. . . What Erasmic intend to do by putting the article on at less than one and sixpence is to cut into Messrs Gibbs' trade which has been built up by a large expenditure in advertising. I am positive that you do not mean this in its full significance, for if you did we should cease to be a family and become a group of belligerants.' As this quotation shows, price cutting within the concern was not wholly stopped; a somewhat similar example, for soap flakes, will be mentioned later.[2] Broadly speaking, however, short-period price competition between the associated firms, and particularly price discrimination concentrated on a few lines only, was successfully eliminated. It was this that Lord Leverhulme appeared to mean by cut-throat competition. His line of thought would indicate that he would not have objected to price reduction made possible by long-period reduction in costs.

Moreover, as will be shown in the next Chapter, whatever may have been the position when the Sub-Committee reported, potential competition from outsiders within the country and keener foreign competition soon limited the power of the combine to fix prices.

[1] *Op. cit.*, Vol. I, p. 248. [2] See p. 256.

CHAPTER 5

The Period of Consolidation and Rationalization 1921 onwards

DURING the inter-war years the nature of the soap market changed radically. Before the 1914–18 war the main product had been hard soap, accounting in 1913 (with the relatively unimportant soft soap) for nearly four-fifths of the weight of Lever's production in the British Isles. Soap flakes and soap powders had been launched on the market, but had not yet captured much of it.[1] By the early 1920's, however, hard and soft soap accounted for only about two-thirds by weight of Lever's home output, due to the increase in the output of flakes, powders and scourers. The efficiency of the powders was greatly increased during the inter-war years and their output expanded to meet consumers' demands for products which made washing easier; the output of hard soap was further reduced.

The table opposite shows the changes in output for all soap producers, and the relative importance of the different types. The Lever family had a rather higher percentage in the inter-war years, both of flakes and powder, than the country as a whole; but their broad pattern was not very different.

By 1938, certainly, by far the greater part of the output was branded, usually by manufacturers, occasionally by retailers. For hard soap about two-thirds of the total, and for soap powder, flakes and toilet soap as much as from 80 to 90 per cent was branded.[2]

After the 1939–45 war the big increase came in powders, and notably in blended powders of the new synthetic variety, some made from natural vegetable or animal oils and fats, others derived from a petroleum base. In 1952 these synthetics accounted for 22 per cent by weight of all domestic detergents sold in Great Britain. In the

[1] See p. 231.

[2] James B. Jefferys, *The Distribution of Consumer Goods*, p. 263.

TABLE I

Production of Soap in the United Kingdom

	Amount 000 tons					Percentage of Total					Percentage Change in Tonnage	
	1924	1930	1935	1937[1]	1951	1924	1930	1935	1937	1951	1924–1937	1937–1951
Hard	316	295	268	258	184	68	65	54	49	32	− 18	− 29
Soft	15	16	19	19	12	3	4	4	4	2	+ 27	− 37
Toilet	24	20	33	35	68	5	4	7	7	12	+ 46	+ 94
Abrasive	29[2]	19	23	26	62	6	4	5	5	11	− 10	+139
Flakes	..	..	42	53	32	..	..	8	10	6	..	− 40
Powders	..	..	107	123	198	..	..	21	23	34	..	+ 61
Flakes and Powders ..	85	94	149	176	230	18	21	29	33	40	+107	+ 31
Other	..	9	6	10	15	..	2	1	2	3	..	+ 50
Total	469	453	498	524	571	100	100	100	100	100	+ 12	+ 9

[1] Census for reduced number of firms and excludes Northern Ireland. [2] Doubtful estimate.

Sources: Years 1924, 1930 and 1935—Final Report on the Fifth Census of Production 1935, Part III, Chemical and Allied Trades, HMSO, 1940, p. 331, Table V C.

Years 1937 and 1951 —Report on the Census of Production for 1951, Vol. II, trade 'J', Soap, Candles and Glycerine, HMSO, 1955, Table II.

United States, which took the lead in the synthetic market after the war, they accounted for 43 per cent.[1]

These technical changes had a considerable effect on the structure of the industry. First, success, even more than before the war, went to the firms that could spot which new products consumers would accept. Secondly, they made more difficult the position of the small firms. These did not, if the Soap Makers' Directory is correct, leave the industry in greater numbers than before until very recently, when synthetics were well established; indeed, fewer gave up per year in the periods between 1920 and 1953 than had in any period up to 1920.[2] But by about the early 1950's far more firms per year began to be recorded as leaving the industry. Fewer firms per year, however, entered the industry from 1920 to 1930 than in the years from 1898 up to the war; and after 1930 the rate of entry fell off further and very sharply. The net result was that the number of firms in Great Britain recorded by the Directory, which had been 280 in 1920, rose to 296 in 1930 and, thereafter, fell steadily to 189 in 1955.

The main reason why the changes have discouraged small firms has been the cost of pioneering research into new materials and into new types of soaps, powders and detergents, and of introductory advertising. On the whole it was the large firms that invented the new types and taught the new technical skills to their employees. Until enough people had been taught, there were none available for the small firms to hire. Economies of scale certainly exist even when the product is established, most notably in the chemical industry to produce the materials for the synthetics. But, if the detergents industry ceases changing so rapidly, the smaller firms may once more feel it worthwhile to come in in greater numbers, to produce the new detergents; it is the expense of establishing a new product that they cannot face.

Thirdly, the new products strengthened the advantage of the north in the production of powders, since both chemicals and petroleum products were available in that locality.

Finally, they brought new and powerful competition for established soap making firms, first from the American soap industry in the form of Procter and Gamble, and then, potentially at least, from the chemical manufacturer who could relatively easily turn to the new synthetics.

[1] 'Synthetic Detergents'—speech delivered by Sir Geoffrey Heyworth at the annual general meeting of Unilever Limited, June 10, 1953, printed by Unilever Ltd for private circulation, p. 9. Toilet soaps are excluded from the calculation and allowance made for the low synthetic content of some products.

[2] See Diagram p. 273.

Lever's had to adapt themselves not only to these changes, but also to the necessity of working out a form of control appropriate to an organization as large as they had become. Moreover, in 1925, Lord Leverhulme died, and was succeeded by professional managers not themselves owning all the ordinary shares, as had Leverhulme.

In 1921, at the beginning of the period we are considering, Lever's controlled about 55 per cent of home soap consumption and about 70 per cent of output. For the moment, the only important outsider was the Co-operative Wholesale Society. Thereafter, although new competition developed, it was met not mainly by the acquisition of the competing firms, but by the development of the new forms of detergents already mentioned and by the consolidation and rationalization of the Lever combine. By the middle 1930's the American soap firm of Procter and Gamble, which had bought and developed Hedley's, a small British firm, was going ahead more rapidly than Lever's. Another important firm had been added to the industry and a definite oligopolistic situation emerged. The idea of a monopoly in the home soap industry had been dropped. The first ten years or more of this period, up to the appearance on the British market of Procter and Gamble, provide an almost classic case of a price leader, but one vulnerable to competition.

To begin with, Lever's were, in any case, prevented from buying up any further home soap companies by the financial difficulties in which they found themselves after 1921. There was one exception, Erasmic, making toilet soaps, which came into the group in 1922 as a subsidiary of Crosfield's. The financial difficulties were due partly to the slump itself; but they were the result also of the orgy of acquisitions of new companies in which Lord Leverhulme indulged after the war, some on behalf of Lever Brothers, some initially for himself. Some of these firms, notably the Niger Company, were bought at inflated prices; many of them were outside the soap industry proper, and some of them were not even very obviously within the sphere of soap, margarine and their raw materials and outlets.[1]

By the time the financial difficulties had been largely surmounted, new competition had again developed, both from the British Soap Company and from the Palmolive Company of America. Competition from the first firm was, for the last time, met in the old way, by acquisition. The new competition developed after 1921, when the British Oil and Cake Mills set up the British Soap Company. At that time both oil milling and margarine production were depressed, but soap looked profitable under the umbrella protection of Lever's. The

[1] Wilson, *op. cit.*, Vol. I, Ch. XVIII.

new firm had to break into the market, and did so with with 'New Pin' household soap, supported by advertising and gift schemes, similar to those which Lever's had tried to drop. Their sales until 1923 were small; but by 1925 they had reached about 34,000 tons, more than three-fifths of the quantity of hard and soft soap that Lever's themselves were selling; by this time the Oil and Cake Mills were almost certainly losing money on their soap business. Lever's own sales of this type of soap were particularly hard hit, falling by about a sixth between 1922 and 1925, almost all the decrease coming in 1925; other firms in the combine were much less affected, and total soap sales in the country almost certainly increased during this period of competition. Lever's tried in 1924 to negotiate with the British Soap Company to stop the violent competition, but no agreement could be arrived at. Possibly the Board of the British Oil and Cake Mills wished to be absorbed by Lever's, and had pushed their soap sales in order to induce Lever's to buy them out. In 1925, certainly, Lever's acquired the Ordinary Shares of the British Oil and Cake Mills, in exchange for their own 20 per cent Preference shares. This ended the competition. Sales of New Pin Soap were immediately cut; the British Soap factory sold no more than 14,000 tons in 1926, compared with nearly 34,000 tons in the previous year, and in 1927 and 1928 only about 6,000 tons annually. Soap production in their Hull factory finally stopped in 1934. The British Soap Company was acquired at least as much, probably more, in order to stop its competition in soap as in order to secure more of the raw materials the combine used.

Lever's were less successful in preventing competition from imports of 'Palmolive' soap from America, which was taking some of their market in toilet soap. This soap, wrapped, marketed in a standard colour and perfume instead of the assortments which were then usual, and heavily advertised, did for toilet soaps what Sunlight had done for hard soaps. Lever's tried to meet this threat by a union with the Palmolive Company of America. They could not bring these negotiations to a successful conclusion, and therefore tried, not wholly successfully, to meet the competition by putting out somewhat similar brands of soap.[1]

Before further strong competition developed Lord Leverhulme died, in 1925, and the company, instead of being dominated by one man, who both owned the ordinary shares and took the crucial decisions, was transformed to one run by professional managers, responsible to other shareholders and having to consider very carefully the costs and consequences to others of their decisions. The change

[1] Wilson, *op. cit.*, Vol. I, p. 280.

in organization, to be briefly described presently, had begun before Leverhulme's death and had many other results than its effect on the acquisition of factories. In fact only two more home soap firms came into the concern after the British Soap Company. Zog, a very small one, was bought in 1926. T. H. Harris, a firm largely non-competitive with Lever's, had been controlled since 1920 by the African and Eastern Trading Company and came into the Lever group incidentally when the African and Eastern in 1929 united with the Niger Company, already bought by Lever's.

In the changed market situation already described[1] it was no longer worthwhile acquiring more small firms, as now they had nothing much to offer Lever's. Most of them made hard soap, and hard soap was clearly a declining market, in which Lever's already had surplus capacity. Lever's had also already developed a nationwide distributive trade and so no longer sought established firms in new parts of the country whose contacts they could develop.

More powerful competition, however, developed from two strong organizations, first the Co-operative Wholesale Society, and then Procter and Gamble of the United States.

The end of the New Pin competition, which about coincided with Leverhulme's death, saw the recrudescence of the expansion of sales by the Co-operative Wholesale Society. After a period of relative stability they rose by about a quarter between 1925 and 1929, while those of the Scottish CWS increased by over one-half.[2]

Yet, in spite of the competition with Palmolive soap, with the Co-operative Wholesale Society, and with the somewhat larger number of small firms,[3] the Lever family, which had controlled about 55 per cent of home sales of soap in 1921, slightly improved on this percentage both in 1924 and in 1927. It shared in the general improvement from the slump of 1921 to 1924, and held its ground in the more stagnant years from 1924 to 1927, apart from the temporary loss of trade in 1925 due to the competition of New Pin. And from 1927 to 1930, when again total sales scarcely increased, Lever's, strengthened by the addition of Harris, sold about 9 per cent more, so increasing their share of the market to just over three-fifths (it was probably even a little higher in 1929). By then they were going ahead rapidly both in flakes and in powders.

Thereafter, both Lever's and the CWS lost relative ground to a further important competitor, Procter and Gamble, the largest soap manufacturer in the United States. In 1930 this American firm bought up T. H. Hedley & Co. of Newcastle, an old-established but

[1] See p. 246. [2] Wilson, *op. cit.*, Vol. I, p. 303. [3] See p. 248.

hitherto small firm. Partly, Procter and Gamble saw profitable outlets in the soap business in England for the new soap powders; partly, they hoped to divert some of Lever's attention from the North American trade in edible fats by hitting them where it hurt most. They added two large factories to the original one at Newcastle, one at Manchester in 1932, the second at Purfleet in 1938. Hedley's sales, small before Procter and Gamble took them over, had by 1936 risen to about 60,000 tons; thereafter the increase was more gradual; in 1939 they were selling 70,000 tons.

Because of this expansion, and in spite of the decline at this time in the number of small firms,[1] the Lever family scarcely shared in the resumed increase in total soap sales after 1930. Although trade was depressed, real wages were rising; and total consumption of soap in the United Kingdom increased between 1930 and 1938 by 90,000 tons, or by just over 20 per cent. Sales by the Lever family rose only by 7,000 tons, less than 3 per cent. The net result was that in 1938 Lever's controlled not much more than a half of total soap sales in the United Kingdom, compared with over three-fifths in 1930. The Co-operative Wholesale Society held about one-eighth of the trade in 1938, a little higher than it had held in 1925, a little lower than its peak share in 1930; by 1938 Hedley's also had captured one-eighth of the total. That left a quarter for other producers.

Lever's made no attempt in this period to acquire the soap interests of the CWS or of Procter and Gamble in this country so as to stop their competition. In any case, it would probably have been impossible to do so. Certainly it appeared more profitable for the concern to develop in other, easier, directions. Procter and Gamble, the CWS and the Palmolive Company of America were all strong firms that might be expected to pursue competitive policies that looked to the long-run situation rather than to the immediate future only. Price wars and what Leverhulme would have called 'cut-throat competition' could not be ruled out; but it could be expected to be intermittent rather than endemic, and directed to some specific purpose, such as launching a new product which it was hoped would capture a wide market. The only way to meet this competition ultimately would be to reduce long-period costs and provide improved types of detergents and an effective selling organization.

Before dealing with the reorganization of the business that began in the inter-war years, a reference must be made to the situation after the 1939–45 war. This was the period when the post-war synthetic powders were being introduced. Here Procter and Gamble, less ham-

[1] See p. 248.

pered in the United States than Unilever in England by war-time difficulties, took the lead, and their subsidiary, Hedley, went ahead fast. This created a new situation, rapidly changing, with at times intense competition both in advertising and in price. Competition of this intense type can hardly be permanent; but too little information is so far available outside the firms themselves to make description or comment useful.

To return, then, to the changes made in the Lever group of home soap factories to adjust to the situation which developed after the 1914–18 war. Meeting the new competition and cutting out waste involved some integration of the companies producing soap at home, and, in the end, a drastic reduction in their number and in the number of sales organizations, of factories and of lines of detergents sold. But before this could be dealt with, the central control of the Lever combine needed reorganization. Much of this, of course, concerned activities outside the home soap trade and so falls outside the scope of this study. But some brief reference must be made to the changes. After the acquisitions following the 1914–18 war, the concern was becoming too large to be run, as in effect it had been before that war, by one man. Leverhulme had to accept this fact, that there had to be, in Mr Wilson's words, 'the substitution of measures for men'.[1] The reorganization of the central control of the business, begun during Leverhulme's lifetime, was pushed much further during the Chairmanship of his succesor, D'Arcy Cooper, particularly after the great merger with the European margarine producers, now amalgamated into the Margarine Unie, which was negotiated in 1929. This combine held very substantial soap interests in Europe, as well as interests in the field of oils and fats, the raw materials common to soap and margarine. The arrangement with Lever's had originally been intended to separate out their respective interests, giving margarine to Unie and soap to Lever's. But this proved impracticable for a number of reasons, an important one being this use of common raw materials. Instead there was what, in effect though not quite in legal form, was a merger with the common name Unilever, but an English and a Dutch parent company, with identical Boards of Directors and working as a unity.[2]

This merger, crucial though it was for Lever Brothers as a whole, had less immediate effect on home soap production and sales, since

[1] Wilson, *op. cit.*, Vol. I, p. 273.

[2] In 1937 a further general financial reorganization led to the titles of the concerns being changed to Lever Brothers and Unilever Limited, and Lever Brothers and Unilever NV, and in 1952 the names were changed back to Unilever Limited and Unilever NV for the sake of simplicity.

Unie owned no soap factories in the British Isles. Its importance, in the field covered by this study, lay, firstly, in the general administrative reorganization of the business, which affected home soap production, and, secondly, in the new experience introduced both by people manufacturing soap abroad and by people who had organized the rationalization of margarine production in Europe.

Reorganization did not stop, but continued, both during D'Arcy Cooper's Chairmanship and during that of Mr Geoffrey Heyworth (now Lord Heyworth), who succeeded him as Chairman in 1941.

From 1923 manufacturing companies in the Lever family in the United Kingdom were grouped by type of product instead of by areas as before, one group being soap. First a committee, then an Executive, both under the Chairmanship of a Director of Lever Brothers, and later of Unilever, exercised general control over the companies in the group. When this rearrangement was started, it provided more formal arrangements for supervision and for the co-ordination of the policy of the different firms than had previously existed. Besides the management group there have been developed central advisory or service departments, dealing with a number of subjects, including advertising, buying, finance, marketing and technical matters and research. The degree of control from the centre has varied considerably; during the process of integration (to be described shortly) much had to be decided centrally. A great deal is now delegated to the individual companies and decentralized, though three crucial matters are subject to central control.[1]

Up to the early 1920's, as already shown,[2] the Associated Companies maintained their own factories and their own sales forces, but had on major decisions to consult Leverhulme. And Leverhulme intervened when he saw advantages in doing so. In the difficult period following 1921, the soap factories, unlike many of his other activities at this time, were making money; but economies had to be sought there too. 'Leverhulme turned his attention to the question of industrial efficiency in the individual factories, bringing to the task a black energy which resembled only in its intensity the driving enthusiasm of his earlier career.'[3] He concentrated on the internal organization of each factory, particularly of Port Sunlight. For he still did not believe that the way to seek economies was to close some factories.[4]

Gradually, after the central control of the concern had been more formalized, the operations of the various home soap companies began to be integrated. While Leverhulme was still alive and the system

[1] See p. 264. [2] See pp. 239-42. [3] Wilson, *op. cit.*, Vol. I, p. 275. [4] See p. 240.

of Committee control being worked out, it was laid down that both the amount spent on advertising and central policy as regards it should be controlled from headquarters.[1] That such control was not fully effective, however, was shown by the setting up, in the process of reorganization which followed Leverhulme's death, of a further committee to examine advertising policy. The committee reiterated that advertising allocations should be determined centrally, advertisement space bought centrally and that advertisements should not clash.[2]

Again while Leverhulme was alive, he attempted to reduce the rivalries which, in spite of their financial union, still continued in the export business between Lever's, Crosfield's and Gossage's, the main exporters, by appointing a single head for the export businesses of the three firms, with an Export Trade Board to help him.[3] Once more, further steps had to be taken later. In 1928, United Exporters Limited was set up to manage the export trade from Lever House in London and stop the 'unnecessary amount of fighting between the various associated companies'.[4] which still apparently continued in spite of the earlier efforts to prevent it. Manufacturing was to be undertaken either at Port Sunlight or at Crosfield's or Gossage's factories 'as circumstances might require'.[5] Some savings in office expenses were achieved by this change as well as the desired aim of reducing competition. Later, after the war, exports of all Unilever products from the United Kingdom came to be marketed by one export organization, Unilever Export, Ltd, drawing the products it sells from the factories run by the various United Kingdom executives.

A third development introduced in 1929 was the establishment of a Technical Committee charged among other duties with evolving a programme of research and of arrangements to secure co-operation between the technical experts of the various companies.[6] It operated for two years, and was then succeeded by a new advisory department, set up in the general reorganization following the merger with Margarine Unie; this department had the same duties as the old one.

Throughout this period, however, certainly until the early 1930's, competition between associated companies continued, in the sense that many offered similar lines, not always at the same prices. For instance, with soapflakes, the Board of Lever's doubted whether the associated companies ought to be permitted to sell flakes of a quality similar to Lux, so heavily advertised. But 'the pressure from the companies was too strong to be resisted. By the end of 1926, the rival

[1] Wilson, *op. cit.*, Vol. I, pp. 271–3. [2] Ibid., p. 300. [3] Ibid., p. 271. [4] Ibid., p. 303. [5] Ibid., p. 304. [6] Ibid., p. 300.

flakes of associated companies were on sale, the Board bowed the knee to the inevitable, and reduced the price of Lux flakes to compete'.[1]

This was the period, too, of intensified competition from the Co-operative Wholesale Society and of stagnant sales by the Lever group. Under these conditions Lever's found irksome the rules of the United Kingdom Soap Makers' Association which prevented price cutting. Some of their smaller firms complained that they could not get trade unless they were allowed to compete with the prices charged by firms outside the Association. These were the firms making hard soap, faced by competition from small as well as large outsiders. The Association, already inactive, decided to disband. Lever's set up a Sales Executive Committee wholly within their group, to be responsible to the Board on sales policy. This body was to try to reduce competition within the concern while permitting its members to fight outsiders. Since the larger firms, with their proprietary lines, were less interested than the small firms in public contracts and 'own-name' soaps, they were told to stand aside here. Districts were allocated to the small firms and prices for these districts fixed by the new Committee; each firm within the Lever group tabled the names of their customers to prevent competition within the group. Thus, by this date, headquarters normally fixed the price levels for the different types of products.

These were relatively small matters, however, compared with the controversial question as to how many sales forces, factories and lines of detergents should be kept going in the detergent industry at home.

By the late 1920's it was becoming clear that the decline in the demand for hard soap[2] was making redundant a number of the older factories producing this product. For the expanding market for the new detergents it was better to increase output in the areas where production could be carried on most cheaply; and this appeared to be at Port Sunlight and Warrington, near the ports and near, for instance, the large Cheshire factory of Imperial Chemical Industries which provided soda ash and caustic soda.

This forced on the concern reconsideration of the policy, so strongly believed in by the founder of the company, of keeping intact the individual entity of its constituent companies, both as production and as sales units.[3] The second Chairman, in his earlier years of office, had apparently not made up his mind on this question. On the one hand, there were 'far too many packs', and 'the ideal position would be to

[1] Wilson, *op. cit.*, Vol. I, p. 301. [2] See p. 246. [3] See p. 240.

concentrate our energies on about five soaps and four powders'.[1] But this would mean closing down the small factories; and the great objection to this 'was the fear that the goodwill of the products of the associated companies would be lost if the companies did not manufacture them themselves and that the goodwill would not be recovered by the remaining companies. The smaller companies also served to protect the larger ones by keeping others out'.[1] These were Lord Leverhulme's arguments some years earlier. The new Chairman was, however, 'ready to close down a factory, on favourable terms, which was not wanted'.[1]

About the time of the merger with Margarine Unie it was decided to proceed, though slowly, with a policy of rationalization. The merger had brought into the business executives who had already organized rationalization in the margarine business in Europe, and it was followed by a reorganization of the central control of the business and the establishment in 1929 of an active Home Soap Executive of three members, C. W. Barnish, L. H. Hartland Swann and Geoffrey Heyworth,[2] which was the body which planned the new policy.

As early as 1929 estimates were being prepared of the economies which might be achieved by ceasing to manufacture soap at specific factories, economies both in manpower and in freight charges. Some clearly had to be closed. But by 1931, when the Great Depression was well under way, a more ambitious policy had been decided on. In a cogent paper delivered by Mr Geoffrey Heyworth to a Conference of Overseas Managers, it was emphasized that the main reason for the proposed change was the necessity of developing a streamlined selling organization to meet competition. At the time, as the paper said, there were forty-nine soap manufacturing companies within the concern in the United Kingdom, with forty-eight separate sales organizations, of which the vast majority handled household soap. Each sold its product in competition with the others and 'control at headquarters had been confined mainly to fixing price levels for the different types of products, to the amount of advertising appropriation and to the production of an agreed final trading profit'. For the future this would not do; 'we must be able to repel the inroads of the Co-operative movement with the minimum of expenditure; to deal quickly with any newcomer that may enter the field, and be ready to market on the most up-to-date lines each advance in soapmaking development'. As already mentioned, this was the period when new types of detergents were being introduced.[3]

[1] Wilson, *op. cit.*, Vol. I, p. 302. [2] Ibid., Vol. II, p. 345. [3] See p. 246.

'From this point of view it has been evident to us that we could not expect to increase our selling efficiency very much further along the line of individual company development. The complications of dealing with so many products and so many selling forces will be evident to you all, as will the difficulties of obtaining the maximum advertising result when so many lines have to be supported. We have, therefore, now mapped out a programme for the future on a new basis.

'Simplification and concentration are its keynotes, and we have based this simplification on meeting the requirements of the consumer.'

Mr Heyworth explained that the Board had set down a maximum number of important uses for detergents in modern households, based on a study of consumer requirements. There were eight of these; and within each use 'we feel that we must offer the housewife a choice rather than let a competitor do so. And we have provisionally placed the maximum of choice at three', in any one use. 'It is our idea that the three products offered for the same use shall, first of all, be substantially different in appearance, and capable of a distinctive advertising and selling appeal . . . Each product in the same field will stress its own selling points to the full limit, without regard to the feelings of its competitors within the family, and each will be improved in efficiency as our experts find ways and means of so doing. The only restriction will be in the number, which, as I have already said, we do not visualize as ever exceeding three, and the advertising appropriation, which will be based on the financial result.'

After indicating the products selected to retain and develop in each group, a selection which had already been tentatively made except for the hard soap group, Mr Heyworth then outlined the programme for selling organizations to give effect to the scheme. 'We are quite clear that the best results can only be achieved in proprietary selling when the salesman is a specialist at it, and when he is able to put his full force behind one line for a particular purpose. In other words, we accept it as a first principle that the same man cannot sell both Rinso and Persil effectively, but he can sell Rinso in the family wash field and Lux in the fine fabric field. We believe that under modern conditions somewhere between six and ten lines are the maximum that one salesman can handle effectively and maintain dealer interest for, and that he can only handle this number if they do not clash with one another.'

Therefore, with three products in each field, and no clashing, three national selling organizations would ultimately be required for proprietary articles. These were to consist of the existing Lever organization and amalgamations of other companies to form two other such groups, with at least 150 salesmen each. In some of the fields, however, it would clearly be a long time before three products were being sold nationally. Choices would not be offered so long as concentration on one product appeared better.

In addition to these three organizations to deal with the advertised leaders there were to be two other organizations arranged by similar amalgamations to cater for existing 'miscellaneous trade based on house goodwill, price and catering to specialized trade requirements. . . . These companies will sell substantially without advertising support, and will work towards the simplification of their price lists. This will be achieved by super-imposing gradually on the existing brands which have area acceptance only, a few leaders which can be sold nationally in this field'.

Specialized organizations were also being built up to 'make more effective the efforts of different companies' in providing soap for industrial use.

Finally, similar developments were taking place on the toilet preparations side (a field outside Mr Geoffrey Heyworth's paper). One organization ought not to cover both fields.

This was the outline of a deliberate plan to reorganize the selling and manufacture of soap by Lever's throughout the country so as to provide cheaply and efficiently what the consumer wanted or could be persuaded to want. The emphasis throughout was on selecting and selling the right products. It was here that the large organization had an opportunity of deliberately choosing a limited number of products which they believed consumers would accept and of pushing these and dropping others. They did not merely have to follow consumers' already expressed wants, as tends to happen when a large number of firms are competing one with another. They could to some extent mould these wants.

In the soap industry selling was the manufacturers' direct problem; over three-quarters of the total soap output in this country in 1938 went direct from manufacturer to retailer.[1] Selling costs, also, were substantial as against manufacturing costs, and could more easily be altered. No figures are available of their relative importance. But, for the soap trade as a whole, manufacturers' distribution costs were estimated to average about a quarter of their sales revenue in 1938, after considerable rationalization had been achieved, rather more for heavily advertised articles, considerably less for soap sold

[1] James B. Jefferys, *The Distribution of Consumer Goods*, p. 262.

unadvertised in a local market.[1] The cost of oils and fats, the main raw materials, may have been of about the same order of magnitude or a little lower. That leaves about half revenue to cover not only manufacturing costs but also the remaining soap-making materials, packing materials, and accounting and administration.

Selling, it was hoped, would be more effective with fewer selling forces and fewer lines. But, besides that, as discussions within the organization made clear, it was hoped to achieve economies both in selling and in manufacture. The economies of selling would result from fewer lines to advertise, from a smaller number of competing salesmen, and from a reduction of transport costs, since each client would get his soap from the nearest factory making it. The economies in production would be of two sorts. First, there would be fewer, larger, factories, so that the less efficient ones equipped to make hard soap could be closed or used for other purposes. Secondly, those that remained would produce longer runs than before, since the total number of lines sold was to be reduced. This would make possible economies of scale in delivery, possibly in buying and certainly in transporting raw materials, and, on the production side, in boiling, in stamping soap mechanically, and in packing. The last economy might be substantial.

Mr Heyworth's paper indicated the direction in which it was proposed to move and did not contemplate rapid integration of the home soap companies. The shortest period for achieving the aim there set forth, of three national selling organizations for household detergents, each selling not more than one product in each of eight groups, was put at five years, the longest at ten. But it was recognized that the programme would need modification as it was introduced, in the light of experience and of changing market and technical conditions. In fact, as will be shown, the reduction in the number of lines and of operating units took much longer to achieve than was contemplated in 1931, and would, almost certainly, but for the war, have taken longer still.

The process was bound to be slow. Much work was required to translate the general decision to rationalize into specific decisions as to which lines and which factories were to be retained for soap production. The crucial point was to assess the merits of the different lines; this had been begun before 1931, but not completed, especially for hard soap. Then the favoured ones had to be pushed, the others dropped. In practice, lines were rarely dropped, except during the war, until they showed definite signs of loss of popularity.

[1] Jefferys, *op. cit.*, p. 265.

Again, before production in any factory was stopped, laborious calculations had to be made on the probable costs of manufacture and of transport in one factory rather than in two, allowing for interest and depreciation on any extra equipment which might be needed in the factory which was to take on the extra work, and for the accelerated pensions or compensation which would be paid to workers in the closed factory who could not be transferred. Unless these calculations showed a profit, no factory was closed or turned over to producing other things. But even if they did, production there might be continued. Account had to be taken of any likely loss of goodwill through abolishing a brand. And the calculations might be wrong; no decision to close a factory was ever taken unless a substantial saving was shown, thus giving an ample margin of error.

Further, some account had to be taken of local opposition. The workers had to be interviewed individually, arrangements made to transfer them to other areas, or help given them to find new jobs where they were, and arrangements made to pension off the older workers or to pay lump sum compensation to the younger. On one occasion it was decided that 'the determining factor' in the speed with which trade should be transferred away from a factory should be 'to make such a gradual one as to prevent anybody making a general issue of the matter'.

And, in addition, the Boards of the Associated Companies had to be got, if possible, to agree to the changes, which might involve their losing their independence, and might be thought to endanger their Preference shareholders. If they would not agree, they had to be forced to do so, as, of course, they could be, since Lever's generally owned all, though occasionally only a majority, of their Ordinary shares. This process might take a great deal of time. Thus, as early as 1929, discussions began on the desirability of closing the two Gossage factories at Blackstock Street, Liverpool, and at Widnes, and by early 1930 a plan had been worked out. Because of local opposition, it was at first decided to close only the first and transfer the trade to the second. By the time production there had stopped in 1931, Lever's were, however, convinced that it was uneconomic to undertake additional capital expenditure at Widnes when ample surplus capacity existed at the other Merseyside factories in the Lever family, and decided to revert to the original plan to close Widnes. Gossage's Board still objected. Since, by then, it was clear that the same problem might arise in other cases, it was suggested, early in 1932, that there should be an agreement between Lever's, Crosfield's, Gossage's, Knight's, Watson's, Pear's and Gibbs' designed to protect their Preference Shareholders by pooling the home trading profits of these companies and providing for each Company to be compensated against capital losses consequent upon factories being closed. Some Associated Companies wanted further concessions and, since Lever's thought the plan anyhow favoured other shareholders at the expense of those of Lever's, the idea was dropped. Lever's did, however, guarantee Gossage's Preference shares. None the less, Gossage's Board persisted in their opposition to closing Widnes. At an Extraordinary General Meeting two additional Directors from Lever's were appointed to Gossage's Board and a resolution passed to accelerate the closing down; by the autumn of 1932, the transfer was taking place, and by early 1933 the factory was closed. The delay, it was estimated in the middle of 1932, was costing from £500 to £600 a week.

And, finally, the process could not be carried out too rapidly without disrupting the efficiency of the organization and the effectiveness of its relation with consumers. After each act of rationalization a pause was needed to rebuild contact with consumers and to re-assess the policy in the light of the existing technical and market situation.

The process of integration and rationalization was a complicated one. It involved three interrelated processes, the reduction in the number of lines, the amalgamation of sales forces and the closing of factories or their diversion to other uses. The number of lines could be, and often was, reduced without stopping factories or amalgamating sales forces; but these two more drastic changes were also necessary for full efficiency. And full efficiency had then to be developed in the new, reduced number of operating units. Amalgamation did not need to be, and often was not either simultaneous or identical on the production and the selling sides. Here an organization as large as Lever's had more flexibility than was possible for a smaller organization. It could more easily concentrate on and push the more hopeful lines while continuing to sell for a time the lines that were to be dropped.

The process began by stopping production in a number of the now redundant factories making hard soap, and by a gradual rolling together of their sales forces, and a very great reduction in their number of packs. This would have been bound to happen in due course in an industry with a large number of independent firms, but perhaps more slowly. Rationalization in selling also went on within the sales forces which remained intact, such as those of Port Sunlight and of Crosfield's at Warrington.

The war enormously speeded up the reduction in the number of brands and of salesmen, and some further factories were diverted from soap production. Some of the amalgamations in sales forces were regarded, at any rate to begin with, as temporary war-time measures. Others, such as the merging in 1940 of the selling forces of Crosfield's, Watson's and Gossage's, had been planned for a long time but postponed. The reduction in the number of sales outlets and of factories went on after the war.

In outline, then, what happened was this. In 1929 there were forty-nine companies and factories producing soaps in the United Kingdom and the Irish Free State, of which two were in Scotland and one in Ireland. They sold both to the distributive trade and to what were called industrial buyers, of which laundries were the most important.

By the outbreak of war, in the soap trade proper, only nine factories still operated in England, one in Scotland and one in Ireland. By 1956 there remained only five factories in England; of these Watson's at Leeds, though they still make soft soap, concentrate mainly on toilet preparations; another produces only small quantities of very specialized products. Of the three main soap factories two, Lever's own factory at Port Sunlight and Crosfield's at Warrington, also manufactured the new non-soap detergents; John Knight, of London, did not. There were no Lever soap factories in Scotland and only one in Ireland.

By the outbreak of war, too, the number of selling organizations, excluding cosmetics, had been reduced to ten, dealing with both the distributive and non-distributive trade, and one additional sales force dealing only with the non-distributive trade. By 1956 there remained only three companies handling the distributive trade proper, Lever's, the amalgamation of Crosfield, Watson and Gossage, and the amalgamation of Hudson and Knight. The industrial trade had been taken away from them and concentrated in one selling organization.

The ten pre-war companies in the ordinary distributive trade handled about 250 brands, just over 150 being hard soap, between twenty and twenty-five each soap flakes, soap powders and toilet soaps and the remainder mostly soft soap, shaving soap and scourers. Over 500 brands were sold to industrial users. By 1956 there remained only two ordinary hard soaps, Sunlight, sold by Lever Brothers and Puritan, sold by Crosfield, Watson and Gossage. Only one hard carbolic soap remained, Lifebuoy, and one soapflakes, Lux, both sold by Lever Brothers. There were two soap powders, Persil, sold by Crosfield, Watson and Gossage, and Rinso, sold by Hudson and Knight. The one scourer, Vim, originally sold by Lever Brothers, had been transferred to Hudson and Knight's. As already mentioned, a new category had been introduced, synthetic detergents; here three existed, of which Surf was sold by Lever Brothers, Omo by Hudson and Knight and Quix by Crosfield, Watson and Gossage. Less than 100 brands were sold to industrial users.

There remained six toilet soaps; two, Lifebuoy and Lux, were sold by Lever Brothers; one each were sold by the two other large sales agencies, Knight's Castile by Hudson and Knight, Breeze by Crosfield, Watson and Gossage; and three by the two specialized toilet selling companies, Astral Cream and Pears Transparent by Gibbs, and Vinolia by Pepsodent.

The managements of the various factories and sales forces, now so greatly reduced in number, are the operating units of the concern, and have considerable autonomy. Each is subject, as already mentioned, to the United Kingdom Soap Executive, presided over by a Director of Unilever; but the control is kept down to a minimum, and is mainly exercised through three devices, the Annual Operating Plan, the Annual Capital Expenditure Budget and the Selection and Annual Review of Remuneration of Top Management.[1]

First, under the Annual Operating Plan, each unit estimates its prospective sales and margins for the year, and hence the following year's profit or loss, and discusses this in detail with the United Kingdom Soap Executive. The plan may be adjusted and then must be brought by the Executive for approval to the Special Committee, the small Committee of the Board which co-ordinates policy. Once accepted, it is made known to all who may be affected, including the Advisory and Service Departments. The operating unit may modify the plan to meet changing circumstances. But its existence means that the central organization can control general policy.

Secondly, the Capital Expenditure Budget provides for firmer control than is exercised on current operations both on the construction of additional plant and on renewals and repairs to existing plant. Each factory makes its plan, which is discussed in detail with the central bodies. The Soap Executive and the operating units may spend up to certain limits, but above these limits only the Board can sanction capital expenditure. For it is this which determines the long-period development of the concern. 'Control of capital expenditure, therefore, will be effective only if it is carried out by a central agency able to look at the whole field of the concern's interests, existing and potential, in relation to the resources available or likely to become available.'[2]

[1] *The Organization of Unilever*, based on a paper delivered by Lord Heyworth to the Institute of Management in 1949, and revised and brought up-to-date in 1952. P. 8.

[2] Ibid., p. 10.

Thirdly, so as to get the best men into the top jobs, to reward them appropriately, and to give them a wide experience in the concern, those holding the higher posts are chosen centrally and their salaries centrally reviewed.

These three controls from the centre are mandatory, and may involve at various stages bringing in the Central Advisory and Service Departments. In addition, the operating units may use these Departments as they wish. They may, for instance, if they choose, delegate the whole of their buying of raw materials to the appropriate Buying Department. They may leave to the Technical Division the drawing up of plans for new buildings and for plant layouts. Or they may seek information and advice from these or other Departments. The head men of the Advisory and Service Departments help as far as possible through personal visits. But the operating units are free, if they wish, to go outside the concern for advice or service.

Besides these regular controls, arrangements have been developed for investigating the organization and methods of parts of the concern which at any time seem to need it and for suggesting improvements.

Thus, it is true to say that the various operating units of the organization now work for a common aim, and as parts of an integrated body. Much is delegated and decentralized, but the crucial decisions are centrally planned.

CHAPTER 6

Conclusions

IN the soap industry the entry of new firms has throughout remained free. Yet one firm, under its dominating founder, Lever, succeeded in expanding until, in 1930, it controlled, with its associated companies, something like three-fifths of British soap sales. The largest part of the expansion came through the acquisition of rival soap firms, mainly between 1906 and 1921. Up to 1906 Lever's had secured about a sixth of the market and only bought one independent soap firm, and that a small one in this country; by 1921, with their associated firms, they held some 55 per cent of the total; thereafter, until 1930, they secured about a further 5 per cent of the market, mainly through innovations; only one important firm, the British Soap Company, was brought in after 1920, brought in mainly in order to stop its competition. Then, from 1930, Unilever accepted a decline in their share of the home soap market at the hands of new and powerful competitors and strengthened their own position by an eventually drastic rationalization of their home soap factories. Unilever as a whole still expanded rapidly into fields now easier than the home soap market.

It is convenient to consider together the extent to which mergers were necessary in order to give Lever's their dominance, and the alternatives to the emergence of such a clearly leading firm. The crucial date is probably 1906, when Lever tried to promote a combine covering over half of the United Kingdom market, and would almost certainly have succeeded but for the largely fortuitous intervention of the *Daily Mail.* By that date, though Lever's were far bigger than any of their rivals, some of these were nevertheless important, with rather wide markets. Although there were many small firms, there was nothing approaching perfect competition. But there was what Lever called cut-throat competition, a state of affairs highly unsatisfactory to the firms concerned. Stability would have been sought in one way or another.

In the absence of mergers the firms might have tried price agreements, as they had in the past. But these could not have secured stability for long. In the soap industry as it had developed, with many branded lines, agreements on price could never be effective. And by encouraging other forms of competition, as in advertising, they resulted in waste.

One possible development would have been the gradual elimination from the industry, after a considerable period of expensive advertising and sales effort, of those firms which were least effective, whose financial resources were least or which could most easily turn to other forms of production. After a time there would have remained relatively few firms in oligopolistic competition with each other, surrounded by small firms supplying mainly specialist markets. The period of elimination would probably have been long, for, as the preceding Chapters have shown, it is difficult to capture other firms' markets without a new product to offer. And really new products cannot be launched all the time. Further, it takes time to drive firms to bankruptcy or to shifting their form of production, since they can cling to parts at least of their existing markets.

Whether elimination would have gone further than this without mergers is highly doubtful. It depends partly but not wholly on the efficiency of scale, a point to be discussed shortly. With imperfect competition an internecine war is not usually worth while. Very possibly, without mergers, growth would have been slow and a number of largish firms as well as many small ones would have remained in the industry. But not certainly. Lever himself so strongly desired expansion that he might perhaps have faced the difficulties of driving out other firms and possibly succeeded.

Alternatively, in the absence of Lever's initiative in 1906 and in the years following it, several of the larger firms might have absorbed a number of small firms rather than eliminated them by competition, thus achieving much the same result as in the previous case.

The most probable alternative, then, to the large combine actually found in the soap industry was a number of fairly large firms competing with varying degrees of energy against each other. In both cases specialist firms would have remained round the big ones; and in both cases new competitors would at intervals have emerged. Which of these alternatives was the most likely to be in the public interest? The answer must turn on what size of firm would be most likely to meet consumers' needs efficiently with the least use of real resources, and on the extent to which one form of organization or the other might be expected to keep prices above costs, long or short term.

To take the last point first. As compared with a large number of competing firms, there can be little question that the large concern not only avoids what Lever always called frenzied competition in advertising, but can also secure greater short-period stability of prices.

As a result, at times, as when the Sub-Committee on Trusts reported, the consumer had to pay more for her soap than she would have done had there been more competition. As compared with relatively few firms, however, the balance here is rather more doubtful. These firms, too, might have refrained from short-period price cutting; but equally they might have adjusted prices downwards more rapidly than did one dominating firm. Yet, with freedom of entry, even a dominating firm was always liable to new competition unless it succeeded in keeping down prices, as Lever's found to their cost with the British Soap Company in the early 1920's. Although, therefore, at times, this factor probably scores against the big firm, it does not score enough to outweigh any important difference in the other factor, the economical use of real resources so as to meet consumers' needs.

In the soap industry as in many others, there are two general factors which tend to favour the large concern. First, research and development; it is generally easier for the large organization to experiment with new products, new raw materials and new methods. In the soap industry, however, until perhaps recently, the advantage here does not seem to have been of enormous importance between the very large- and the medium-sized firm. It was thought to be important, but in practice did not prove so, when fat hardening was being tried before the first world war. It may be important now with the new synthetics.

Secondly, applying to research but also much more widely, the best use of ability and skill. Ability is always scarce, technicians skilled in a particular art very frequently so. The large firm can afford to hire ability and, where necessary, give it training in a technical skill. It may, too, be able to use more fully than can the smaller firm special abilities and skills through the greater ease with which it can shift people from place to place and the extent to which it can relieve them of routine duties. And, even more important, if there is one man with exceptional energy, drive and marketing sense, as Lever had, possibly only a very large organization can use his talents fully. But this does not, perhaps, require a concern as vast as Lever's had become by 1920. Lever himself was not, apparently, an ideal delegator; and the concern had by then become too large for him to run it effectively single-handed. Men with his type of talent may never be good delegators.

Yet, so far as the difficulties and costs of delegation are concerned, the large firm appears normally to have some advantages over the fairly large. Only the small firm can avoid establishing some formalized channel of command and of information. The necessary organization may be more expensive per unit handled for the medium-sized firm than for the large. And the large firm can afford to employ specialists to study the changes which ought to be made in a dynamic industry, and to concentrate first at one point, then at another.

These two considerations, then, may favour the large firm at all stages of operation, but in general not decisively as between the very large and the fairly large. There are also possible differences in economies of scale at the various stages of production and selling.

Raw material costs are an important item for soap; but it does not seem that the large-scale organization can normally secure its raw materials more cheaply than the medium sized. Lever's may have spread its risks by building up and owning large sources of raw materials and thus at times prevented fluctuations in shareholders' earnings. So far as the public interest is concerned, however, this factor does not seem of great importance.

On manufacturing and on selling (more costly than manufacturing) there are advantages of scale, and there are advantages of specialization, of producing and selling a large volume of a particular line.

In the soap industry advantages of scale in manufacturing are not decisive between the large- and the medium-sized organization provided each factory does not produce a large number of lines. When Lever started, economies of large-scale manufacturing were small; they have become more substantial as time has gone on, particularly in packing and, recently, with the introduction of synthetic powders, in the early stages of manufacture. In this field the large factory now has a definite advantage; but these economies could be realized with an appreciable number of reasonably specialized factories in the industry.

In the marketing field the small firm with a specialized or localized market may be able to sell cheaply. Such firms will persist, but not over the whole field. Once a wider market is aimed at and the product advertised, there are advantages in selling a large volume of one line, and advantages of a large total volume of sales. The larger the sales of any line, the less is the cost of advertising each unit sold. Large sales need a wide marketing network; generally, the salesman can handle effectively several lines (in 1931 Mr Heyworth suggested from six to ten); unless, therefore, the sales of any one line are very large, the firm with a number of largish lines gains. Yet again, it would seem, to achieve these economies it is not indispensable to have an organization of the size that Lever's became in the home soap industry. Thus Lever's themselves operate three sales organizations for the distributive trade, not one.

Further, in an industry such as soap where both the nature of consumers' demands and the knowledge of new ways of meeting them are changing, the large firm has some advantages in production and marketing combined. To launch new products and even new brands may be expensive, and, unless they can be launched quickly, the costs of production and of selling may be very great in the pioneering stage. A medium-sized firm can produce one very successful line and sell it widely, for a time at least; but this line may then be superceded by other lines, produced by other firms. The large firm can let the line whose popularity is declining fade out gradually, and it is much more likely than the medium-sized firm to have a new line coming along which it can push with its existing sales organization and manufacture in its existing factories. Moreover, the large firm has here a certain flexibility that the medium-sized firm lacks. Its production and its sales units need not be identical. Any sales unit which ceases to push a line whose popularity is waning can take on a new line from any conveniently situated factory in the organization.

So far, none the less, the issue must be regarded as rather open between the large concern and relatively few rather smaller ones, provided that both types of firm reduce the lines they sell fairly drastically, only meeting consumers' real needs. The crucial question in the soap industry appears to be which type of organization is most likely to do this.

As has been shown in some detail earlier, Lever's did not rationalize for many years and, until they did so, selling was very expensive, from the point of view of the public interest almost certainly unnecessarily so. But in the end they rationalized; and, as Chapter 5 has shown, the final process was based on deliberate selection from the centre of a limited number of lines that it was decided would meet consumers' needs and a gradual but none-the-less drastic reorganization of their home soap industry both on the manufacturing and the selling side.

Part of the rationalization process consisted in reducing the number of lines of hard soap sold, and the number of units producing and selling this product. This change was, in effect, forced on them by the decline in the popularity of hard soap as new and better forms of detergents were developed. Some similar change would have had to be made even with a number of firms in the industry.

But part of the process was something more than this. Unilever took a view on what consumers could be got to accept, and formed consumers' demand rather than merely adapted to it. This is certain; what would have happened in the absence of a dominating firm is surmise. On the one hand the pressure of competition would have been greater than in fact it was was for many years. On the other, if a fair number of large firms had remained, the fear of losing customers to other firms, so potent among producers until the 1930's, might have prevented enough lines being dropped, enough factories from being closed, or enough sales forces amalgamated. Moreover, the firms that remained might well not have been able to integrate in the planned way that was possible for Unilever's, with the aim of economizing on transport. Imperfect competition—and competition in the soap industry could never have been perfect—does not force on the producer the most economical methods; indeed, it may have the reverse effect if advertising is important. With a very few firms there may be a *modus vivendi* about frenzied competition; it is unlikely with many.

On balance and in the end, it seems likely that bigness in this industry benefited the consumer. It did so by a decision drastically to limit the number of lines offered to the consumer, to judge what they needed and would accept and to concentrate production and sales efforts on them.

APPENDIX

Number of Soap Producers in Great Britain at Selected Dates

'The Soap Makers' Directory'[1], published annually since 1888, gives the names of all firms reporting that they were making soap in Great Britain, with their addresses and, in general, the types of soap they claimed to make. Subsidiary firms are included separately. The lists are not entirely accurate; some firms are certainly listed after they had ceased to manufacture; and newcomers are not always at once included. None the less, the Directories give a rough indication of which firms were manufacturing at any date. Hence, by comparing different dates, it is possible to estimate how many new firms came in, and how many old ones went out of soap production (ignoring any that may have come in and gone out between two successive selected dates).

For the purposes of this study the names of soap producers were listed for chosen years only, 1888, 1898, 1906, 1914, 1920, 1930, 1938, 1946, 1953 and 1955. The number producing soap in each of these years in London, in the rest of England and Wales (called 'country' in the Directory), in Scotland, and in Great Britain as a whole are shown on the accompanying diagram, the chosen years being joined by a thick line. The slopes of this line indicate the average net change in numbers per year.

The lines radiating from the selected years show the number of firms entering and leaving the industry between the selected year and the next selected year, and their slope the average number entering and leaving per year between any two selected dates.

Thus, for Great Britain there were 345 listed soap producers in 1888; between 1888 and 1898, 153 firms left the industry. Thus the exit line falls from 345 in 1888 to 192 in 1898. As sixty-five new firms were listed the entry line rose to 410; the number of firms in the industry in 1898 was $345 - 192 + 65 = 257$. (Since, apart from the period 1888–98, the number of entries and exits in Scotland were small, the radiating lines are not visible for later periods.) Over the ten years 1888–98 about fifteen firms per year left the industry, in the next period (1898–1906) just over nine; this is indicated in the diagram by the fact that the exit line is steeper in the first than in the second period. The diagram shows that the rates of exit and entry became progressively slower. It is the figures for average rates of exit and entry which are discussed in the text.[2]

The figures for makers of different types of soap have not been tabulated as they are not sufficiently reliable. They are, nevertheless, interesting and some very broad qualitative statements have been based on this information.[3]

[1] London, Chantry Publications Ltd.

[2] See pp. 218, 219, 231–2, 248. [3] See p. 219.

NUMBER OF SOAP PRODUCERS AT SELECTED DATES

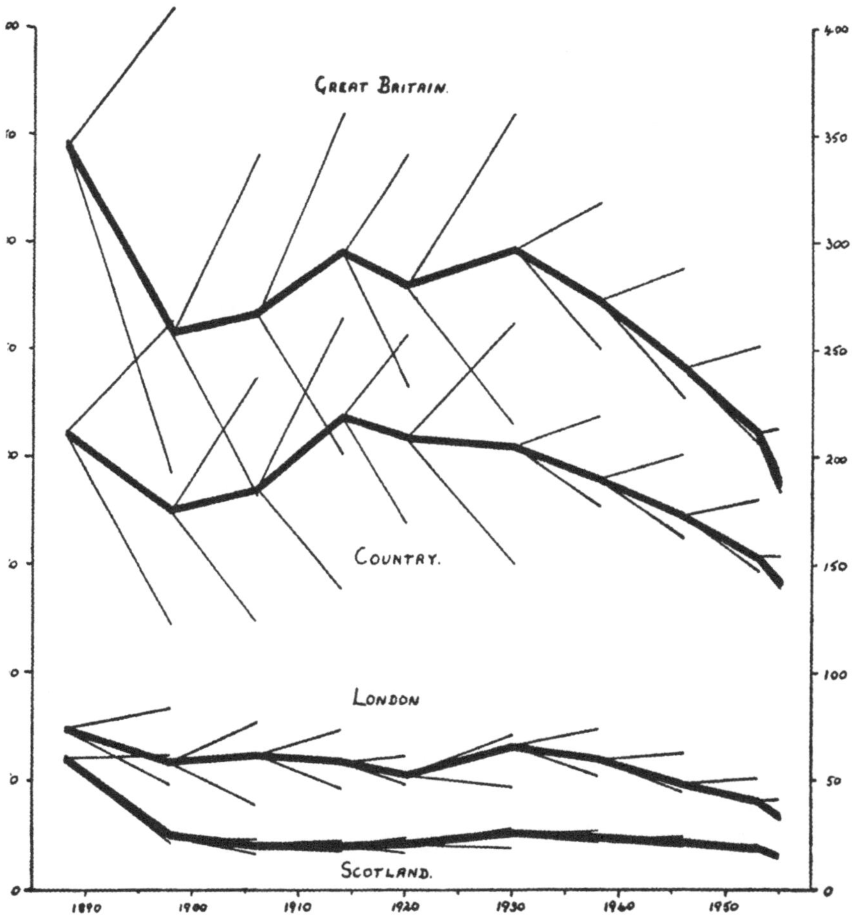

IV

THE FLAT-GLASS INDUSTRY

CHAPTER 1

Introduction

THE flat-glass industry has an interesting history in which mergers have played only a small part. The reasons for this are closely linked with the peculiar circumstances of the industry and its rapidly changing techniques; for these reasons interesting comparisons may be made between this and other industries in which mergers have played a more prominent part. In all these studies of mergers in particular industries, we are concerned with the effects of mergers and with the question as to why there were mergers rather than other developments; by looking at an industry in which mergers were of relatively little importance some light is thrown upon the circumstances in which the concentration of industry takes place by means other than mergers. In this industry, as in others, there are tremendous economies of scale and it appears that in the main processes, particularly in the production of plate glass, one can think in terms of inevitable elimination of competition and concentration of production. In sheet glass the concentration of production was less inevitable than the restriction of competition and in rolled plate glass neither was quite inevitable, although free oligopolistic competition is improbable.

The flat-glass industry has several extremely important characteristics which have persisted and which give rise to possible generalizations about the relationships between the characteristics of industries, their efficiency, and the development of their structure. There are four particular themes which are illustrated by the history of this industry. Firstly, there is the extent to which the survival of a firm (and industry) depends upon its being multi-product; when there are numerous firms in an industry, multi-product firms may be able to be less efficient in some respects than would single-product firms; where the industry consists of only one or two firms, subject to foreign competition, it may be necessary to accept periods when some products are being supported by others, for the alternative is losing the industry altogether, and either becoming dependent upon imports or having only a subsidiary of a foreign company which pays out both profits and royalties.

The second theme is related to the first. It is the examination of the results of having an industry in which the rate of decay of substantial firms may be rather slow. In this industry the core of strength of the bigger firm depends upon glass technology which can be used for the production of many different glass products.

Thirdly, the flat-glass industry has been distinguished by a very rapid rate of expensive technical change which has meant that any firm which lagged or became inefficient became practically valueless to its direct competitors and ceased to be a threat to the progressive firm.

Finally, marginal costs are low compared with average costs and price competition, since the product is homogeneous, can be extremely effective; as a result price agreements are not too difficult to arrange since all parties are anxious to have them. The willingness to accept the restrictions of price agreements is reinforced by the fact that firms are usually making different types of glass in different proportions and each firm is, therefore, in a position to cut prices where his competitor will be hurt most; because of this an uneasy equilibrium based upon localized retaliation may be established even in the absence of formal agreement.

The major reasons for the absence of mergers in this industry are the rapid elimination of backward firms which results from technical change and the prevalence of price agreements; mergers have not been required either to mitigate short-period competition or to make it possible to secure the economies of scale.

In this study the period up to 1914 is considered historically, but the post-1918 period is somewhat more analytical; here the major technical changes are discussed first and these are then treated as important determinants of the commercial history, thus emphasizing the distinction between the more durable and the temporary determinants of policy.

CHAPTER 2

The Establishment of the Modern Industry

THE repeal in 1845 of the excise duty on window glass resulted in big changes both in the quantity and type of glass demanded, and this is, therefore, an important date in the development of the industry. As the excise laws limited the thickness of window glass to a thickness of a ninth of an inch or less, a definite distinction was drawn between window glass and plate glass; the latter was a luxury product taxed at a high rate. There were at this date fourteen factories engaged in the manufacture of window glass,[1] two substantial plate-glass manufacturers—the London and Manchester Plate Glass Company of Ravenhead, St Helens, and the Birmingham Plate Glass Company—and a number of small plate-glass manufacturers in the London area. Only two of the firms which were in existence in 1845 survived as active flat-glass manufacturers into the twentieth century; both were makers of window glass. The first was Chance Brothers, already a large firm in 1845, and the second Pilkington Brothers, founded in 1826, which, although prosperous, had reached no more than average size by 1845. The other firms of importance in 1845 were Hartley's, which had moved to Sunderland, and the old firm of Cookson's at Newcastle-on-Tyne, which in 1845 became R. W. Swinburne & Co.

Before 1845 improved techniques had stimulated Chance Bros, Hartley and Pilkington Bros (then called Greenall & Pilkington), to reintroduce sheet glass made by opening and flattening glass cylinders. This glass began to compete with crown glass which, although clear and brilliant, had to be cut from circles of glass which had a boss in the middle and which could, therefore, be produced only in small sizes for small window panes. Cylinder sheet-glass also began to compete with plate glass as a method was found for grinding and polishing it; this glass was cheaper than plate glass, and did not incur the higher rate of duty which was imposed on plate glass.

As methods of making cylinder sheet glass improved, so demand,

[1] T. C. Barker, *Pilkington Brothers and the British Flat Glass Industry*, an unpublished typescript, p. 113.

both at home and abroad, increased. By 1842 sheet glass had become important, and it became more so after the repeal of the excise duty which removed the thickness limit; it came to be specified more and more frequently in orders for window glass.

The concentration of the British window-glass industry began shortly after the repeal of the excise duty which coincided with the fairly rapid replacement of crown glass by sheet glass. The immediate reaction to the repeal was an expansion of the industry; ten new factories were built in 1845, the majority making sheet glass. The boom only lasted until 1847 and in the depression of 1848–9 the new companies just coming into production were killed at birth or in early infancy.

The firms on Tyneside which had been the great producers of crown glass also failed during this period. Swinburne's started sheet-glass production, but the majority clung obstinately to crown glass. This trade shrank fast, and *The Builder* reported in 1849 that the Tyne glass industry was 'reaching the climax of its decline'. Of the numerous Tyneside firms formerly engaged in the window-glass trade two alone faltered on, and these appeared to be 'not only languid but expiring also'. By 1856 the only crown-glass furnace still at work was at Swinburne's in South Shields where sheet glass was also manufactured. Early in the following decade no window glass of any kind was being made on the Tyne.[1]

The failure of many firms by the early 1850's left Chance's, Pilkington's and Hartley's, the three major firms which had entered the sheet-glass trade before 1845, in a very strong position. They were able to buy up a number of firms which were in financial difficulties and which were offering, or might offer, further competition. In at least three cases the firms were bought jointly; Joshua Bower, of Hunslet, near Leeds, was purchased in 1861, and the Stourbridge Glass Works in 1867.[2] The most aggressive competitor was acquired in 1855; this was Robert Gardner who had himself bought an existing works. He was prepared to sell because he was not skilled in glass technology and he had no faith in the technical direction of his works.

The predominant position of the three major firms is also shown by the decision, made in 1854, not to license to other firms Hartley's patent method for manufacturing rolled plate. One firm, belonging to a Richard Hadland, who had been connected with the Liverpool Crown Glassworks, began to make rolled plate soon after 1850, but

[1] Barker, *op. cit.*, p. 137.

[2] J. F. Chance, *The History of Chance Brothers & Co.*, privately published, p. 94.

a case was brought against him for patent infringement and his defeat led to his bankruptcy.[1]

The concentration of the British window-glass industry thus took place remarkably rapidly between about 1846 and 1862. By 1860, the three major firms together produced 75 per cent of all the window-glass produced in the country,[2] and by the early 1860's few competitors of any importance remained. (The Nailsea works were bought by Chance's in 1870.)

The three firms also dominated the Crown and Sheet Glass Manufacturers' Association, and 'it was a simple matter to bring swift and crushing pressure to bear upon any manufacturers inside Britain who refused to sell at list prices. When, for instance, Samuel Brown and John Powis took a lease of the Nailsea works in 1862, and tried to flood the market with cheap, rolled-plate glass their initial success was short-lived . . . other manufacturers cut their prices . . . and the lessees of Nailsea were driven out of business'.[3]

The glass trade had regulated competition to some extent for many years. The Association of Crown-glass Manufacturers of England and Scotland was established before 1827, at which time it 'met twice a year, regulated prices and general conditions of sale of crown glass, prohibited the employment of each other's workpeople, established penalties for breaches of rules, and arranged for the adjustment of production to demand'.[4]

In 1846 the name of the Association was changed to the Crown and Sheet Glass Manufacturers' Association. The prices it fixed were almost certainly higher than they would otherwise have been, but they were low enough to drive many firms out of the industry as the differences in costs between firms were substantial. These substantial differences were partly the result of the rapid technical progress and partly due to the inherent difficulties in maintaining quality in glass manufacture. Prices were fixed relatively low, partly because of the growing Belgian competition. The Belgian glass industry made great strides after 1825; in 1850 12,000 tons of glass of all kinds were exported, and by 1857 this had risen to 29,000 tons. Much of this went to the United States, but after the abolition of the United Kingdom tariff in 1858, and particularly after the beginning of the American Civil War in 1861, exports to the United Kingdom grew substantially.

The importance of these figures is shown by a comparison with British production. 'In the middle of the 1860's the three great glass-

[1] Barker, *op. cit.*, p. 138. [2] Ibid., p. 142. [3] Ibid., p. 156.

[4] J. F. Chance, *Chance Brothers & Co.*, *op. cit.*, Ch. XIV, by W. L. Chance, p. 276.

making firms in Britain—Chance's, Pilkington's and Hartley's—were, together, making 17,000 tons of glass per year.'[1]

Exports of Belgian Window Glass, 1866–9

	To GB	To USA
	Tons	Tons
1866	14,000	11,891
1867	13,000	13,837
1868	16,487	6,369
1869	18,583	9,906

The account of the process of concentration shows the extreme importance of technology; in this field the industry was highly competitive, although in the short-period price competition was largely eliminated by the effective regulation of prices.

The rate of technical change continued to be very rapid; in particular the introduction of the Siemens gas-fired regenerative furnace was an important innovation which affected the bulk production of all types of glass. Chance's and the London & Manchester Plate Glass Company, of Ravenhead, St Helens, both installed a Siemens furnace in 1861. Pilkington's did not follow suit until 1863. The really significant feature was, however, the fact that Pilkington's found their furnace to be a decided success, commercially, whereas J. H. Chance confided to W. B. Pilkington on July 28, 1864:

'How does your gas furnace answer? We don't find any saving—fuel is more.'[2]

As Barker points out, this was, perhaps, the first real sign of the weakening of Chance's ascendancy in technical matters.

The successful introduction of gas furnaces by Pilkington's became of the utmost importance since, in 1870, Siemens took out patents for tank furnaces,[3] and Pilkington's were remarkably quick in taking up the new invention. The final specification was sealed on May 21, 1873, and by the beginning of February 1874 the firm was already bringing a successful tank into operation.[4] This was not achieved without difficulty, the first experiment having been a failure. Nevertheless, by May 1877 there were twelve tank furnaces in opera-

[1] Barker, *op. cit.*, p. 155. [2] Ibid., p. 161.

[3] The raw material was to be fed in continuously at one end of the tank, and with the temperature controlled along the length of the tank, the molten glass could be drawn off continuously at the other end, This was a vast improvement upon the system of melting the raw material in pots.

[4] Barker, *op. cit.*, p. 171.

tion and the ground was being prepared for more.[1] Much of the credit for the very successful introduction and development in design of the tank is attributed to Mr William (Windle) Pilkington.

Walter Lucas Chance wrote: 'It was the adoption of the tank system for making sheet glass by their St Helens competitors (Pilkington's) about this time that finally deprived them (Chance's) of the predominant position which they had hitherto held.'[2] It appears that this failure was largely a reflection of the general decline in the relative technical competence of the firm.[3]

The relative strengths of the managements of Chance's and Pilkington's were also reflected in the results of their entry into the manufacture of cast plate glass. Trade was booming in the early 1870's, and the demand for plate glass had increased enormously, both in the UK and in America. 'In previous years the three window-glass firms had agreed among themselves not to make plate glass by the casting process. This may have been a safeguard for Hartley's rolled-plate patent. By the 1870's this patent had expired and both Pilkington's and Chance's chose 1873, when the Belgian glass industry was temporarily weakened by internal difficulties, as a suitable time to embark upon plate-glass manufacture themselves.[4] Chance's bought the Birmingham Plate Glassworks in 1873, and re-equipped it in the following two years. They sustained losses in 1874 and 1875, and for 1876 the loss was £20,000. The works was closed in 1877 and eventually sold in 1889. John Chance recorded 'our conviction that the management has been radically bad from beginning to end',[5] and the story given in *Chance Bros and Co.*,[6] pp. 109–116, makes it quite clear that all was not well with the management, especially the technical direction, of Chance's.

Pilkington's put up an entirely new works and cast glass successfully in 1876. By 1879 output of plate glass at Cowley Hill (Pilkington's) was on a scale comparable with that of the London & Manchester Plate Glass Company of Ravenhead, St Helens, which had been making more than half the total plate glass in the country. By 1888, output of polished plate was almost double that of 1879.[7]

As has been seen, Pilkington's had during this period a very high standard of technical skill, and it is this, above all, which enabled them

[1] Barker, *op. cit.*, p. 172. [2] *Chance Brothers and Co.*, p. 279.

[3] In the postscript written in 1919 to 'Chance Brothers and Co.' the work of three directors is mentioned and it is said that they 'have raised the factory from a state that was certainly a backward one to one of first rate efficiency' (p. 284).

[4] Barker, *op. cit.*, pp. 176–7. [5] *Chance Bros. and Co.*, p. 110.

[6] pp. 109–116. [7] Barker, *op. cit.*, p. 179.

to survive despite large reductions in the price level and the appearance of very severe foreign competition. In 1887, prices were 45 per cent below the level of 1876. At this point the British manufacturers succeeded in combining and fixing prices with the result that in 1891 prices were only 35 per cent below the 1876 level. However, by June 1893 prices had slumped again and were 60 per cent below the 1876 level. New and efficient works had been opened in Belgium, France and Germany, yet demand had fallen. The fall in demand was partly due to general trade depression, but the imposition of the McKinley Tariff in 1891 caused a reduction in imports into the United States,[1] and this had major repercussions on the London market; prices fell and competition was severe. The English Plate Glass Manufacturers' Association remained in existence, but foreign competition was such that it had little effect upon the general level of prices: it is, however, probable that local price discrimination was checked.

Pilkington's great local competitor in cast plate glass, the London and Manchester Plate Glass Company of Ravenhead and Sutton, which employed 1,500 in 1889,[2] could not survive the crisis precipitated by the McKinley Tariff. They were technically behind Pilkington's, having failed to keep up with the very rapid rate of progress throughout the 1880's and early 1890's. Their position was also made difficult by the fact that, unlike Pilkington's, they were largely dependent upon their exports to the United States and sales to the big London merchants and in both markets they came into direct competition with the Belgians.

The other competitor in plate glass, the Union Plate Glass Company Ltd, of the Pocket Nook Works, a smaller concern, was in financial difficulties by 1889. Despite considerable re-equipment in the mid-1890's, glass ceased to be cast before the end of the century.[3]

The Ravenhead and Sutton Oak works were reopened, in 1895 and 1896 respectively, by new and separate companies, but were mere shadows of their former selves. The British Plate Glass Company Ltd sold Ravenhead to Pilkington's in 1901 for £95,000. These works were used to augment the capacity of Pilkington's. The new London and Manchester Plate Glass Co. Ltd cast their last plate glass at Sutton Oak in June 1903, and these works were sold to Pilkington's in 1905 for £80,000, but were used only as warehouses. (The new company had bought the works for £150,000 in 1896.)[4] The two other British plate-glass works had also closed, the Thames Plate Glass Company in the 1870's and the Tyne Plate Glass Company in 1891.

[1] Barker, *op. cit.*, p. 181. [2] Ibid., p. 183.
[3] Ibid., p. 182. [4] Ibid., p. 183.

The failure of their British competitors left Pilkington Brothers the sole British manufacturer. Pilkington's survival was due partly to technical superiority and partly to the indirect effects of their being a multi-product firm. They were able to press forward with developments in plate-glass manufacture, temporory losses in plate-glass departments being covered by the profits from sheet glass and rolled plate. Quite as important was the fact that as they were distributing a full range of flat glass they had depots all over the country and in many places abroad; this sales and distributive organization gave some protection against the full blast of competition from the Belgians, and it made Pilkington's somewhat less dependent upon the US market which was largely cut off by the McKinley tariff of 1891.

Mergers have played practically no part in the concentration of the plate-glass industry; only two works were bought by Pilkington's and in neither case were they taken over as going concerns. Only the Ravenhead works were used for glass manufacture. Pilkington may well have thought that it would be wise to buy lest at some future date it might be re-opened by a new company as it had been in 1896. There was also always the slight chance that a foreign competitor might wish to have a fighting company. The extra capacity was, in fact, useful as a counter in the bargaining with foreign competitors in 1904.[1]

During the period when Pilkington's were establishing themselves as the sole producers of plate glass, they were also strengthening their position in other types of window glass.

The only firms which remained were Chance's and Hartley's. The Nailsea works had been bought by Chances in 1870 and was closed in 1874 after large losses had been incurred. No window glass was made on the Tyne after the mid 1860's.

Little is known about the last period of James Hartley & Co., of Sunderland. T. C. Barker merely says:[2] 'The concern was always smaller than either Chance's or Pilkington's. The economic struggle of the later nineteenth century proved too much for Hartley's. James Hartley died in 1886 and his successors at the works did not have his sure grip. The crisis of the early 1890's drove the firm out of the business. The Sunderland works ceased to make window glass in 1894.' The failure appears to have been largely technical, and is a further illustration of the fact that in the last quarter of the nineteenth century only exceptional drive and competence combined with large resources were enough.

Chance's, having failed in their attempt to make cast-plate glass,

[1] Barker, *op. cit.*, p. 213. [2] p. 185.

were also in difficulties with sheet glass. Their quality was poor and much was scrap. They tried larger and smaller pots and larger and smaller furnaces, all at considerable cost, but without much success. In 1880, and again in 1887, the question as to whether the manufacture of sheet glass should be discontinued was discussed.[1] The rolled-plate departments on the other hand were doing well, rolled cathedral (glass with an indefinite pattern imprinted on one surface) being particularly successful; by the end of the 1870's these departments were displacing the sheet-glass departments in importance.[2] Rolled plate did not become subject to severe foreign competition until after 1900, and Chance's held several important patents for the manufacture of rolled plate and figured glass. After the depression in 1891–2 demand increased considerably. Tank furnaces were at last introduced. Chance's also undertook the manufacture of 'muffled' glass, impressed with patterns by blowing into moulds and they succeeded in capturing practically the whole home trade.[3]

An important development during this period was that of continuous lehrs[4] for annealing glass. These were introduced in 1887 at Chance's and, after some difficulty, they were made to work satisfactorily and were used for both rolled and sheet glass. This is one of the few major improvements during this period in which Chance's preceded Pilkington's, but according to T. C. Barker,[5] Pilkington's installed continuous lehrs shortly after Chance's, having sent a man out to America to find out about the new method of annealing. Between 1870 and 1900 Chance's lost their predominant position in the industry, and were largely maintained by their trade in rolled plate, although their production of coloured glass, lampshades, lighthouses and optical glass was also important.

Under the impact of the severe foreign competition during this period, the Window-glass Manufacturers' Association declined in importance. 'There was great temptation to undersell the others, and to justify such action by claiming that foreign competition made it impossible to sell at a higher price. This created much bad feeling within the Manufacturers' Association. Robert Lucas Chance wrote (to Hartley's), of Sunderland, in January 1878:

'I . . . can quite understand your feeling of irritation at the treatment we are receiving at the hands of Pilkington Brothers and if I thought it advisable to consult my feelings only, I should fall in with

[1] *Chance Bros. and Co., op. cit.*, p. 116. [2] Ibid., p. 117. [3] Ibid., p. 129.

[4] A lehr, lear or leer is an annealing furnace for glass. In the early lehrs the glass was put in and the lehr allowed to cool. The continuous lehr is a long chamber through which the glass is passed.

[5] p. 175.

your views and say, dissolve the Association. But we cannot always allow our feelings to rule us and I am inclined to think that it will be better to swallow the annoyance and retain the Association than stand upon our dignity and throw it over. There is no doubt that it has been a substantial benefit to us in the past, checking the downward tendency of the time and putting us right when we were getting all abroad. What it has done in the past, it is competent to repeat in the future; although at present it certainly does not show symptoms of producing much fruit.'[1]

It appears that prices continued to be discussed between the British manufacturers. For many years the actual level of prices depended largely upon the price of imports. It is important, however, that the industry has generally operated under conditions in which prices were discussed and kept stable over short periods; of course there were times when the arranged prices had to be changed drastically and rather frequently. Pilkington's, who were increasing their share of the market, appear to have been dominant in fixing the price level. Chance's were more interested in rolled plate and patterned and figured glass, which are differentiated products for which the market is more imperfect. It appears that on the whole Chance's were prepared to agree not to cut prices below those agreed between themselves and Pilkington's in the light of foreign competition.

A picture of the situation at the turn of the century is incomplete without further reference to the foreign competition: it was severe; about 70 per cent of the sheet glass used in the country was imported and the proportion of plate glass was even higher. A London merchant replying to the Tariff Commission in 1907 even said: 'In the sheet-glazing trade I use about 90 per cent foreign and 10 per cent English. Polished plate is principally foreign as I believe there are not many manufacturers in England. . . The polished plate trade has almost entirely vanished.'[2] These extreme remarks are a reflection of the situation in the London area rather than the country as a whole, but they serve to illustrate the strength of foreign competition.

THE CONCENTRATION OF THE BRITISH FLAT-GLASS INDUSTRY, 1845–1900

Between 1845 and 1900 the flat-glass industry became concentrated and by the beginning of the twentieth century there were only two flat-glass manufacturers in Britain. As has been seen, the concentra-

[1] Barker, *op. cit.*, p. 157.
[2] Report of the Tariff Commission, 1907, Vol. VI, Para. 125.

tion took a relatively long time and, although the mergers were unimportant, the reasons why this was so varied.

Until about 1860 weak firms were eliminated very easily. Firstly, their fate depended to a large extent upon the capacity of the management, and many found it extremely difficult to keep up with the developments in techniques which were taking place. Secondly, their capital value was low, the works consisting of little more than the actual glass house and furnaces. For example, the Eccleston Crown glass works, which was by no means one of the smallest, was sold for just over £2,000 in about 1845 and it was mortgaged for £6,333 in 1847. As the fixed overheads were relatively low these small works left the industry without any prolonged struggle for survival. A number of those which were unable to compete successfully in the flat-glass trade were able to enter the expanding glass-bottle industry.

After the majority of the unprogressive and small firms had been driven out, the industry consisted of about a dozen more substantial firms, and the period between 1855 and 1865 is the only one in which mergers were of any importance; firms were bought out by their more powerful competitors in order to limit competition. Despite loose price agreements, competition tended to develop both when firms were in great difficulties and when new people tried to expand old businesses. By this time firms were more substantial, each had a greater influence upon the market, and was more difficult to eliminate.

After about 1865–70 there were practically no new firms and very few new people came into the industry by acquiring existing firms. The technical problems had become so difficult and the rate of change so rapid that very great risk was involved.

The last stages of the concentration of the industry were brought about largely by the intense foreign competition which caused a number of the remaining firms to fall. The concentration of plate-glass production was due almost wholly to the fact that Pilkington's was the only firm which managed to survive the Belgian onslaught.

The rate and nature of technical progress dominated the industry during the period of concentration. This continued to be a major factor in the twentieth century and, although the industry has consisted of only two or three firms since 1900, much that has been said of the nineteenth century also applies to the twentieth.

CHAPTER 3

1900-14

BY the beginning of the twentieth century the modern flat-glass industry had taken shape in this country. There were only two firms of significance in England; Pilkington's were by this time more important than Chance's who made no polished plate and very little sheet glass. During this period international competition and international negotiation and manoeuvre came to be important. This was foreshadowed in 1894 when Pilkington's built a new plate-glass works at Maubeuge in France.

The intense foreign competition was one of the main factors which forced Pilkington's to extend their activities in embossing, brilliant cutting, bevelling and bending. 'Bending and embossing were introduced at Cowley Hill (the plate-glass works) in 1900 as a countermeasure against the London dealers. An old employee has recalled how "we found that our not doing that kind of work meant that orders for the actual glass were going to the people who could do it, with probably foreign glass being used".' Henry Enever, a London glass bender, joined the firm in 1902 and reorganized the bending department with good effect . . . The introduction of the Offenbacher machine about 1905 also speeded up the process of bevelling straight edges.'[1] The result of these activities was to diversify the product and to make it possible to sell direct to smaller customers without special facilities, and in this way to create a less perfectly competitive market which was less directly affected by foreign competition.

Another reaction to intense competition is diversification into other usually related products, as this spreads risks. A firm which sees a profitable line is likely to exploit it so long as it has the managerial and financial resources available, as it often will have when expansion on existing lines becomes difficult. By 1900 Chance's had already gone a long way towards switching from the relatively homogeneous products of the flat-glass trade and Pilkington's were making an increasingly wide range of products. They continued to make coloured

[1] Barker, *op. cit.*, p. 216.

and cathedral glass and glass shades and they had 'smoothers' making a patent plate glass for the photographic trade. In the 1890's they began to make cells for electric batteries; this trade fitted into their organization particularly well as batteries were required in large numbers and used a large quantity of glass.

It is very clear that around 1900 Pilkington's were suffering from the pressure of intense competition in the flat-glass industry. 'A loss can only be withstood if there is solid hope of turning it into a profit; if it is a temporary affliction and not a chronic drain on resources. By the end of the 1890's Belgian competition was beginning to look more like the latter than the former and we have it on the authority of Mr Cecil Pilkington that during the last years of the nineteenth century the firm's strength was slowly ebbing away.'[1]

During the period of most intense competition in plate glass, the sheet-glass trade was still profitable, and it was thus possible to bear the losses on the manufacture of plate. The Canadian tariffs of 1898 gave some preference to British glass. Profits were also made on rolled glass for which there was a high demand at the time.

In 1900 Pilkington's acquired their first subsidiary—the Anglo-Belgian Silver Sand Co. Ltd, which owned property at Moll in Belgium. 'This move was made . . . in order to avoid having to pay very high prices to the Belgian Syndicate which cornered all existing supplies of silver sand.'[2] This property has not, in fact, been used and the strategic move was apparently enough to make adequate supplies available at reasonable prices. The acquisition has been of little importance since as early as 1914.

Just at the time when competition with the Belgians was at its fiercest, a strike broke out in Belgium which lasted from August 1900 to May 1901. 'From Pilkington's point of view, the strike was a remarkable stroke of luck.'[3] After the strike, competition became fiercer than ever. In 1904 imports of plate glass into Britain from Belgium exceeded 20,000 tons. This was 25 per cent more than the average for 1895–9.[4] Nevertheless, attitudes were changing because the Belgians 'who had previously been in a position to undercut their way into the world's markets', were prepared to consider agreements. 'It is significant that immediately after the great strike, a leading member of the American Window Manufacturers' Association' which included the American Window Glass Company, a combine formed in 1895 and controlling over fifty factories in the United States 'was able to go to Brussels and propose the formation of a Belgian glass syndicate

[1] Barker, *op. cit.*, p. 212. [2] Ibid., p. 209. [3] Ibid., p. 212.
[4] Report of the Tariff Commission, 1907, Vol. 6, Para. 224.

in which the Americans were to hold upwards of one-third of the capital. The Belgians lent a most attentive ear to this proposal. *The Times* correspondent reported that it was the attitude of the men that was "largely responsible for the readiness with which Belgian manufacturers have responded to the advances made by the trust".'[1]

International collaboration was discussed with increasing purpose and in 1904 the international syndicate of plate-glass manufacturers was formed. This included all the main European producers but not the American firms. 'Prices were fixed and outputs controlled on an international basis, much as the manufacturers had done in Britain in previous years.[2]

The British Consul-General in Belgium reported, a year after the syndicate had been formed, that prices had advanced by 25 per cent.[3]

'In 1907 the British Consul-General in Belgium recorded that "the general assembly of plate-glass manufacturers had decided to keep the supply at a level with the demand, and do away with the bad results of over-production by settling upon certain days when work shall not be carried on during the month".'[4] For a time, however, the syndicate contented itself with fixing prices only.

In 1908 a depression in trade in the United States, then still an importer of European plate glass, had a severe effect on European manufacturers. Representatives from Great Britain met those of the Plate Glass Convention who controlled works in Austria, Belgium, France and Germany. They met at the Grand Hotel in London, and decided to regulate their output. Each firm was permitted to operate a fixed area of grinding surface. Pilkington's, who were not members of the Convention, possessed several strong bargaining counters. Firstly, the factory at Maubeuge, secondly the fact that their Cowley Hill works were very modern and efficient and, thirdly, that they had potential capacity at Ravenhead and Sutton Oak.

The extent to which Pilkington's area of grinding surface was limited is not known. The following table shows a fall in imports between 1908 and 1910, but this was relatively small and could have been largely accounted for by market changes.

[1] Barker, *op., cit.*, p. 213.

[2] Various attempts to enforce production quotas on crown glass manufacturers were made from 1838 on, but the more progressive firms, such as Pilkington's, would not join the agreements except during periods of very poor trade. The question of organized output restriction does not appear to have been considered seriously after about 1850.

[3] Barker, *op. cit.*, p. 213, quoting from Annual Series of Diplomatic and Consular Trade Reports, 1905 (Cd. 2682).

[4] Ibid., p. 214, quoting from 1907 Consular Trade Report (Cd. 3727).

TABLE I

Plate Glass Imports from Belgium to Great Britain

	tons
1904	22,000
1905	20,000
1906	17,800
1907	18,400
1908	15,000
1909	13,400
1910	13,000
1911	14,700
1912	16,000
1913	19,200

Source: Annual Statement of Trade.

The syndicate broke down in 1910. Imports began to rise and, at the same time, Pilkington's sales of plate glass fell, so that imports took an increasing share of the market, the figures being approximately 48, 53 and 58 per cent in the years 1910, 1911 and 1912.

It is not surprising that the syndicate broke down after only two years. It was trying to exert extensive control over both prices and production, despite the fact that it did not include all the main producers in the world. In addition, it was a period in which extensive technical developments were taking place. Many improvements were made in the techniques for annealing, pot making, handling of pots, the handling of the plates of glass, and in the grinding; there was also closer quality control. It was extremely unlikely that all firms should continue to progress at the same rate and those which improved fastest were likely to wish to exploit their strong position by expanding their share of the market. Further, the more progressive would be unwilling to allow those who did not belong to the syndicate to expand their share of the market by increasing production and, perhaps, reducing prices.

The fact that the syndicate broke down so rapidly indicates that, at least during a period of rapid technical change, extensive international agreements are likely to be temporary and unable to hold prices much above the level of long-period average costs of the more efficient for any length of time. It appears that agreements of this type will limit competition and be maintained when the industry is faced with the possibility of acute short-period competition, but that they are broken when the restrictions of the agreement prevent firms from maintaining or improving their long-period position.

After the breakdown of the syndicate there was no full return to the intensely competitive conditions prevailing prior to 1904. 'Although this (the syndicate) came to an end in 1910, drastic price reductions by the English makers, coupled with certain private arrangements with the more important of the Continentals, considerably curtailed foreign competition in British markets up to the outbreak of the war.'[1] Although Chance's were largely engaged in the production of rolled glass and did not make polished plate, Mr W. L. Chance's statement is applicable to trade in all the main types of glass. The reason for the maintenance of private arrangements in a situation in which general agreements could not be maintained appear to be related to the fact that the large firms could do each other such damage that they were prepared to limit competition between each other while preserving freedom of action against 'outsiders'.

The private agreements took two forms. Chance's made 'arrangements which in 1912 resulted in the transfer of shares of the company to the St Gobain Company in France, the oldest and still the premier plate-glass manufacturing company of the world. The close connection between the two companies of late years has been of the greatest mutual benefit to them'.[2] No further information about the nature of the benefits is given, but it must be supposed that they were both technical and commercial. Pilkington's did not form any financial connection, but there are references in correspondence to a tacit agreement with the members of the Continental Plate-glass Convention which, at that time, seems in practice to have been controlled by St Gobain.

The industry thus appears to have developed to a point where unrestricted competition was regarded as intolerable but complete agreement was impossible; the more general agreements broke down, and the private arrangements were limited. Arrangements made in these circumstances appear to have two features which modify considerably any conclusions about their significance. Firstly, they are often loose agreements which may be broken. Secondly, the very circumstances which make agreements possible may be such that in the absence of agreement the firms' behaviour is in a large part similar to that demanded by the agreement.

It is not clear whether the mitigation of competition by agreement was carried over into the sheet-glass trade. It seems probable that it was not. Competition in the home market was severe and according to W. L. Chance[3] not less than 70 per cent of the sheet glass used came from abroad. This being the case, Pilkington's could only follow the

[1] W. L. Chance in *Chance Brothers and Co.*, p. 283. [2] Ibid., p. 132.
[3] Ibid., p. 283.

price set by the imports. At that time they were selling largely to the merchants up and down the country and not to the London merchants; the basic price had to be decided in the light of the price of imports, but they could generally obtain some premium. Chance's were by this time very small producers of sheet glass and they normally followed the prices fixed by Pilkington's.

Technological developments in sheet glass were rapid, but at this time the older methods were able to survive. Machinery for blowing large cylinders (which were later cut open and flattened) was greatly improved around 1900. The main change, however, came with the development of drawn cylinders. This process involved drawing cylinders straight out of the molten glass. It was patented by Lubbers in 1903, but both before and after this date enormous sums were spent by the American Window Glass Company in developing and perfecting the machine. At first the quality of the glass was poor but the process soon became a commercial success. Pilkington's were aided considerably by the changes in patent laws which came into operation in 1908 and said that a United Kingdom patent must be worked within three years. Partly as a result of this the firm was able to obtain the process in 1909, for the Americans were anxious for the patent to remain valid in the United Kingdom and Canada. This process, which had been so expensive to develop, was certainly obtained more cheaply by Pilkington's than by the American firm which had developed it. The machinery was set up immediately and worked on two tanks in 1909. Mr William (Windle) Pilkington improved the machine and took out two more patents.

During this period the bargaining and the negotiating between firms was extended from the realm of prices and markets to that of patents and processes. Research and development entered a phase in which it was important not only because it reduced costs and improved the product, but also because new processes could only be obtained on reasonable terms if the firm had enough technical strength to do without the other patents, if necessary. As it was necessary for the Lubbers' patent to be worked in Canada and the Canadian tariff had given protection to British glass and so enabled Pilkington's to capture much of the Canadian market, Pilkington's set up a sheet-glass works in Canada.

While Pilkington's were strengthening their position in the flat-glass industry in the ten years before 1914, Chance's were declining in importance, if not in actual size. Their strength lay in their rolled-plate section (which is discussed below) and they were also making wired glass. Sheet-glass production was of relatively small importance and they did not install the new drawn-glass system. Their lighthouse works were important, but this is a small industry; in the optical department 'in face of the subsidized competition of the Jena (Zeiss) glasses, the manufacture had frequently been conducted at a loss, and more than once it was proposed to abandon it'.[1] They did not, in fact, do so, as they considered it to be of national importance and hoped for government support. In 1902 they began to manufacture opal tiles for the interior lining of walls, but although several patents were applied for and the tiles made successfully 'low prices made the venture unremunerative'.[2] In 1909 a similar type of article, 'vitreous tiles' was made but 'again the very low selling prices could not be met. On the outbreak of the war the manufacture was suspended, and in default of prospect of profit, and from other causes, has not yet been resumed'.[2]

In other words, Chance's appear to have reached a stage where they were holding their own successfully in some departments (e.g. rolled glass), and were continuing on a small scale in sheet glass, coloured glass (which is a semi-small scale business), shades of various kinds, lighthouses and optical glass. They also continued to try to expand their range of miscellaneous businesses, but without any real success. During the period they did not enter any field which enabled them to recover their important position in the industry, or even to give them a position of strength and security in a new line which might replace other lines diminishing in importance as fashion changed or foreign competition grew.

In rolled glass, beside the successful use of new methods and the introduction of new patterns, Chance's acquired the Glasgow Plate Glass Co. Little information about this acquisition is available. 'Negotiations of 1895 with the Glasgow Plate Glass Company for the formation of a joint Limited Liability Company fell through, but twelve years later Chance Brothers & Co. purchased the works, and in 1908 transformed them into a Limited Liability Company. The Glasgow vendors were Messrs. Brogan and Mallock, and the services of the latter were retained to direct the works. In 1911 the new company was taken over by Chance Brothers & Co., who, as a first step, decided upon alterations and additions estimated to cost £11,000.'[3]

In the absence of further information one may hazard several guesses concerning the circumstances and motives of this acquisition. First, the Glasgow company was not very large and would, therefore, be finding it difficult, for both technical and financial reasons, to introduce tanks and new equipment for rolling plate. Secondly, finance must have been a predominant motive since the discussions which

[1] J. F. Chance, *op. cit.*, p. 183. [2] Ibid., p. 130. [3] Ibid., p. 132.

started as early as 1895 appear to have centered around the formation of a joint limited liability company. There were thus clear reasons why the vendors wished to sell. The point had been reached where the manufacture of rolled plate required large technical and financial resources and these were only available within the industry. The acquisition was likely to benefit Chance's in several ways. First, they were technically competent in the production of rolled plate and the product was in demand. Secondly, they had resources available because they were not expanding in other directions. Thirdly, they were, and had been for some time, short of top management and were thus in a position where expansion by acquisition was more likely to be successful. Fourthly, rolled plate is cheaper in comparison with its weight than other types of glass and, therefore, a works in the north enabled them to compete better with Pilkington's in an area which was less subject to foreign competition.

Pilkington's made no effort to acquire the Glasgow firm; quite apart from the fact that this firm had entered Chance's orbit and fairly close connections had probably developed between them, there are several reasons why neither Pilkington's nor the vendors would have been enthusiastic about the matter. Firstly, Pilkington's were heavily engaged in expansion and technical development which from a long-term point of view were much more important. Secondly, the works was very small, having only one tank and an equivalent increase in output could easily have been made at St Helens. Thirdly, competition with Chance's was a relatively small problem compared with the competition abroad and with imports. Further, Pilkington's being a family business with plenty of good top management available, would not, perhaps, have wished to incorporate a going concern and give its executives the sort of position which they could demand and would obtain from Chance's.

CHAPTER 4

The Industry Since 1918

INTRODUCTION

SINCE 1918 the flat-glass industry in this country has been dominated by Pilkington's and the history of the period is concerned with Pilkington's struggles with foreign competition and technical progress. There has been only one merger, the absorption by Pilkington's of Chance Brothers; this merger is, however, of the greatest interest since the actual financial merger was simply one stage of an increasingly close association between the two firms. Out of all the cases studied this is the one example of a monopoly which is now so strong in the home market as to approach the classical text-book pattern. Examination of the way in which such a 'monopoly' conducts its affairs gives rise to interesting comparisons between this and the workings of an oligopolistic industry.

The discussion of this period is divided into six sections. The first gives an outline of the major technical changes and related events in sheet- and plate-glass production. The second section analyses the cost structure and the characteristics of the market. This section is largely introductory to the four sections on the commercial history of the various sections of the industry, since much of a firm's policy is determined by the relationship between its cost structure and the structure of the market. The advantage of this arrangement as compared with a single historical treatment is that the continuous importance of the rate and nature of technical progress is emphasized. Whereas the technical developments have had permanent effects upon the industry, the results of the commercial policies have in many cases been merely transitory, since they have been designed to solve the relatively short-period problems of competition.

(a) THE MAJOR TECHNICAL DEVELOPMENTS IN SHEET GLASS

At the end of the war, Pilkington's were making sheet glass both from hand-blown and from machine-drawn cylinders and Chance's were making a little by the hand-blown process. A great technical advance had, however, begun and by the early 1920's the process known as the flat-drawn process was coming into general use. Flat-drawn glass is drawn straight out of the tank in a ribbon and has the great advantage that it has only to be annealed. The whole business of cutting open the cylinders and flattening them is thus dispensed with. Experiments had been going on and patents had been taken out from the beginning of the century, but the process was not a commercial success until the end of the war. There were then two main patents, firstly the Fourcault, which was developed in Belgium, and secondly the Colburn, which belonged to Libby Owens, the big American firm.

In the early 'twenties, the flat-drawn glass was of poor quality; nevertheless, production by this method increased rapidly both in the United States and on the Continent. The product improved as the many technical difficulties were solved. In the United States, where labour costs were particularly high and demand was increasing fast, 80 per cent of the sheet glass was made by one of the flat-drawn processes by 1929, although 59 per cent had been made by the cylinder process in 1926.[1]

Competition from the flat-drawn glass became serious in the mid-'twenties as the quality increased and it became competitive with the cylinder-drawn sheet in more uses. By about 1929 it had to be recognized as being fully competitive in practically all uses. During this period, Pilkington's prices fell from about 85*s*. per box in 1923–4 to 77*s*. in 1925, 75*s*. in 1926, 66*s*. in 1927 and 54*s*. for the three months, June to September 1928. These reductions in price were, however, insufficient to maintain their sales which fell by about 25 per cent between 1924 and 1928. These price reductions also give an indication of the very great importance of the technical advances being made in sheet-glass production.

Like all the major firms with technical strength, Pilkington's had been experimenting with flat-drawn processes for some time. 'Mr Cecil Pilkington had tried to draw a ribbon of glass from a pit over a roller (on the Colburn principle) as early as 1908. After the war experiments on the flat-drawn process were resumed at St Helens under his direction. The first experimental draw took place . . . on October 29, 1921, and the trials were continued until 1926. Although much experience was gained a workable machine was not developed.'[2] Pilkington's were at this stage optimistic that they could develop a

[1] US Tariff Commission, 1937, Report No. 123, Ch. II.
[2] Barker, *op. cit.*, p. 244.

flat-drawn process. The Fourcault patent licence could, perhaps, have been obtained, but they had no confidence in the process, as they thought that the glass would inevitably suffer considerable devitrification. Although they were experimenting with the flat-drawn method they felt, almost up to the end of the 1920's, that the cylinder-drawn glass was superior. The sole rights in the Fourcault process were actually obtained by a new company, British Window-glass Co. Ltd, which will be discussed below.

Pilkington's suspicion of the flat-drawn process is shown by the fact that in 1926 a large new tank with drawn-cylinder machines went into production. In 1925 Mr Austin Pilkington stated that, owing to flat-drawn competition from Continental works, hand-blown cylinder sheet glass was being produced at St Helens at a loss, though the drawn-cylinder process was just paying its way.

In March 1926 Mr Cecil Pilkington announced that the loss on hand-blown sheet glass amounted to ½*d.* a foot. Although machine-drawn glass did pay for itself, hand- and machine-made sheet glass, taken together, did not.[1] In November 1926 a new, large tank with drawn-cylinder machines went into production to replace the hand-blown production. It had, perhaps, been hoped to avoid this and move straight to flat-drawn machines, but by this time Pilkington's were very much on the defensive in sheet glass. 'The quality of flat-drawn glass was improving and by the middle of 1928 even the cylinder process was proving to be of doubtful value. Mr Austin Pilkington was obliged to confess that: 'the firm had been gradually driven out of the export trade in sheet-glass by foreign competition, and had to face the fact that the trade was practically lost to them. The Libby-Owens and Fourcault system produced sheet glass at such low cost and improved quality that we could not compete with the foreigners' prices . . . all the sheet glass we were now producing was sold at a loss'.

Looking back in March 1931 over the previous five years Mr Austin Pilkington revealed that, with the exception of one period of six months, the firm had constantly been losing money on its sheet-glass, the worst being 1926 and 1927, 'each of which cost the industry over £100,000 (a very large sum indeed in those days), and the loss of many customers who have not been regained'.[2] The magnitude of these losses is shown by the fact that they were equal to the capital cost of the large, new manufacturing unit built and equipped for the cylinder process in 1926, and they took no account of the obsolescence on existing plant.

[1] Barker, *op. cit.*, p. 243. [2] Ibid., pp. 223–4.

By 1926 it had become obvious that Pilkington's could not afford to wait for their own experiments with the flat-drawn process to produce a successful machine and efforts were made to obtain a licence to work the Libby-Owens process which was thought to be considerably better than the Fourcault process. Long negotiations took place in 1926 and 1927, between Pilkington's and the Belgian Libby-Owens company, but they finally broke down in the middle of 1927.

In the meantime the Pittsburgh Plate Glass Company had developed a third method of drawing sheet glass; patents on the process were taken out in 1926 when it was in the early stages of development. Pilkington's arranged to work the Pittsburgh Plate Glass (PPG) patents in Britain and made the first attempt to draw glass in March 1930. In April 1931, after some difficulties, the PPG machine was declared a success.[1]

Immediately after the success of the pilot plant, four machines were erected at a tank and began to operate in November 1931. In July 1932 a second tank for drawn-sheet glass came into production, and in May 1933 the last drawn-cylinder tank and its attendant flattening kilns were closed.[2] These changes involved considerable capital expenditure, and large losses through obsolescence. For example, the new cylinder-drawn unit, installed in 1926, at a cost of £200,000, was changed over to the new process at a further cost of £100,000, plant which had cost £110,000 being wholly destroyed. The successful introduction of the new PPG process was a great technical achievement. This is shown by the fact that only Pilkington's and the Pittsburgh Plate Glass Company were able to make a success of it until after 1945. Even now the Fourcault process, which produces less good glass, is used in India, Argentina and Brazil because it is easier technically.

The flat-drawn process for the manufacture of sheet glass gives a very high rate of production. Four or five machines are attached to each tank and there are in this country at the present time (1956) only seven sheet-glass tanks. The one at Queensborough[3] was closed and kept in reserve, but the recent high demand has made it necessary to start it up again.

The innovation of the flat-drawn process has several features which must be emphasized. The first is that the inherent advantages of drawing flat glass, instead of drawing cylinders and then flattening them, were obviously so great that the reward for success was likely to be very considerable. All the major companies in the world had been experimenting since the early nineteenth century and the de-

[1] Barker, *op. cit.*, p. 275. [2] Ibid., p. 245. [3] See Ch. 4 (a), p. 302.

velopment work had been extremely expensive. The second point is that, although the basic idea is simple, the difficulties in the detailed design of the machines and of their control are very great indeed. The relatively slow rate of development of the process and the poor quality of the product even after it was being produced commercially are a genuine reflection of the extreme difficulties of the technological problems, difficulties which lay both in the solution of the fundamental problems and in the exact control of an immense number of variables. It was necessary if the process was to work successfully for the molten glass to be of exactly the right consistency, free from impurities or unfused lumps; it had also to be drawn at the right speed and cooled at the right temperature along its width so that it did not either narrow or distend while cooling. Further, crystalization had to be avoided, for, if any sticks on the grilles, the glass which follows is ruined. To get all these variables right and keep them right is the basic problem. Even today it is almost impossible to make good-quality sheet glass all the time. When the machine itself was in an experimental stage the problem was thus extremely difficult.

Pilkington's had been outstandingly successful in developing machinery for plate glass. They had managed to flow glass straight from the tank for the manufacture of polished plate. They had made continuous lehrs successfully at an early stage, and they had used and improved the drawn-cylinder process. With these technical achievements behind them it is not surprising that they should have thought that they could develop a flat-drawn process. On the other hand, they knew the expense of experimenting in this field with unsatisfactory machines and, not having found a good machine, they were, perhaps, hesitant to take a patent they thought doubtful. Although it is perfectly clear that they fell very much behind in methods of producing window glass, it is important to realize how fast things were moving and how difficult were the problems. The failure of Pilkington's to produce a satisfactory machine, despite their technical competence in other matters, is a sign of the extreme difficulty of drawing flat glass. This is also indicated by the failure of Sheet-glass Ltd to make satisfactory glass in 1928–9 and in 1932, although they had the Fourcault machine which was, by that time, being used extensively.

The obvious potential advantages of the flat-drawn system not only led all the major firms to experiment with the new methods, but also attracted other interests into the industry. In 1919 the British Window Glass Co. Ltd was formed; this company obtained the sole rights for the manufacture and sale in Britain of window glass made by the Fourcault process. These rights were obtained at a time when Pilkington's had no confidence in the Fourcault process. The authorized and issued capital of the company was £450,000, and the works were at Queensborough in Kent. This was already a glass-producing district, having one of the factories of the Canning Town Glass Works Ltd.

The British Window Glass Company was closely connected through interlocking directors with other companies in the glass industry. One of the directors, Sir Walrond Sinclair, was also on the board of United Glass Bottle Manufacturers Ltd, and both he and A. C. Bidworth, another director, were on the board of British Glass Industries Ltd. British Glass Industries Ltd was a holding company which controlled, among other things, United Glass Bottle Manufacturers' Ltd, other glass bottle manufacturing companies and, for a time, the Triplex Safety Glass Co. Ltd. (This company was then small and did not become important until after 1927.) Another member of the board of the British Window Glass Company was C. C. Hatry, the financier.

The British Window Glass Co. failed to utilize the process successfully, and by 1922 no dividends had been paid and only about £47,000 cash in hand remained. A Receiver was appointed in September 1924 and a resolution to wind up the company was passed. In 1928 a new company, Sheet Glass Ltd, was formed; this company acquired the assets of British Window Glass Ltd, most important of which was the right to work the Fourcault process. Lord Beaverbrook was a leading shareholder and the company is said to have had some connections with major building interests. Its object was to compete in the London market which was conveniently near. This meant that it would compete with foreign glass as much as, or more than, with Pilkington's.

Sheet Glass Ltd started production at Queensborough in 1928, but they were unable to make any glass of reasonable quality, and what was produced had to be sold at very low prices, mainly to the horticultural trade. The factory was closed after about a year with a loss of something of the order of £25,000. After devaluation and with the prospects of tariff protection the situation in 1931 was very different from that of 1928. There were rumours of reopening in 1931 but, in fact, no saleable glass was produced until 1932, by which time negotiations for the purchase of the company by Pilkington's had already proceeded some way. Sheet Glass Ltd were quite unable to compete with Pilkington's or with the foreign imports; their costs were high and the quality of the glass very poor. Pilkington's experience enabled them to improve the working of the plant and the quality of the product so that the works has proved a satisfactory addition to capacity. Nevertheless, a rather high price was paid for a firm which was very much on its last legs; this may be attributed partly to the fear that it would be taken over by a foreign producer, so giving him a production unit behind the tariff protection.

The other firm concerned with sheet glass was Chance Brothers Ltd, but their interest in this part of the glass trade had become very small by the mid-1920's. They had not installed the machine-drawn cylinder process and, while Pilkington's were struggling with the new flat-drawn process, Chance's sheet-glass production was confined to a little made by the hand-blown cylinder method and a little crown glass made for special decorative uses. Their technical resources had shrunk to small proportions and they had become no more than a long-period potential competitor; a revolution within the company or an extreme boom would have been necessary to bring them back into sheet-glass production.

It is probably very fortunate that they had not tried to develop their sheet-glass manufacture after 1918, as they would have used much capital in putting in the cylinder-drawn machines and then made such large losses, due to their obsolescence, that the company would have been very much weakened. By the middle of the 1920's the relationship between Chance's and Pilkington's had become very close; Pilkington's actually reserved for Chance's the right to use two PPG machines. This was, however, largely the result of their agreements concerning the production of Vita glass which are discussed in Chapter 4(f).

This section on the major developments in the sheet-glass industry shows that they have been of such outstanding importance that many of the questions which are asked about industries where the rate of historical change is slow are of relatively little interest. For example, the questions as to how the less efficient may be driven out of the industry or whether the market imperfections prevent the expansion of the efficient assume a very different aspect when the rate of change is so fast that differences in costs are large. Similarly, when machinery so quickly becomes obsolete, long-term problems of adjustment of the size of the industry such as those seen in the cotton industry scarcely exist.

The entry of both the British Window Glass Co. Ltd and Sheet Glass Ltd into the industry, during this period of great technical change, indicates clearly the importance of potential competition from those engaged in other sections of the glass industry. Their appearance is also an illustration of the general point that new firms are likely to appear at times when there are new opportunities and cost differences are large, rather than at times when techniques are more stable, and the new firm will be rather similar to the established firms. The failure of both these firms is largely a reflection of the very great importance and the complexity of the technical problems of this industry.

(b) MAJOR DEVELOPMENTS IN PLATE GLASS

In 1918 Pilkington's, the only producer in the United Kingdom, were in a very strong position, for much of the European plant had been destroyed—including their own works at Maubeuge. Not only were the works at Maubeuge rebuilt but also a new, modern plate-glass works was put up at Doncaster. The first plate of glass was cast there in August 1921, and by the end of 1922 production was in full swing.[1]

In this period, however, the rate of technical development was rapidly making existing plant obsolete. There were two independent inventions of immense and almost equal importance. The first was Pilkington's development of a continuous grinder which enabled the glass to be passed under a series of grinding heads, instead of being bedded down on a circular grinding table. A machine was run experimentally in 1920, and by February 1922 was a 'useful machine'. Expenditure of £26,489 was authorized for a third in October 1923.[2]

The other development was the successful use of a continuous flow direct from the tank to replace the casting of plate glass from pots. This development was made by the Ford Motor Company in America, working in close liaison with Pilkington's. Ford had decided to enter the glass industry since there was, at that time, a tremendous potential demand for glass by the American motor-car industry, which was not only expanding but also producing saloon cars, instead of open cars. The US industry, although expanding fast, could not meet the demand and the US became the most important export market.

Henry Ford wrote in *Today and Tomorrow*:[3] 'It seemed to us that we ought to be able to manufacture glass continuously in a big ribbon and with no hand work at all. The glass experts of the world said all this had been tried and that it could not be done. We gave the task of doing it to men who had never been in a glass plant. They started experimenting at Highland Park' (Ford's factory). 'They ran up against every trouble that had been predicted and a number that had not been, but eventually they achieved their result . . .'

'By 1921 the Detroit plant was producing a ribbon of glass 42 in. wide and ½ in. thick, which was assessed by J. H. Griffin, of Pilkington's, to be of "very fair" quality.'[4] Experiments with wider ribbons

[1] Barker, *op. cit.*, p. 234. [2] Ibid., p. 235. [3] p. 52. [4] Barker, *op. cit.*, p. 237.

were conducted at St Helens, and improvements were made; a tank flowing a 60 in. ribbon was built and came into use in October 1923.

The two developments, continuous flow and continuous grinders, made the new plate works at Doncaster obsolete, and in 1926 the flow process was introduced there. This was only three years after the works had got into full production with the old method. In the late 'twenties two more tanks were built at St Helens. During this time techniques continued to develop and the width of the ribbon was increased to 100 in.

Meanwhile, attempts were being made to devise a twin grinder which would grind both sides of the glass simultaneously, thus making the process continuous up to the polisher. Experiments went on successfully, and an entirely new plant for 100 in. glass with a twin grinder came into use at St Helens in 1937. At about the same time a continuous twin polisher was developed so that the whole process became continuous. These technical strides had taken the relatively short time of seventeen years, and were largely responsible for a reduction in the price of plate glass from 3*s*. a square foot for large sizes in 1922–4 to about 2*s*. a square foot in 1939.

Technical developments have by no means ceased although they are less spectacular. Since 1937 it has become possible to draw the glass more than twice as fast from the tank. This has resulted in making one of the two tanks at St Helens obsolete. All these developments have been accompanied by a high rate of obsolescence and large new capital expenditure. Since the war the plant at Doncaster has been completely rebuilt and the twin grinder and polisher installed. At St Helens the increase in output from the tank resulted in the grinders being unable to keep up, more grinding heads had to be put in the place of the polishing heads and a new high-speed polisher installed.

There was not room to make it continuous as it would have had to be in a straight line with the rest of the machine, and there were other buildings in the way. This break in the continuity is, however, not a great disadvantage and in many ways it is an asset for it makes it possible to vary the amount of polishing done and it gives greater flexibility. Experiments with the processes are continuing and particular emphasis is placed upon the successful production of thin, polished plate for laminated safety glass.

Pilkington's are still in the lead in the technique of producing plate glass, and are receiving very considerable royalties on patents, but they are liable to suffer from the fact that they do not require a new machine and the most modern machines tend to be somewhat more economical.

Thus, in plate-glass production, as in the case of sheet glass, the technical developments are of overriding importance, and it is against this background that the commercial events must be considered in the next section. It may be pointed out here, however, that Pilkington's failure to develop an adequate flat-drawn sheet-glass machine was fully offset by their success in plate.

(c) COST STRUCTURE AND MARKET STRUCTURE AND THEIR RELATIONSHIPS WITH PRICE AND OUTPUT POLICY

Having discussed the technical developments one can turn to the cost and market structure of the industry. There is much that is common to the production of the different types of flat glass, so that many of the points made in relation to sheet are relevant to the production of other types. Sheet glass costs and their effect upon policy are discussed first; there is then a shorter section on the costs of plate glass. Both in the case of sheet and of plate glass the data relates to the present time, but many of the magnitudes are relevant to the whole period after the introduction of the PPG flat-drawn process.

COST STRUCTURE OF SHEET-GLASS PRODUCTION

Long-period decisions about expansion are affected by the relationship between costs and the scale of output. In the manufacture of sheet glass there appear to be some economies of scale, but compared with unpredictable changes in cost due to technical change and to variation in the level of capacity worked, they are not outstanding. The magnitude of the economies of scale cannot be estimated with any accuracy since the installation of more tanks would probably make other changes worthwhile and so reduce the long-period cost curves below those calculated on the basis of existing methods. It may be said, however, that when more can be sold at a price which already yields a profit, expansion is always profitable.

It is easy to exaggerate the economies of scale by taking the view that all the costs of development and of gaining experience in working the plant can be regarded as fixed costs. This is, of course, true in the sense that a given total profit may be earned with lower profit margins, the larger the output. There is, nevertheless, a distinction which may be drawn between a falling cost curve, reflecting lower *costs* the larger the output on the one hand, and the ownership of a patent or special skill or knowhow on the other. Special skill and knowhow give an advantage over competitors, make it possible to earn a larger profit margin and to increase total profit by expanding output whenever more can be sold at the going price. However, the important point is that, except in so far as a smaller margin may be accepted when output is increased, a firm which has knowhow or patents does not necessarily strengthen its long-period competitive position by expanding. The opposite is true of expansion by a firm which can gain real long-period economies of scale; in this case the firm reduces its costs per unit *because* it expands and so strengthens its long-period competitive position. (The history of the automobile industry illustrates this point.)

In most industries, including the glass industry, the cost structure affects short-period price and output decisions more than long-period decisions, because economies of scale over the relevant range are seldom large compared with the variations in unit total cost due to different levels of activity.

The sheet-glass industry is highly mechanized and the value of the capital employed is approximately equal to the value of sales. The fixed *expenses,* plus return on capital employed but not including profit, are in the region of 30 per cent of total cost at 'capacity' output. This is high compared with most industries but not, perhaps, as high as might have been expected in view of the low cost of raw materials (about 10 per cent). The reason for this is the very high output per machine which makes the cost of actually drawing the glass low as compared with the handling and packing, etc.; fuel costs are about 10 per cent of total costs.

It is generally supposed that when fixed costs are high prime costs will be low and a firm will, when faced with a fall in demand, reduce prices in order to maintain sales, and so make some contribution towards the high overheads. Examination of the magnitudes involved shows, however, that when fixed costs are 30 per cent of normal price (assumed to be equal to total cost plus normal profit) it cannot be worth reducing the price over the whole output unless the elasticity of demand is greater than five, i.e. such that a 10 per cent reduction in price gives an increase in sales of more than 50 per cent. If the fixed costs were as high as 35 per cent a general price reduction would be worth while only if the elasticity of demand was at least four. The importance of these considerations can only be discussed in relation to the structure of demand, but they do show that even with a relatively highly capitalized industry price reductions over the whole of the output depend upon high elasticities of demand facing the individual firm.

As a high proportion of costs are fixed in the very short period these calculations apply only to situations which are likely to persist for long enough for all costs except true overheads to vary.

As soon as one introduces the possibility of price discrimination the relatively high fixed costs give scope for price reduction even though the elasticity of demand for the product as a whole is not high. For example, it is worth while to bring an idle tank into production so long as the extra output can be sold at a price sufficient to cover the extra costs incurred, provided it does not affect the price obtained on the rest of the output. The extra cost incurred is actually about 65 per cent of the total normal cost and it is, therefore, worthwhile to bring an idle tank into production if its whole output can be sold at a price equal to 65 to 70 per cent of the total cost, including normal profit. There is in other words considerable scope for dumping. This measure may over-estimate the scope if the tank has been idle for more than about a year, for some of the supervisory staff may have been dispersed. It will also be an over-estimate if the tanks vary in efficiency and the marginal tank is the least efficient.

Changes in the number of tanks in use involve large changes in output; very considerable scope for dumping arises when some, but not all, the output of a tank can be sold at the ruling prices, since the marginal cost of the remainder of the output of a tank already in use is very much less than 60 per cent of the average total cost.

The cost structure not only affects a firm's willingness to make price reductions, but also affects their more long-term decisions with regard to profit margins. When fixed costs are an important fraction of total cost the break-even point tends to be high unless the profit margin is substantial; that is to say, the higher the percentage of fixed costs the higher the break-even point at any given price level, and the greater the sensitivity of profits and losses to changes in output. Where fixed expenses (or fixed variable costs) are high, absolute losses may be very great when output falls below the break-even point. As there are considerable changes in the demand for glass and individual firms cannot affect the quantity sold very much by making temporary price changes, the cost structure makes it necessary for them to pursue a relatively cautious price policy with profit margins high enough to give them a fairly low break-even point. The break-even point must be such that output can rise above it sufficiently to give profits which will more than offset the losses incurred during periods when demand is low. Capacity cannot be increased quickly, so that if the break-even point is high, any losses made are unlikely to be offset when demand is high. (This point applies only to industries in which factors in the demand situation make it undesirable to raise prices when demand is high.)

COST STRUCTURE OF PLATE-GLASS PRODUCTION

Much of what has been said about sheet-glass production applies also to plate glass, but the latter is a very much more extreme case. The cost structure is relatively simple as there are in the UK only the two plate-glass tanks belonging to Pilkingtons. One is at St Helens and the other at Doncaster. The output of these tanks is quite adequate for the whole of the plate glass required in the UK, and an approximately equal amount of exports. It is very expensive to put a tank out of production for a short period and three to four months is regarded as a minimum; as a result it is quite common for very large quantities of plate glass to be held in stock. The technical characteristics of plate-glass production thus give only two situations which can usefully be discussed. Firstly, there is the marginal cost of putting the second tank into production. An order of magnitude only can be given, but it would not seem misleading to say that a 25 per cent reduction on the 'long-period average price' would reflect marginal costs. As in the case of sheet glass, it is unlikely that the elasticity of demand would make any short term price reduction worth while, but it might be necessary for long term purposes. (This point is discussed further in the next section.) The other case which is of some importance is the case of the marginal cost of additional production from one of the tanks already in use. We have no data on this; but, as labour costs are predominantly maintenance costs and as raw material is little over 10 per cent of total cost and the fuel cost on marginal output must be considerably less than 10 per cent, the marginal cost of additional output is low in relation to total cost. This means that the scope for dumping at low prices, provided that the price in other markets is not affected, is considerable although handling and packing costs are fairly heavy.

The scope for dumping is the most important influence on the pattern of international trade in plate glass; it dominates the relation between producers at home and abroad, and makes agreements concerning prices and market areas extremely important to producers. In the section on the commercial history of plate glass the results of this peculiar cost structure and the actual demand situation are discussed in some detail.

MARKET STRUCTURE

Glass is sold to a large number of customers of various types and of various sizes all over the country; merchants, both large and small, motor-car manufacturers and large builders are the most important, but a number of other users of glass such as the photographic plate manufacturers deal directly with the manufacturers.

Despite the many uses to which glass is put the demand is, except possibly in the very long run, extremely inelastic. Not only in the two most important uses, in building and in motor cars, but also in most other uses, the cost of the glass represents a small proportion of total cost of the item in which it is incorporated. The low-price elasticity of the demand for glass is of particular significance since demand fluctuates considerably, both over fairly long periods, hitherto associated with the trade cycle, and seasonally. Demand shows a peak in April, a dip in July and August and a minor peak in October. Sales in the April–September half year are not in general as high as sales in the September–March period. These seasonal fluctuations are also accompanied by more random fluctuations and there are very considerable changes in stocks held, particularly by importers; as a result of changes in demand, deliveries from the manufacturer fluctuate considerably.

As the product is relatively homogeneous, the manufacturer announces his selling price. Some firms get larger discounts than others on account of the quantity they buy or on account of their standing as a stock carrying merchant in their district. The whole price structure tends to move together, although the relative prices of different types of glass may alter. In plate glass, the manufacturer announces the prices of cut sizes to the builder as well as the price of stock sizes to the merchant, thus, in part, determining merchant's margins. The fact that much of the market is made up of numbers of relatively small customers in competition with each other inevitably leads to this type of pricing by large manufacturers. Such pricing is also the result of the desire to limit the number of price changes as much as possible; this minimises alterations of stock values and reduces risks. The manufacturers find it more convenient if the merchants hold a fairly steady level of stocks and refrain from speculation rather than carry minimum stocks except when they think that prices may rise. This will not be achieved by steady prices if the seasonal fluctuations are large and regular, but as they are not, manufacturers maintain that steady prices result in greater efficiency and that seasonal changes in price would not be profitable.

The natural imperfections in the market for flat glass are of two main types; there are those associated with the value of regular trade connections, and those associated with differences in the product (this distinction is somewhat blurred since the particular services rendered to individual customers may amount to differences in the product).

Regular trade connections are particularly important in relation to the trade with the smaller customers. These expect and get somewhat better service by remaining loyal, the salesman is anxious not to antagonize them and he gets to know their requirements. When trade is highly competitive there is some tendency for the smaller customers to be retained by giving them extra service to an extent which amounts to price discrimination. When demand is high the regular customer expects to receive adequate supplies at reasonable prices.

A manufacturer 'has customers' from whom he expects orders so long as his price is not out of line with competitors' prices. He may succeed in increasing his number of customers, but this is not easily done and increased orders are more usually obtained by increasing the proportion of the customer's requirements which he supplies. As the larger customers generally deal with more suppliers and do not require special services, they are the more price conscious.

Regular trade connections are particularly important in those sections of the trade where the customer has special requirements and buys not simply stock sizes but glass which has been further processed by cutting, bending or bevelling, etc. There are a number of very large buyers of semi-processed glass, of whom the most important are the motor-car manufacturers and safety-glass makers; but there are also the railway coach builders, greenhouse and cloche manufacturers and the photographic plate manufacturers (large buyers of very thin sheet glass). Supplies of glass for these purposes are generally obtained direct from the manufacturers and special prices may be negotiated. As the orders are large and, therefore, particularly important, the prices may be somewhat lower than other prices. On the other hand, they usually require special services, for example, the glass may have to be cut to size and bent, or a particularly high quality may be needed. Meeting these requirements may, therefore, need special adaption of production and in this case orders once obtained are likely to be retained. They may be retained despite slightly lower quotations from competitors because the customer does not wish to upset arrangements which are working satisfactorily; on the other hand if the order looks like being taken elsewhere there is a great incentive for the manufacturer to cut prices in order to keep it. As both the customer and the manufacturer place emphasis upon the regularity of the contracts, the prices are unlikely to be determined by very short-period considerations.

The imperfections associated with differences in the product are very much more important in rolled, figured, and cathedral glass; as with all products which vary in artistic value there is scope for price differentials which bear little relation to costs. Although sheet glass and plate glass are relatively homogeneous products, at some periods and in some uses differences in quality have been very important and have given rise to market imperfections. Imperfections are also found in the markets for semi-finished glass products such as mirrors, bevelled glass, glass shelves, etc., in countries which have no well-established glass-merchanting or glass processing industry.

The policy of entering to some extent into semi-manufacturing may be regarded partly as a defence against temporary price reductions, partly as an insurance against dumped foreign glass, and partly as a way of selling more glass into foreign markets which are not well served by home merchants and may be supplied by foreign merchants using another manufacturer's glass.

GENERAL PRICE AND OUTPUT POLICY

Certain general price and output policies are likely to be adopted as a result of the persistent characteristics of the cost structure and the market structure. The analysis which follows relates to 'normal' conditions in which there are some changes in demand but no major historical changes taking place.

The length of time under consideration is of great importance in relation to price policy and inability to specify accurately makes generalization difficult. This inability to specify stems in part from the fact that the larger the movement being considered, the shorter is the relevant period.

Price reduction designed to meet situations which are thought to be going to last for less than about a year are rare. This is because the market imperfections due to the advantages of regular trading are such that trade is retained as long as prices are similar to those quoted by competitors, but trade can only be regained or increased by the quotation of lower prices. This asymmetry gives a strong incentive to follow temporary price reductions and thus tends to make the short-period demand curve facing the individual firm inelastic.

The question of the incentive to reduce prices in order to maintain sales or increase a firm's proportion of the market is usually a longer period problem, and the elasticities of demand over periods of two or three years are relevant. Examination of the relationship between fixed and variable costs has shown that *general price* reductions on *all sales* are only worth while if the elasticity of demand facing the individual firm is as much as four or five. As the demand for glass is inelastic the increased sales must be largely at the expense of other producers and elasticities of the order of four or five are only likely when there are a number of firms each with a small share of the market. Such elasticities are unlikely to face large firms since, given the elasticity of demand for the product as a whole, the elasticity of demand facing the individual firm is smaller the larger the proportion of the market held by that firm. This point is made clear by considering a hypothetical case: If a firm's overheads are such that a reduction of price of 10 per cent is only worthwhile if the elasticity of demand for its output is three, then a firm which has already 60 per cent of the market must be able to win 20 per cent more of the total market; this is equal to 50 per cent of the market of its competitors. In more extreme cases, where, for example, a firm has 80 per cent of the market, an elasticity of demand of three is not possible if the demand for the product as a whole is very inelastic.

Thus, a firm which initiates price reductions which are likely to be other than permanent is unlikely to find the policy successful, and in fact general price reductions for short-period purpose are rare when there are firms competing in a single market. Such general price cutting is part of the long-period policy of firms and is initiated by efficient firms who wish either to expand at the expense of their less efficient competitors or to discourage their competitors from expanding in a growing market.

The importance of this conclusion lies in the fact that it shows why agreements between firms serving the same market can be reached rather easily. Agreements between Chance's and Pilkington's appear to have become a more-or-less normal and accepted practice and have not generally been subject to any great strains. The point is also confirmed by the history of the industry; in the middle of the nineteenth century the importance of price fixing was considerable although at the time few industries could be organized successfully. It is probable that the agreements were relatively easy to arrange and there was not much tendency to break them except under long-term influences, when new price levels had to be agreed.

R. L. Chance said of the association in 1878—'There is no doubt that it has been a substantial benefit to us in the past, checking the downward tendency of the time and putting us right when we were getting all abroad.'[1] In other words, it appears that agreement made it possible to find new levels of prices more quickly and without the experimental price cutting which did not indicate the long-period equilibrium clearly. It becomes difficult to plan ahead when current prices are known to be temporary.

[1] Barker, *op. cit.*, p. 157.

The conclusion that there would be little price cutting for short-period purposes if firms were *competing in the same market* also throws some light upon the question as to the effects of price agreements in the public interest. The indication is that the situation is affected very little by price agreements so long as they break down under long-period influences and so long as firms are competing in the same market. They do, however, prevent the price cutting which might appear when one firm, having lost a market, thinks it worth trying to regain it and the other thinks of the newly-gained market as being its own. In other words, agreements prevent the price cutting which might ensue when firms are taking a different view about the long-term equilibrium.

It has been seen that *general price* reductions, except when they reflect long-period costs, are likely to be infrequent. Instead, the sales policy of a large firm is generally directed towards trying to sell more without reducing the price on the bulk of its sales. This may be achieved either by persuasive selling and by such devices as offering better services or by price discrimination. The firm will try to find special markets and special customers to whom additional sales can be made if 'special' prices are charged. Although search for extra sales at prices below the listed prices becomes more important when there is excess capacity, it may be possible to operate continuously a discriminatory price structure which gives different profits in different markets. The possibility of price discrimination makes price and sales policy very much more complicated. The time factor becomes of increasing importance, for the length of time for which different prices may be charged in one market without its affecting another, varies. On the whole, it seems that in the glass industry within a country, apart from the special orders from big customers, a single manufacturer cannot maintain different prices for any length of time. The effect of this is to make the amount of permanent price discrimination within the UK market small, but on the other hand, it does not preclude its use as a preliminary to general price cuts. It is impossible to generalize but, when some basic change in relative costs was taking place, a price agreement might delay the cutting of prices, but, on the other hand, an agreed price might result in an earlier change in the general level.

On the home market two types of price discrimination may be distinguished. Both have already been mentioned. The first is the different prices which may be quoted to large customers with special requirements. These contracts, as has been argued, usually involve a price which remains stable; it is thus a type of discrimination which must either continue for some time or herald a general change in price levels. The price on orders of this type is likely to be a price which is relatively low in relation to long period costs, as foreign competitors can meet a few large orders more easily than a multitude of small ones. The second type of discrimination is between small customers who require considerable service and take small orders and the large customers, particularly the London merchants, who are very price conscious and can very easily turn to imported glass. It is possible to fix discounts so that, with the differing amounts of service taken into account, there is still some degree of discrimination. This may normally favour large merchants but when the future is uncertain it may be better to cultivate the smaller outlets where the market imperfections are greater and more durable. It is, however, difficult to pursue a policy of expanding sales to minor distributors and cut out the larger merchant because it creates distrust and many customers are liable to be lost. When the manufacturer absorbs some of the cost of doing the large merchant's work and increases, by sales effort, his orders from small distributors and users, there is an element of price discrimination; this policy is largely defensive and it must be pursued with extreme caution if goodwill is not to be jeopardized.

The most important case of price discrimination, which may be combined with one of the forms discussed above, is dumping in a foreign market; it is most profitable in markets where the firm is not already selling any significant quantity. As has been discussed in the previous section, the price may be as much as 40 per cent below the price which would give normal profits at a normal level of activity. (This would be rare and would not be continued indefinitely; but a price 20 per cent below might be continued for several years.)

Dumping into a market which is dominated by one or a small number of powerful firms is fairly common; in this case the elasticity of demand is likely to be high because the firms already in the market would lose considerably if they followed a reduction in price. Dumping usually involves sales to large merchants who are extremely price conscious. It is not worth establishing a sales organization, or arranging for particular services for a market which may not be permanent. Only if the dumping becomes extensive, or if it goes on for some time, will any home manufacturer be likely to be forced to reduce prices lest the more stable trading relations become upset and the normal channels of trade begin to change; in particular, the smaller customer may begin to buy from the big importing merchants rather than from the home manufacturer.

The home manufacturer, when deciding upon his reaction to the dumping, must estimate both the quantity likely to be dumped and the length of time over which the dumping is likely to continue. If he thinks that the quantity will be small and the time short, he will simply suffer a reduction in sales; but if he thinks that cheap imports are likely to continue for some time on an appreciable scale he is likely to reduce prices.

When dumping is initiated by a foreign manufacturer it is often possible for the home manufacturer to retaliate by dumping in the foreign market. This may cause such a considerable reduction in profits that it may very well be relatively easy to reach agreement upon the division of markets or upon prices; it will only be difficult if one firm thinks that it can bring about a major readjustment in the relative strengths of the two industries. In other words, unless the relative costs of manufacture in the two countries are substantially different and major readjustment is called for, there is a method of retaliation which is strong enough to make formal agreement easy to reach, and may even make formal agreement unnecessary.

The situation is, however, very different when one of the countries has a tariff barrier sufficient to make retaliatory price cutting in the home market impossible. In this case, a permanent policy of price discrimination may be used by the manufacturers with a protected market. Dumping on a permanent basis is likely to be combined with the dumping of surplus output and prices may fall enough to cause the manufacturers in the unprotected markets to curtail production and make very low profits.

Another situation in which there may be price discrimination between home and foreign markets can be distinguished. This is when the low prices are charged in markets where there are relatively few importers and no established sales organization. In these markets, notably such as the South American and Asian, buyers are extremely price conscious and any manufacturer quoting a low enough price may sell; prices tend to fluctuate considerably and competition is intense. These markets offer an outlet for surpluses and a sphere in which manufacturers may compete without doing each other great damage. In periods when there is surplus capacity these markets probably get the cheapest glass in the world and no indigenous producer could survive; at other times, however, they may find that their prices are relatively high and supplies rather short as they are the markets which are the first to have their supplies limited in times of shortage.

This somewhat general section on the demand for glass shows some of the persistent characteristics of the industry but it is largely an introduction to the following sections on the commercial history of the inter-war and post-war periods.

(d) COMMERCIAL HISTORY OF THE SHEET-GLASS TRADE

In the immediate post-war period the war-time destruction of much of the French industry, the disruption of the Belgian industry and the post-war boom made Pilkington's sheet-glass production very profitable. By 1920, however, Belgian production had returned to pre-war levels and thereafter competition became more intense. The price fell steadily from 140*s*. per 200 sq. ft. at the end of 1920, and was down to 77*s*. per 200 sq. ft. by November 1922. 'The Belgians continued to work a seven-day week while Pilkingtons actually reduced their hours in April 1920 . . . The depreciation of the Belgian franc from fifty-seven to the £1 in June 1922 to eighty-nine to the £1 in 1923 gave Pilkington's competitors a further advantage.'[1] Pilkington's prices were reduced but their sales, particularly to the London merchants, fell. The Belgians, producing more cheaply than the British manufacturer, were making a concerted effort to regain and increase their share of the British market, a large proportion of which they had come to regard as their own. They offered extra discount to individual merchants who would either refrain from buying English glass or buy only a specific proportion of it.[2] These agreements, which were a form of fidelity agreement, were not an anti-dumping device, as is usually the case with agreements of this type; they were a form of discriminatory price reduction in what was the most vulnerable section of Pilkington's market. Pilkington's followed a policy of making price reductions 'when they were inevitable' but they refused to give concessions of price to anyone who had signed agreements with foreign producers.[2] During the 'twenties long-period adjustments were taking place and Pilkington's, unable to meet the Belgian prices on a long-period basis, were prepared to lose some of the market. The market was by no means perfect and some of it could be retained at slightly higher prices, although these often had to be accompanied by greater selling effort and good service.

In 1923, the general level of activity was rising and in March it was possible to increase the price to 85*s*. per 200 sq. ft.; in April 1924 the price was again raised and reached 88*s*. It was reduced again in June 1924 to 83*s*., and after that it fell in six main stages until it was down to 54*s*. in July 1928. This relatively slow rate of price reduction in a period in which Pilkington's were losing 15 per cent of their sales of sheet glass and a greater percentage of the market shows that even

[1] Barker, *op. cit.*, p. 240. [2] Ibid., p. 241.

when competition is severe and prices are determined by market considerations, prices change relatively slowly and steadily, and show short-period stability. This behaviour is in accordance with the previous analysis; there is too little data available for any generalization to be made about the importance of 'special' prices at this time. Certainly Pilkington's were making considerable efforts in the Commonwealth market in the early 'twenties; in 1923 the Commonwealth took 58 per cent of its glass from Great Britain, compared with only 34 per cent in 1914.[1]

In the 'twenties, Pilkington's sales and price policy must have been extremely difficult. From 1926 to 1929 they made losses on sheet-glass production because of their backwardness in technique,[2] and throughout the period they made little profit. As they would not wish to maintain sales at prices which actually involved a loss the problem appears to have been to maintain the output of such plant as could be used profitably. Sales policy during this period involved a series of decisions as to when, where, and how much to reduce prices; in general it was the problem of deciding how great a proportion of the market must be surrendered how quickly.

The slump did not affect demand in the home market very much as activity in the building and motor-car industries was maintained; there was a slight decline in 1928, but after that sales rose. During 1928 Pilkington's were able to raise home market prices from 54*s*. to 58*s*. per 200 sq. ft., and during 1929 to 62*s*. In February 1931, when foreign competition was particularly severe, prices were reduced to 58*s*., but when Britain went off the gold standard prices were raised to 64*s*. and they remained at that level until the end of 1932.

By 1928 world capacity had increased enormously, particularly in the United States. As many new flat-drawn machines had been installed and most of the cylinder-drawn machines were still in use, there would almost certainly have been excess capacity in the industry even if demand had not fallen. Both Pilkington's and Belgian exports were continually reduced and competition was severe. Pilkington's were in an extremely difficult position both on account of the unfavourable exchange rate and because of their failure to introduce the flat-drawn process. For several years prior to 1932 they handled Belgian sheet glass in their Canadian warehouses. It was more profitable to sell the Belgian glass than sell glass made in the United Kingdom. After the conclusion of the Ottawa Agreements in 1932 these warehouses again handled only British sheet glass.

[1] Barker, *op. cit.*, p. 241. [2] See Ch. 4 (a), p. 300.

The following table shows Pilkington's sales at home and abroad in these years and the volume of imports.

TABLE II

Pilkington's Sheet Glass Sales and U.K. Imports

(million sq. ft.)

	Home	Ex-port	Total	U.K. Imports	
1925 ..	—	—	60·2	70·8	other plate and sheet glass
1926 ..	38·4	11·4	49·8	88·6	,,
1927 ..	38·4	10·2	48·6	93·4	,,
1928 ..	37·5	8·2	45·7	89·7	,,
1929 ..	39·3	10·1	49·4	95·9	,,
1930 ..	37·9	6·3	44·2	99·4	,,
1931 ..	34·3	2·8	37·1	108·0	other plate and sheet glass (including rough glass, cast and rolled, figured and cathedral)
1932 ..	46·4	3·7	50·1	89·6	other plate and sheet glass (including rough glass, cast and rolled, figured and cathedral)
1933 ..	70·4	10·2	80·6	71·9	plain sheet window glass
1934 ..	75·6	11·3	86·8	88·9	,,
1935 ..	..	..	..	90·1	plain sheet window glass (including thick drawn)

Sources: Pilkington's and Annual Trade Statistics

In the period between 1928 and 1932, when competition was so particularly severe, it was not possible to make agreements with the Belgians as the firms there were in the midst of a process of regrouping.

The year 1932 was a very important turning point for Pilkington's in the sheet-glass trade. They had installed a successful flat-drawn process[1], and were given a 15 per cent tariff protection in the home market and increased preference in the Commonwealth markets. In addition, the general recovery from the slump was beginning. The increase in sales, as shown in the table, was spectacular, especially in the home market. The change was made somewhat more spectacular by a tremendous hailstorm in the London area, which broke much horticultural glass. Immediately large orders were secured where hitherto only very small orders of a box or two had been taken.

It was in the new epoch after 1931–2 that Pilkington's bought Sheet Glass Ltd of Queensborough.[2] This has already been discussed from the technical point of view, but there are several points relating to the commercial situation which must be made. The first question

[1] See Ch. 4 (a), p. 300. [2] See Ch. 4 (a), p. 302.

is whether the independent existence of Sheet Glass Ltd, had they succeeded in making good glass, would have made much difference. It appears that the additional competition would not have been of great significance beside the existing foreign competition, since either Pilkington's or the foreigners could probably have crushed a relatively small single-product firm. Alternatively, there might have been a situation in which the small firm simply followed the market price which was set largely by the strong Belgian firms (until 1935 half the home market was supplied by foreigners); in this case the value of the competition would have depended on the efficiency of the firm, for it would have been of little value if it survived simply because it held so small a share of the market that it could work to full capacity by making special price cuts which its larger competitors would not find it worthwhile to match. Whatever the possible outcome, Pilkington's were anxious that there should not be an independent competitor and they were even more anxious that the firm should not be taken over by one of their foreign competitors. If a foreign manufacturer had set up inside their market, protected after 1932 by a 15 per cent tariff, their bargaining position would have been very considerably weaker.

The situation in the 'thirties was very different from that of the 'twenties. The technical revolution was more or less complete and the major firms were competing on a more equal footing on an equally strong technical basis. No firms were fighting a rearguard action, as Pilkington's had been in the 'twenties, and the competition was now unlikely to change the relative strength of the major firms.

There was, however, intense competition for markets; Pilkington's in particular were striving to regain their lost ground. At the beginning of 1933 prices were reduced from 64*s*. to 56*s*. per 200 sq. ft. This, however, is an indication rather than a measure of the competition since the published price did not reflect the special prices or special discounts, or the competition in export markets. Dumping had become increasingly important as tariff barriers were strengthened in Europe, particularly in Eastern Europe. By 1934 the competition in sheet glass had become so severe and the effect upon prices so great, in comparison with the effect upon each producer's share of the market, that international agreement became more possible.

Negotiations were pursued between the principal producers and the Belgians and Czechs came together in 1933. A conference was held at Ostend in 1934[1] at which all the principal established manu-

[1] Statement in support of the application to the Import Duties Advisory Committee for an increased duty on Sheet Glass.

facturers were represented. Pilkington's made it clear that the alternative to voluntary limitation was application for increased tariff protection. They proposed a gradual reduction in the proportion of the British market taken by foreign producers. Although the principle of reduction of imports was accepted, the meeting adjourned for the European groups to consider counter proposals. No general agreement was reached and it, therefore, became necessary to negotiate separate agreements with each national group. 'After lengthy negotiations Pilkington's succeeded in 1935 in concluding separate agreements with the principal exporting groups in Belgium, Czechoslovakia, Germany, France and Italy. In general, these agreements provided for the import of quantities decreasing yearly.' 'In October 1935 agreement was made with the Russian Export Authority under which the British Manufacturers accepted responsibility for the disposal of the permitted Russian imports.'[1]

The agreements were accompanied by the general understanding that firms would not undercut prices in each other's markets. This was particularly important to countries like Britain and Belgium where the amount of tariff protection was slight. Pilkington's quoted prices were only altered once (a rise of 2*s*. per box of 200 sq. ft. in 1935) between 1932 and the end of 1936. After 1935 they were the main price leader in the British market.

During the period of the agreement, Pilkington's sales in the home market remained practically constant. The agreements probably prevented imports from capturing a larger share but did not achieve the intended reduction in the share held by imports, owing to the action of non-participating firms and countries. 'In March 1935 immediately after the conclusion of the agreement with the Belgian sheet manufacturers, Belgium devalued her currency by 28 per cent; this induced two former manufacturers who were not parties to the import agreement to re-equip derelict plants.' 'Throughout 1935 and 1936 imports from outside manufacturers, whose imports were not regulated by agreement with the British manufacturers, continued to grow and disturb the market. Although the biggest quantities have come from the two outside Belgian works, there were considerable shipments, mainly of a dumping character from Sweden, Latvia, Estonia and Eire.'[2] These competitors could not be induced to join any agreement as they themselves were not vulnerable to retaliatory dumping; they were either protected by high tariffs in their own home markets, or, in the case of the Belgians, by the fact that any retaliatory dumping would have had severe effects upon the other Belgian manu-

[1]IDAC, Case. [2] IDAC, Case.

facturers who were parties to agreements. Negotiations for modification of the import agreements took place towards the end of 1936. The Russian agreement was left unchanged but it was decided that for 1937 the quota provisions of the other agreements (except as to thick-drawn sheet)[1] should be suspended.[2]

The severity of competition during 1936 resulted in greatly increased sales efforts by Pilkington's. They managed to sell an additional 900,000 sq. ft. of sheet to their smaller and more scattered customers such as builders, ironmongers and picture framers at a time when their sales to merchants, large and small, fell by 3,300,000 sq. ft., and their total sales of sheet in the home market by 2,740,000 sq. ft. The sales efforts were designed to ensure that the final consumer bought as much of Pilkington's glass as possible. The policy had, however, two grave difficulties. It required extreme care to conduct the policy without antagonizing the merchants who were customers by cutting them out. To some extent it was necessary to introduce customers to loyal merchants. The other difficulty was that such sales efforts were inevitably expensive, both in travellers and in the cost of meeting the smaller orders which were received from the smaller customers. Long-period efficiency in marketing had to be subordinated to the need to take advantage of the imperfections of the market.

In December 1936 Pilkington's reduced their prices in order to meet the foreign competition. The energetic sales policy, although fairly successful, had led to protest from the merchants who found themselves losing trade because sales were made direct to their customers. Prices were reduced by 10 to 15 per cent and certain discriminating discounts were introduced. These discounts were applied so generally that they amounted to a further price reduction of nearly 5 per cent. In addition, the thickness of the glass supplied under the chief trade description was increased, in effect giving a further price reduction.

Despite the difficulties in 1936 the agreements with foreign producers had strengthened Pilkington's position very considerably. Price cutting in each other's home markets by the principal producers was more-or-less eliminated and, after 1935, Pilkington's were the price leaders on the home market. Further, in the atmosphere of agreement and negotiation, it was possible to make gentlemen's agreements not to put up works in other people's territories. During the 'thirties, the firms went to considerable lengths to make sure that, in manufacturing as well as in sales, they respected one another's

[1] See Ch. 4 (e), p. 330. [2] IDAC Case.

spheres of influences. Pilkington's acquisition of the works at Queensborough is an example of this.

There was also another case of Pilkington's taking steps to avoid having an independent competitor on the home market. Much of the story is told in the following message which was sent (in code) to the firm's representatives abroad on March 11, 1937.

'For your private information, for use at your discretion, we learned recently that German inventor had almost completed arrangements establish two works England manufacture and grind and polish Fourcault glass. German had obtained promise Government support, because both works located distressed areas. We made strong representation, having regard to surplus capacity idle St Helens, but if glass works must be built, should be built by us. Government accordingly withdrew support German and announcement made House Commons March 10 PB Ltd establishing factory South Wales, probably sheet glass.'

Pilkington Bros (South Wales) Ltd was formed in 1938 and a factory at Pontypool was equipped with a two-machine unit for making sheet glass.

Although the German inventor, Eckert, had claimed that he would use new patents to grind and polish sheet glass, there was almost certainly no market for this, as it would have been more expensive than plate glass made by the most modern methods. His real intention was simply to start a sheet-glass factory. Although Pilkington's representations to the government were successful in making them withdraw support from Eckert, they had to put up the small factory at Pontypool despite the fact that they had already some spare capacity at St Helens. In 1937 there was a tank out of use which could have been brought into production within two months.

After the breakdown of the agreements, competition became even more severe and the dumping continued despite Pilkington's efforts to combat it both by general and by specific price reductions. The specific price reductions included: a reduction in the price of horticultural glass in February 1938 to meet exceptional prices quoted by Estonian producers, a reduction of prices in Northern Ireland in 1937 to combat dumping by Eire, a reduction in the price of thick glass to meet competition from Belgium, and a reduction in 1938 in the price of a type of glass used mainly for safety-glass manufacture.

The British firms appealed to the Import Duties Advisory Committee for an increase in tariff; their first appeal was refused, they appealed again in 1938 and the case was accepted in 1939 just before war broke out. The acceptance appears to have been based upon the great ease with which foreign producers could dump on the London market and the fact that the British producers had little way of retaliating because foreign tariff barriers were so high.

The Simon Committee report on the Distribution of Building Materials and Components (1948)[1] preferred official tariffs to private agreements, involving price fixing, special discounts and exclusive dealing. The building materials trade was, however, reported as feeling that 'tariffs were a slow and imperfect method of dealing with the problem'. This contrast is not entirely relevant to the sheet-glass trade just before the war as they were apparently unable to organize and maintain the necessary agreements. Nevertheless, it should be pointed out that agreements may, if they are reasonable, eliminate dumping (particularly intermittent dumping), while having no great effect upon the regular trade of the parties to the agreement. Tariffs, on the other hand, cannot be made to distinguish between regular trade and dumping and may, therefore, be a more drastic step in cases where a substantial proportion of the product is normally imported. The case for tariffs, as opposed to agreements, in this type of situation, depends upon the view that the agreements are likely to be particularly restrictive, in other words, to do very much more than simply prevent dumping.

On the outbreak of war the situation was immediately changed completely and Pilkington's found themselves in a very strong position. As in 1914 'Pilkington's took the opportunity of the removal of cut-throat competition to introduce a stable price policy and to treat all their customers with equal favour'.[2] In particular, it was no longer necessary to charge different prices in different parts of the country to counter foreign competition.

In 1942, partly on Pilkington's initiative, the Sheet Glass Merchant's Association was formed. The turnover required to become a member was low and the subscription was small. The formation of the association, which already had a parallel in the more stable plate-glass trade, was in part the result of the reduction of competition; it reflected the more stable trade relationships. Initially, the merchants were not graded, but in 1952 two categories were introduced. The categories were distinguished on the basis of size and range, and the larger merchants received a bigger discount. On the whole, Pilkington's accept the Association's merchant categories, although they have the power to object and would do so if they thought that the Association was being unduly restrictive. Pilkington's are in so strong

[1] Report of the Committee of enquiry appointed by the Ministry of Works on The Distribution of Building Materials and Components, 1948, p. 25–6.

[2] Barker, *op. cit.*, p. 255.

a position that they prefer to leave the question as to who should receive the different levels of discount to the merchant, but they would revise this policy if they found that any of their prices left substantial scope for price cutting by the merchants. The strength of Pilkington's allows them to take a firm line on the question of which orders they will supply direct and which they will supply through the merchants.

During the war and immediately afterwards, the proportion of trade going to the different types of customers changed relatively little since, when supplies were short, only existing customers were supplied. There was, however, some tendency for rather more to go to the larger merchants as no new small merchants were given deliveries and a number of the old ones left the trade. The structure of the market remained more or less frozen until 1950, but after that the effects of the reduced competition can be clearly seen.

The proportion of sales going into different types of sales outlet in 1936 as compared with the proportion in 1935 is an interesting illustration of the effectiveness of sales policy. Sales to large merchants were 7·8 per cent lower in 1936, but sales to small merchants only fell by 5·5 per cent and sales to most other trades fell by only 0·6 per cent, this fall being concentrated almost entirely in the photographic plate trade. A stronger reflection of the relationship between the intensity of competition and the distributive system is to be found in the contrast between the inter-war and post-war periods. After the war, it was no longer necessary for Pilkington's to sell energetically to the smaller customer in order to meet the foreign competition. They preferred the more efficient system of selling in large lots to the bigger customers, since this not only reduced the need for salesmen but also made it possible to take greater advantage of 'loose loading'. Loose loading means sending glass loose in special lorries or trucks instead of putting it into packing cases. It saves much labour and timber, but the economies are only gained if large loads are delivered and the customer has unloading and storage facilities. Since 1950 the quantity sold to large merchants has increased by nearly 20 per cent, to smaller merchants by about 15 per cent, and the quantity going to ironmongers, plumbers, decorators, builders and contractors, large works and mills, and to shop fitters has actually decreased. These changes in the distribution of sheet glass have their parallels in the distribution of other types.

Pilkington's do not think that there are at present any appreciable 'soft spots' in the market which make one type of trade much more profitable than another. In other words, there is little price discrimination and no part of the trade which would be particularly vulnerable to price cutting, on a long-term basis, if there were effective competition. Nevertheless, it is extremely difficult to charge prices which reflect exactly the cost of supplying a customer. There are four variables, the size of individual orders, the total value of orders over a period, the regularity of orders month by month, and the regularity of orders over the years. Since the value of a customer depends upon all these variables it is extremely difficult to devise a price list which does not contain an element of discrimination.

Pilkington's strong position as the only supplier during the war has continued since; their efficiency has increased and their costs are now below those of their European competitors. The high Belgian exchange rate has weakened competition from that source and high level of world demand has reduced incentives to dump. It is largely this greatly increased strength of Pilkington's position which has brought about the changes in the structure of the home market. Sales policy is now dictated mainly by long-period cost considerations and it is no longer necessary to consider market imperfections and to conduct a sales policy which takes them into account. All elements of price discrimination cannot be eliminated, but they can be reduced to a minimum compatible with reasonable degrees of stability and flexibility.

(e) COMMERCIAL HISTORY OF THE PLATE-GLASS TRADE

Pilkington's have been the only producer of plate glass in the United Kingdom since soon after 1900 and, thus, the commercial history of the inter-war period is the history of the competition between Pilkington's and foreign producers in both the home market and in export markets. Immediately after the war world demand was very high compared with capacity and new equipment was being put in all over the world. The rate of technical improvement was fast,[1] and price competition in the early 'twenties, despite the slump, appears to have been largely long-period competition in which prices were reduced only when it was justified by the long-period cost structure. One of the chief reasons for this was that the demand for plate glass by the automobile industry increased phenomenally fast, especially in America.

Up to 1926 demand was high and competition was not severe except on a long period, mainly technical basis. However, there can

[1] See Ch. 4 (b).

have been little incentive to expand output other than cautiously because all producers were expanding, especially the Americans. In 1926, Pilkington's exported 10 per cent of their production to the United States, 90 per cent of this going to the Ford Motor Co. However, 1926 was the peak year; production in the United States increased and the market for imported plate fell sharply. By 1927 competition had become severe and Pilkington's exported only 1 per cent of their output to the United States. Prices were reduced at the beginning of 1927 for the first time since 1924. The reduction was 3*d.* per square foot to 31*d.* per square foot. A further reduction of 4*d.* per square foot was made in the middle of 1927, and the new price of 27*d.* per square foot was maintained until mid-1929.

One of the most important developments of the 'twenties was the increased use of glass in automobiles. The patent for safety glass was obtained before the war and the Triplex Safety Glass Co. Ltd, which had the licence of the main patent, was registered in 1912. The company got into great difficulties and was liquidated by the senior official receiver in 1921, It was, however, reformed and registered as a private company in 1922 and made into a public company in 1925. The Stock Exchange Intelligence of 1922 shows British Glass Industries Ltd as holding a controlling interest in Triplex Safety Glass Co. Ltd, but by 1925 the connection was not mentioned. Triplex Ltd did not make glass themselves but concentrated on the laminating process. The market was growing fast in the 1920's and Pilkington's were contemplating the desirability of getting a sub-licence to manufacture Triplex safety glass.[1] It appears that in 1925 the Triplex company were importing a proportion of the glass they used. Pilkington's were thus in a rather insecure position in a market which was becoming extremely important. At this stage they decided not to embark on the manufacture of safety glass, but they were very anxious to continue to supply the glass for lamination to the Triplex Company. In November 1927, for instance, it was reported that Triplex expected to gain the Austin Motor Company's order for 1,400,000 ft. of safety glass;[2] the Board at Pilkingtons recorded:

> 'We wish to have the whole of this order and a special price will be quoted . . . Considerable discussion as to whether the firm should obtain some option or licence to make Triplex themselves in view of the fact that the firm's contract agreements with many of its customers will be jeopardized if all supplies take place through the Triplex Co.'

It would seem that the very large Triplex orders contained a con-

[1] Barker, *op. cit.*, p. 248.
[2] This quantity must have represented a long term contract.

siderable element of risk for Pilkington's since, in the absence of some form of agreement, Triplex could at any time obtain their glass from continental producers. The interests of the two firms were closely linked, but Pilkington's must obviously have disliked their somewhat uncertain position. In 1929, the two firms came together and formed Triplex (Northern) Ltd., a jointly-owned subsidiary, and a new factory was opened at St Helens in 1930. This is a clear example of a merger to secure outlets for the product.

Although Triplex Ltd was by far the most important maker of safety glass there were others, most of which started in the late 'twenties. The most important was Protectoglass which was the main supplier of three of the smaller motor-car manufacturers. The goodwill, assets and some of the plant of the firm were bought in 1933 by the Triplex Company.

British Indestructo was formed in 1927 to acquire an exclusive licence to manufacture Indestructo in England, Scotland and Wales. They had a factory at Dagenham near the works of the Ford Motor Company Ltd. This firm had a chequered career and frequently paid no dividend. In 1951 large interests in it were bought by the Austin Motor Co. Ltd, Briggs Motor Bodies Ltd, Ford Motor Co. Ltd, and Pressed Steel Co. Ltd. The firm is, however, smaller than the Triplex Company and supplies only a proportion of the requirements of the Austin and Ford companies.

In 1937 the Triplex Company bought up the Lancegaye Safety Glass Company of England, and its subsidiary, the Gilt Edge Safety Glass Ltd; Lancegaye Ireland remained independent and continues to manufacture safety glass independently in Ireland.

Other firms worth mentioning are the Tyneside Safety Glass Company, which is in association with Suntex Ltd, and the Tudor Safety Glass Company: both of these continue to produce laminated safety glass, but they do not sell to the big motor-car manufacturers. Another is the Splintex Company which was registered in 1928, having been formed to acquire the Splinterless Glass Co. Ltd (registered February 1926). It acquired the Newtex Safety Glass Co. Ltd in 1932. The firm has never paid an ordinary dividend, its paid-up capital was reduced in 1932 and again in 1954, when there was a major reorganization and the preference dividends for 1931 to 1954 were cancelled. It now makes plastic mouldings and, although still making some laminated safety glass, is not important in this trade.

Pilkington's entry into the production of Triplex, which made a part of their market very much more secure, was not, however, the most important reaction to the intensified competition which resulted from the enormous increase in productive capacity in the United

States as well as in Europe. Even more important were the market-sharing agreements, negotiated with the European producers at the discussions which followed the intense competition of 1927. Pilkington's had a large stake in the United Kingdom market and in the Dominions, and were thus vulnerable to dumping in these markets. The European producers supplied most of the Continent and, although many countries were protected by tariffs, firms such as St Gobain had works in several countries. Pilkington's were also established on the Continent at Maubeuge, and were thus able to compete from within the Continental market. There was thus a situation in which the producers were able to do each other great harm in each other's markets, the extent of their power being indicated by the low marginal costs of producing extra glass from tanks already in production. This type of situation makes agreements relatively easy to reach, as even in their absence the scope for retaliation against price cutting is considerable. If a firm cuts prices in a market in which it has only small sales, the producers with a substantial interest in that market may cut prices in the main market of the price cutter.

Agreements were made in 1929; prices were fixed, the markets were divided, and each industry was given quotas. In the cases where one producer had a major share of the market the quotas fixed a quantity of imports and not a share of the market; this allowed the major supplier to meet all increases in demand.

Pilkington's bargaining position was rather weak at this time. They had very little tariff protection and this, together with the well-organized and large London market, made dumping into the United Kingdom particularly easy. The agreements were made to last for a period of ten years, 1929 to 1939, and were then to be reviewed. In 1932 devaluation, the tariff protection and the Ottawa Agreements strengthened Pilkington's position very considerably and thus the Plate-glass Agreements became unfavourable and involved a considerably smaller volume of sales than would have been possible in their absence, both in Commonwealth markets and in the large London markets. The nature of the agreements did, however, allow Pilkington's to meet the expanding demand of the United Kingdom motor-car industry.

During the 'thirties Pilkington's position was strengthened still further by their technical achievements and they threatened to re-equip the Maubeuge works with the most modern plate-glass equipment. New discussions with the foreign producers were started, and in 1935 Pilkington's sold the Maubeuge works to the St Gobain Company and obtained a number of important concessions in markets outside Europe.[1] These arrangements accord with the big manufacturers' general policy of defining and preserving their particular spheres of influence.

By 1939 Pilkington's position was further strengthened since the new twin-grinding and polishing plant had started production in 1937, and the firm had a definite technical lead over its competitors. The Convention Agreements were renewed in 1939 on terms more favourable to Pilkington's, but the new terms never became effective as the war intervened.

Although Pilkington's position in plate glass had become so much stronger, there was, during the 'thirties, increased competition from traders who were not parties to the agreement; important among these were certain trading corporations, mainly of New York, who bought plate glass at domestic rates in the United States and resold it in other markets at a narrow margin of profit. Their activities undermined the efforts of the American producers to keep to their agreed share of the market. The response to this type of competition was to make increased use of 'fidelity' agreements. Customers were supplied only if they did not buy from firms who were not parties to the main agreements. Customers accepted 'fidelity' agreements as the outside competitors seldom supplied a full range of glass and their supply was not always regular. Fidelity agreements are also the obvious, and almost the only, response to dumping by firms protected by high tariff barriers. Outside producers, if protected in their home markets, would be quite unlikely to make any agreements until they had achieved a high volume of sales in foreign markets.

One of the features of the competition in plate glass in the 'thirties was the competition from thick-drawn sheet glass: improved techniques had made this an adequate substitute for plate glass in some uses. Pilkington's did not sell thick-drawn sheet glass on the home market until after 1937, when imports were such that the competition had to be met. In the sheet-glass agreements made with other producers,[2] clauses limiting imports of thick-drawn sheet glass and fixing prices were inserted; these were not suspended until 1937. The sale of thick-drawn sheet was also regulated to some extent by agreements between Plate Glass Merchants' Association and the producers who were parties to the plate-glass agreements. In the years just before the war Pilkington's sold large quantities of thick-drawn sheet; since the war they are selling even more. Practically all of it goes to the motor trade and, even so, the demands can scarcely be met. Given total sheet capacity the proportion of thick sheet which can be drawn is limited

[1] Barker, *op. cit.*, p. 251. [2] See Ch. 4 (d), p. 322.

by the fact that only a proportion can be drawn thick. Further, in times of shortage, thick-drawn can only be produced at the expense of a much larger footage of thinner sheet. The British market is peculiar in that the proportion of thick-drawn sheet to thinner types of sheet is abnormally high. For these reasons, Pilkington's do not supply the whole of the demand for thick-drawn sheet and a quantity is imported from Belgium. Incidentally, these features probably lead to a slightly larger sale of plate glass.

Since the war, Pilkington's have been in a very strong position in the plate-glass trade and have declined all suggestions to renew the pre-war quota agreements. They have maintained some of their technical lead by further developments and are receiving royalties from producers who have installed the twin-grinder and polisher. In addition, their costs are lower than those in the United States, for in this industry the higher costs of labour are not offset by greater efficiency. In this strong position they require no specific agreements; the threat of retaliation, including the use of fidelity agreements, is sufficient to eliminate short-period competition.

(f) ROLLED, WIRED, FIGURED AND CATHEDRAL GLASS

It is very much more difficult to generalize about trade in rolled, wired, figured and cathedral glass, but it is here that, in Chance's, Pilkington's had an important competitor in the United Kingdom. In the second part of this chapter the merger between Pilkington's and Chance's, which was the only big merger in the flat-glass industry, is described and analysed.

The cost structure of these types of glass is not unlike that of sheet glass, but rolled and wired glass are much heavier in relation to their value, and thus not only the world market, but also the home market, is somewhat less perfect. In figured and cathedral glass the design is of considerable importance and, thus, the product by no means homogeneous. The market for rolled and wired glass is largely with the big merchants and the patent glaziers. The patent glaziers are generally large concerns which both make the bars and fittings which hold the glass and do the actual installation. The market for the figured and cathedral glass coincides very largely with the market for other types of glass used for building.

In the home market Pilkington's and Chance's agreed not to cut each other's prices. This does not, however, appear to have been done without some friction in the earlier years. Towards the end of the war in 1917 there was even the tentative suggestion that 'one way of affecting some closer working was offered in Scotland where a joint control of the Glasgow works' (purchased by Chance Bros. Ltd, in 1908) 'might solve many of the questions which produced friction. This friction he thought was aggravated by the action of the merchants who had their own axes to grind . . .'[1] Nothing came of this suggestion, but it was finally agreed that prices should be fixed and competition confined to sales efforts. Pilkington's were in the stronger position of the two, but it appears that so long as Chance's did not expand their share of the market Pilkington's were content to allow them to remain. Any effort to force them to contract or even close would undoubtedly have been extremely expensive; but, in any case, the friendly relations between the two great glass-making concerns in the country made this policy undesirable so long as Chance's did not pursue aggressive policies.

The prices were fixed mainly with reference to foreign competition and, as far as possible, on a long-period basis. Perhaps one of the reasons why Pilkington's were content with the situation was the fact that they had obtained, in 1925, a method of making wired glass which produced a product much superior to that produced by Chance's, and this wired glass was tending to replace rolled glass upon which Chance's very largely relied.

In the export market there has generally been severe price competition, particularly in rolled and wired glass for which the orders tend to be so large that individual quotations may be made. In some markets, especially those in which there were no home producers, there has been little to moderate the price competition except in particular corners of the market. In others, however, there have been some private agreements between producers which have tended somewhat to mitigate the competition. It appears, for example, that Chance Brothers Ltd and the St Gobain Company probably did not compete severely after 1912 when some of Chance's shares were transferred to the St Gobain Company. Similarly, competition was limited both by the Continental Convention in 1904 and by the private arrangements made after 1910, which followed the Convention agreements.[2] In the inter-war period competition was severe, but it may have been somewhat reduced by the willingness of the major producers of Germany, Belgium, France and the United Kingdom not to cut each other's prices unless it was necessary to keep out other competitors.

[1] Barker, *op. cit.*, p. 232, Data from the Board Minutes of Pilkington's, in which a conversation with E. F. Chance was reported by Mr. Cecil Pilkington.

[2] W. L. Chance, Ch. XIV, of *A History of Chance Brothers and Co.*, by J. F. Chance, p. 283.

In the inter-war period the relationship between Pilkington's and Chance's became progresssively closer. Not only was competition between them limited to their sales efforts, but more formal arrangements were made tying the two companies together. In each case the predominant position of Pilkington's became clearer.

The first example of the closer association is found in their joint actions concerning 'Vita' glass. 'Vita' glass is a special glass which has the characteristics of a special transparency to ultra violet, and thus does not cut out the ultra violet rays from the sun. The special glass was invented by F. E. Lamplough, who was associated with Chance's; an agreement between them was made in 1926 and Chance's began to market the glass under the trade mark 'Vita'. In October 1927 a new agreement was substituted in which Pilkington's and Chance's jointly obtained the rights to make the special glass. If they thought it advisable, they were to form jointly a new company for the purpose of manufacturing the glass. A further agreement was made at the same time between Chance's and Pilkington's, defining their co-operation and their respective interests, and Pilkington's agreed to pay Chance's £7,500.

Pilkington's were at that time convinced that 'Vita' glass was an important development and in March 1928 a new agreement was made assigning to Pilkington's firstly, 'all that business of Chance's as manufacturers of and dealers in the special glass now carried on by Chance's at Smethwick and the goodwill thereof', and secondly, 'all the said British Trade Marks . . . and thirdly, almost all the interest and benefit of Chance's under the first agreement (1927)'.[1] In return Pilkington's agreed to pay to Chance's a share of the profits made on the manufacture of the special glass to compensate them for loss of profit. Chance's share was based on the assumption that they would have supplied a proportion of the 'Vita' glass market; the proportion had of necessity to be fixed somewhat arbitrarily. In sheet-glass Chance's annual share was 60 per cent in 1928–9, 30 per cent in the years 1931–43 and then remained at 20 per cent. In rolled glass their share was based on the assumption that they would have supplied 50 per cent of the market.

In addition Chance's were to have 'in order to compensate them for the increase in the cost of their manufacture of other lines of manufacture, arising out of the Assignment',[1] £60,000 of Pilkington's 5 per cent debenture share. It was envisaged that sales of the special glass would exceed 10 million sq. ft. per year, and Pilkington's liability to make any payment under the sub-clause relating to the

[1] Agreement between Pilkington's and Chance's.

transfer of shares was to cease if sales averaged less than this amount for three consecutive years.

The very close working between the two companies is shown by the fact that the agreement included an option by which Chance's could supply to Pilkington's not only special sheet glass to meet a small proportion of the market, but also such quantities of rolled, special glass as Pilkington's required to fulfil their orders. Pilkington's, however, retained the right to manufacture rolled glass if the demand required it, or if Chance's costs were too high.

It was the clause giving Chance's the option to supply a proportion of the 'special' sheet glass which led Pilkington's to reserve for Chance's the right to work two Pittsburgh Plate Glass flat-drawn sheet machines.[1]

The close association between the companies at this stage partly represented the friendly relations between them, but it was also a reflection of the greater technical and financial strength of Pilkington's, for it was they who were prepared to invest in the new product. The 'Vita' glass enterprise was of considerable importance because it strengthened the bonds between the companies, but it was not a commercial success. Pilkington's had paid heavily to obtain control of the patents and trade marks, but events showed that they had completely misjudged their importance. In 1928 a 'Vita' glass marketing board was set up and a considerable publicity campaign was organized. This, however, met with very little success and although 'Vita' glass continued to be made by Pilkington's up to the outbreak of the war, the quantities were small.

There was no occasion for Chance's to install the PPG flat-drawn machines for sheet glass and they ceased to make sheet glass.

The agreements concerning 'Vita' glass were followed fairly soon by the beginning of the merging of the two companies, for it was in the early 'thirties that Pilkington's began to buy an interest in Chance's.

The immediate cause of the merger was the desire of the Chance family to take some of its money out of the firm, for the number of members of the family closely associated with the management of the firm was by this time very small. One possible course was to convert the firm into a public company and float it on the Stock Exchange. This would have been difficult as the firm was not very prosperous, and its position depended almost entirely upon the goodwill of Pilkington's, who, if they wished, could have ruined Chance's by reducing prices. Pilkington's were more efficient and, at some cost to

[1] See Ch. 4 (a), p. 303.

themselves, could have driven Chance's out of the rolled-plate trade. The alternative course was to sell to another manufacturer. This had to be either Pilkington's or a foreign company. The firm was probably of greater value to Pilkington's than to any other firm since a lively foreign competitor with international interests might well have reduced very considerably Pilkington's freedom of action. Further, Chance's probably preferred Pilkington's as the two families were well known to each other and had had mainly friendly relations in their struggle against foreign competition for many years.

The arrangement made was that Pilkington's should buy the shares of Chance Brothers Ltd as and when the Chance family wished to sell them, at a price fixed by an independent valuer. Purchases of the shares by Pilkington's continued slowly until 1951, when the whole transaction was completed by a big final purchase.

During the 'thirties the firms continued independently to sell against each other at agreed prices, but Chance's did not enter any new field in which Pilkington's were engaged. The two firms also operated a number of joint enterprises. In 1938 a jointly-owned company began to produce rolled plate in the Argentine, and in 1939 this company began to make sheet glass as well.

More important was the case of fibreglass production. Chance's had been interested in glass fibre products since the early 'thirties and had been manufacturing them at their Glasgow works. By 1938 it had become clear that there was a future in fibre glass and a jointly-owned firm, Glass Fibres Ltd, was formed. Large-scale production was started at a new works at St Helens, largely financed by Pilkington's. The establishment of their jointly-owned firm may be compared with the suggested jointly-owned 'Vita' glass firm which was not formed, the whole development being undertaken by Pilkington's. In the case of fibre glass the development was largely in Pilkington's hands, although the firm was jointly owned. This project has been a great success and is still expanding rapidly.

Another field in which Pilkington's effectively took over from Chance's, under the guise of a jointly-owned company, was optical glass. The industry in this country has always been comparatively small on account of the competition from Germany, but Chance's were the main producers. Soon after the outbreak of war Umbroc Ltd, a jointly-owned subsidiary, was started by Pilkington's and Chance's and a large new works for optical glass was started at St Helens.

The merger was completed in 1951 when Pilkington's bought the remainder of the Chance ordinary shares. The policies pursued prior to the final amalgamation must, however, have allowed for the fact that it would take place. In the post-war period Chance's were in a difficult position, their management was weak and an unsuccessful attempt to enter the pressed-glass trade had proved expensive. This failure was to a large extent technical, for the glass was of low quality. No ordinary dividend has been paid since 1950–1. Although the higher financial policies of the two companies were merged in 1951 they continued to be run independently for a while. In the last few years, however, the process of merging the two firms has gone forward, and now both sales and production are largely merged, and there are no longer two selling organizations in competition with each other.

This is the most important merger which has taken place in the history of the flat-glass industry since it is the only case of a merger between two major companies. Although Chance's were weak compared with Pilkington's, they were producing large quantities of rolled glass. Further, it is the only case since the 1860's where the merger made a substantial difference to the degree of competition in the home market.

There are two outstandingly important features about this merger from the point of view of the general study of the role and importance of mergers.

The first is that the merger might have taken place at almost any time since the beginning of the century and that, even when the purchase by Pilkington's started in the early 'thirties, it had been preceded by proposals for quite extensive joint working on 'Vita' glass. Further, the acquisition of Chance's took place over nearly twenty years (including the war). This appears to have been a direct result of the fact that the industry is such that two firms, of even only approximately equal efficiency, can, rather easily, come to agreements not to compete on price, for in any case the prices quoted must be the same, as all price cuts will be met by the competitor. In addition, there is the point that, although the acquisition was complete in 1951, the changes in organization which are the direct result of the merger were by no means complete four years later.

The second feature of this merger stems from the fact that Chance's technological skill had apparently declined to such an extent that, had a major technical change occurred in the production of rolled plate, the firm would quite likely have shrunk and ceased to be a factor in the flat-glass industry. In other words, Chance's were only able to remain in the flat-glass industry because there was a section in which technique changed relatively little after the beginning of the century. In this section they were able to maintain a reasonable level of efficiency. The extent to which their efficiency fell below that of Pilkington's was largely offset by the fact that in rolled, figured and cathedral glass the market is very much less perfect, the product being less homogeneous and the transport costs higher in relation to value.

Further consideration of these points, and the light which they throw upon the role of mergers in the flat-glass industry, is reserved for the final section in which general relationships between the characteristics of the industry, the nature of competition and the role of mergers and of agreements and restrictive practices are discussed.

CHAPTER 5

The Subsidiary Activities of Pilkington Brothers

PILKINGTON'S is based on large-scale production of various types of flat glass, the relative importance of which has changed from time to time. The commercial history of the main types has been discussed in some detail in the preceding chapters. In order to complete the picture of the scope of the firm its other activities must now be considered.

When sheet glass was made by hand, and before the introduction of tanks, this could readily be combined with the production of shades. The shade department was started between 1845 and 1848,[1] and continued until the beginning of the twentieth century. At about the same time the ornamental department came into existence and coloured glasses were made. Again, this was technically closely related to the production of window glass, as all glass was made in pots so that small batches were normal practice.

Another departure from the production of flat glass was the introduction, at the end of the 1890's, of a section making pressed ware. The chief product was cells for batteries. These took relatively large quantities of glass and were thus a suitable product to turn to when demand for other glass was shrinking due to the very severe foreign competition; it enabled spare glass house capacity to be used. The demand for cells increased enormously when the battery wireless became common and in 1927 an American Miller machine, which was really an adapted bottle-making machine, was installed. By this time the pressed-ware department, although relying upon the firm's knowledge of glass technology, was less obviously related to the production of flat glass and was in competition with the producers of bottles and pressed ware. This department has, however, continued to be of importance and in the 'thirties the manufacture of glass blocks (bricks) was started. This again is a product which requires large quantities of glass and is semi-mass produced. It also combines well

[1] Barker, *op. cit.*, p. 144.

with the production of flat glass, being distributed through many of the same channels.

In the 'thirties Pilkington's began to produce glass insulators for electric power lines. Like glass blocks, these can be mass produced, and they require a large volume of glass. Although the sales outlets are quite different from those of the other products, the number of customers is small and each order large so that no elaborate sales organization is required.

Since the war the production of the glass part of cathode-ray tubes has been developed on a large scale. The demand promises to be very large, and it is certainly a product which can only be produced by firms with the highest standards of glass technology. It is also one which is suitable for large-scale production and which will use a considerable volume of glass. Further, it fits into the Pilkington organization without making it necessary to have a large, new sales organization, for the orders can only come from the relatively few makers of cathode-ray tubes. This field is one in which technical development has been rapid and the production methods are changing, but nevertheless the heavy initial expenditure may well give a position of considerable strength. It is a case where the initial risks and costs are high, but the possible rewards are also high, particularly in terms of security.

These characteristics may be compared with the research and development in methods of plate-glass production. Firms with large and successful research and development facilities can go forward into new long-term projects, financed in the initial stages by the proceeds from their past success. This is a pattern which must repeat itself unless the firm is to change its characteristics and regard itself in some sense as having reached maturity and so turn its attention to low costs and the maintenance of a given secure position. This stagnant approach to the business is always possible and might be profitable, but it involves accepting the risk of an eventual decline such as that of Chance Brothers Ltd.

Fibreglass Ltd has become an exceedingly important subsidiary and is expanding very rapidly. The production of fibreglass is related to the production of flat glass in two ways. Firstly, both use large quantities of glass and are mass produced and, secondly, a high proportion of the output goes to the building industry. Nevertheless, like the production of cathode-ray tubes, the relationship is not very close and Fibreglass Ltd, as the uses for the product increase, is tending to lead an independent life of its own. In other words, it is a case of real diversification into a different, although related, field, a diversification which was undertaken because the field appeared profitable and the firm had the managerial and technical strength to enter it successfully on a large scale.

Another activity which was largely taken over from Chance Brothers Ltd is the production of optical glass. Pilkington's now have a monopoly of the production of most types of optical glass and does a considerable amount of processing. They also make raw glass for spectacle lenses.

Some of Pilkington's other activities were taken up for a different type of reason, to ensure that their own glass should be used. A prime example of this is Triplex (Northern) Ltd which has already been discussed.[1] There are also a number of overseas safety-glass subsidiaries. These have plants in Australia, South Africa, New Zealand, Brazil, the Argentine and interests in a plant in Canada. Another example, already mentioned[2], is the cutting, bevelling, bending and decorating of glass, and the production of mirrors. All these processes make it possible to take large, important orders direct from big customers, such as shop fitters, railways coach builders, etc. They also make it possible to sell more glass direct to merchants in countries where the glass-processing industry is undeveloped. These activities may be regarded as taking advantage of markets which are less subject to short-period price fluctuations and severe short-period competition, because they are more imperfect.

Somewhat similar, although the circumstances were peculiar in that the firm was in great difficulties, was the acquisition of O. C. Hawkes Ltd in 1932. O. C. Hawkes was a Birmingham firm of merchants, makers of mirrors (especially Venetian mirrors) and of bathroom furniture. The firm was removed from Birmingham to Ravenhead at the outbreak of war in 1939, and closed in 1941–2.[3] The acquisition was not of great importance to Pilkington's and no others of similar nature were made. It was, nevertheless, an indication of the general wish at that time to ensure outlets for their glass.

The range of Pilkington's activities was also increased by entering into the production of special types of glass of which 'Vita' glass, 'Calorex' and 'Vitrolite' are three important examples. 'Vita' glass has already been discussed.[4] 'Calorex' is a glass which allows only a small proportion of the heat of the sun to pass through it and it is thus useful in the tropics. Like 'Vita' glass, it was one of the results of increased knowledge of basic glass technology. 'Vitrolite' is an opaque glass for the surface of buildings. When space became available at Doncaster because of the changed methods of making plate glass, the production of 'Vitrolite' was started there in 1932, an agreement

[1] See Ch. 4 (e). [2] See p. 289. [3] Barker, *op. cit.*, p. 251. [4] See p. 333.

having been made to work an American process. The first big order received was for the Mersey Tunnel which was opened in 1934. 'Vitrolite' made it possible to use glass in a new way and thus constituted an addition to total demand. It needed energetic advertising and skill was required both in installing it properly and in giving advice as to where it could suitably be used. The British Vitrolite Co. was formed as a pioneering company to fit and fix the glass properly so that its reputation would not be damaged by unskilled installation. The British Vitrolite Co. Ltd continued to perform these functions for about ten years, but now the product is sufficiently well known for no further efforts to be made in this direction and the work can be left to the usual merchants, glaziers and builders.

Double glazing (two layers of glass sealed together with a small airspace between) is another example of promotional work. It doubles the area of glass required for windows and Pilkington's are more interested in developing the processes for making it efficiently, and in promoting its use, than in keeping its manufacture to themselves.

Toughened glass became a definite possibility in the 1920's, and in 1930 Pilkington's began to operate a French process successfully. This development resulted in major changes in Triplex (Northern) Ltd, as production was switched from laminated to toughened safety glass. The other effect was the development of the uses of 'Armour' plate which was the trade name given to the Pilkington-toughened glass. Again Pilkington's found it a good thing to go into the production of semi-finished and finished products, such as assembled 'Armour' plate-glass doors. They did this mainly to promote their use, and, as soon as other glass processing firms were prepared to take over the job, were quite willing to let it go so long as it was done competently.

There is thus one range of activities broadly connected with the question of ensuring the use of Pilkington's glass, and another range broadly connected with promoting the use of glass. Other subsidiaries were less directly connected with the main activities of the firm.

In 1936 Triplex (Northern) Ltd bought H. E. Ashdown (Birmingham) Ltd, a struggling firm in the plastic industry. The chief reason for this acquisition was the desire to obtain an interest in plastics because it seemed possible that plastics would replace glass in a number of uses. The firm was moved to St Helens in 1937, partly because of unemployment there and partly to fill part of the works left unused after the transition by Triplex (Northern) Ltd from laminated to toughened safety glass. It did some plastic mouldings for windscreens, but on the whole had to take whatever orders it could get. Pilkington's took it over from Triplex (Northern) Ltd, and it is still doing a variety of things, including some shaping of perspex. It has never really come into its own and on balance has not been profitable. It may, perhaps, become profitable making things which require a combination of plastics and fibre glass. The acquisition of Ashdown's was not the only step taken to ensure against the possibility of the replacement of glass by other plastics. Before the war an agreement was made with a major perspex manufacturer that, if sales of perspex rose above a certain figure, a jointly-owned firm should be set up in which Pilkington's would hold 51 per cent of the shares. Thus, in effect, an arrangement was made by which Pilkington's could buy themselves into the 'perspex' industry on a co-operative rather than a competitive basis. This agreement has been abandoned since the war, the threat of plastics having been found to be slight.

Pilkington's have also had interests in two other glass firms which are only remotely connected with their main activities. From 1933, part of the Doncaster works was occupied by the Rockware Glass Syndicate Ltd, a bottlemaking firm in which Pilkington's obtained an interest.[1] This connection was made partly because something was needed to fill vacant capacity at Doncaster ('Vitrolite' production being only on a small scale.) The Rockware Glass Syndicate Ltd was chosen mainly on account of personal considerations, but also because there was no danger that Rockware would attempt to make flat glass. These main considerations were reinforced by the feeling that a small interest in the bottle industry might be useful.

The other firm was James A. Jobbling Ltd, the makers of Pyrex. Pilkington's came into possession of this firm as a result of personal friendships and a series of peculiar circumstances.

In the early 'thirties, when Pilkington's were still anxious to diversify and reduce their dependence upon the very risky flat-glass trade, Jobbling's wished to make provision for the future. It was arranged that Pilkington's should put some money into Jobbling's and it was agreed that Pilkington's, the Corning Company of America and Rockware Glass Syndicate Ltd should buy the rest of the shares as Jobbling's wished to sell them. Corning and the Rockware Glass Syndicate left the agreement and in 1948 Pilkington's bought the rest of the shares. The company had by this time expanded considerably so that very much more capital was involved than had been anticipated. Further, Pilkington's had no wish to diversify further and had many other opportunities open to them.

James A. Jobbling Ltd is an excellent firm, with considerable scope for continued expansion, but the whole business is rather

[1] Barker, *op. cit.*, p. 248.

different from Pilkington's other lines. Nowhere else are they selling what is practically a fashion product in a highly competitive trade to a vast number of small and large distributors. Although Pilkington's could have undertaken it wholeheartedly, and their knowledge of glass technology would have been useful, the success of the firm depended to a much greater extent upon a large number of smaller special developments and upon marketing, than does their success in the major lines. It would, thus, have involved a major expansion into a rather different line at a time when there were tremendous opportunities in fields to which they were better adapted. Another influence was the fact that Pilkington's did not want to expand beyond all possibility of remaining a family firm.

When the opportunity arose, Pilkington's sold 60 per cent of the capital to Tilling's Ltd, who were looking for opportunities to invest the resources they had available as a result of the nationalization of road transport. Tilling's did not wish to have the entire share capital as they were anxious to maintain contact with an experienced glass producer. In 1954, however, arrangements were made for Pilkington's to sell the remainder of their shares to the Corning Company in return for certain cathode-ray tube patents. In this way one of the world's major glass producers has become established in this country and it appears that this is likely to have some effect upon the competitive strategy and bargaining power of the American firm. They might also expand here rather than be willing to license patents; this could be important as they have very large research laboratories.

This case of the relationship between Pilkington's and Jobbling's is of particular interest; the merger was dictated partly by personal considerations and partly by the particular situation of the 'thirties which made Pilkington's wish to diversify. The main considerations which led Pilkington's to sell the company were by contrast very long-period strategic considerations. After the war they aimed to concentrate upon those products which they were particularly well suited to make and were prepared to cease to produce those things which could equally well be produced by others. This long-term policy was pursued despite the fact that it meant selling a currently profitable subsidiary in return for the potential profits to be made from cathode-ray tubes and from the increased investment in other sections of the business. The selling of Jobbling's was thus a remarkable instance of untying a somewhat fortuitous merger.

Finally, it is necessary to discuss Pilkington's activities in relation to their supplies of raw materials and equipment. These are a reflection of the size of the firm and of its emphasis upon long-period continuity. The first two cases of backward integration were into coal and alkali production. Pilkington's began to work the coal measure in the immediate vicinity of the works just before 1860. This developed rapidly and new pits were opened. The firm gained considerable advantages in buying their coal at preferential rates and the colliery was also expanded and merged with others so that it became a substantial business in its own right. This continued until the nationalization of the coal mines. As it was customary for coal proprietors of the St Helen's district to operate a brickworks in conjunction with their collieries, a colliery brickworks was started in 1872. Pilkington's had actually had a brickworks before this which was referred to in the Board Minutes of 1865.[1]

Pilkington's entered the alkali trade in 1865, but it had been discussed earlier and one attempt had been made in uneasy partnership, which broke down, with an ex-employee, William Deacon. Entry into the industry was made necessary partly in order to ensure increased supplies, but largely because an especially high-quality product free from iron was required. The Mersey Chemical Works of William Pilkington & Sons was not under direct control of the board of Pilkington's. The first deliveries from the works resulted in considerable improvement in the quality of the glass.[2] Technical developments in the production of alkali challenged the Leblanc process at the end of the nineteenth century, and after intense competition the works were incorporated into United Alkali Co. Ltd, which was later absorbed by ICI. Now regular supplies are obtained from ICI who can be relied upon to supply the quantity and quality required.

Pilkington's have obtained most of their sand from near-by sources, but some for the whiter types of glass has had to be imported. In about 1900 the firm bought the Anglo-Belgian Silver Sand Co. Ltd, which owned property at Moll in Belgium. 'This move was made on the advice of the firm's chemist in order to avoid having to pay very high prices to the Belgian Syndicate which had cornered all existing supplies of silver sand.'[3] This company has been completely inactive and of little or no significance since before 1914. It was wound up in 1954.

A different type of subsidiary is Khasia Sillimanite Co. Ltd, which owns a sillimanite quarry in Assam. This company was formed as a result of research work on the problems of refractories (used for lining furnaces), which have become in many cases the limiting factor in furnace design and operation. It was found that sawn blocks of unfired sillimanite gave good service and the company was set up to

[1] Barker, *op. cit.*, p. 204. [2] Ibid., p. 152. [3] Ibid., p. 209.

produce and market the blocks. This company has, however, proved uneconomic and is to be wound up or sold.

As the major producer of flat glass and the only producer of the most important types in the country, Pilkington's have had to be, to a large extent, their own machinery makers. They have, therefore, a substantial engineering department as well as design and drawing offices. Their heavy demands for machinery of particular types and mainly to their own specifications have led to close relationships with the engineering firm of Entwhistle and Gass Ltd.

Finally, Pilkington's have a major interest in timber and the manufacture of packing cases. The cost of packing is, in a few cases, greater than the cost of the glass and in most export markets it is substantial. The difficulty is that the final customer is often small and the case must be small enough to be handled without special equipment. In Canada and the United States of America all cases of sheet glass must weigh less than one hundredweight. This means that where the sheets are large the case must be very narrow. Within the United Kingdom the cost of cases is less serious, for since the 'thirties methods of loose packing have been used successfully. The amount of timber used is so large that Pilkington Brothers were on the 'Approved List' of timber importers. In general, the lists of importers were confined to merchants and Pilkington Brothers were the only exception. This exception was largely due to the long standing direct connections with Swedish exporters and the large amount of timber used.[1]

CONCLUSIONS

Pilkington Brothers Ltd is then a very large concern which is based on flat glass. Its other activities, even where large themselves, are, in the main, subsidiary. Where the other activities are not directly related to flat-glass production or marketing, they have in general several characteristics in common. These are large-scale production, requiring big volumes of glass and extensive glass technology. On the whole, they are the result of long-term plans which aim to give good results over a long time. This is particularly true of fibreglass, cathode-ray tubes and insulators. Another point is that in general the product is sold in markets which are free from short-period day-to-day price competition. The competition is in basic technology, efficiency and in the promotion of the product. This long-term outlook is not necessarily incompatible with undertaking the production of goods

[1] Monopoly and Restrictive Practices Commission: *Report on the Supply of Imported Timber*, 1953.

which require short-term price and product decisions, but the two are sufficiently different to require very different types of managerial organization. James A. Jobbling Ltd was sufficiently different in this sense for Pilkington's, which is still essentially a family firm, to be quite willing to relinquish it. Similarly, Pilkington's sold rather than used and developed the engineering subsidiaries of Chance Brothers.

Consideration of the general structure of the firm and the emphasis upon technical efficiency in mass-production explains why the firm, in common with others of similar types, finds its monopoly position burdensome; it feels compelled to accept many special orders which cannot be placed elsewhere. This is a responsibility because a short-period refusal or really very high prices would be exploitation of their position. It may also be necessary from a very long-term point of view, as repeated refusals would perhaps lead to the development of competitors who would enter the field and take some of the regular trade just because they were prepared to do special orders as well.

This general survey of the firm is relevant to the present study, partly because it emphasizes the continuity and desire for stability of a particular large organization which is taking long-term decisions of great importance. These features have very considerable effects upon the nature of competition and on the relationships between competition, mergers and agreements.

CHAPTER 6

Conclusions

MERGERS have played a very small role in the development of the flat-glass industry, but its history shows the way in which the objectives of mergers have been achieved by other means. Production of flat glass is now in the hands of a single firm and, therefore, all possible economies of scale can be exploited; although there is competition from foreign manufacturers there is only potential competition from home producers.

The flat-glass industry is comparatively simple in that it is relatively well defined and the products are fairly homogeneous. In addition, the main features are well marked; the long period is very long, technical change has been extremely important and the number of firms has been small. The most difficult features to assess are those related to price discrimination and its possible effects in the absence of price agreement. On the whole, however, as a relatively small number of characteristics are of overriding importance, generalizations about the relationships between the characteristics of the industry and its structure, and judgments as to the relative merits of different structures, have been rather easier in this case than in the other more complicated industries where there are more features of moderate importance.

Mergers have been unimportant in the flat-glass industry because they have been unnecessary. Firstly, short-period price competition has seldom been severe. This has been partly due to the fact that there have been so few firms that either tacit or formal agreement has usually been maintained, and price cutting would have been expensive. The fact that price discrimination is possible usually makes it necessary to have formal rather than tacit agreements. No merger could ever have raised prices significantly since it has generally been necessary to fix the price in relation to the prices of imports.

The second major objective of mergers is expansion to obtain economies of scale. Again mergers have not been required. The rate of technical progress was such that market imperfections have been unimportant compared with the very large reductions in costs and prices which have taken place. As a result the efficient firm has been able to drive out its competitors. This elimination was stimulated by the very intense foreign competition during the crucial period at the end of the nineteenth century. The efficient firm, Pilkington's, gained both at the expense of Chance's and at the expense of those which were forced out of existence; it then expanded whenever foreign competition allowed. When an industry becomes concentrated the concentration is frequently accompanied by the acquisition by the strong firm of the assets of the other firms; in this industry, however, these assets, even if acquired, have been of little value or significance.

The gradual merging of Chance's and Pilkington's took the form of a series of agreements which were followed by increasingly strong financial links. Almost thirty years elapsed before the two were fully integrated. The process of integration appears to have been closely related to the importance of the various types of economies of scale; Pilkington's first took over the new products which required technical skill, research and finance, and not until three years after the full financial merger was the amalgamation of the sales forces completed. It appears that the expansion of Pilkington's might have followed a rather similar pattern even in the absence of merger, but it is not clear how long Chance's would have remained either in existence or independent; it might have been acquired very much sooner or ruined quite quickly if it had refused to follow Pilkington's leadership.

In the absence of price competition the elimination of weaker firms is almost entirely associated with technical change. This is illustrated by the fact that Chance's survived upon the basis of their rolled-plate departments which were those least affected by technical change. In the absence of a high rate of technical change the industry, with its durable capital equipment, might have become relatively inefficient since the inefficient would have tended to remain in existence.

It is partly the importance of technical change which makes firms willing to agree to short-period price stability, as long-period positions have depended upon ability to make technical improvements resulting in cost reduction. Those reductions have been so great that the successful have been able to expand and grow while still pursuing a policy of charging prices equal to average costs. The technical changes have given rise to such large differences in efficiency that change in the relative strength of firms has been the result of historical development, not the cumulative result of short-term price policies.

The glass industry was highly concentrated by the end of the nineteenth century and since then it has become completely concentrated as a result of two mergers, one of which was of considerable importance. The question is now whether the high degree of concentration is in the public interest. Again discussion turns upon price policy and upon economies of scale, including research and development. With regard to prices, it appears that if there had been a small number of firms, agreements would have been reached. This indicates that the monopoly cannot be regarded as being against the public interest simply because it charges prices related to average rather than marginal costs. In a naturally oligopolistic industry, monopoly price-policy cannot be compared with competitive price policy, unless price agreements are either illegal or too difficult to negotiate.

If there had been several firms with price agreements the industry would probably have been less efficient because of the wastes and inefficiencies of competitive selling. This is not, perhaps, an important consideration since there has been foreign competition, but nevertheless the foreign producer has shown less tendency to develop elaborate sales organizations than might have been expected from a home producer.

A number of firms without price agreements would have produced a situation in which price discrimination would have become of considerable importance. It is possible that the different price levels would have varied considerably over time, and that the average price might have been very similar to the non-competitive alternative. The major effect would probably have been found in the alterations in the share of the market going to the different firms, and this might not have been closely related to productive efficiency. It thus appears that in the flat-glass industry short-period monopoly pricing is not markedly inferior, from the point of view of the public interest, to any of the possible alternatives. However, although Pilkington's are substantially a monopoly producer in this country, there is foreign competition and considerable potential competition; both would develop if Pilkington's fell behind in any way. The big Continental and American producers could manufacture in this country, the Corning Company, which has control of J. A. Jobbling & Co. Ltd, being in a particularly strong position to do so.

The existence of a monopoly rather than competition appears to be little or no disadvantage from the point of view of development and research. The glass industry seems to be one of those in which research must be done on a large scale beyond the scope of the smaller firm. By the end of the nineteenth century competition in basic research had become international and the existence of a number of smaller firms in this country would have been of little significance. It may even be suggested that they would have been less effective than Pilkington's and that they would have been unable to make such good bargains in patent negotiations; they might even have been unable to reach the price-cum-patent agreements which enabled this country to use some foreign processes.

Expansion and, to a lesser extent, mergers have made Pilkington's into a multi-product firm as well as into a very large firm. A great firm with technical strength and a spirit of enterprise may be expected to develop along several lines both because its ability makes it profitable and because diversification gives greater security. The survival of Pilkington's as a major producer of flat glass might well have been impossible if it had not made both plate and sheet glass, for there have been considerable periods during which one or the other has been unprofitable. It has sometimes been argued that inefficiency is protected within large, conglomerate firms because one product can subsidize another. However, if one product has high costs, these may be offset by charging only marginal costs for the services of departments shared by other products. This should not necessarily be regarded as subsidizing inefficiency, for, if it is profitable to continue to do this indefinitely, the 'inefficiency' is simply being offset by economies of scale, a form of efficiency. This point is of some importance since it gives recognition to the fact that the production of flat glass involves a great deal beyond the main processes of drawing and rolling. Any discussion of the comparison between situations in which there are single-product firms rather than multi-product firms is quite misleading, and ignores the fact that new producers of any particular product are extremely likely to be those already producing related products. In this industry a large single-product firm, even if it existed for historical reasons, would be very unlikely to remain specialized; the technical problems are so difficult and the capital investment so heavy it seems probable that single-product firms would have been subject to an intolerable degree of risk.

Such is the importance of long-period technical development that the modern flat-glass industry is one in which only the large firm, protected in some way from the full rigour of short-period competition, can survive in competition with the great glass enterprises in other countries. This protection is obtained partly from diversification and partly by agreements. In this industry, more than in any of the others which we have studied, a structure which is favourable to major technical development is required; this is found in the large firm whose prosperity depends largely upon its success in solving long-period cost problems rather than short-period problems arising from temporary market situations.

V

THE MOTOR INDUSTRY

by G. Maxcy

CHAPTER 1

Introduction

THIS chapter is concerned with the development of the industry which manufactures and assembles private cars. The purpose of this enquiry has made it necessary to adopt this limited, and somewhat arbitrary, definition of the motor industry; one which excludes producers specializing in heavy commercial vehicles, and the numerous manufacturers of parts and components. Attention is, thereby, concentrated on firms whose products are in fairly close competition, and whose conditions of development and survival are similar. It so happens that the manufacturers and assemblers of private cars also make most of the commercial vehicles and tractors, so that nearly all of the final output of the industry is covered by this definition.

Mergers have not been important in this industry and the recent formation of the British Motor Corporation by the amalgamation of the Morris and Austin companies is quite exceptional in this respect. The real interest in this study lies in the way in which the motor-car industry, which once had over eighty firms, has become concentrated into the hands of five, who now produce 95 per cent of all cars, and some 90 per cent of all commercial vehicles and tractors. This has been achieved by expansion and competitive elimination, rather than by merger. The historical analysis examines the reasons for this pattern of development and discusses the special circumstances which gave rise to the mergers that did take place.

The motor industry has enjoyed an almost continuous increase in demand so that it has never had to face the complication of adjusting to lower levels of output. Within this expanding framework, firms have been pre-occupied with problems of growth, design, technique and styling, and have in general refrained from intense short-period price cutting. Throughout its existence, the industry has been affected by ever increasing economies of scale to a greater extent than, perhaps, any other.

The history of the industry has been divided into five periods: the early, experimental years (1896–1901), the period of small-scale competition (1902–22), the beginning of mass production (1923–9), price and model competition between larger firms (1930–9), and the post-war expansion (1945–55). There is also a section on the industry in the United States, which offers interesting comparisons indicating the very considerable effects of apparently minor differences in circumstances.

CHAPTER 2

The Early Experimental Years, 1896–1901

IT is not often that an exact date can be said to represent the beginning of an industry, but the year 1896, with the repeal of the 'Highways and Locomotives Act' of 1878, certainly marked the birth of motor-car production in the United Kingdom. By imposing impossible conditions on the use of roads by self-propelled vehicles, the 1878 Act had stifled the development of the new form of transport. Pioneers such as Knight, Austin and Lanchester had been quietly experimenting with engines, and F. R. Simms had gained possession of the patent rights of the Daimler engine for the United Kingdom. However, no attempt had been made to exploit the commercial possibilities of the new invention prior to the 'Emancipation Act' of 1896.

Manufacturers were quick to enter the new industry as soon as the legal barriers were removed. Six years later, in 1902, there were fifty-odd producers of cars exhibiting at the first official Motor Show. Very few of them were long-established businesses of any size and importance. The great majority were either new companies organized expressly for the purpose of making cars, or small, general engineering firms trying their hands at the new product. For both types the risks seemed small, while the gains open to new ideas and enthusiasm appeared unlimited. Obviously, it must have been easy to enter the industry and not too difficult to turn out a car that would run—at least until after the sale had been completed!

The production of the early experimental models required very little capital. The new product needed no heavy equipment, no huge outlays on plant and machinery before manufacture could commence. The production techniques, for the most part, were simple and widely known. For the established general engineering firm, the making of cars was primarily a question of adapting existing equipment to a new use. Very little reorganization or training of the labour force was involved; the men merely turned out a different product with the same general purpose tools.

But if entrance into the new industry was easy, survival proved much more difficult. This was partly due to the intense competition and partly to the rapidly changing nature of the product. The latter problem was acute in this period when even the basic layout of the chassis and engine had not been decided and there was fundamental disagreement among the engineers as to whether cars should be powered by petrol, steam, electricity, oil, etc. Even as late as the 1912 Motor Show, although the majority of the cars exhibited had petrol engines by then, there were over a dozen different steam cars on the stands as well as a number of electric vehicles. The Liquid, Air, Power and Automobile Co. of Great Britain presented a car 'driven by atmospheric air, in the form of a liquid at a temperature of 312 degrees below zero'. The following claim was made by Botsword's, of Ipswich, for their offering on Stand Number 7:

> 'With this car other fuels than petrol can be used, such as, pure alcohol, benzolene, or any good spirit, such as, gin, brandy, whisky, etc.'[1]

This extreme uncertainty over the major lines of development of the new product naturally added to the hazards of the industry, and increased the number of entrances and exits. Recruits were lured from wider areas of industrial background, and many young hopefuls raced off in the wrong direction, never to be heard from again.

But even those fortunate enough to have joined the petrol camp right at the start, soon found themselves in a technological race for survival. Every year significant improvements were made in the design and performance of the primitive petrol engine, while radical changes were taking place in the body work. It was vitally necessary for a firm to keep pace with these developments, to initiate improvements of its own, and to find public support for its version of the march of progress. No firm could stand still and keep its place in the industry.

The highly fluid structure of the industry and the very rapid rate of product development presented a barren field for mergers. With the annual unit output of even the largest companies only measured in hundreds, combination could provide little in the way of economies of scale. The existence of so many small firms, coupled with complete freedom of entry, rendered it impossible to limit competition and to secure a significant market share by amalgamation. The rapid product change weighed against the acquisition of firms with a model enjoying current success; today's purchase might well be tomorrow's failure. Under these conditions it seemed preferable to devote one's resources to internal expansion and model improvement. In union

[1] Catalogue, p. 23.

there was no strength. No mergers worth mentioning took place in these early, hectic years, except the absorption of Wolseley in 1901 by Vickers, the armaments manufacturers.[1]

However, a bold attempt was made to seize monopoly control of the industry by buying up patents instead of firms. The man behind this move was Harry J. Lawson, a dynamic and colourful individual, who had grown rich promoting companies in the cycle and kindred industries.

'His scheme was to make a complete corner of the still unborn British motor industry, petrol, steam and electric, by buying up every hopeful-looking patent on which he could lay his hands, in the hope that one day he would come across some "master" patent which would prove a gold mine.'[2]

Lawson relied upon the public, of course, to provide the money for his patent-monopoly scheme, and he was not disappointed. A public issue of £100,000 by the newly-formed Daimler Motor Co., of which Lawson was chairman, was oversubscribed, and speedily recompensed him for the £35,000 he had paid to Simms for the patent rights to the Daimler engine. This was followed by an issue of £750,000 by the Great Horseless Carriage Co., another Lawson creation. These, and subsequent flotations enabled his 'parent' company, the British Motor Syndicate, to indulge in an orgy of patent speculation. The aim was to acquire enough patent rights to cover the manufacture and use of all motor engines in the United Kingdom, and thus to be in the position to extract royalties from every British car manufacturer, importer or owner. So confident was the Syndicate of its supremacy that its secretary, Charles Jarrott, declared in November 1897:

'So far all attempts to excel the patents and inventions belonging to the Syndicate have signally failed, and all tests indicate that our systems are the only ones of any value, and will be the controlling powers in the industry for years to come.'[3]

The future of the Syndicate, and indeed of the whole industry, depended upon the validity of its patents, which were subject to considerable litigation. In this the Syndicate was not without some early successes. The Courts, for example, found C. S. Rolls guilty in 1897 of importing and showing a French Peugeot in the United Kingdom without the permission of the holder of certain British patent rights, and ordered him to pay the British Motor Syndicate £15. Herbert

[1] The reasons behind this merger are discussed in the following section.
[2] St John C. Nixon, *Daimler*, 1896–1946, p. 29.
[3] D. H. Noble and G. M. Junner, *Vital to the Life of the Nation*, 1946, p. 9.

Austin abandoned all thought of developing the first Wolseley he built because it so closely resembled the French Bollee, the patent rights of which were held by the Syndicate. After several years of confusion and litigation, the deciding case came in 1901 as the result of an action brought by the Automobile Material Protection Association Ltd, an organization formed by members of the industry for the express purpose of fighting the patent monopoly. The association contested the validity of one of the Syndicate's major patents and won the case. This Court victory put an end to the only serious attempt at monopoly control of the British motor industry.

Lawson undoubtedly realized that, at this early stage in the development of the industry, it was ideas and not firms that were of value, and in his bid for monopoly control he bought up patents, not firms. He was a farsighted man whose ideas were on the grand scale; he realized from the start the great possibilities of the motor industry, and he even envisaged the coming of the aeroplane. What Lawson could not see was that his attempt to corner the market in ideas was bound to fail. The rate of progress was so rapid that no patent was of value for any length of time, and his hope of finding a 'master' patent controlling the whole future course of development of the industry was merely wishful thinking.

There is no evidence to suggest that the Lawson episode was anything more than a grandiose attempt to hold the new industry at ransom. His operating companies appear to have been little more than excuses for public issues to provide the money to buy more patents. When his patent claim collapsed, they disappeared into thin air. Lawson, the promoter, was not the man to use monopoly gains to build up a great productive organization of his own, one capable of developing and improving the new product and of initiating the large-scale manufacturing techniques that were to come. Nor were the times ripe for such an organization, which would require sweeping changes in attitudes, relationships, and in the structure of the entire industry. The stage had not been reached when large resources were essential, or even could be used with advantage. In the meantime, progress continued to be made by numerous small firms, free from concern over patent litigation.

CHAPTER 3

The Period of Small-scale Competition, 1902–22

THIS was a period of slow, but steady, expansion in production. The combined output of cars and commercial vehicles rose from about 4,000 in 1905 to over 10,000 in 1908. Before the First World War intervened, production had climbed unspectacularly to 34,000. No breakdown of this figure exists, but it seems likely that about a quarter of these were commercial vehicles, which leaves some 25,000 as the number of private cars made.

Roughly fifty manufacturing firms contributed to this total. The largest of these was Ford, with car sales in 1912 of 3,000 rising to over 6,000 a year later.[1] Ford at this time was established in Manchester, primarily as an assembler of the well-known Model T, parts for which were obtained from the parent company in Detroit. The largest British producer was said to be Wolseley, with an output of about 1,600 cars in 1911, and a planned output of over 3,000 for 1914.[2] Morris had only started production of the famous Morris-Oxford in 1913, and turned out about 1,300 by the end of the following year.[3] After considerable plant expansion in 1911, Austin is said to have planned for output to reach 1,000 vehicles a year.[4] Singer and Rover were probably also producing in this range, leaving the vast majority of manufacturers with an output numbered in the hundreds. In short, the industry expansion up to the First World War was accompanied by very little concentration in manufacturing, and production for the individual firm continued on a very small scale.

As a result it continued to be extremely easy to enter the industry, and to compete on fairly equal terms, although the large number of competitors led to many failures. In 1913 there were thirty-five producers exhibiting at the Motor Show who had not been present at the

[1] H. G. Castle, *Britain's Motor Industry*, 1950, p. 141.
[2] St John C. Nixon, *Wolseley*, p. 90.
[3] P. W. S. Andrews and Elizabeth Brunner, *The Life of Lord Nuffield*, Blackwell, 1955.
[4] Castle, *op. cit.*, p. 146.

same event in 1902. This seriously understates the ease of entry since not all producers were represented at the Show, and it makes no allowance for firms which were born and had died between the two dates. A PEP Report[1] states that up to 1913 there were 198 different makes of British cars placed on the market. Obviously, the requirements for entry in the form of capital, equipment and technique could still be easily met. However, survival was another matter, for of the 198 makes, 103 had disappeared by 1913. Many failed in this severely competitive situation for technical reasons, some were unable to turn out cars that were sound from an engineering standpoint and some failed to incorporate the latest mechanized improvements. Most of the successful companies not only kept abreast of these technical advances but also made their own contributions towards the improvement of the product, something far beyond the powers of many enthusiastic entrants into the industry. Others failed in their designing, were not able to produce a model which appealed to a fickle public surfeited with choice. Nor was one successful model a guarantee of survival in this period of rapid, and often fundamental, change in the product. It was a success that had to be repeated reasonably often if the company was to remain in business.

The surviving firms quickly ran into the perils of success, that is to say into the very real dangers encountered in attempts to expand output. Indeed, the outstanding economic feature of this period is the extremely slow rate of growth of successful firms in an expanding market. The answer lies mainly in the structure of British manufacturing industry, which threw almost the entire capital burden of expansion on to the shoulders of the car manufacturer. Conditions were such that he had to build most of the car himself because of an inability, in most cases, to rely on suppliers for parts and components. This imposed no great financial burden on to the general engineering firm-cum-car manufacturer—as long as output remained small. However, a major increase in output meant that large outlays in fixed plant and equipment were necessary. Perhaps as much again would be needed as working capital to finance a costly and slow-moving inventory.

The early experiences of the Wolseley Co. provide a good illustration of the supply position. That company started its career as a manufacturer of sheep-shearing machines, assembling the shears out of parts which were nearly all manufactured by outside firms in Birmingham. Despite their best efforts to prevent the use of faulty parts and to remedy bad workmanship:

[1] Political and Economic Planning: *Report on Motor Vehicles*, p. 5.

'They continued to suffer from the same difficulties in obtaining, from outside firms, parts of a sufficiently high standard of workmanship to satisfy their requirements. . . . The situation finally became so acute that the Directors decided, in spite of funds being low . . . (to) remove to larger premises, install new plant, and undertake the manufacture in their own works of all parts previously bought-out.'[1]

This lesson was not forgotten when the company turned to making cars. Typical of this early period was the Star Motor Co., which in 1899 boasted, 'One car per day, all of our own manufacture, except for chains and tyres'.[2] The Daimler Co. certainly made all its own engines, bodies and other major components. This situation slowly altered as reliable components manufacturers appeared with the growth of the industry. The 1913 Morris-Oxford had the engine, carburettor, gear box, wheels, body, axles and other parts made by specialist components producers who were already supplying other car manufacturers.[3] However, as Morris was to find out, this did not solve the problem of financing expansion, because he was unable to get the *quantities* required from suppliers even at this relatively late date.

Those companies that met this situation by enlarging their own fixed plant and equipment, quickly found that the highly integrated production of cars in any quantity required, at that time, large amounts of working capital to finance a costly, slow-moving inventory. At the first annual general meeting of the Daimler Co., the chairman pointed out that 'it was not possible, however well equipped and managed a factory might be, to produce a motor car complete with a body, etc., in less than two or three months'.[4] At practically every annual general meeting the chairman remarked on the need for more working capital. Just how tight the financial position was is reflected in the table overleaf.

In such a situation, which was typical of the company during its early years, it was not only difficult for it to expand, but also it was very vulnerable to any fall in sales. A good demonstration of this vulnerability was provided by the smash of 1907 which resulted in the failure or reconstruction of numerous car companies. Among them was Argyll Motors, one of the largest at that time, which the previous year had stock on hand valued at over £200,000 or 27 per cent of total assets. The plight of the company was responsible for the chairman's famous discovery that 'cars are not cash'.

[1] St John C. Nixon, *Wolseley*, p. 19.
[2] D. H. Noble and G. M. Junner, *Vital to the Life of the Nation*, p. 22.
[3] P. Andrews and E. Brunner, *The Life of Lord Nuffield*, p. 62.
[4] St John C. Nixon, *Daimler*, 1896–1946, p. 48.

TABLE I

Summarized Balance Sheet—Daimler Motor Co.—30 September 1900[1]

Current Assets	£	*Current Liabilities*	£
Cash	1,000	Accounts Payable ..	15,000
Accounts Receivable ..	9,000	Customers' Deposits ..	9,000
Inventory	46,000		
	£56,000		£24,000
Fixed Assets		*Long-term Liabilities*	
Plant, Machinery, Tools	26,000	Mortgage Loan ..	10,000
Experimental and Research	7,000		
Furniture and Fixtures	2,000	*Net Worth*	
Land and Buildings ..	16,000	Capital and Surplus ..	73,000
	£51,000		£83,000
Total[2]	£107,000	Total	£107,000

In good years, of course, these companies made high profits on turnover which financed the expansion that did take place. But large additions to fixed capital in these highly integrated firms resulted in relatively small increases in volume, and left them chronically short of working capital.

Very few mergers took place under these conditions, in fact, no merger before 1914 has had any significant effect on the present structure of the industry. Most of them seem to have been motivated by the need for capital and the desire to enter the industry via the acquisition of a going concern. The Vickers-Wolseley amalgamation referred to earlier grew out of the interest of the prosperous armament firm in motor vehicles, and the reluctance of the directors of the Wolseley Co. to embark on the programme of expansion necessary to exploit the success of the early Wolseley cars.

'If, however, the car business were to be given the support that it called for, larger premises would have to be obtained, together with the expenditure of considerable capital outlay on plant and machinery, and this was an undertaking on which they hesitated to embark.'[3]

[1] St John C. Nixon, *Daimler*, p. 89. [2] Excludes £40,000 patents, goodwill, etc.
[3] St John C. Nixon, *Wolseley*, p. 43.

A more mixed bag of reasons probably lay behind the amalgamation of the Birmingham Small Arms Co. and the Daimler Motor Co. in 1910. Daimler had survived its earlier difficulties and had prospered since its reorganization in 1904. However, profits fluctuated enormously, and the stockholders probably welcomed the additional security that the combination with the older, more solid company afforded. BSA had made several attempts to enter the industry with a BSA car which had not been successful. The amalgamation assured a prominent place in the industry, and perhaps also the possibility of economies through the supply of parts and components to Daimler by the BSA factories. Or, the aim may have been as the BSA chairman stated in the Annual Report, 'to secure additional departments, thus ensuring a better average earning power and avoiding dependence upon the continued prosperity of any particular branch of the business'.

The purchase price of the Daimler Co. was a little over £600,000 and the merger was referred to by the *Financial Times*,[1] in the following words: 'The combination is one of the most important ever effected in the motor industry.' One can use this quotation as an indication of the relative *unimportance* of mergers up to 1910, for even this 'famous' amalgamation had remarkably little effect on the industry. Daimler sales policy remained unchanged and the company retained its position as a producer of high quality, relatively expensive cars for a limited market. Various attempts were made to market a BSA model, which met with little real success. This merger, like the Vickers-Wolseley amalgamation, resulted in a change of ownership—and very little more.

It does seem rather surprising that more firms did not resort to merger as a means of raising capital to finance expansion. But apparently the public would not support further stock issues, and without this the merger of two capital-starved car companies offered no solution to the problem of expansion. Mergers with strong-established firms outside the industry might have helped, but the latter apparently took the view of the banks that the car business was too much of a gamble. Only a few outsiders such as Vickers and BSA took the plunge, and even these companies can hardly be said to have gone 'all out' in their new sphere. As a result, each little integrated firm expanded as best it could, much in the manner of an undeveloped country slowly and painfully industrializing itself without the aid of foreign capital.

The 1914–18 war had remarkably little effect on the structure of the industry. The expansion was quickly resumed after the war, with

[1] September 27, 1910.

sales greatly stimulated by the post-war boom, and a much strengthened desire for car ownership. Official figures are lacking for the early 'twenties, but one observer has estimated that total production of vehicles in 1920 was about 40 per cent higher than the previous peak in 1913.[1] This expansion in output was mainly achieved by an increase in the number of firms of almost 50 per cent, rather than by much greater volume on the part of existing concerns. Small-scale production, with many entrances and exits from the industry (given a strong fillip by the post-war boom and the short slump in 1921), characterized the industry as it had before the war.

The large number of new firms that appeared to cash in on the post-war boom in cars provides a clue to an important development that had slowly been taking place behind the scenes. This was the gradual appearance of a parts and components industry able and willing to supply car manufacturers with their requirements. For the newcomers, for the most part, were mainly assemblers of bits and pieces made by these outside specialist suppliers. These parts and components manufacturers were not yet equipped for mass production any more than the car manufacturers themselves—but they were there at least, as an essential part of the industry.

The speculative atmosphere of the immediate post-war years saw a revival in public interest in motor shares, and a number of car manufacturers unwisely recapitalized at the inflated values of the boom period. During these hectic years there were several unsuccessful attempts at combination which had very little effect upon the industry. One such was Harper Bean Ltd, 'iron founders, metal workers and manufacturers and distributors of motor vehicles', financed by a new stock issue of £6,000,000 which was oversubscribed. It acquired a financial interest in several companies and was quickly swept into oblivion by the 1921 slump. What is often referred to as 'the first combine in the motor industry' also took place at this time when the makers of Sunbeam, Talbot, and Darracq cars joined forces along with a spring manufacturer and a general engineering concern to form STD Motors Ltd. This ill-assorted group dragged out an unsuccessful and much-reorganized existence until its liquidation in the mid-'thirties. These ventures seem to have been inspired mainly by the feeling that putting together a number of companies into one big company was the thing to do. The polyglot nature of the combinations suggests that it did not matter what companies were chosen to achieve this goal of bigness. The results proved highly disappointing to all concerned—except possibly the promoters.

[1] Andrews and Brunner, *op. cit.*, p. 105.

CHAPTER 4

The Beginning of Mass Production, 1923–9

RECOVERY from the short-lived slump in 1921 was rapid and continuous; by 1929 annual output of cars alone had trebled to total 182,000. For the first time in the history of the industry, the expansion was accompanied by a major reduction in the number of firms. The number of new entrants was reduced to a handful while, at the same time, over sixty companies were forced out of the industry. Clearly, a new factor had been introduced, one which favoured the concentration of production and discouraged firms from entering the industry. In short, for a few firms mass production had begun. The effect of this on the industry structure is shown in Table II, which is based on the number of manufacturers exhibiting at the annual Motor Shows.

TABLE II

Estimated Number of Entries into and Exits from the Motor-car Industry

Date	Entries Since Previous Date Examined	Exits Since Previous Date Examined	Number of Firms
1897	—	—	9
1902	46	5	50
1913	35	37	48
1919	35	13	70
1922	37	19	88
1929	5	62	31
1933	2	9	24
1938	3	5	22
1948	4	3	23
1956	1	4	20

There were eighty-one British makes of cars produced in 1920 which went out of production within the next eight years.[1] It is com-

[1] Andrews and Brunner, *op. cit.*, p. 104.

monly believed that what is still remembered as 'the biggest slump in the motor industry' was responsible for this thinning out of producers. However, despite the large number of concerns which failed to survive the slump, there were more companies producing cars when it was all over in 1922 than ever before. As can be seen from Table II, the great changes in the structure of the industry came *after* 1922, in a period of prosperity and expansion. It was not hard times that brought about this great reduction in the number of firms, but the impact of mass production. The phenomenon of economies of scale had at last reared its lovely head in the British motor industry.

Motor-car manufacture is usually cited as the outstanding example of the economies of large-scale production. This popular notion received the wholehearted support of the National Advisory Council for the Motor Manufacturing Industry in its 1947 Report:[1]

'In respect of two characteristics, elasticity of demand and production under a law of sharply increasing returns (i.e. increasing quantity production of a unit results in substantially diminishing unit costs) the use and production of motor cars are believed to constitute a case *almost without parallel* among the major economic activities. . . . In batch production, to step up the rate of output from 1,000 a year to 2,000 a year may well lead to a saving of, say, 7½ per cent in the cost per unit. But in flow production, an increase in the rate from 1,000 a week to 2,000 a week may well give savings of 15 per cent in the cost per unit.'

It is believed that there is a limit to this state of affairs but the council were unable to indicate the 'optimum' level of production. However, they were sure that 'mass production, as it exists in this country is still far short of the stage where increasing mass production would cease to yield substantial economies'.[2]

This was a fairly recent comment. In the early 'twenties, a few manufacturers such as Morris and Austin were just setting out on the long, long trail of increasing returns. This was reflected in their sales, profits, quality and prices. The SMMT Index of Retail Car Prices dropped by 25 per cent between 1924 and 1929.[3] It was this severe price competition stemming from the introduction of elementary mass production techniques, and the growing popularity of the small, light car, which were mainly responsible for the structural changes that took place in this period. By 1929 the number of producers had been reduced by more than half, and three firms accounted for 75 per cent of the market.

[1] HMSO, p. 23. [2] Ibid., p. 11.
[3] Society of Motor Manufacturers and Traders, *Motor Industry of Great Britain*, 1939, p. 46.

TABLE III

Estimated Production of Cars 1929

Firm	Output ('000)	Share of Market Cumulative %
Morris	63	35
Austin	46	60
Singer	28	75
Ford	7	79
Standard	6	82
All others (twenty-six firms) ..	32	100

This concentration of production was brought about by internal expansion and the competitive elimination of other firms—not by mergers. Of the three dominant firms, only Morris combined with another car company (Wolseley) during this period, and that was *after* he became the largest producer. Morris was a relative late-comer in the industry for he never really got underway before the First World War. His most rapid expansion took place in the four years from 1921 to 1925, when sales jumped from 3,000 to 55,000.[1] The acquisition, two years later, of the Wolseley Co. made no increase in Morris's share of the market worth noting as sales of the Wolseley were then little more than a few thousand a year.

Nevertheless, the Morris-Wolseley amalgamation was the most significant merger of the period, and marked the withdrawal of Vickers from the car industry. Morris acquired the company at a receivers' sale for £730,000, bidding against a number of concerns including the Austin Motor Co. and, it is said, the American firm of General Motors. His biographers list a variety of reasons for this move,[2] but it appears that the major considerations were the desire to secure the large, modern and integrated Wolseley plant, and to extend his range of products into the higher price class, with the help of the very good distributors' organization built up by Wolseley.

The remaining horizontal mergers that took place in this period may be touched on very briefly. In 1928 General Motors (USA) absorbed Vauxhall, just in time to save that company from bankruptcy. The purpose of this acquisition was, of course, to gain a local foothold in the UK market, a foothold carrying with it a highly respected name in British motoring, and a site which could be reorganized and developed on mass-production lines. But the purchase brought with it

[1] Andrews and Brunner, *op. cit.*, pp. 112 and 185.
[2] Ibid., p. 155.

nothing worth mentioning as regards a share of the market, for Vauxhall output was probably less than 1,000 cars a year. The growth in size to its present status as one of the Big Five was to be accomplished entirely by internal expansion.

Although not destined to survive as an independent entity, Humber effected several mergers in the late 'twenties. Commercial Cars Ltd went into receivership in 1923 and was later acquired by Humber to become a subsidiary known as Commer Cars Ltd. In 1928 Humber, now in financial difficulties itself, joined forces with the Hillman Motor Co. Ltd. Chief interest in the Hillman-Humber-Commer combination lies in the fact that it was to form the basis of the Rootes Group which became one of the 'Big Six' in the 1930's.

But the merger that did not take place is, in some respects, more interesting than the mergers that did. This was the attempt by Sir Herbert Austin to merge his company with Morris and Wolseley in the spring of 1924. With the coming repeal of the McKenna duties in mind, Austin wrote in a letter to Mr Thornton, Morris's accountant:[1]

'Under the rough suggestions of figures I forwarded to you, Mr Morris would have control of all the share capital and would virtually be in command of a concern capable of meeting any competition likely to be met in the near future, and at the same time remove the two most formidable interests he will naturally have to deal with of the home manufacturers.'

This frank statement of the aims and terms of the merger would seem to have met Morris's previous objection to the proposition on the grounds that he preferred the complete freedom of running his own business as he saw fit. However, in his reply, Thornton says again that Morris 'does not see his way to give up the freedom which he so much prizes', and adds that the stumbling block to all such negotiations has always been Morris's 'firm aversion of being responsible for other people's money'.[2]

Nevertheless, within two years, Morris overcame this 'firm aversion' and became responsible for £3 million of the public's money in the form of Preference Shares in Morris Motors (1926) Ltd![3] One cannot help feeling that Morris, intoxicated with rapidly-rising sales and tremendous profits, was not at all concerned over his ability to deal with the 'two most formidable interests' and turned down the proposition out of hand. Had the offer come later, say in 1926, when

[1] Andrews and Brunner, *op. cit.*, p. 153. [2] Ibid., p. 153.

[3] His biographers lamely comment on p. 136, 'It was only because he thought their capital would be safe that he had overcome his reluctance to be responsible for other people's money'.

Morris sales were falling in the face of rising industry sales, the answer might have been different. As it was, this crucial decision reflected the personality of Morris and the mood he was in at the time; it also appears to have been based largely on non-economic grounds.

It is difficult to judge whether Morris's decision was right or wrong from the standpoint of the industry as a whole. We cannot be certain whether this big firm would have retained the 60 per cent of the market that it would have acquired at the outset; whether it would have dissipated its potential economies of scale in variety and inefficiency or whether it would have used its superior resources to develop new techniques and better, cheaper products. The answers we give to considerations such as these will determine our assessment of the decision.

But if Morris turned this merger down, he was responsible for a number of others in the 'twenties in addition to the Wolseley acquisition. These, however, were vertical rather than horizontal combinations, and were more or less forced on him by the need to obtain sufficient supplies of certain components to match his rapidly expanding output of cars. Morris's policy was to make use of the services of specialist suppliers wherever possible, and the supply situation with regard to parts and components had improved considerably since before the war. Nevertheless, to avoid potential bottlenecks in engines, bodies and radiators, he acquired, as from January 1, 1923, the Coventry Works of Hotchkiss et Cie SA (France), Hollick & Pratt Ltd and Osberton Radiators Ltd.

Even before these mergers, Morris had been taking the entire output of the last two concerns, so that amalgamation was almost the inevitable accompaniment of his further expansion. The larger, and more independent, Hotchkiss company did not wish to become dependent on any one customer nor were they anxious to expand appreciably total output of their English subsidiary. This led them to refuse a Morris offer of a contract to take 500 or 600 engines a week, saying that the best they could do was something under 300 a week.[1] As it would have been extremely uneconomical to split an engine order among several firms, the quickest and safest way for Morris to get more engines was to buy the plant. Six months after acquiring it, output was up to 500 engines per week, and by the end of a year, with reorganization and overtime, the desired 600 per week was achieved out of the identical factory space.

Morris subsequently acquired two other businesses which made his

[1] Andrews and Brunner, *op. cit.*, p. 127.

enterprise still more vertically integrated. However, these transactions were not motivated by the need to ensure an adequate flow of supplies; Morris purchased them because he thought they were 'good buys'. The first of these was E. G. Wrigley & Co. Ltd, makers of motor components and small tools who were in receivership in 1923. The other acquisition came in 1926, and was the S. U. Carburettor Co., the initiative in this case coming from the proprietors of the acquired concern, who had been losing money on their enterprise.

During these few years of rapid expansion, Morris spent over three-quarters of a million pounds on these vertical acquisitions. It must not be concluded from this that the absorption of suppliers is an inevitable concommittant of expansion. Indeed, a rapidly rising volume may put pressure on car manufacturers to do just the opposite; to have more bits and pieces made outside so that all available resources can be concentrated on final assembly. Austin and Singer also expanded rapidly at this time but Morris was the only producer who bought up suppliers, and his policy was determined by a set of circumstances peculiar to himself. He had come into the industry relatively late, at a time when one could start in a small way simply as an assembler of cars, so that at the beginning of this period he was less integrated than his main competitors. Secondly, his extraordinary early success gave him the cash that others lacked. Austin, for example, struggled throughout most of the 'twenties under a top-heavy capital structure. Lastly, the policy was partly the result of the personal characteristics of the proprietor, always an important consideration in the early days of the motor industry. Most observers agree that Morris's great talents were more those of the merchant than of the engineer, and it is not surprising that he chose to buy production units (complete with management) to meet his need for supplies, rather than to build them himself.

But these mergers, and the four horizontal combinations referred to earlier, were only incidental events accompanying the basic structural changes brought about by the coming of mass production. They were the product of special circumstances peculiar to individual firms, and were primarily motivated by production requirements rather than by market considerations. They had little direct bearing on the concentration of production that was taking place. It is noteworthy that all four horizontal combinations involved firms in liquidation or financial difficulties of some sort. A good name, dating back to the earliest days of the industry, plus physical assets, useful to the acquiring company, which could be bought at bargain prices; these seem to have been the prerequisites of survival by merger for car manufacturers in the 'twenties. Only a handful met these requirements; the vast majority of the many failures simply disappeared like the unfortunate *entrepreneurs* in economics textbook demonstrations of the workings of perfect competition. Those who had been merely assemblers had little to lose in leaving the industry, while the small-scale builders of cars who could not compete probably retreated back into general engineering.

This mass exodus and the concentration of production brought the industry close to its present structure of a few large concerns and a more numerous group of specialist producers. However, the gap between the large and the small producer was not yet too great to prevent a small company from moving into the first ranks. The competition in the 'thirties was to determine the final contestants for the mass market, and to reduce further the number of independent producers.

CHAPTER 5

Price and Model Competition, 1930–9

IN marked contrast to the major set-back experienced by car producers in the United States, the depression of the early 'thirties had little effect on the British industry. Output for 1931, the worst year, was less than 10 per cent below the previous peak in 1929. The experience of individual firms varied, of course, with those making expensive, luxury cars being particularly hard hit. Recovery from this minor setback was rapid, and the level of output in the latter 'thirties averaged well over twice that of 1929.

This period was marked by intense price and model competition. Retail car prices fell by about one-third by 1934, then remained fairly stable at the lower level until the war.[1] With much publicity, both Morris and Ford came out with a car selling for £100, but the resulting increase in volume was not sufficient to sustain the prices at this level. Quality competition became more important than price competition, and there was tremendous emphasis on variety.

Although it is extremely difficult to define what is meant by a new or different 'model', the trend was definitely toward variety as manufacturers sought to stimulate sales by frequent model changes and a wider range of models. The *Economist*[2] made the following estimate of the number of models for the ten largest manufacturing groups.

1929–30 ..	.. 46
1930–31 ..	.. 55
1931–32 ..	.. 60
1932–33 ..	.. 64

By 1938 the six largest groups were producing forty different engine types and an even larger number of chassis and body types. The *Economist*[3] estimated that twenty-six out of those forty models had sales of less than 5,000 units, which was an uneconomic level in the 'popular' class.

[1] SMMT, *The Motor Industry of Great Britain*, 1939, p. 46.
[2] October 21, 1933, p. 756.
[3] April 16, 1938, p. 131.

Morris, Austin, and to a lesser extent Singer, dominated popular car production at the beginning of this period, with a volume many times that of their nearest rivals. It is strange that they did not take advantage of their greater size to widen the gap and to consolidate their supremacy. The great emphasis on variety and frequent model change certainly made it easier for small producers to compete, and even to increase their share of the market at the expense of the leaders. Whatever the explanation, the result on the structure was that the period ended with a 'Big Six' rather than a 'Big Three', and there were rather more specialist producers left than might otherwise have been the case. These six firms, who accounted for over 90 per cent of the market, were Austin, Ford, Morris, Rootes, Standard and Vauxhall.[1] All of these producers attained their 'Big Six' status by means of internal expansion rather than by merger. Austin, Ford, Standard and Vauxhall did not combine forces with any other car company during these years. Morris absorbed Riley Motors in 1938, but this had no effect on his position in the industry. Riley output had been running well below 1,000 cars a year, and the business was on the verge of liquidation when its managing director appealed to Morris to take it over. The subsequent purchase for some £143,000 might conceivably have been listed amongst Lord Nuffield's benefactions, for his biographers write of the merger:

'This did not arise out of any direct need of the existing Morris motor business; the Riley company was bought by Lord Nuffield because he wanted to make sure that an enterprise which had done so much to enhance the prestige of British cars should go on.'[2]

The rise to 'Big Six' status of the Rootes Group requires special consideration, for the history of mergers in the 'thirties is largely a history of the Rootes Group, just as the history of mergers in the 'twenties is largely concerned with Morris. The Rootes Bros had been established for many years as sales agents and distributors, and had taken over the old car building firm of Thrupp & Maberly in 1926. Their policy was to acquire control of a number of companies in financial difficulties, reorganize their capital, rationalize their production and distribution, and knit them together into an integrated structure. Entrance into the industry proper was secured by gaining control over the Humber, Hillman, Commer group in 1932. This was followed in 1934 by the acquisition of Karrier Motors Ltd, commercial vehicle producers in Huddersfield. In 1935 the Sunbeam Motor Car Co. Ltd and Clement-Talbot Ltd were salvaged

[1] Singer was no longer a major producer.

[2] Andrews and Brunner, *op. cit.*, p. 217.

from the wreckage of the STD combine. All of these companies were either facing bankruptcy or already in receivership so that their shareholders had little choice but to accept the terms for survival offered by Rootes. Again, it is noteworthy that every one of the firms singled out for amalgamation bore a well-known name and had been established in car producing before the First World War.

Rootes purchased a place in the industry, probably at bargain prices, by means of mergers, but this did not give them their position as one of the 'Big Six'; that came from their development of the assets they acquired. The combined car output of all these companies could hardly have been more than 5,000–6,000 before the Group was formed. By 1939, total sales for the same companies had increased by nearly 600 per cent to give the Group over 10 per cent of the car market. This improvement came not only from a reorganization of these properties into an integrated whole, but also from considerable standardization of the various products made possible by the amalgamation.

The only other merger between car companies in the 'thirties involved specialist producers of expensive, luxury cars whose sales suffered severely in the depression. In 1931 Bentley Motors went into voluntary liquidation and later was taken over by Rolls-Royce. The latter company probably felt that extending their range to include a world-famous sports car would stimulate sales. In the same year, the Lanchester Motor Co. was taken over by BSA (Daimler) which gave the latter control over the two oldest names in the industry. A purchase price of only £26,000 indicates that BSA acquired little in the form of assets other than the use of the name of the first British-built petrol-driven car. The subsequent production by BSA of the 'Lanchester Ten' suggests that the motive for the merger was the desire to extend their range to include small, high-class cars.

As in the 'twenties, all the mergers between car companies in the 'thirties involved the acquisition of old-established firms in financial difficulties. No attempt had yet been made to integrate the assets of two *successful* producers. Failure continued to be a prerequisite to horizontal combinations. Because of this, these mergers contributed nothing toward the growing concentration in the industry and had no limiting effect on competition. Indeed, it could be argued that, in the case of the Rootes Group, mergers actually increased competition by making possible a 'Big Six' instead of a 'Big Five'.

Vertical combinations were not important in the 'thirties, proof that it was quite possible for the industry, and for individual firms, to grow rapidly without the necessity of absorbing suppliers. Apparently the latter were well aware by this time that it was imperative for them to expand without hesitation to meet the growing needs of their customers. The few acquisitions that took place would be entirely insignificant were they not all connected with body-building capacity. Rolls-Royce gained control in 1936 of Park Ward, an old-established firm of coach builders, and the Rootes Group took over British Light Steel Pressings in 1937. These moves, when linked with the establishment of a new pressings branch by Morris in Birmingham suggest the beginnings of pressure on available supplies of bodies. This pressure was to become acute in the post-war period of expansion.

CHAPTER 6

Post-war Expansion, 1945–55

EXPANSION was the keynote during this ten-year period; expansion in the face of an almost chronic shortage of supplies, especially sheet steel. This shortage became acute in 1951 and 1952 under the pressure of rearmament, and car production, which had by then surpassed pre-war levels, actually declined. The expansion was resumed in 1953, and output grew very rapidly to more than double that of the best pre-war year.

In the sellers' market which characterized this period, competition took the form of a production race rather than a battle for sales. This had its repercussions on the structure of the industry, for the need to assure supplies in an expanding market led to eight vertical combinations with suppliers of car bodies, among which were two of the largest producers. The following is a chronological list of these mergers, including, for the sake of completeness, one which took place before the end of the war:

1944 The Morris Garages Ltd—Charles Raworth & Son Ltd.
1946 Austin Motor Co. Ltd—Vanden Plas (London) 1923 Ltd.
1947 Birmingham Small Arms Co. Ltd—Hooper & Co. (Coachbuilders) Ltd.
1947 Birmingham Small Arms Co. Ltd—Barker & Co. (Coachbuilders) Ltd.
1953 Ford Motor Co. Ltd—Briggs Motor Bodies Ltd.
1953 British Motor Corp. Ltd—Fisher & Ludlow Ltd.
1954 Birmingham Small Arms Co. Ltd—Carbodies Ltd.
1954 David Brown & Sons Ltd—Tickford Ltd.

The absorption of Briggs and Fisher & Ludlow, each with assets in the region of £5 million, were events of major importance, and they left the Pressed Steel Co. as the only independent large-scale producer of car bodies in the industry. The Ford-Briggs merger, in the spring of 1953, preceded the BMC acquisition of Fisher & Ludlow by about six months. There can be little doubt that the Ford Company made the move to safeguard body supplies, but it may well be that the company's hand was forced by the position of the Briggs parent company in the USA.

'On October 26, 1953, the financial newspapers published reports on the Chrysler Corporation's newly announced plan to buy the auto-body plants and equipment of Briggs Manufacturing Co. It is reported that the Briggs family interests were active in promoting this acquisition. . . . It was also reported at this time that *negotiations had been carried on between the Chrysler Corp. and the Briggs Manufacturing Co. for over a year*, and that on at least two previous occasions the companies had come close to a deal . . . Finally on December 29, 1953, the deal was closed, and Chrysler Corp. acquired the automotive properties of Briggs Manufacturing Co.'[1]

The Ford Co. must have known that these negotiations were taking place, and could not have relished the idea of having the supplier of almost all their body requirements controlled by Chrysler.

The subsequent merger of BMC and Fisher & Ludlow suggests a counter move in the struggle over body supplies. This merger was particularly interesting in that Fisher & Ludlow also supplied most of the body requirements of the Standard Motor Co., and Standard now became dependent on one of its main competitors for its bodies.[2] Although Fisher & Ludlow publicly announced that there would be no change in their policies as a result of the merger, and that they would continue to supply customers other than BMC, Standard subsequently found it desirable to conclude a long-term agreement with Mulliners, one of the smaller producers of car bodies, and to have the new Vanguard III bodies made by Pressed Steel.[3]

The six other companies absorbed by car manufacturers were all specialist coachbuilders rather than mass-producers of steel pressings. Some of the chairmens' statements issued with the annual accounts make outspoken references as to the reason for these mergers.

Birmingham Small Arms Co., 1954/55

'During the year we purchased Carbodies Ltd. . . . Our primary aim was to assure the supply of certain classes of motor bodies.'

[1] Federal Trade Commission, USA, Report on Corporate Mergers and Acquisitions, May, 1955, pp. 76–7.

[2] The BMC strike in 1956 revealed that Fisher & Ludlow supplied underbody pressings for the Ford Consul and Zephyr.

[3] The Standard Eight and Ten bodies continue to be supplied by Fisher & Ludow (1956).

David Brown and Son, 1954/55

> 'Again the steady absorption of motor-car body capacity by "Big Four" make it imperative that supplies of this commodity be assured and to this end the old-established business of Tickford Ltd of Newport Pagnell was acquired towards the end of the year.'

Just how serious the situation was can be illustrated by the fate of the old-established concern of Jowetts Cars Ltd, who were forced out of the industry in 1954. The chairman's statement accompanying the accounts for 1953 stated:

> 'Company have completed limited programmes for Javelin cars and Bradford commercial vehicles which availability of bodies permitted and only continuing vehicle production is small programme of Jupiter sports cars which is now also drawing to a close. . . . Company must, however, face hard facts that events of latter half of 1952 and first half of 1953 affected company so severely that organization had to be reduced to such an extent that a resumption of production now would be almost equivalent to starting *de novo*, especially as some sources of supply are no longer likely to be open to us.'

The shortage of bodies may not have been the only cause of Jowett's difficulties, but there can be no doubt that it was a major contributing factor towards the disappearance of the company.

There were only two other vertical combinations of note in this period. They were also motivated by the need to safeguard supplies. One was the acquisition of the foundry business of Thomas Butlin & Sons, Wellingborough, by Morris Motors in 1947, to provide castings for the Nuffield Universal Tractor introduced in 1948. The other was the absorption of the Kelsey-Hayes Wheel Co. by Ford, also in 1947. While official comment on this move is lacking, it seems likely that the proprietors of Kelsey-Hayes preferred to sell out to their main customer rather than to finance the expansion necessary to keep pace with the rapid post-war rate of growth envisaged by Ford.

All these mergers illustrate how changing circumstances provided the motives for combinations. Companies moved in response to particular events; their actions, in a sense, were 'forced' by these events. There was no general move on the part of the industry in the direction of vertical integration, no drive to reduce costs by making more parts 'inside'. Despite the fact that a finished car body represents about 40 per cent of the total cost of a car, these major companies who still lacked their own car-building facilities made no move to amalgamate until impelled to do so by the need to expand in the midst of a steel shortage. In general, unless forced by particular circumstances, companies preferred to devote all their available resources to expanding output, rather than in increasing the 'made-in' content of cars.

Important as some of these vertical combinations were, they were overshadowed by the amalgamation of Austin and Morris in February 1952 forming the British Motor Corporation. This involved the two largest car producers (with the possible exception of Ford), and was by far the biggest merger the industry had seen. It was also the first time in the history of the British motor-car industry that a horizontal merger had occurred between two *prosperous* companies. Heretofore, every such amalgamation had involved a firm in liquidation or in financial difficulties. For this reason alone the merger is highly significant and calls for further consideration of the forces at work and the motives behind it.

Official comment on the reasons for the merger and the benefits expected from it are meagre and general in nature. The prospectus for the new company states:

> 'The boards of both Austin and Morris are confident that such an amalgamation will be in the national interest and to the advantage of the share and stockholders of each company by bringing about more efficient and economical production and furthering the export drive, particularly as respects manufacture and assembly abroad.'

These points were repeated in almost the same words by Lord Nuffield and L. P. Lord in a joint statement issued at the time of the formation of the holding company and the exchange of shares. All the emphasis here is on production, and the statement clearly implies that a big car company can produce more efficiently than a small one. In other words, the aim behind the merger was to get economies of scale which, in turn, would make the company both more profitable and more competitive in export markets.

Not inconsistent with this motive would be the desire to reduce competition in the home market. Any merger which results in control over a large share of the market (roughly 40 per cent in this case) is open to suspicion on this score. And after all, this was one of the principal reasons given by Austin when he first proposed the merger of these same two companies in the 'twenties. However, as the US Federal Trade Commission in its recent study of mergers is most careful to point out, '. . . while market share information is relevant to an appraisal of the competitive effects of an acquisition, it is not conclusive'.[1] Included in the appraisal must be 'consideration of the

[1] Report on Corporate Mergers and Acquisitions, May 1955, p. 180.

effects of particular acquisitions against the competitive marketing setting in which they occur'.[1]

The most relevant aspect of 'the competitive marketing setting' is shown in Table IV.

TABLE IV

Estimated Percentage Share of Unit Car Production—Selected Years

1929–54

	Austin and Morris	Ford and Vauxhall	All Others
1929	60	5	35
1932	60	11	29
1935	54	25	21
1938	44	28	28
1947	43	25	32
1950	40	28	32
1954	38	36	26

For the past twenty-five years, the two American-controlled companies have been steadily increasing their share of total British car production. The bulk of this increase has been at the expense of the two largest British companies. From the end of the war up to the time of the BMC merger, Ford and Vauxhall had been investing large sums in new plant and equipment, and huge expansion schemes were then under consideration. It was subsequently disclosed that these plans involved a capital expenditure of £65 million for Ford and £36 million for Vauxhall. Sir Leonard Lord, chairman of the new British Motor Corporation, replied to these announcements in a most revealing speech in September 1954 in connection with the introduction of a new Austin model. After referring to the recent visits to this country of Mr Henry Ford and Mr Harlow Curtice (president of General Motors), and pointing out that the Ford Company was controlled from Detroit and Vauxhall was controlled by General Motors, Sir Leonard said that he was not prepared to 'bandy millions' with the Americans, who were preparing to use production in this country as a 'springboard for the Commonwealth markets'. He then indicated that BMC was also expanding, here and in Australia, New Zealand and South Africa. He concluded by saying, 'We expect keen competition, but we have a few shillings in the bank and friends who will lend us money. We are feeling pretty comfortable'.[2]

This review of the 'competitive market setting' strongly suggests

[1] Report on Corporate Mergers and Acquisitions, *op. cit.*, p. 143.

[2] *Financial Times*, September 28, 1954.

that the motives behind the largest and most important merger in the British car industry were largely defensive. The combination appears to have been designed to bring into existence a British organization large enough to prevent the seriously threatened domination of the popular-priced market, here and in the Dominions, by the American-controlled UK companies. The new company became the fourth-largest car producer in the world, and for the first time in the history of the British industry, a merger was responsible for appreciably increasing the concentration of production.

The remaining post-war mergers had little effect on the structure of the industry, and require only brief comment. They followed the familiar pattern whereby a firm in liquidation or financial difficulty is acquired for the sake of its name, or because its physical assets can usefully be fitted into the productive structure of a going concern. In 1945, Standard purchased the assets and goodwill of the Triumph Motor Co., a concern which had gone into receivership in 1939 and was no longer producing cars. In 1947, David Brown & Sons entered the industry by buying up two small specialist makers of sports and racing cars—Aston Martin and Lagonda. David Brown was an old-established general engineering company, noted for its production of gears and tractors. The Rootes Group added to their organization by acquiring the commercial vehicle firm of Tilling-Stevens, and its subsidiary, Vulcan Motors. Production of these makes was discontinued and the facilities used for general Group purposes. On December 30, 1955, Rootes took over the old-established firm of Singer Motors which was on the verge of bankruptcy. The directors of Singer issued a report on December 2, which indicated that Singer, like Barkis, was willing:

> 'Loss incurred in year was due to an insufficient volume of sales of motor cars . . . company is in a somewhat unfavourable position in the motor industry because it is a comparatively small producer of passenger cars. . . . Directors have therefore come to the conclusion that if a favourable opportunity occurred of negotiating a merger, or making arrangements with a business of a like nature to solve the problem they would enter into negotiations.'

The output of the unfortunate Singer Co., once one of the major producers, had fallen to about fifty cars per week, so that the merger had no appreciable effect on market shares. Had it not been for the potential usefulness of the Singer properties to the Rootes Group, these assets probably would have been withdrawn from the industry, for another bid for Singer was made on behalf of a firm reported to be in the engineerings trade and not interested in the motor industry.

And so, by the end of 1955, about 95 per cent of total car production was concentrated in the hands of five companies—BMC, Ford, Rootes, Standard and Vauxhall—each producing over 100,000 units. The remainder was scattered amongst a dozen or so serious specialist manufacturers, including Rover and Jaguar, both with an output of cars in the 10,000–15,000 range.

CHAPTER 7

A Comparison with the USA

AN historical study of the changing structure of an industry in one country runs the risk of jumping to the conclusion that the observed development was inevitable. Reasons are sought and, of course, found, to explain particular events, or groups of events, and the more convincing these reasons are, the greater the danger of concluding that no other course of development was possible. Because of this tendency, some sort of comparison, if it can be done, is salutary. Fortunately, enough material is readily available to make such a comparison with the car industry of the USA.[1]

The technical development and commercial production of motor vehicles in the USA lagged behind France and Germany. Most of the successful American companies such as Ford, Buick, Chevrolet, etc., were not established until the early 1900's. Hence, it would be fair to say that the US and the UK began the commercial production of automobiles at about the same time. Both were advanced industrial countries, possessed of sufficient inventiveness, technical ability, and resources in skilled manpower and equipment to produce the new complex product. Both underwent similar experiences in the early days of the new industry. There was the same rush of many producers to enter the new field, and the same high casualty rate in the face of an uninterrupted industry expansion and high profits for the successful companies. There was the same early uncertainty over the choice of steam, electricity or petrol. Both suffered from speculative ventures, patent litigation, the hostility of bankers, and preoccupation over models.

And yet by 1913 the US industry was nearly *fifteen* times the size of its British counterpart! Total US production in that year was 485,000 as against 34,000 for the UK. Ford alone in Detroit had turned out over 100,000 cars in one year. No British producer had yet exceeded

[1] See especially L. H. Seltzer, *The Financial History of the American Automobile Industry*, 1928, and US Federal Trade Commission, Report on The Motor Vehicle Industry, 1939.

N

2,000–3,000 units a year. In short, the overwhelming superiority of America in the production of motor vehicles was firmly established before 1914. It has remained with the US ever since, for pre-eminence in a mass-production industry, especially one subject to great economies of scale, tends to stay with whoever 'gits thar furstest with the mostest'.

Greater potential demand in America is often cited to explain this great disparity in the rate of growth in the early days of the new industry in the two countries. The US certainly was, even then, a much bigger and wealthier country, with a greater need for private transport and a greater income per head to spend upon it. Important as these market considerations may have been, they fall far short of accounting for a growth ratio of 15 to 1. And they ignore the fact that growth stems from the interplay of supply and demand; that a mass market for a new product never *exists*, but must be created. Furthermore, the demand approach fails to provide any explanation of *how* the new American industry was able to expand so rapidly.

The answer here lies in the tremendous advantages derived from the greater division of labour and the much wider sharing of capital burdens made possible by the existence from the start of a parts and components industry:

'As a result of the previous development in the United States of the technique of standardized interchangeable parts manufacture—a technique which had been extensively employed by the sewing machine, bicycle, wagon, and other American industries—numerous establishments were in existence equipped with the tools, machines, and technical skill for the manufacture of wood and metal sub-products . . . The chief business of the automobile producer, after the design of his product and the placing of orders for parts, was the assembling of the major components, and the sale of the completed vehicle.'[1]

The effect of this on capital requirements can be seen from some quoted remarks of Mr Roy D. Chapman, chairman of the board of directors of the Hudson Motor Car Co., and one of the pioneers of the American industry:

'It is said that the Ford Motor Co. started with $28,000. We started with much less than that . . . Dealers' deposits often paid half the sum necessary to bring out a full year's production; and if the assembling were efficiently directed, drafts against the finished cars could be cashed as rapidly as the bills from parts-makers came in . . . We sold directly to distributors from the first.'[2]

[1] Seltzer, *The Financial History of the American Automobile Industry*, pp. 19–20.
[2] Ibid., p. 21.

The large profits which were made by the successful producers could be used directly to expand the volume of production. The British manufacturer, on the other hand, had no such 'bits and pieces' department at his beck and call. This proved no handicap as far as entry into the industry and small-scale production were concerned, since he did possess general purpose engineering equipment and skilled labour which could readily be adapted to new products with little expense. But rapid expansion and efficient large-scale production depended upon either heavy fixed-capital investment by the car manufacturer on an integrated plant and in sufficient working capital to operate such a plant, or the development of a components section willing to share the capital costs of expansion. No manufacturer had the resources to undertake the former, and a components section worthy of the name simply did not exist. No better proof of this can be cited than the early experience of Morris, the first British producer to plan for quantity production:

'Even as early as the end of 1913, however, Morris ran into the difficulty that suppliers were not in fact big enough to take the orders he wished to place with them, and could not or would not at this time meet him by expanding.'[1]

As a result Morris went to the US for parts and the 1915 Morris-Cowley was made with American engines, gear boxes, axles, steering gears and transmissions.[2] It is barely credible that in 1913, when American production was nearing the half-million mark, Morris was unable to place components orders in the UK to match a planned production of a mere 1,500 units! Given the situation in this early period in which American producers were, for the most part, assemblers, and British producers were forced to be manufacturers, it is hardly surprising that producers in the US could put cars together a great deal faster than their British counterparts could make them. And on top of that, America had Henry Ford!

The basically different technical and financial conditions under which cars were produced in America were primarily responsible for the sharp contrast with the UK in the extent of merger activity. Mergers were rare and isolated events in Britain before 1914, having little influence on the structure of the industry. The early history of the American industry, on the other hand, reflects large numbers of combinations and acquisitions, particularly in the years leading up to 1914 and in the short period after the war and preceding the 1921 slump. The industry during this time can best be described as a highly

[1] Andrews and Brunner, *op. cit.*, pp. 70–1. [2] Ibid., p. 74.

competitive, exciting and risky scramble for high stakes on the part of large numbers of more-or-less undercapitalized producers.[1] To the victors went the spoils—spoils in the form of very large profits which, if reinvested in the business to expand volume, brought competitive advantages in the form of economies of scale, and a more effective sales and service organization. Those who failed to produce a successful model, even for one season, faced bankruptcy—for any drop in sales meant inability to meet suppliers' bills, or even their own wage bills. In such a situation, a combination of many 'makes' increased the chances of always having some popular cars.

This idea of mergers as a form of insurance was expressed by the organizing and promotional genius who put together General Motors, William Crapo Durant:

'They say I shouldn't have bought Cartercar. Well, how was anyone to know that Cartercar wasn't to be the thing ? It had the friction drive and no other car had it. How could I tell what these engineers would say next? Maybe friction drive would be the thing. And then there's Elmore, with its two-cycle engine. That's the kind they were using on motor-boats; maybe two cycles was going to be the thing for automobiles. I was for getting every kind of car in sight, playing safe all along the line.'[2]

In addition to the car firms he acquired, which included Buick, Cadillac, Oldsmobile, and Chevrolet, he was also 'for getting' dozens of parts and accessory manufacturers as well, partly, it is said, for the purpose of protecting sources of supplies. This seems highly plausible at a time when the industry output of vehicles was expanding in the decade following 1909 from 130,000 to nearly 2,000,000 units. It is likely also that the high profits of suppliers encouraged such mergers, as did the possibilities of large promotional gains to individuals. Then, too, the entire list of well over forty combinations and acquisitions, both horizontal and vertical, initiated by Durant on behalf of General Motors may have aimed at complete domination of the industry; for the desire to 'play safe' easily shades into the 'need' for monopoly control. The Federal Trade Commission concludes flatly that, 'It is apparent that William C. Durant intended to gain control of the entire motor-vehicle industry'.[3] Had he succeeded in his attempts to acquire the Ford Motor Co., he might well have achieved that aim. Whatever his motives, his merger activity served to amalgamate almost all the necessary constituents for what was to

[1] Census figures show 265 automobile producers in 1909. Seltzer, *op. cit.*, p. 25.
[2] Seltzer, *op. cit.*, p. 157.
[3] Report on the Motor Vehicle Industry, Washington, 1939.

become in time one of the largest and most profitable business concerns in the world. Here we have a good example of the road to heaven being paved with 'bad' intentions.

The history of General Motors indicates that it was possible, under the conditions prevailing in America at the time, to build a highly successful concern by means of merger. It does not prove that 'merger was the best policy', any more than the history of Ford Motor Co. proves the reverse. The large number of mergers does suggest that conditions were conducive to combinations. Some of these, such as the merger of Studebaker and Everitt-Metzger-Flanders Co., were moderately successful, while many others failed. The most spectacular failure was that of the United States Motor Co., formed in 1910 with the merger of one of the important early producers, the Maxwell Briscoe Co., with four other minor vehicle manufacturers. After a policy of rapid expansion and the purchase of numerous parts and car companies, the combine ended in receivership two years later. At that time it was found to control more than 150 distinct corporations! The guiding light behind this venture was Benjamin Briscoe, a man with Durant's outlook, who later cited the chaotic, speculative, and undercapitalized nature of the industry as the reason for 'a combination of the principal concerns in the industry, not with a desire to sell all the automobiles that were to be sold, but rather for the purpose of having one big concern of such dominating influence in the automobile industry, as for instance, the United States Steel Corporation exercises in the steel industry, so that its very existence would prevent many of the abuses that we believed existed'.[1] Thus, it can be seen that the stability looked for in the more ambitious attempts at amalgamation involved a high degree of monopoly control.

The large number of mergers before 1914 naturally increased the degree of concentration to some extent, but the immediate influence was not as great as might be supposed. Ford's dominant position, with 40 per cent of the market in 1913, was obtained entirely by internal expansion. The share of General Motors was less than 15 per cent, and the large remainder was distributed amongst about sixty concerns producing vehicles on a commercial scale.

Demonstrations of the extent of concentration in American car production are apt to prove misleading if based on the market share of x-number of producers. It is a curious fact that the combined share of Ford and General Motors in almost every year from 1919–37

[1] Seltzer, *op. cit.*, p. 33.

stood at 60–65 per cent of the market.[1] Yet it was during this period that the real concentration of American car production took place and the 'Big Three' came to control 90 per cent of all car production. Three major developments are mainly responsible for this concentration, and in none of them have mergers played a major role. First, there was the change in the relative position of Ford and General Motors, which began to take place after 1925. This gradual rise to supremacy on the part of General Motors was clearly the result of internal development and expansion, rather than merger, as its last acquisition of a car company (Chevrolet) came in 1918.

The second major development was the remarkably rapid growth of the Chrysler Corp. to become one of the 'Big Three'. The Chrysler Corp. was formed in 1925 to take over the Maxwell Motor Corp., which had gone bankrupt in 1920 and had been successfully reorganized under the leadership of Walter P. Chrysler. The Maxwell Co. had been formed in 1913 out of the remains of Briscoe's United States Motor Co., but the links between the present Chrysler Corp. and that ambitious failure are extremely tenuous, and it would be incorrect to maintain that it owes anything to the merger policy responsible for the United States Motor Co. On the other hand, the acquisition of Dodge Bros Inc. in 1928 did give Chrysler a boost towards its 'Big Three' status. Dodge output of vehicles in 1926 was 332,000 units and, although there was a subsequent serious decline from that peak, the Chrysler share of the market increased from 6·2 per cent in 1927 to 8·2 per cent in 1929,[2] the first full year after the merger, largely because of the acquisition. However, this increase is to be compared with the internal growth of Chrysler after the merger when output increased to over one million vehicles in 1937, or 25 per cent of the market.[2]

The third development leading to concentration was the wholesale elimination of small producers. The number of car manufacturers increased until 1921, when it reached a peak of eighty-eight. By 1926 this figure had been reduced to forty-four, and by 1937 there were only eleven independent firms actually in production.[3] This was accomplished without any noticeable rise in merger activity. Most of the casualties were mainly assemblers, with no great investment in plant and equipment. They had nothing to gain by merging with each other, and nothing in the form of assets that might interest the sur-

[1] Federal Trade Commission: Report on the Motor Vehicle Industry, Washington, 1939.

[2] Ibid., p. 29. Table 8,

[3] Seltzer, *op. cit.*, p. 65 and FTC, *op. cit.*, p. 26.

vivors, and they simply vanished. Of the more firmly-established independents, who were also having difficulties, such as Nash, Packard, Studebaker, etc., only Studebaker attempted a merger (Pierce-Arrow 1928), and that was a failure. Noting the shift in demand to cars in the lower price brackets, these companies were convinced that their survival depended upon breaking into the mass market monopolized by General Motors, Ford and Chrysler. To be competitive, the new model had to have a volume of about 100,000 units per year under the technical conditions existing in the 'thirties.[1] Each of the independents apparently felt that such a goal lay within the limits of its own resources, and a number of attempts were made to produce such a model, for example, the Lafayette (Nash) and the Terraplane (Hudson). However, they were not successful, and the big companies continued to dominate the popular-car market.

The recent behaviour of the six remaining independents in the post-war years is in sharp contrast to their moves in the 'thirties. Circumstances have so altered that merger now appears to be the only alternative to extinction. The Kaiser-Willys merger in 1953, and the Nash-Hudson and Packard-Studebaker mergers in 1954 received the approval of the Federal Trade Commission on the grounds that these amalgamations 'would strengthen the ability of the combining companies to compete with the big companies which already firmly set the pattern of production and distribution in the automobile industry'.[2] Statements to the Press in connection with the Nash-Hudson merger by the Presidents of the two companies indicates how they felt competitive ability was to be strengthened:

> 'Advantages of the merger, according to Mr Barit and Mr Mason were: pooling of executive abilities, research and engineering resources, and purchasing power. . . . Opportunities for new manufacturing economies and improved methods; reduction of the individual overhead and administrative charges; diversification of products, which tend to stabilize earnings in periods of high and low business activity, and a spreading of tooling costs over more units with less cost per unit.'[3]

The most interesting point about this rather dull list is that it does not explain why the merger took place when it did. These advantages of amalgamation are *always* present, to a greater or lesser extent; the real question is why these economic arguments for merger give rise

[1] Testimony of Paul Hoffman, Temporary National Economic Committee Hearings, December 6, 1939, Part 21, pp. 11181–11224.

[2] FTC, Report on Corporate Mergers and Acquisitions, May, 1955, p. 135.

[3] Ibid., p. 72.

to combinations at certain periods and lack influence in this direction at other times. Specifically, why did competitive weakness lead to mergers in the 'fifties and not in the 'thirties?

As might be expected, major changes in technique have taken place during this period. This has culminated in the much publicized place of 'automation' now in progress. The industry spent over $7·5 billion on new plant and equipment in the years 1946–55.[1] Total car output for the 'fifties has been running at considerably more than double that of the level of the 'thirties. On a grand scale, this is another illustration of a common phenomenon in the automobile industry; more expensive, but much more efficient equipment and techniques, especially when coupled with higher volumes. There can be little doubt that the optimum level of production for the individual firm has been raised, probably from 100,000 to at least 500,000 units, and that the chances of any of the independents achieving salvation by breaking into the low-priced field are now very remote. This conclusion is strengthened by the inability of the independents to gain any advantages through vertical disintegration, for the individual output of most parts and components by each of the highly integrated 'Big Three' companies is now many times that of 'industry' suppliers.

Fortunately for the independents, survival may no longer depend on producing a successful low-priced model. The large increase in real incomes since the 'thirties has noticeably increased the demand for medium- and high-priced cars. The larger sales of Buick, Mercury, Oldsmobile and, in particular, Cadillac, reflect this trend. The demand for variety has been strengthened by the growth of two- and three-car families. It may be possible for a few 'small' companies to compete in this field with the 'Big Three', producing a variety of 'models' with a total volume in the neighbourhood of a quarter-of-a-million units. Catering to the odd corners of demand in a very large and rich market may provide a modest reward to those independents who can continue to hang on, and their ability to hang on under such supply and demand conditions has been enhanced by the mergers which have taken place.

A study of the vertical acquisition made by the major American companies discloses no more of a pattern than do the horizontal combinations. The industry is much more vertically integrated than in Britain, but this is mainly a function of the great size of the major companies, rather than of mergers. Most of the vertical acquisitions took place in the early days of the industry, when men like Durant

[1] Automobile Manufacturers' Association (Annual): *Automobile Facts and Figures*, January, 1956.

and Briscoe were busy putting together almost anything they could get their hands on. Briscoe's efforts failed, but Durant succeeded in laying the groundwork for the development of General Motors' highly-integrated operations. Ford, on the other hand, achieved a similar status almost entirely by internal expansion. In general, after about 1920, this type of amalgamation took place sporadically, as in Britain, in response to particular circumstances affecting particular companies. The merger of Chrysler and Briggs in 1953 provides a good illustration of the influences of special conditions.

This merger stemmed from the death of the founder, W. D. Briggs, in 1952. The Briggs family interests were active in promoting the merger with Chrysler, who took 80 per cent of Briggs body output and who were rumoured to be considering building their own body plant. The desire on the part of the family to diversify stock holdings in a trust set up by Mr Briggs, and largely composed of Briggs stock, which they considered to be too speculative and vulnerable, lay behind this move.[1] This was the only such merger with a body-builder in the post-war period, there being no scramble for these facilities as in Britain. This merger and the $3 million acquisition of Universal Products Co. Inc. (universal joints, propeller shafts, etc.), in 1955 has brought Chrysler more in line with the two other firms. It appears now that the 'Big Three' have each achieved the degree of vertical integration deemed necessary or desirable.

[1] Federal Trade Commission: Report on Corporate Mergers and Acquisitions, May 1955, pp. 76–7.

CHAPTER 8

Conclusions

THE British motor industry, like the motor industry in the other major producing countries, is highly concentrated. Mergers have played a minor role in bringing about this concentration. This may well be true of any mass-production industry that enjoys more-or-less continuous expansion, and which makes a durable product subject to constant development and improvement. Out of this historical survey as far as Britain is concerned, very few of the two dozen or so horizontal combinations that have taken place emerge as being memorable events, exerting a significant influence on the development of the present structure of the industry. Certainly the formation of the British Motor Corporation was an event of major importance—but beyond that? Only the Morris-Wolseley merger and, perhaps, one or two others stand out at this date as having any real significance. If one lumped together all the acquisitions of the Rootes Group one would be entitled to say that they provided the foundation for one of the major producers. But no more than that; for it was clearly the internal expansion of these purchases which gave the Rootes Group its position as one of the 'Big Five'. In some respects (if one ignores scale) this resembles the experience of General Motors.

Merger in the rapidly expanding car industry, with its rapidly changing product, may succeed in putting together the pieces required for success, but it cannot confer permanent status. That must be gained by growth. The subsequent internal growth *after* amalgamation has been the essential requirement of success, and this expansion has far outweighed in importance the influence of mergers in the case of every existing company in both countries, with the possible exception of General Motors. The very high degree of concentration in the car industry is derived from the internal growth of successful firms, the resulting economies of scale and the outright elimination, in time, of all but a few mass producers. Size has been handsomely rewarded, but size has not been achieved by merger. Amalgamations have played, for the most part, only an indirect and minor role in this all-important process of growth.

Of the mergers that did take place in the UK two characteristics stand out as prerequisites. One is that the acquired firm possess desirable physical assets and be in, or on the verge of, liquidation, so that the purchase represents a 'bargain' to the acquiring concern. This means that mergers did nothing to limit competition in the industry. Another requirement of merger is that the acquired firm possess an old and highly-valued name in the industry. Pioneer names have an appeal which is rarely achieved by later entrants. Apparently a car by any other name does not sell as sweetly!

In addition to being highly concentrated, the British car industry is, to some extent, vertically integrated. Here too, mergers have played a minor role, and have been the product of special circumstances. The majority have involved the acquisition of body builders. This is partly due to the importance of the body as a major part of the total cost, and partly because of the race to expand in the midst of the post-war steel shortage. However, there is no evidence to support the conclusion that expansion necessarily involves the absorption of suppliers. Whether it does or not depends on a variety of circumstances prevailing at the time.

There have been more mergers in the US than in the UK, but this is not the main explanation of the greater concentration in the US. Put crudely, that has come from a much faster rate of growth. It is as simple as that. There was no conscious attempt to rationalize the industry in the US anymore than there was in the UK. The industry in both countries grew like Topsy, and each had its mergers, depending upon particular and local circumstances. The major difference on the supply side is that the American Topsy had a happy childhood and quickly grew to fifteen times the size of her British sister, while the latter was out scrabbling for parts and components.

The minor role of mergers makes it difficult to assess whether or not such combinations were in the public interest. Certainly they did no harm. The only question is whether the industry would have benefitted from a larger dose. Even this question is purely academic as regards the USA. All roads may lead to Rome, but when it comes to car production they all emanate from Detroit. For Britain, on the other hand, the industry seems headed for further concentration if it remains competitive. (And it is bound to do so if it remains a major export industry.) With a volume of only one-tenth that of the United States, it is highly unlikely that it will permanently support five mass producers as against three in the larger market. Mergers depend on circumstances—and circumstances are now favourable to mergers.

VI

THE BREWING INDUSTRY

by J. E. Vaizey

CHAPTER 1

Introduction

AMALGAMATIONS between firms and acquisitions of subsidiaries are a usual process of expansion in the brewing industry, so that an attempt to describe them, and suggest reasons for their occurrence and for their results, is an attempt briefly to describe an important aspect of the behaviour of the firms in the industry. It is also an excursion into economic history, because at different times different causes have come to the fore.

Mergers have been frequent since modern industrial brewing began, and especially since 1880, and many of the causes and results have been persistent. In this study, after a short survey of the condition of the industry up to 1886, several subsequent periods are considered in order to elucidate the causes and results of mergers in differing economic and political atmospheres. This necessarily brief study is an attempt to describe the changing situations which have faced the industry and to give weights to the importance of different factors relating to mergers in the different periods.

THE BACKGROUND TO THE MODERN INDUSTRY

Beer has always been brewed by what is basically the same process. Water is infused with malt in a mash tun; it is then boiled with hops; the liquor is then cooled and yeast is added to ferment it. The yeast acts on the sugars dissolved from the malt to turn them into alcohol. The beer is then allowed to mature for periods which depend upon its composition and its market. Nevertheless, although the basic process remained, and remains, the same, substantial technical changes in brewing began to take place in the eighteenth century, when the trade began to apply the scientific approach to technical problems. This advance accompanied the development of large breweries, employing substantial amounts of capital, and using ancillary measuring equipment, large vats which economized in fuel, and carefully chosen raw materials bought in bulk, and enjoying other economies of scale. The use of steam power, of large vessels, of hydrometers and thermometers, reduced waste; more precise measurement raised the extraction of beer from raw materials, and helped to ensure reliable products. In the eighteenth century these economies in manufacture helped in the growth of the London breweries. As large towns grew, so did the possibility of large breweries, because the common brewers required large populations to consume their outputs, and their delivery area was limited by transport costs. The late nineteenth century saw a number of modifications in technique. The chief of these were in the cooling and fermenting of beer. Biological discoveries and the realization of the importance of infection gave a premium to the technically skilled firms, which were usually the bigger firms. These tendencies to growth were not offset by any organizational limits to growth.

Few people relative to the capital used are employed in breweries, and the main problems of organization on a large scale are technical and not problems of man management. To a considerable extent economies of large output arise from the technical ability and skill of the men in charge, although the superiority of the industrial brewers arose mainly from their superior equipment. The importance of the skilled brewer has diminished over the years; originally he was probably the most important factor in a firm's success or failure because of the unscientific nature of the brewing process, which depended on his art. In the 1870's and 1880's the larger breweries began to employ chemists and establish laboratories. But even today a skilled staff is of great importance, and amalgamations sometimes envisage the possibility of concentrating all brewing operations into one brewery where the skill is available, and usually result in the closing of the smaller breweries.

In 1880, there were over 11,000 breweries.[1] These varied considerably in size, as did the firms which owned them. First and foremost, there was Arthur Guinness, the brewers of Dublin stout, probably valued at this period at over £10 million, with an extensive English trade and a virtual monopoly in Ireland. The other large firms were broadly of two types. There were the Burton brewers Allsopp, Bass and Worthington, and the Scottish brewers who made pale ale and had a widespread wholesale market, mainly developed after the railways were built. In 1897, pale ale was only some 5 per cent of the total beer produced, but its retail value was higher (about two-and-a-half times that of ordinary beer), and so more able to bear transport costs. Some of these breweries were large and at this time relatively little interested in tied houses. The other large brewers were those

[1] Licensing statistics.

brewing in big towns, particularly in London, where industrial brewing began in the eighteenth century.[1] There the bulk of the trade fell into the hands of twelve great brewers who pioneered advances in the technique of brewing and into whose enormous breweries, producing 100,000 to 200,000 barrels a year, steam engines and other mechanical equipment were early introduced. The names of Whitbread, Barclay Perkins[2] and Hoare's, were redolent of power and wealth before the Northern 'industrial revolution' really began. As a result of the better and more reliable products and the cheapness of the manufacture in bulk by these great brewers, the small publican brewers and families who brewed at home were placed at a considerable disadvantage. Their products were unreliable, the rate of extraction of beer from the raw materials was low, and the rate of wastage high. Restrictive licensing also enabled the bigger brewers to 'tie' publicans by using their capital reserves to advance loans, or to extend credit. This prevented the growth of new rivals because the free retail market always diminished and never grew.

Below these two groups came many of the country brewers, producing over 10,000 barrels a year, which were substantial local businesses, but even so in a provincial town like Norwich four or five fairly large breweries and dozens of publican-brewers was quite a usual number. The bigger firms, together with their tied houses, were worth something of the order of £50,000 to £100,000. The size of local markets was limited until the coming of motor transport, because the effective limit of road delivery was some five miles by dray, or slightly longer by local railway.

Alongside these firms there were innumerable semi-domestic brewers who brewed on a small scale. They were usually publicans. Sometimes, like Butler in Birmingham, they bought out other publicans and developed into brewers. Some of them deteriorated in status and became customers of the wholesale brewers from whom many publicans, brewers or not, bought their expensive specialities. These small brewers reflected the origin of brewing as a domestic craft industry, and by the later nineteenth century, even in the provinces, this craft industry had been replaced almost entirely by industrial brewers. The decline of the publican brewer began in London in the early eighteenth century and took some two centuries to complete. His methods were archaic and his product was often inferior.

[1] Industrial brewing superseded domestic brewing gradually; previously commercial brewing was a small-scale craft (J. Clapham, *The Early Railway Age*, pp. 170–1).

[2] Originally Thrale's brewery, about which Dr Johnson made his 'potentialities beyond the dreams of avarice' remark.

Any commercial brewer was eventually able to supply him with beer more cheaply than he could brew himself. Therefore, the nineteenth century marked the rapid elimination of these petty brewers as commercial brewing spread with the urbanization of the Kingdom, and as restrictive licensing raised the prices which commercial brewers were prepared to pay for the tie of a public house.[1] The percentage of beer brewed by publicans fell from 40 in 1841–5 to 20 in 1871–5, to 10 in 1886–90, and, by the First World War the volume was negligible.[2]

Since there were substantial economies of production to be obtained as scientific techniques were established, the quality of the product raised and more modern large-scale equipment became available, the smaller wholesale brewers, who were producing under 10,000 barrels a year, were at an increasing disadvantage. Not only were publican brewers replaced by commercial breweries, but the commercial firms themselves became larger and there was a continuous and strong incentive for mergers to occur.

This was closely connected with the market situation, as well as with technical changes. Originally, the establishment of large breweries was essentially a process of vertical disintegration between manufacturing and retailing as the publican brewer was replaced. This development was succeeded by a movement forward into retailing by the industrial brewers, which became the dominant characteristic of the retail market for drink, and provided powerful conditions giving incentives for mergers to take place. Very early in commercial brewing history, brewers found advantages in controlling their retailers. There were some technical reasons why brewers found reliable exclusive retail outlets economical. Beer was perishable and had to be handled carefully because bad handling and slow turnover could ruin the reputation of the product. Public houses with small sales could not economically stock the supplies of more than one brewer if the beer was to be sold in good condition. Above all, draught beer, because it was unbranded, was a product on which reputations could easily be lost by misrepresentation. The relative security of sale in exclusive outlets enabled the brewer to estimate demand more closely and so to avoid the waste of overbrewing his perishable product. The resources and advice of the brewer also helped the publican in his sales policy. More important, the capital resources of the brewer were available to the publican.

[1] A small publican brewer whose beer was unsuccessful might buy some stock from a local commercial brewer. If he was short of cash, he would require credit; the *quid pro quo* would be a tie for beer. Later, outright purchase might occur.

[2] The absolute volume began to fall in 1871–5.

For these reasons the tied house system was an early feature of commercial brewing, and by 1800 over half the ordinary publicans and, for some types of beer, publican-brewers were tied to some kind of commercial brewer. The tie became more important as the century progressed and it was by means of loans and mortgages that the big brewers came to acquire the exclusive right to deal at certain outlets.

The tie was thus in part a result of the characteristics of the trade but its strength lay fundamentally in the licensing system. The sale of alcohol has been, broadly speaking, under the control of the licensing justices for some centuries.[1] At times the number of licences has been severely restricted, as in the period 1780 to 1800. The more stringent licensing justices became in granting licences, the more valuable an exclusive dealing arrangement with an existing licensee became. The advantages of the tie were increased by the restriction of freedom of entry. In the period 1830 to 1869 there was 'free trade in beer', and the number of beer licences was unrestricted. The tie remained important; probably over half the houses were tied to brewers in 1830, and a not significantly lower proportion in 1869, when restrictive licensing was reintroduced. The tie from 1830 to 1869 was accompanied, however, by freedom of entry of new firms, and a number of existing brewers date from that period. The restriction of this freedom of entry gave the tie its contemporary importance, dating from the period after 1870, to which we now turn.

The importance of the tie increased as the population rose and the number of licences was reduced, a reduction reinforced by the movement of people from abundantly licensed town centres to suburbs where few licences were given. The licensing system reinforced the natural imperfection of the retail market which arose both from the spatial competition between public houses on different sites and from consumer loyalty. Loyalty seems to rest mainly on affection for the publican rather than on a positive preference for the products he sells.[2]

The tied-house system, therefore, has been extensive since the earliest days of commercial brewing and as commercial brewing expanded so the importance of the tie increased. While there were numbers of free houses available the commercial breweries could expand by selling more at wholesale, attracting more trade to their

[1] S. and B. Webb, *The History of Liquor Licensing in England* (London, 1903), Ch. III. The tied-house system was extensive by 1800. In 1830 Parliament adopted 'free trade' in beer, partly as a remedy for the tied-house system; as a policy it was unsuccessful and had unfortunate social consequences.

[2] Loyalty was probably of less importance when the quality of beer varied more widely and there were more publicans to choose from.

houses and by obtaining more tied houses. As the number of these dwindled after 1869 a competitive rush arose for the remainder. Between 1886 and 1900 the proportion of tied houses rose by one-third from about 70 per cent to more than 90 per cent. When the supply of free houses had practically gone, the main means of expanding sales for most firms was by merger and acquisition of other firms.

Throughout the eighteenth and nineteenth centuries to 1900 the demand for beer continued to expand. Output rose from twenty-eight million bulk barrels in 1884 to thirty-two million standard barrels in 1890, and to thirty-seven million in 1900, and this expansion was merely a continuation of what had been happening for well over a century.[1] Many firms in the industry were exceedingly prosperous and the families who owned them had great financial resources which enabled the firms to expand and to change to take advantage of opportunities offered to them. The economies of scale of commercial brewing were not often open to new firms, for the lack of free entry arising from the tied-house system, whose strength lay in the licensing law, meant that few new firms arose. Some *entrepreneurs*, for instance Mitchell and Butler, did begin in the mid-nineteenth century in the expanding Midlands, but except in a few of the expanded industrial areas almost all brewing firms were (and are) old family firms, and even in the industrial areas some family firms are still to be found.

[1] Output had been some fourteen million standard barrels in 1831.

CHAPTER 2

The First Period of Mergers, 1886–1901

IN the 1880's another factor was added to those already mentioned which caused a 'snowballing' of the merger movement. This was the financial gain which, as a result of the development of the Stock Exchange, could be made from the flotation of companies.

In 1886 shares of the biggest brewing firm, Arthur Guinness of Dublin, were floated on the London stock market. The succeeding years came to be known as the 'Brewers' Wars', for they were marked by the competitive buying of public houses. There were many mergers between brewers, based on public issues of shares; with the increased capital, breweries were rebuilt and production economies were gained. The very small commercial brewers and the very small publican-brewers were rapidly eliminated. The larger breweries were soon competing for public-houses and as the supply of these dwindled, the brewing firms amalgamated.

The speed of the movement was partly due to the rising demand for beer and a tightening up of licensing, and partly to the new possibilities of using the Stock Exchange. This period was the heyday of joint-stock company formation, and since breweries had local, and sometimes, national, reputations as prosperous businesses, and most of their capital assets were in real property, they were good subjects for public issues.[1] The extent to which brewing companies were formed during this period is shown by the fact that in the fourteen years, 1886 to 1900, £185 million of brewing issues were made.[2]

The mergers in this period were of several types. Examination of a few cases shows something of the conditions in the trade which led to their formation. The usual case was of a bigger firm buying up small businesses, either tiny breweries, brewer-publicans, or public houses. Often, small local firms combined. Sometimes, big firms combined. These three types of expansion were carried on simultaneously

[1] By September 1890, in under five years, over 200 British brewing companies had been floated, as well as twenty-four foreign concerns. Many of these flotations involved the amalgamation of existing firms.

[2] *Statist*, October 1903.

and persistently and, with the progressive elimination of small businesses, the merging of big firms became relatively more important.

The most important mergers at this time, both numerically and strategically, were those between the local breweries with several thousand barrels output a year. They were smaller than the national brewers and the big London and provincial commercial brewers, but they were larger than the multitude of very small publican breweries. There were many flotations of shares of companies of this intermediate size and, although some of these did not involve mergers, a great number were based on the amalgamation of three or four businesses in order to provide a large enough basis for a public issue.

For instance, in February 1890, four local breweries on Tyneside formed the Newcastle Breweries Ltd; three breweries were closed and the fourth brewed for the retail trade of the other three. The tied houses were supplied from one brewery and one wine and spirit department. The Board was a joint committee of the partners of the constituent members of the amalgamation. A firm of London financiers floated the company, and then retired from the scene. The same tale could be told of firms, large and small, all over the country, for example, Northampton Breweries, in which two small breweries joined, later joined by another (The Lion); Manchester Breweries (five local brewers); Russells and Wrangham of Malton (Yorkshire) combined with two other local breweries in 1897; Plymouth Breweries was an amalgamation in 1889 of five local firms at a purchase price of £317,650; Bristol United Brewery, formed in 1889, consisted of four firms, to which others were soon added.

There were, besides mergers of brewing firms, many cases of larger firms buying up such individual public houses as became available, which smaller local firms would have regarded as purchases of some importance. By a series of such changes many small firms became substantial. The major stock market flotations were those of the large wholesale brewers, of which the £6 million issue of Guinness was the outstandingly successful inauguration. This was followed by Ind Coope, in October 1886, and then by Allsopp's Burton brewery, Bass, and the London firms. Some of these brewers, like Guinness and Bass, had national markets, or were of great importance over wide areas, although the total national trade was then a relatively small proportion of the total trade.[1] The early flotations of these companies were seldom mergers and may be regarded as part of the contemporary movement into public companies by large concerns and

[1] Probably some 7 per cent of the total consumption in 1900.

partly as a way of getting more finance for expansion. What happened in individual cases seems to have depended in part upon how far the piecemeal buying up of outlets had gone and the relative sizes of the firms competing in the area. Many flotations were of private family firms and did not involve any merger as a basis of issue, e.g. Parkers' Burslem Brewery, Threlfalls Brewery, Taylor's Eagle Brewery and Massey's Burnley Brewery; however, most of these firms expanded by merger subsequently.

It is not surprising to find growth and merger going on side by side; in some cases the extension and improvement of a large brewery could only be undertaken if accompanied by amalgamation which gave the firm control of additional retail outlets for the larger output. The technical changes described earlier gave larger and newer breweries significantly lower unit costs as long as output was maintained at a high level. Firms with resources available used their money to extend or rebuild well-sited breweries. This was an optimistic period in which firms 'built big' for the future; costs were falling and good firms expanding rapidly. Firms undertook major expansion partly because the industry was prosperous; in addition, they knew that their new, larger works were substantially better than many of the existing older works of their competitors and should, therefore, be able to compete successfully in the long run; further, there was always the possibility of buying whatever additional outlets were required to sell the additional output, should their estimates of the natural increase in demand prove over optimistic. In some cases it was necessary to buy outlets rapidly in order to sell the output of the increased capacity. Even the traditional wholesale brewers like Bass, who suffered as other firms began to exclude their products, came to meet the competition by investing in better-class public houses all over the country.[1] Allsopp's, a big Burton firm with customers mainly in the free trade, were unable to do this to the same extent and their trade suffered. As early as 1888 Captain Townshend, the chairman of Allsopp's, commented on the serious difficulty his firm found in selling their well-known products because of the growth in the number of houses tied to other brewers. Money was spent on rebuilding public houses so as to attract custom from a growing population with rising incomes which was moving into new suburbs. Since the justices were beginning, after 1880, to close public houses, or to refuse to grant licences freely although demand was still rising, the competition to buy retail outlets drove their prices up to two or three times their pre-1886 levels. This had serious results.

[1] O'Hagan, *Leaves From My Life*, 1923, p. 241.

To take one notorious instance, in July 1898, Watney & Co., Combe & Co. and Reid's Brewery Co. were amalgamated with an issue of £15 million of shares. This was £6 million more than the combined value of the three businesses before flotation.[1] The extra capital was used almost entirely in the purchase and rebuilding of tied houses and this real property in turn provided security for the debenture holders; but although the prices paid for this property were justified at the time of purchase by the rise in share values, eventually it was seen that the capitalization was based upon over-optimistic estimates and serious financial difficulties followed.[2]

The whole of brewing finance had become extremely speculative. The initial share issues were so successful and the industry so prosperous that the early issues soon rose to substantial premiums, and in the 1890's the share promoters allowed no more than 7 to 8 per cent on ordinary shares because the shares came to be regarded as sound commercial risks. The floating of brewing companies yielded great capital gains to the brewing families, and to the company promoter and brewery financier.[3] Some brewers had share holdings in other breweries, and in many cases care was taken to allot shares within the trade, especially to publicans.[4] Much of the underwriting was also done by the big London brewers.

The capital gains were made largely from the capitalization of goodwill, rather than from any hope of attempting to establish local monopolies and making extravagant profits from them. The archetype of amalgamation for monopolistic motive is not to be found in this country but in the brewing trust in the United States, where British financiers arranged for the formation of brewing trusts. One firm combined nearly all the breweries in St Louis, in an amalgamation of eighteen local firms, and another tried to gain control of the trade in Cincinnati, Chicago and Indianapolis. The ultimate aim of the financiers, however, which was to control all the breweries in America, was not achieved because the national brewers did not join the syndicates.[5] Since the tied-house system was absent in

[1] As each of the parties to the new issue was already a joint stock company capital gains had been realized earlier on a substantial scale.

[2] Had the demand for beer continued to rise (see p. 401) with population, most of these expectations would have been justified. But at the turn of the century demand fell off and the initial capital gains were lost.

[3] The Brewing Investment Trust was concerned with some of the issues and its activities led to later mergers. The company had interests in several companies and directors on some of the boards.

[4] Failure to do this was a contributory factor in Allsopp's decline.

[5] *The Economist*, February 22, 1890; T. C. Cochran, *The Pabst Brewing Company*, New York, 1948, pp. 151 *et seq.*

America, this experience suggests the importance of the financial factor in the genesis of mergers.

Thus we see that, in this period of great prosperity before 1900, the impulse to forward integration was substantially but not entirely due to the fear of exclusion from the market because of the competitive growth of the tied-house system; this fear was particularly acute for the firms which had relied traditionally on a wholesale market and for firms in areas where licence reduction was proceeding. There were substantial profits, however, to be made in retailing, which also encouraged forward integration; the retailers' margin varied around a figure of 20 per cent,[1] and the organization of the brewing company has often been aimed at the exploitation of this margin rather than merely at the economies of large-scale production.[2] In addition, there were substantial cost savings to be achieved by the larger merged firms if they could rebuild their plant and renew their equipment. This was, in itself, a powerful motive for merger.

The 'Brewers' Wars' resulted in the extension up to 90 per cent of the tied-house system and the reduction in the number of breweries from 11,322 in 1890 to 6,460 in 1900 and a more than proportional reduction in the number of firms. These changes represent the fulfilment of changes begun nearly two centuries before in London. They occurred at this time chiefly because they were made possible by the new financial institutions, particularly the increased importance of joint stock-company finance, which in turn rested on the great prosperity of the industry, a prosperity apparently so great that large projects and expansions could be undertaken with what seemed little risk. Breweries came on to the market for family reasons and because many firms could see that without rebuilding they could not make profits which would justify the refusal of the prices to be obtained from the large firms. The choice had, for some, become one of modernization or selling, but on the whole many of them were making adequate profits and with their tied houses and the restrictions of new licences they had considerable market security. So the merger movement was limited by the good profits that many private firms were making which made them unwilling to sell. Those which came on to the market were bought eagerly. After this period a steady trickle of firms has been available each year and consolidation has taken place more slowly, except in the depression of the inter-war period and since 1948.

[1] The variation of this margin for different beers is important in the anatomy of competition; this broad figure is given in order to indicate the importance of retailing as such.

[2] Over three-quarters of brewing companies' capital is now estimated to be in the retail business.

CHAPTER 3

Mergers in a Depressed Period, 1900–14

AFTER 1900 the output of beer not only ceased to increase but fell,

UK Output of Beer (m. Standard Barrels[1])

1899	37
1904	35
1909	33
1914	35

Source: Customs and Excise Reports.

and this caused financial difficulties for many of the firms which had bought tied houses at high prices, and which had been capitalized with heavy burdens of debentures and preference shares on the basis of the high profits of the earlier years. The margins on which brewing firms operated appear to have been narrow and, in some cases, even a slight falling off of sales led to insolvency.

The Burton breweries, Bass and Allsopp, which had suffered when they lost much of their wholesale trade in pale ale, fell into difficulties. Ind Coope was in the hands of the receiver from February 1909 to December 1910, although it made considerable amounts of beer in this period. Insolvency was, however, unusual. More often, dividends were passed and capital written down. Watney, Combe & Reid, for example, passed their dividend in 1901 and in 1905 their capital was written down. The actual output of Watney, Combe & Reid fell relatively little.[2] A rough calculation suggests that from 1900 to 1910 the capital structure of companies controlling over a quarter of brewing output in the United Kingdom was reconstructed.

Brewing shares stood at low prices as the earlier enthusiasm for the issues was now followed by an equally extreme public distrust. The new issues market was no longer open to the brewing industry. This affected all firms, except Guinness, although all firms did not suffer

[1] The strength of beer, measured in degrees of original gravity, is an indication of the volume of raw materials relative to the amount of water. Beer is measured either in bulk barrels, or in standard barrels, which indicate both bulk and strength.

[2] Annual Report, 1909.

equally from the depression and many firms, especially those with compact market areas and secure local outlets, remained prosperous, despite occasional trade depressions and the increased licence dues that Liberal legislation imposed.

The period of financial difficulty in the trade took place in a tense political atmosphere, and when the number of licensed premises was being rapidly reduced.[1] In 1886 there were 104,792 on-licences in England and Wales, in 1906, 98,742, and by 1914 only 88,445, and this reduction took place at the same time as the adult population increased rapidly. The reduction took place originally and most rapidly under the pressure of local benches, and the process was impeded somewhat by the legislation of the Balfour administration,[2] and then speeded up by the Liberals.

The 1904 Licensing Act established a statutory principle of licence reduction and set up a compensation fund for licences suppressed by the justices on other than grounds of misbehaviour; until then the reduction was in the hands of the justices without compensation. The Liberals objected strongly to the mildness of the 1904 Act, and temperance advocates were influential in the Liberal government of 1906 to 1916. Lloyd George revised the licence duties in the Budget of 1910, and when war came the trade was strictly controlled by the Liberal government and the Coalition, and in some areas it was nationalized.

In 1904 the three associations, the Country Brewers' Society, and the London and the Burton Brewers' Associations formed the Brewers' Society to protect the interests of the industry. Its membership was extensive and its influence considerable in political matters. Local regulation took place in local associations and there were local agreements on prices, although these sometimes broke down. The general tendency to reduce competition was, however, largely based on *ad hoc* arrangements between firms; for example, there were cases of breweries exchanging tied houses so that each achieved economies of distribution and obtained a stronger local position.

Price competition was also affected, and on the whole checked, by strategic moves; cases have occurred of firms buying properties in other firms' areas. These properties would give a firm a powerful bargaining counter *vis-à-vis* its competitor because it could threaten

[1] The political atmosphere was not unconnected with the view of the market about brewing company prospects.

[2] After 1870 the brewing industry became closely identified with the Conservative party, and the temperance movement with the Liberals. R. C. K. Ensor, *England*, 1870–1914, pp. 20–2.

to reduce prices in its competitor's area. Price competition may be eliminated if two firms are in a situation in which each can inflict considerable damage on the other. Aggressive and defensive policies of this type have become unusual in recent years. Another type of agreement which tended to reduce competition was an arrangement to exchange the trade in a group of houses for the right to sell bottled beer throughout the outlets of the other firm. This type of reduction of competition combined with rationalization is an indication of the spirit of consolidation which came to replace aggressive expansion. These agreements usually depended upon traditional friendships, but they were sometimes facilitated and encouraged by the financial links between breweries through finance houses; in a number of cases they were followed by full amalgamation.[1]

A typical example of the process of amalgamation between small firms may be given: it is East Anglian Breweries Ltd, of Ely, Cambridgeshire. In 1894, there were three brewers at Ely: Hy. Hall, who subsequently became, by 1914, Arthur and Bertram Hall, of the Forehill Brewery; the second was E. W. Harlock, of the Quay Brewery; and the third was T. and H. Legge of Market Street. In Littleport, north of Ely, Wm Cutlack and Sons were brewers. By 1912, Cutlack and Harlock were brewing at Ely, and after buying out T. and H. Legge during the war, Hall's and Cutlack and Harlock amalgamated in 1930 as Hall, Cutlack and Harlock. They then became, jointly, the biggest proprietors of tied property in the south of the Isle of Ely. In 1938, the business of Mill's Brewery (Wisbech) Ltd, at Wisbech, in the north of the Isle, was acquired, giving them interests throughout the Isle of Ely. Meanwhile, in Huntingdon there were two brewers, Jenkins and Jones, and Marshall Bros. In 1932 they were amalgamated, closing one brewery, and the new firm amalgamated with C. S. and R. H. Lindsell of Soham, Cambridgeshire, who had interests in St Ives, Huntingdonshire (where their brewery was closed in 1912); the combination became Huntingdon Breweries Ltd.; C. S. and R. H. Lindsell were the successors to Cutlack and Treadway at Soham, and in 1928 their brewery at Soham became the Soham stores of Cutlack and Harlock of Ely. In 1951, Hall, Cutlack and Harlock, and Huntingdon Breweries Ltd, became East Anglian Breweries Ltd, with breweries at Ely and Huntingdon, owning over 500 tied houses in Huntingdon, the Isle of Ely, Cambridgeshire and adjoining counties. In September 1954 the Huntingdon brewery was closed and all brewing was concentrated at Ely. Out of at least nine breweries

[1] A contemporary (1954) example is that of the Wenlock Brewery Co. which was acquired by Bass who had supplied them with draught beer for a long time before amalgamation.

only one remained. This story is typical of many. But despite this history of amalgamations, a considerable number of rivals operate in the East Anglian company's area; there are brewers at Cambridge, Wisbech, Bury St Edmunds, Norwich, Great Yarmouth, Northampton, Luton and Bedford who all own public houses in these counties. Almost all of these brewers have themselves a long history of mergers and acquisitions. In addition, the London brewers and the national brewers sell an appreciable proportion of the beer sold in the region.

During this period, as well as the mergers between smaller brewers which were similar in kind to those which had taken place earlier, there were mergers which were influenced by the desire to maintain output and make full use of the large breweries built earlier. Since fixed expenses (short period overheads) were important there was considerable economy in working at higher levels of capacity, and long-period overheads could also be spread over larger output. The capital investment undertaken in the optimistic period before 1900 was mainly in durable buildings and plant. This durability makes the time taken for reduction of capacity in the industry very long; in addition, such adjustment is prolonged by the fact that a brewery consists of many pieces of equipment which are renewed at different intervals. This feature is accentuated because temporary local booms often led to the renovation of equipment which then remained in existence but was only partially used for many years. For these reasons there is a chronic tendency for excess capacity to remain in the industry for very many years, and in view of this tendency, the importance of the fall in demand, which began in 1900 and has continued with few exceptions, cannot be over-emphasized; it has dominated brewing economics since 1900. In particular, enterprising managements have been constantly aware of the possible economies to be obtained from expanding sales.

CHAPTER 4

Continuous Concentration

THE inter-war period somewhat resembled the period 1900 to 1914, but the effects of the war itself were considerable. Consumption shrank, the number of breweries was further reduced but the brewing companies' finances were restored by the inflation which enabled them to meet their fixed commitments, even though output was lower than for many years. In 1918 indeed, output fell to half the 1914 level, but profits were higher than ever before.

UK and Ireland (*m. Bulk Barrels*)

1919	33	1930	27
1914	37	1935	22
1918	19	1940	26
1920	35	1950	29
1925	27		

Source: Brewers' Almanack.

The fall in consumption was partly due to changed taste and consumption patterns and partly to the increase in excise duty. Cheap draught beer, sold at 2*d.* a pint in 1914, rose to 6*d.* or 7*d.* at various times between the wars and after 1939 to 1*s.* 2*d.* a pint. The beer in 1939 was only about three-quarters as strong as it was in 1914, so that the fall in value for money has been even greater.

The accompanying table shows changes in the cost of living index and of the level of beer prices for ordinary draught beer in London, taking 1914 as 100 in both cases:

	Cost of Living Index	*Index of Draught Beer Prices*
1914	100	100
1920	269	350
1925	177	300
1930	155	300
1935	147	250
	Source: LCES.	Source: Whitbread & Co. Ltd.

Duty rose from about 15 per cent of the total ex-brewery cost to about 60 or 70 per cent.

The reduction in breweries (plants—not firms) was as follows:

1900 ..	.. 6,460	1930 ..	.. 1,418
1910 ..	.. 4,482	1940 ..	.. 885
1920 ..	.. 2,889	1950 ..	.. 567

Source: Excise Returns.

The fall in the number of firms has been even more rapid; in 1954 there were about 350 compared with some 11,000 in 1890. By 1920 a high proportion of the old-fashioned small breweries had been closed and the industry had assumed its modern shape.

Price competition in the form of independent changes by individual firms had become a relatively unimportant feature of the industry except in the bottled beer trade. Local brewers competed through their tied houses in quality and amenities, and the local minimum price agreements were fairly well observed. The main reason for this is the fact that the demand curve facing the individual firm is kinked. The elasticity of demand at prices above the ruling price was illustrated in 1910: Watney, Combe & Reid was the only firm to raise prices as a result of the Lloyd George budget increase in excise duty, and this independent action caused them to lose trade rapidly. The incentives to avoid price competition were reinforced by the fact that the marginal costs are fairly constant over normal ranges of output.

As a result of these features high-cost producers which found themselves losing trade because of their poor beer or their bad public houses, found it infinitely safer to sell out their public houses (which always have a market value), rather than incur the danger of hastening their own death through ruinous competition. The same applied to breweries who were losing trade, and thus running at much below full capacity, because of movements in population.

Competition has actually been strongest in bottled beers and this section of the trade has become increasingly important. The proportion of bottled beer rose from 16 to over 35 per cent in quantity from 1900 to 1950, and from about 15 to over 50 per cent by value. This change has altered the relative prosperity of different types of firm, and has changed somewhat the advantages and disadvantages of different forms of organization. Some of the bottled beer is brewed and bottled locally, but most of it is brewed by bigger brewers who sell it wholesale, sometimes to independent bottlers, and it is then sold at retail in other brewers' public houses. The biggest firms, like Guinness and Whitbread, have national markets, maintained by advertising, where competition is in substantial degree in quality and prestige. However, only Guinness, the biggest brewery concern in the British Isles, has been able to maintain and increase its sales without entering the retail trade; this has been possible because of the peculiar reputation and special characteristics of its product which has been extensively advertised. Guinness's unique position has been achieved at the expense of generous wholesale and retail margins over which no control is exercised. Since the proportion of Guinness sold at each outlet is only a small proportion of the total sales, its entry into wholesale bottling and retailing might well have antagonized its other brewer customers, by providing them with an overt rival instead of a supplier of a product with generous margins.

The 'free' trade, which in 1954 was over 15 per cent of the market, is partly in 'free' houses, but mainly in licensed clubs, which are less restricted than ordinary licensed premises.[1] Here, price and margin competition is strong, particularly where there are 'club' breweries which sell beer some 10 per cent below the usual wholsesale prices of other brewers to member clubs. Some of the free trade is served by independent bottlers and wholesalers. Brewers have tended to acquire these firms (and so, incidentally, a hold in mineral water manufacture) in order to control this trade, as well as to acquire bottling plant.[2] The mineral water trade is a small one, but brewers have moved into it as the sales of soft drinks have grown and the sales of beer have fallen. The margins obtained by bottlers and retailers have been unstable, and there are examples of the repeated breakdown of local wholesale bottling price agreements. This is, however, the only form of price competition which has been important.

The incentive to acquire breweries with retail outlets was increased as bottled beer became more important. The additional retail outlets gave the big brewers a larger and more secure share of the bottled beer trade; this enabled them to run near full capacity and to obtain economies of scale in the marketing of bottled beer. Where the large company obtained a high proportion of the public houses in a district, improvement expenditure could be limited to a smaller number; business also could be acknowledged to be redundant with less fear of

[1] The retail trade for beer is divided into three categories: public houses, of which 95 per cent are owned or controlled by brewers; off-licences, about 40 per cent of which are owned or controlled by brewers; and clubs, none of which are owned by brewers. About 75 per cent of beer is sold in public houses, 10 per cent by off-licences, 10 per cent by clubs and 5 per cent in other ways.

[2] By 1954 about half the wholesale bottlers were brewer controlled.

losing trade to competitors. Many small houses were closed by the justices, or by brewers with a strong local market position.[1]

During the first world war, there was a radical tightening up of licensing restrictions. The output of beer was restricted, licensing hours were halved, and the public concern over 'bad conditions' in licensed premises intensified. Mitchell's and Butler's, an amalgamation of two Birmingham firms, formed in 1898, and Ansell's, had initiated a policy before the war, in conjunction with the Birmingham bench of magistrates, of 'fewer and better' public houses,[2] that is to say of reducing the number of licences, and raising the standards of those that remained. This entailed 'fewer and better' tied houses for those firms which drove the policy through. After the end of the war the 'fewer and better' policy was widely adopted by the industry which undertook a considerable expenditure of capital on licensed property at a time when profits were depressed and the capital market was not easily available.

The secular reduction in the demand for beer which followed the first world war was accentuated during periods of trade depression, and at these times the need to maintain the output of the newer, large breweries became a more important incentive for amalgamations, expecially in areas where the depression was severe. As the chairman of Meux's said in April 1924: 'what we really want is more trade to enable us to run our brewery[3] more nearly to its real output capacity. This probably can only be achieved by absorption of some other brewery undertaking, as individual houses are becoming extremely difficult to acquire at a reasonable price'.

Throughout the period there was a general increase in the size of businesses which were acquired. This was partly because the supply of small businesses was dwindling, and partly because transport costs were not as significant in limiting the area of the mergers of the larger companies, as they had been at an earlier period. The transport costs of beer are surprisingly low at present; one great national brewer has transport costs of some 1½ per cent of retail price, and the transport costs of local brewers vary between 2 and 4 per cent of retail price: in general, transport costs only rise as high as 4 per cent when the

[1] An example of this is in the State Management District. In Carlisle, the state monopoly is almost complete, and the reduction in licences has been substantial. In Maryport there is competition with a commercial brewery and there reduction has been less fast because some customers from closed houses would move to those belonging to the competitor.

[2] H. Mitchell, annual meeting, Mitchell's and Butler's, August 13, 1908; E. A. Ansell, Chairman's Speech, Ansell's Ltd, November 23, 1912.

[3] Which was a new one, built with an eye to a considerably larger trade than the firm had actually achieved.

radius of the delivery area exceeds about thirty miles. Two factors were important in reducing transport costs to their present low level. The first was the rise in the price of beer which took place because of the increase in the excise duty. This reduced the relative importance of costs other than the duty. The second was the early development of motor transport in areas where communication had been poor. In 1921, for instance, E. Robins and Sons, of Hove, were delivering by road in Kent, Surrey, Hampshire and Sussex, an area where rail transport had been expensive. The combination of brewers in these counties was hastened by the growth of their delivery areas. The acquisition of brewing firms has usually been closely related to the cost of transport between their tied houses and the acquiring brewery. For example, in August 1922, Watney's bought Cobham United Breweries Ltd, whose houses lie within the area of delivery between (Watney's) Mortlake Brewery and Farnham agency.

The history of a big amalgamation and the minor amalgamations associated with the firms concerned may be taken to summarize some of the factors at work. In 1934 Ind Coope amalgamated with Allsopp & Co. Ltd. These two large Burton firms had both had a history of acquisitions and amalgamations. Allsopp's had entered late into the race for tied property. It then bought unwisely at high prices,[1] and became burdened with a heavy rate of fixed interest payments.[2] In 1906, Allsopp's made an attempt to amalgamate with Thos. Salter, Ltd, then in liquidation, and the Burton Brewery Co. Ltd, which was in considerable difficulty. The plan was thwarted by a preference shareholders' committee of Allsopp's who were driven to change the Board of the company after losses of over £1 million had been incurred. It was only in 1910 that the amalgamation was allowed to proceed, and two of the breweries were closed. In December 1913, the firm united with Showell's, an old-established and sound concern. The process of acquisition continued after the first world war. For example, in 1926, Allsopp's bought Hall's Oxford Brewery and Ind Coope bought the new London Brewery of Coggeshall and Colchester.[3] Sir George Courthope's last speech as Chairman of Ind Coope summarizes many of the factors which were important during this period.

'In order to maintain economic production and profitable business it is necessary to maintain the output of our breweries. This has only been possible by an increase in the number of licensed houses which

[1] *Country Brewers' Gazette*, October 1889.

[2] Allsopp's was called by *The Economist*, on August 11, 1990, 'a grossly mismanaged business'.

[3] *Brewers' Journal*, August 1922.

form our distributing agencies. To achieve this, both Allsopp's and ourselves, in common with other large concerns, have acquired from time to time smaller brewing businesses, whose houses have been added to our own. But the supply of small brewing businesses is dwindling . . .'

Then Sir George turned to production economies: 'The two breweries at Burton are side by side, the different departments . . . could be consolidated in one set of premises or the other. A single analytical laboratory could serve both breweries . . .'

These quotations emphasize that the advantages to be derived from brewing to capacity cannot be dissociated from the need to expand the market available to the brewery. In part this arises from the movement of population and the contraction of the total demand for beer. The population of the County of London, for example, fell by 17½ per cent from 1938 to 1953 and, in consequence, London brewing firms have had to acquire businesses in the provinces.[1] The acquired breweries are usually closed and the licensed houses supplied from the parent concern. Occasionally, where licensing restrictions were less severe, new public houses became available in the areas to which the population had moved.

The fall in the demand for draught beer has strengthened the bigger brewers and weakened the smaller firms because the latter find bottling plant expensive to acquire and a reputation for good bottled beer difficult to achieve. Thus, small firms tend to become dependent on other concerns for their bottled beer, and the production of beer in their own breweries tends to fall; in this way the increase in the bottled beer trade has provided additional incentives for amalgamation. The shrinking of sales of draught beer made by the small brewer makes him increasingly willing to sell and the increased importance of the outlet for bottled beer makes the larger brewer more anxious to buy.

When large firms buy small firms the subsequent policy of the new organization tends to follow certain patterns. This is most particularly the case when the acquiring firm is a national brewer with an established market for well advertised brands of beer.

First, the newly-acquired outlets obtain their bottled beer from the large firm and their outside purchases are restricted. The local brewery may be left to produce draught beer for a while, but it is usually closed in the end. These features are illustrated by the examples of Whitbread and of Ind Coope & Allsopp who have both tended to supply their bottled beer to the outlets of the breweries they have acquired. For example in 1954 Whitbread bought Dale's

[1] E.g. Watney, Combe & Reid, *Financial Times*, October 22, 1954.

brewery in Cambridge and the bottled beer is supplied by Whitbread, while the draught beer is bought locally, the brewery having been closed.

The time-lag between the acquisition and the subsequent reorganization and the closing of small breweries varies considerably. Tollemache, for example, have kept both the Star Brewery and their other brewery in production. Frequently, however, the rate of change is fairly rapid, as may be seen from the following examples. After a recent amalgamation, the chairman of Joshua Tetley & Son Ltd[1] said: 'Our board has been engaged since last March in co-ordinating the working of Duncan Gilmour & Co. and its subsidiaries with the activities of the parent company. We have taken over already the production of beer to be sold by certain of Duncan Gilmour's subsidiaries and over a period of years we hope, gradually, to supply the demands of the whole Duncan Gilmour group from our Leeds brewery'.[2] Another example is from the report of Flowers, a brewing firm which has been expanding rapidly by acquiring other businesses. 'You will have noted that a feature of this expansion has been the re-grouping of the various brewing units involved. For instance, in 1950 the output of the Royston brewery of J. and J. E. Phillips Limited was concentrated at the Luton brewery, and only last month a further addition of output to this brewery was made by the closing of the Ashwell brewery of E. K. and H. Fordham Limited. In 1950 the output of George Ware and Sons Limited was absorbed by the Tunbridge Wells brewery of E. and H. Kelsey Limited. In 1951 we acquired Soulby, Sons and Winch Limited, of Alford, Lincolnshire, and this was followed a few months later by the acquisition of all the ordinary shares in Mowbray and Co., Limited of Grantham. In September of this year the Alford brewery ceased to brew, and its output has been absorbed by the Grantham brewery.'[3] Flowers now operate four breweries and have closed four since 1950.[4]

[1] Annual Report, January 3, 1955; the chairman goes on to mention the co-ordination of transport and wine and spirit interests.

[2] *Financial Times*, January 3, 1955.

[3] J. W. Green Ltd (now Flower's as a consequence of further expansion). Annual Report, *Times*, December 19, 1952.

[4] Strong and Co. of Romsey Ltd, Annual Report, *Financial Times*, December 18, 1954.

CHAPTER 5

Conclusions

MERGERS in brewing have taken place both at times of good trade, and at times of bad trade, because, fundamentally, the drive to amalgamate rests on growing economies of scale and on the imperfect retail market to which entry is restricted by the licensing system. Despite the extent of the merger movement there are still over 300 firms in the industry; by comparison with other industries the degree of concentration[1] is not high, although it is increasing rapidly. In any area there is usually a choice of tied houses and within many of these houses there is some choice at least of bottled beers.

How far has the trend to merge restricted competition?

In the retailing of beer, as of any commodity, competition is inevitably imperfect. Although the differences of price in different outlets are largely the reflection of different amenities, retail prices are not as rigidly controlled by agreement as in other trades;[2] it appears that the conditions of retail demand are such that there is little incentive to make short-term price changes. The high rates of duty on beer make brewing costs an insignificant proportion of the price; however the variation of gravity, especially if undetected, can effect considerable changes in profits. Over longer periods, however, changes in price and gravity relations do occur, and these changes are long-term competitive factors.

The value to the brewer of secure outlets in a restricted market led to the tied-house system and, as soon as the policy of vertical integration had begun, it inevitably continued to spread rapidly as brewers feared exclusion from the market. At times of tightening up of the licensing laws the process has been strengthened and there have been no counteracting factors tending to weaken it at times of relaxation of the law, except in the contemporary case of clubs which are

[1] H. Leak and A. Maizels, *The Structure of British Industry*, Journal of the Royal Statistical Society, 1945. The proportion of output by the three biggest firms in the brewing and brewing and malting trades was between 23 and 27 per cent in 1943.

[2] Retail prices other than for draught beer are not necessarily established even by one brewer for his tenants.

virtually unregulated. The secure market, given by the ownership of tied houses, has limited short-period competition.

The almost complete dominance of retailing by the tied-house system has, in general, prevented concentration of production on more efficient units by means other than merger, so that restriction of free competition has probably delayed concentration of output on these efficient units. Few firms, since 1800, have disappeared or failed completely. Yet, especially in conditions of falling demand, the technical incentives to the concentration of production have been strong. There were the general economies of scale and improved techniques which became widely available with the spread of technical knowledge at the end of the nineteenth century. These were partly responsible for the rebuilding of many breweries at that time. More recently, the growth in the bottled beer trade has gradually raised the minimum size of efficient brewing operation. The small brewers cannot now ignore the trade, and they are in a weak position if they do not sell bottled beers in their houses. The increased trade in bottled beers has, however, given the brewers who are large enough to advertise nationally some opportunity to expand without merger. Expansion in this way is nevertheless somewhat chancy, since many of the outlets where trade is to be found are owned by rivals or potential rivals, and a change of ownership, or the decision to start bottling, may close the outlet overnight. Control of the market is thus essential for large and secure increases in sales.

The fall in the demand for draught beer which has been the predominant trend for fifty years has made fixed expenses a frequent preoccupation to most firms. Not only is fixed equipment extremely durable, but also it is made up of a large number of different items, each of which has to be replaced at different intervals. Firms do not shrink, they simply have idle capacity and they continue to replace equipment so long as the total return constitutes sufficient profit on the one item to justify its replacement. There is thus a persistent tendency for excess capacity to remain in the industry, and a persistent incentive to maintain or expand sales.

Beer now provides only some three-quarters of the profit in retailing, and only about one-half or two-thirds of this profit is attributable to the tying brewers' own beers. Therefore, brewing firms, which are especially adapted to the exploitation of the peculiarities of this trade, have an additional incentive to expand their retail holdings; this incentive is quite distinct from the production economies of a larger output.

The survival of independent firms, despite the continual process of merging which has gone on steadily for many years, arises from the protected market position of brewers which reduces the likelihood of forced sales of their businesses; the mergers must wait upon a steady supply of businesses becoming available. This happens both for family and individual reasons and because their costs of operation become relatively high and profits fall below the possible return on the capitalized value of their goodwill. High prices must be paid for the acquired concerns, especially when trade is good. The value of the smaller, independent business is generally enhanced because a number of larger suppliers are competing for the business.

If there were no tied-house system small, inefficient breweries might not be protected, and the concentration of production in efficient units might proceed more quickly as it would not then require the purchase of outlets at great cost.[1]

Although the licensing system raises the value of outlets and so raises the proportion of fixed payments which follow a merger, it is possible that consumer loyalty and other imperfections are such that in the absence of licensing the goodwill of local brewers would still be valuable to an acquirer. It is probable that the elimination of high-cost producers and the expansion of the more efficient firms, which would follow greater retail freedom, would result in lower brewing costs than the present multi-firm vertical structure, with its protected market, allows.

The effect of this upon the final price to the consumer is, however, uncertain. At present the most competitive part of the trade is in the supplying of houses and clubs which are not tied and in the supplying of bottled beers to tied houses which belong to breweries, who do not bottle. In both cases the competition takes the form of large retail margins rather than the reduction in the final price paid by the consumers. Bottled beer retail profit margins vary from 20 per cent to over 25 per cent, those for draught beer are between 15 and 18 per cent. However, lower retail prices would be probable in some districts[2] so long as there were not price agreements between the brewers. Although the market would continue very imperfect it is quite possible that competition between the brewers in a declining market would prove so severe that they would be driven to make binding price agreements. Intense competition in an industry with a persistent

[1] In the USA, where the output of beer has risen from 9·6 million bulk barrels (American) in 1873 to 80–90 million bulk barrels in 1949, the number of breweries has fallen from 4,131 to 450 (*Collier's Encyclopaedia*, New York, 1954; *Encyclopaedia Britannica*, Chicago, 1954). This is in a market without vertical integration between manufacture and retailing.

[2] In the areas like Tyneside where clubs are strongest, local retail prices tend to be lower than elsewhere, and local gravities higher.

tendency towards excess capacity and with high fixed expenses would be very painful.

The growth in advertising and retail amenities which has marked the last fifty years is so closely connected with the existing retail restrictions that it is difficult to say whether these forms of competition would be intensified at the expense of price competition.

Concentration of the brewing industry has increased and is increasing because of the growing economies of scale and the tendency of demand to fall. The degree of forward integration has made mergers the only possible method of growth. The forward integration has been increased by the licensing laws, but even in their absence it would probably have been substantial, and some quite definite legislation such as the prohibition of tied houses would probably have been required to prevent links between brewers and public houses. (This might not have been necessary if the taste for bottled beers had developed earlier.) The possibility of competition in retail margins and the possibility of price agreements makes it difficult to judge whether the greater concentration of the industry which might have resulted from a horizontal industry structure would have been in the public interest. As concentration proceeded a situation would probably have been reached in which a few big firms were price leaders and did not find it worthwhile to drive out the remaining small competitors. In other words, an oligopolistic situation would have emerged which would not, perhaps, have been unlike the actual development which is taking place, despite the vertical structure of the industry. The vertical structure has, however, made concentration slower then it might otherwise have been; but an oligopolistic situation is now emerging from the existing system in which so many historical anomalies persist.

GENERAL CONCLUSIONS

THE preceding case studies have tried to bring out, for each of the six industries surveyed, the relationship between the technical and market conditions and the tendency for firms to amalgamate by merger or absorption. They have also attempted to suggest what alternative developments might have been possible and, in the light of this, to evaluate the extent to which the process of concentration was in the public interest.

Judgment in each case has depended both upon the relative importance of the different characteristics of the industry and upon the type of changes which have been needed. As the relevant characteristics are very numerous and the changes required to be made in each industry have been rather different, conclusions about one situation are seldom relevant to another; the number of factors to be taken into account is so great that particular situations are rarely found to be repeated in different industries. Useful generalizations appear to be either very general indeed or to relate to rather closely defined situations.

In all the six industries surveyed there has been a noteworthy concentration of economic power during the period covered. We have not included any industries where conditions have encouraged the persistence of small-scale business. This limitation is, of course, arbitrary and, perhaps, unfortunate; an industry in which competition between many firms has remained, although a merger would seem to have been possible, would have been of great interest: the worsted spinning industry constitutes just such an example.

The size of the unit of control can be increased not only by mergers—the main subject of this study—but also by internal expansion. If this process goes far enough to increase substantially the share of the market of the expanding firms, other firms must be driven out. The distinction between the two types of expansion is not clear cut. The expanding firms may take business away from their less successful rivals, force them to the verge of failure and then buy them up at very low prices.

In this final chapter the particular conclusions relating to the case studies are summarized. This is done because a feature may be fairly obvious when related to a particular industry, but is extremely cumbersome to define in general terms. From the summaries a considerable list of the main determinants of events has been drawn up. This list is of some importance in itself, for it contains distinctions which are often neglected and features which are often regarded as mere peculiarities in much orthodox theory. The list is long but not unmanageable since many of the items can be grouped; for many particular problems whole groups of features are of little importance and can be explicitly disregarded. It must be stressed that features should be disregarded explicitly rather than simply ignored, since a conclusion based upon one set of features may be quite misleading if there are other features of some importance.

Discussion of the main determinants is followed by consideration of the main difficulties which are encountered when one tries to reach conclusions about the effects of mergers. (The 'effects of mergers' is understood as the difference between the situation after a merger and another situation which might have arisen.) It is shown that only in rather simple cases can the 'effects' be stated with any certainty.

Finally, the problems of judging the effects are discussed. This is extremely complicated, and again conclusions can only be reached for simple cases. There are, however, a few general relationships which make tentative judgments easier than would appear at first sight.

No attempt is made in this chapter to show how far existing theoretical models can be applied to actual situations. This exercise is regarded as useless since any theory 'applies'; the main variables generally exist, but the real question is whether or not they are important and whether or not any conclusion reached is more, or less, important than that which would have been reached by the application of a different theory based on different variables. Conclusions are complementary rather than mutually exclusive; all throw some light upon the situation but they will not indicate a clear course of action unless they can be weighted.

SUMMARIES OF THE CONCLUSIONS FROM THE INDUSTRY STUDIES

I. CEMENT

In the cement industry a number of important mergers took place between 1900 and 1950, and as conditions changed new factors became important. This has made it very difficult to summarize the conclusions, and it has been necessary to indicate the period to which each applies.

Causes of Mergers

1. The main cause of the first two big mergers (the formation of the APCM and its subsidiary, the BPCM) was the intensity of short-period competition. The competition, though intense, did not result in the reduction in the capacity of the industry. It was characterized by price discrimination both in the form of freight absorption and in discrimination between customers, and it was made more severe by the variations in demand between different districts and at different seasons. The competition was considered intolerable (it showed no sign of giving 'normal' profits in the long run), and firms were prepared to join the combines in order to avoid it.

2. Both the great differences between the many firms in the industry, particularly those differences in equipment and efficiency which made their long-term prospects diverge, and the characteristics of short-term competition, made price agreement between many firms impossible to maintain.

3. The rapid rate of technical change, increasing economies of scale and the larger capital requirements made large companies seem likely to become profitable.

4. Although the cement industry was seldom very profitable before 1935, the long-term outlook was usually good, as demand was increasing and new uses for cement were being found. This made financiers ready to invest in the industry when there was some hope of price control in the relatively near future.

5. The concentration of a multi-firm industry in which there are economies of scale may be achieved by a mixture of mergers and competitive elimination. In the cement industry a number of the firms acquired in the inter-war period were very weak and the concentration is to be attributed partly to competitive elimination.

Effects

1. The existence of the APCM-BPCM Group certainly limited competition. The extent to which it did so varied; but it was very important both in the period 1900 to about 1905 and 1911 to 1924. Price competition was restricted both by the existence of a price leader and by the fact that there were a smaller number of firms. Although the existence of a price leader made breaking away from agreements less dangerous, it seems unlikely that price agreements would have been reached and maintained as effectively in the absence of the combine.

2. The competitive elimination which would have taken place in the absence of major mergers would have led to concentration and the possibility of price agreements in the end. It is difficult to guess when this would have happened but, having regard to the technical changes, some time in the late 'twenties or early 'thirties seems probable. After this date the restrictions of price competition cannot be attributed to mergers as the alternative was no longer intense competition between a larger number of firms.

3. The APCM and the BPCM improved the average efficiency of the firms taken over by promoting technical progress (particularly the introduction of the rotary kiln), by causing interchange of ideas, and by eliminating the most inefficient.

4. The relative stability of the industry due to the combine encouraged new entrants who saw increased demand and knew that they had lower costs than many of their rivals.

5. Favourable conditions of entry ensured that price could seldom be maintained for long at levels above average total cost of new, efficient works.

6. Mergers made competitive elimination relatively unimportant. This would have taken place in the absence of mergers, but the rate would have been slow since equipment is very durable.

Judgment

1. The mergers promoted efficiency both within the combines and in the new firms in the rest of the trade; it also encouraged expansion in a growing industry. Really intense competition, had it been possible, might have caused periodic shortages of cement. Only such shortages would have made normal profits possible.

2. Prices were higher than they would otherwise have been during most of the period up to about 1925–6, but after this it seems possible that increased efficiency and the possibility of restricted price competition in the absence of mergers made the actual price no higher than it would otherwise have been.

3. The present high degree of concentration tends to minimize idle

capacity, but is not so great that competition in techniques and efficiency is reduced to any important extent.

4. In the absence of mergers the rate at which efficiency increased would very probably have been lower, but it seems probable that growth and minor mergers would have given rise to a situation not very different to that which exists today.

II. CALICO PRINTING

Causes of the Formation of the Calico Printers' Association

1. Intolerable, imperfect competition appeared likely to continue indefinitely.

2. The failure of attempts to maintain price agreements was due to lack of faith, the importance of non-price competition, and the great differences between firms and their prospects.

3. Potential progress in the industry was thought in 1900 to be sufficient to give economies of scale.

Effects

1. The immediate effect was to raise prices. The alternative situation was competition modified from time to time by price agreement, but it is fairly clear that the agreements would seldom have been effective.

2. The favourable position of independents immediately after the formation of the combine allowed them to grow.

3. Efficiency was raised as a result of the elimination of the least efficient within the combine.

4. There was great rationalization within the combine and the necessary contraction, which was inhibited by imperfect competition, was achieved more quickly than it would have been in the absence of the combine. The size of the combine allowed some specialized works to be maintained.

5. The combine contributed towards the improvement of technique to some extent, especially in the inter-war period and post-1945.

Judgment

1. In this declining industry with much imperfect competition, the combine and the other large firms contributed substantially towards the maintenance of efficiency.

2. More firms would have increased competition which was checked by the existence of a price leader, but as this competition could have been very imperfect the effects are uncertain. The combine was partly responsible for the 1949–54 pools and quota scheme. This was

restrictive, but it was short lived, and the circumstances changed so quickly that the effects are doubtful.

3. The combine has been almost entirely dependent upon a high level of efficiency, and on the whole has set a sufficiently high standard to offset adverse effects which have resulted from the restriction of competition.

III. SOAP

Causes of Mergers

1. Competition between a large number of firms involved heavy selling costs since products differed, new ones had to be launched, and advertisement was potent. This led to a situation which was found intolerable by the firms concerned and was, therefore, liable to be altered by some means.

2. Changing product, variations in the efficiency of firms and the large number of small firms made price agreements difficult to maintain despite the fluctuating price of raw materials (particularly the fats).

3. Economies of scale exist, especially in marketing, research and in risk spreading, but they are not overriding.

4. Expansion by firms has generally been rather slow and expensive because of market imperfections and the cost of price wars. Expansion was not, however, impossible; in the absence of Lever it would, no doubt, have been important in bringing about a greater degree of concentration.

Effects

1. The economies of scale, which were largely related to new processes, became increasingly important but were only achieved gradually; rationalization within the combine was rather slow. There are few real grounds for believing that up to the end of the 'twenties competitive elimination would have been less effective than the rationalization which took place within the combine.

2. Selling costs and some of the wastes of imperfect competition were reduced. The combine had so large a share of the market that it could decide upon the extent to which choice should be limited in the interest of economies. The strength to mould demand, if used effectively, as it probably was after about 1930, speeds up the rate of adjustment in an imperfect market and enables the firm to take advantage of possible economies of scale.

3. Vertical links with retailing only developed to a very small degree; this suggested that the combine was efficient. Market imper-

fections are increased by vertical links and can shelter considerable inefficiency, especially in a changing industry.

4. The combine prevented prices from falling when they might otherwise have done so, e.g. during periods of low demand. This was probably important from about 1912 to the early 1930's, but after that the alternative, oligopoly, achieved by minor mergers and competitive elimination, would probably have prevented continuous price cutting, and even price wars would have become rare.

Judgment

1. Unilever became efficient and they were kept on their toes by potential and actual new entry. New entrants into the mass markets had to be efficient to meet Unilever price levels, and had to be fairly large in order to obtain the economies of scale. All the important firms are now such that they tend to take a long-term view.

2. The day-to-day competition is not as expensive as it would be in a more competitive industry and prices are probably lower. This is partly due to the fact that the choice offered is smaller because the large firm will withdraw less popular types more quickly.

3. The actual situation is not now very different from what would have come about in the absence of Levers, but the number of firms is smaller and this makes for greater efficiency because there are economies of scale.

IV. FLAT GLASS

Reasons for the Comparative Unimportance of Mergers in Bringing About the Concentration of the Industry

1. High rate of technical progress and the competition from progressive firms abroad resulted in the elimination of many firms. Their works were normally out of date and there was little of value to be sold. Market imperfections were unimportant compared with the cost differentials which resulted from the progress.

2. The importance of know-how and developing techniques made entry into the industry after about 1860 both difficult and risky.

3. Large economies of scale developed, particularly after 1870.

4. Temporary price agreements were relatively effective. The mergers in the middle of the nineteenth century were due to the fact that this was a period when they were effective in reducing competition. Foreign competition had not become so important at this stage, techniques were not changing so fundamentally and new entrants were feared. These mergers probably resulted in somewhat higher prices for a short time. The Pilkington-Chance merger was partly the result of special personal relationships, but technical economies of

scale, the relatively slow rate of technical change in the manufacture of rolled plate-glass, the possibility of eliminating the wastes of very imperfect competition, and the failure of Chances to maintain technical progress, were all-important.

Mergers were unimportant in this industry and it is misleading to summarize their possible effects since many other factors were so much more important.

As Pilkingtons have remained enterprising and efficient it is difficult to suggest any development which would have increased the efficiency of the industry.

V. THE MOTOR INDUSTRY

The conclusions relating to this industry must be divided as a long period of great interest in which mergers were of negligible importance was followed by a big merger.

Reasons for the Absence of Mergers

1. Rapid rate of product change made goodwill rather unimportant.
2. Firms which failed in the early years were generally small and their equipment not very specialized.
3. Product competition overshadowed price competition in importance. This product competition was seldom the equivalent of price reduction, since the improvement of the product resulted from new ideas and technical progress, rather than increased costs and lower profit margins. This type of competition could not be mitigated by mergers in an industry which new firms could still enter freely.
4. By the 1920's the growth of a components section had eased capital requirements and this made it possible for successful firms to grow quickly.

Effects of Relying upon Competition

1. There was a waste of resources which might have been averted by a large 'efficient' firm; there is no guarantee, however, that in the early years such a large firm would have been efficient.
2. One or more large firms at earlier dates might have hastened the introduction of mass-production methods.

Judgment

1. Mergers might have created one or two firms, capable of a greater rate of progress in the inter-war period. This view turns upon consideration of the outstanding success of the American motor-car industry, but the fact that Morris did not consolidate a dominant

position makes the effect of fewer larger firms in the British industry a matter of pure conjecture. The mergers which formed the basis of the Rootes group were discussed at length, and it was shown that very small firms were acquired and that the development of the group depended primarily upon growth.

The Austin-Morris Merger: This has been the one important merger in the industry.

Cause

1. Economies of scale developed with the increasing use of mass-production methods.
2. Economies existed on the sales side, especially in the export markets associated with the growing importance of service in spare parts and of guarantees.
3. There was severe competition from the American subsidiaries, Ford and Vauxhall, who had advantages of scale due to the fact that both are world-wide organizations.

Effects

1. It must be presumed that the merger has, in fact, yielded economies of scale and that with good management it will continue to do so.
2. Competition from American subsidiaries, Ford and Vauxhall, is such that shares of the market rather than prices are likely to have been affected.

Judgment

The formation of the BMC was almost certainly in the public interest in that it enabled economies to be made and better service to be given. These economies are likely to be passed on to the consumer because of the continuing need to meet competition from the other large firms. The British pattern is tending towards the American pattern and the latter shows no lack of competition.

VI. BREWING

Causes of Mergers

1. There were economies of scale.
2. Excess capacity persisted due (*a*) to declining demand; (*b*) to the fact that the capacity of a brewery cannot be reduced as there are not a large number of similar pieces of equipment.
3. No method of expansion except by merger is available because of the tied house and the licensing laws.

Effects

The industry became more concentrated and costs were reduced.

Judgment

Mergers were in the public interest, given the circumstances. In the absence of mergers, the small firms would have been small protected monopolies, which could survive, however inefficient.

THE MAIN DETERMINANTS

The determinants which gave rise to the particular conclusions in the individual case studies may be grouped under three heads. Firstly, those features which relate to the intensity and persistence of short-period competition, secondly, the features which give rise to economies of scale and, thirdly, those which determine the conditions of expansion by existing firms and the ease of entry into the industry. These three groups cover the features which cause mergers, determine their 'effects' and give rise to favourable or unfavourable judgments; generalizations about these problems are made easier by the fact that a classification of the main determinants is common to all three.

Throughout the discussion of the three groups of determinants which follows, each group is illustrated from the case studies; particular emphasis is placed upon the less familiar points and the distinctions which the case studies have shown to be important.

1. Intense and persistent short-period competition is a major factor tending to bring about changes in the structure of industry; further, the judgment of the effects of the changes in the structure often depends upon whether or not the short-period competition has been in the public interest.

The case studies show that intense and persistent short-period competition is particularly associated, not only with features such as homogeneity of product and high overheads which are stressed in orthodox competitive theory, but also with a number of others which are less amenable to systematic theoretical treatment.

Short-period competition tends to be particularly intense when there are considerable opportunities for price discrimination. Firms anxious to increase sales but reluctant to cut prices over the whole of their sales often find it profitable to make discriminatory cuts. In the cement industry discrimination between customers and freight absorption have been common and important. They have frequently been the prelude to general price reductions, but they have also been a source of considerable wastes in cross haulage and sales effort. In the calico printing industry, also, price discrimination has led to price reductions in situations in which prices would probably have been maintained by tacit collusion in a more perfect market. In this industry the possibility of price discrimination has tended to increase risks and to cause considerable diversification.

Short-period competition is also found to be particularly intense in industries such as the soap industry where raw material prices fluctuate. In a competitive situation each firm is reluctant to initiate price increases and, therefore, rises in the price of raw materials tend to reduce profits.

2. The existence of economies of scale in manufacturing is the most powerful factor leading to concentration, but that concentration may be achieved either by merger or by the elimination of the weaker firms. If there are not economies of scale, large combines are seldom successful since they are likely to be weakened by the appearance of new competitors. The development of economies of scale is associated with progress. An important distinction must be made between a change or series of changes in methods which give rise to permanent economies of scale, and continuous progress which can be exploited most easily by the large firm. In many cases permanent economies of scale and continuous progress are found together.

Economies of scale played a different role in each of the cases studied. In the brewing industry economies of scale led to merger, growth without merger being impossible. In the soap industry Unilever's position was strengthened as new processes were developed, but pure economies of scale were comparatively unimportant. In the glass industry progress eliminated the weaker firm and the economies of scale, rate of progress, and the importance of know-how made new entry extremely difficult. The Calico Printers' Association would have been stronger had progress been faster, for it generally depended upon scientific knowledge and know-how, both of which were more readily available within the combine. Among the cases studied the cement industry was exceptional. Here fairly fast progress in manufacturing techniques did not give rise to great economies of scale, nor did it give many great advantages to the combine. Progress was made by foreign producers and by machinery manufacturers; consulting engineers and machinery manufacturers could install new plant and teach the owners to operate them. New entry into the industry was easy and the economies of scale limited to those available within a single plant. The concentration of the motor-car industry was partly the result of the rapid change and progress in design and partly the development of economies of scale. This form has resulted in the competitive characteristics of firms; the latter has made the development of substantial new firms extremely difficult and has led to the highly important Austin-Morris merger.

Competition is normally severe when there is excess capacity; in orthodox theory competition eliminates the excess capacity and equilibrium is restored. There are, however, a number of combinations of factors which tend to cause persistent idle capacity. The most important is rapid fluctuations in demand and changes in the demand in different areas and for specific large projects.

The intensity and persistence of short-period competition in any situation is then partly the result of unrestricted competition and partly the result of the factors which cause the interests of different firms to diverge, thereby making collusion difficult.

There are many types of marketing economies of scale, and the case studies indicate that a number of distinctions are important. In the case of the cement industry the economies related mainly to the advantages to be obtained from a wide sales network which could be served by the most conveniently situated works; the larger the network the smaller the amount of excess capacity which had to be carried in order to meet peak demand in any particular area. These economies of scale constitute reductions in real costs but not necessarily immediate reductions in the price to the consumer. In the case of the motor-car industry there are economies of bulk buying, which are mainly related to the technical economies of scale in the components industry; and these economies are usually passed on to the consumer.

In the soap industry and to a lesser extent in the glass industry the marketing economies of scale are related to monopolistic or semi-monopolistic positions. In the glass industry selling and distribution costs have been reduced because it has been possible to pursue a policy of maximum efficiency which disregards the competitive behaviour of competitors and makes it unnecessary either to take steps to protect markets which are prone to short-period competition or to develop the imperfections in the already somewhat imperfect sections of the market. In other words, a degree of price discrimination designed to maintain profits, at times when demand is lower, is made unnecessary.

The case of the soap industry is even more interesting. Here it is claimed that Unilever is in such a dominant position that it can offer to the consumer the selection which is thought to give the best compromise between choice and price. The firm does not have to compete at every point lest other firms gain a larger share of the market; it can mould demand so that the consumer can be offered the advantages of the economies of scale. Competition might lead to a similar compromise between choice and price in the end, but in an imperfect market adjustment would be very slow; where change in the types of product demanded is continuous, competitive adjustment would probably be too slow and an unnecessarily large choice, at a higher price, would persist. The large firm is able to cut out the less good lines without risk or fear of loosing sales to competitors. The more drastic steps may sometimes reduce immediate profits but they strengthen the long-period position of the firm by introducing a cost structure which no smaller competitor can match.

Although there are economies of scale in marketing which give rise to lower long-period average costs there are a number of important disadvantages associated with being large; these are particularly related to price policy. These points play little part in the stationary analysis of orthodox theory and cannot be regarded as simple diseconomies of scale.

Firstly, the large firm is faced by a low elasticity of demand since it already has a large proportion of the market. The Calico Printers' Association could not cut prices without affecting their own trade, whereas smaller competitors could often maintain sales by cutting prices in markets in which they were selling very little. In the case of the cement combine the difficulty lay in the fact that they dominated the large London market and could only meet the price reductions, made by smaller competitors from other areas, if they were prepared to incur considerable losses.

The second disadvantage which results from a dominant position is the fact that the large firm is often forced into a position of price leadership. It is forced to announce its prices although it knows that they will, whatever the level, be undercut by the smaller competitors unless demand is very high. Thus, if demand fluctuates, the small competitor may, on average, gain at the expense of the larger. The level set by the large is, on account of economies of scale, usually such that the smaller are not encouraged to expand; if this is not the case the large firm is very likely to lose its dominant position.

A third disadvantage of size arises because the large firm must pursue a relatively rigid price policy which can be operated by salaried salesmen. This position is somewhat akin to the first two and is related to the whole question of short-period price discrimination.

Thus, in the cement, calico printing and, to some extent, in the soap and glass industries, the dominant firms have had to maintain their position despite this weakness of their market position *vis-à-vis* their better small competitors.

The points of weakness of large firms are seldom emphasized. This is generally due to the fact that there are many industries where these weaknesses are amply offset. The cement industry is of some interest in that it has been delicately poised. Where there is a very large group and only a very few small firms, the threat of local price discrimination may make the small firm very frightened; on the other hand when there are a number of small firms it is the large firm which becomes frightened unless there are great economies of scale.

The weaknesses of the market position of large firms are of great importance in relation to mergers because they exist from the moment a combine is formed, whereas in some cases it may be several years before the genuine economies of scale can be obtained. Both the Calico Printers' Association and the Associated Portland Cement Manufacturers were in considerable difficulty in the early years, and even Levers made little headway, except by further acquisition, in the period up to 1914. The studies have shown the importance of the early years of combines; they appear to require true monopoly power until such time as real economies of scale are realized; where these do not exist a big multi-firm combine is only successful in very special circumstances.

3. The factors which govern the conditions of expansion of firms constitute the third group of important determinants. Where expansion is difficult economies of scale can only be obtained by the merging of firms.

Several rather fine distinctions must be made under this head. Freedom of entry is not quite the same thing as expansion; it may be fairly easy to enter an expanding industry, such as the cement industry, but exceedingly difficult to grow at the expense of existing firms. In the calico printing industry it has often been easy to enter the industry, relatively easy for some good small firms to grow, but extremely difficult for the large firm to expand significantly. This is also true of the soap industry; the small firm with initiative and some luck or good judgment may grow, but the large firm is able to do so only at great cost unless it finds a successful new product. The more imperfect is competition, the more difficult it is to cut into other firms' markets. Thus, the introduction of branded products and the development of advertising tends to encourage expansion by absorption rather than by elimination. Further, when the size of the total market for a product is declining or even increasing at a rate less rapid than is aimed at by the expanding firm, absorption becomes more likely. Both these factors were important in the brewing industry and in the soap industry.

The easiest conditions of expansion are found where firms differ very much in efficiency; the really big differences in efficiency are generally related to progress and change. In the motor-car industry expansion has come from firms with successful models and the enterprise and determination to produce them on as large scale as possible in order to reap the economies of scale and reduce costs. Successful growth on this basis made mergers of little importance in this industry; when they did take place they merely involved the acquisition by the strong firm of a weakened firm which could be bought cheaply. The important Austin-Morris merger appears to have been largely the result of the appearance of new economies of scale available to the very large; in the previous period sheer size does not appear to have been as important as it is now.

The glass industry is another example where expansion has been achieved by successful development of techniques. The rate of change was sufficiently fast for less progressive firms to be of little value. Again, the only important merger, Pilkington's with Chance's, occured when technique in a particular branch of the industry, the rolled-glass section, was changing relatively slowly.

The case of the soap industry is very different. After the early growth of Levers the concentration of the industry was largely the result of a series of acquisitions. The rate of technical progress was not dramatic and did not lead to the rapid elimination of the less progressive; on the other hand it was almost continuous, and it appears that Levers were able to make a number of acquisitions because their competitors were becoming frightened that they would be unable to keep up with the rate of progress and would become weaker and weaker. (The acquisition of Chance's by Pilkington's may also be analysed in these terms.)

In general the conditions of expansion appear to be very closely related to the rate of change unless, as in the case of the brewing industry, there are permanent and important market imperfections. If there is little historical development, expansion leading to concentration of the industry will be difficult. (If there are, and always have been, important economies of scale the industry will be concentrated and there will be no reason for changes.) Where there is very rapid historical change, whether firms merge or simply expand will depend upon the speed and nature of the change. Sometimes there will be mergers designed to take advantage of the change; the first cement merger was partly of this type. Sometimes, as in the glass and motor industries, a few firms will develop sufficiently rapidly to drive out the others without any significant mergers taking place. Sometimes a moderate rate of progress exploited by the large firms will weaken the others and make them prepared to sell; they will be bought if their acquisition offers a cheaper method of expansion than prolonged competition. This point can be illustrated from the brewing, soap, cement and glass industries, but only in the brewing industry was it of continuous importance.

The three groups of factors which have been discussed are the basis of general propositions relating to (a) the causes of mergers; (b) the effects and (c) the judgments as to whether or not these effects are in the public interest.

CAUSES OF MERGERS

Mergers take place in order to secure economies of scale or to reduce intense short-period competition, or, more frequently, to do both. These objectives may be achieved by merging but they may also be achieved either by price agreement or by internal expansion. The former may deal effectively with intense competition, the latter may bring economies of scale and, eventually, a reduction of competition. A merger will only take place if it offers the best method of achieving the objectives, one or both of which may be attained either by internal expansion or by price agreement.

Although one can often determine, *ex post*, the conditions in which a combine might have been successful, it must be stressed that the formation of a major combine may be such a big undertaking that a possible opportunity may be lost because there is no individual able or willing to undertake the task. The analysis of changes in the structure of industry must be based upon the assumption of rational behaviour and a fairly elastic supply of entrepreneurs, but it is clear that these assumptions are not entirely valid for situations where very big changes are indicated.

It would have been possible to divide each industry study into periods and to discuss the presence or absence of mergers in that period in terms of the general conditions which give rise to mergers. This, however, would have been a long process full of pitfalls because, as always, the problem of weighting arises. For example, in a situation in which competition is 'moderately' intense and expansion 'fairly' easy it is not clear whether or not there will be mergers.

A merger will almost certainly take place if:

1. Unrestricted competition is intense, persistent and painful.
2. Price agreement is unworkable.
3. The concentration of the industry appears profitable.
4. Expansion by individual firms is slow, difficult or expensive.

Not all these conditions are necessary but all are relevant. The major difficulties arise from the fact that each may prevail to a greater or lesser degree, and in order to assess the importance of each, a great many questions must be considered.

Competition may be intense, persistent and painful if:

1. There are a large number of firms and no tacit agreement on prices.

2. The efficiency of firms varies to such an extent that some wish to expand at the expense of others.

3. Some or all firms find it profitable to exercise considerable price discrimination and will not sacrifice freedom in this respect, although it is known to spoil the market.

4. There are high, fixed expenses.

5. (a) Fixed equipment is durable; (b) fixed equipment consists of various large items; as these have usually to be replaced at different intervals such firms are reluctant to close and there is often a tendency for persistent over-capacity.

6. Fluctuations and changes in demand give rise to a persistent tendency for over-capacity.

7. Demand is tending to decline.

8. The price of raw materials fluctuate so that new price levels have to be established frequently. Where there is a somewhat kinked demand curve this is particularly difficult because prices fall easily but are difficult to raise.

Conditions 2 and 3, and to some extent condition 1, make price agreement unworkable.

The concentration of industry will be profitable if:

1. There are economies of scale either in manufacturing or marketing.

2. The reduction in competition reduces selling costs.

3. Progress is likely to be of the type best promoted by large organizations.

4. The large firm is not in too vulnerable a market position *vis-à-vis* the remaining independent firms.

Concentration can only be achieved by merger if:

1. Market imperfections are so durable that expansion is difficult and expensive.

2. Progress is insufficient to assist in the elimination of the inefficient and unprogressive firms.

This breakdown of the general conditions which indicate that mergers are likely shows that analysis of the causes of mergers depends upon distinguishing between the persistent and immediate influences. What we generally call 'the cause' is generally the last change which suddenly gives rise to a merger in a situation which was already sufficiently favourable in other respects. When several changes take place simultaneously, as is usually the case, the situation is only fully explained if the importance of each is weighted and these interconnections explained.

THE EFFECTS OF MERGERS

The assessment of the effects of mergers is closely related to the assessment of the causes; in those cases where the causes are fairly certain the effects are likely to be more predictable. For example, if, as in the case of calico printing, the reason for the combine is the elimination of intense short-period competition, then it is usually found that, for a time at least, short-period competition is eliminated. If, as in the brewing industry, merging was caused by the desire to obtain economies of scale in the only possible way, then it is probable that such economies will be found.

Mergers tend to reduce competition and to give scope for economies of scale; these are sometimes regarded as the 'effects' of mergers, but as has been pointed out, this is misleading. The true 'effects' are the differences between what would have happened in the absence of mergers and what did happen after the merger. Where the alternative to mergers is the competitive elimination of firms the final situation reached may be very similar whether or not mergers take place. In this case the effects of mergers will be (a) to reduce competition for some length of time; (b) either to cause greater efficiency more quickly because internal rationalization is quicker and more efficient than competitive elimination, or to delay rationalization because management is less ruthless than competition; (c) if the process of elimination by competition were long and profits very low, then the merger might make the rate of progress greater. This type of case is of considerable theoretical as well as practical importance, because it illustrates very clearly that the true 'effects' of mergers are, to a very large extent, or even wholly, a matter of timing. Both the soap and cement industries conform, to some extent, to this type of pattern.

A second type of example is where the alternative to merger is price agreement. In this case it may be that a merger would result in somewhat lower prices than those maintained by effective agreement. It may also be argued that efficiency would increase faster if a merger took place. However, there are pitfalls. These conclusions do not hold unless the price agreements are maintained for a considerable time and the increases in efficiency, particularly economies of scale, cannot be obtained by individual firms. These are just the type of uncertainties which have arisen and it has been found impossible to generalize about any but the most clear-cut cases.

JUDGMENTS

The effects of mergers can only be judged if they can be clearly determined and, as we have seen, there are many cases where this cannot be done sufficiently accurately. Even when it can be done there are a number of further difficulties; the most troublesome arise when there are both good and bad effects which must be weighed against each other. For example, the immediate effect of the formation of both the Calico Printers' Association and the Associated Portland Cement Manufacturers Ltd was to raise prices, and while both tended to raise efficiency in some ways, they were inefficient in others. Judgment was difficult in the case of Levers, because here again reduced competition and price maintenance were accompanied by long-run economies. Judgment is only easy in the very rare cases where there is either only one important effect or where all the effects are either good or bad. The nearest approach to this simplicity is found in the case of the Austin-Morris merger where it appears that economies of scale may be gained at the cost of very little reduction in the degree of competition.

The good and the bad effects can seldom be weighed against each other in general terms and more often assessment of the importance of the different effects depends upon what is required of the industry. For instance, if the industry is expanding, as was the cement industry during the inter-war period, the maintenance of prices at levels which cover average costs, even during periods of low demand, is much less damaging to the public interest than it is in industries which have had, like the calico printing industry, to contract; in the expanding industry, the 'excess' capacity is likely to prevent periods of very high prices. In the case of the glass industry there was immense scope for technical development, and any artificial maintenance of prices was likely to be unimportant in comparison with the reductions made possible by technical progress; in this industry the large firm with capacity to do research was desirable, whereas in the calico printing industry the large unit capable of doing research could not be justified simply on these grounds as there was relatively little basic technical development during the first thirty years of the life of the combine.

Where there is a divergence between the short-period effects and the long-period effects judgment is particularly difficult; this is partly because it is difficult to weigh a temporary disadvantage against a more-or-less permanent gain and partly because the longer the time under consideration, the less certain are the results of alternative developments. It is, for example, impossible to be sure that progress made by a combine over a period of thirty or forty years would not have been matched or even exceeded by the progress made by a number of independent firms. In general it has been found that the disadvantages of mergers relate to the short rather than to the long period, and that as a result the longer the period under consideration the more likely is the verdict to be favourable to mergers.

It has been found that the following types of development may be aided by mergers.

1. (a) Promotion of progress of techniques and efficiency; (b) promotion of efficient and rapid expansion in growing industries.

2. Elimination of inefficient firms and capacity.

3. Reduction of the wastes of imperfect competition, including the reduction of risks.

When there is considerable scope for increased efficiency in any of these ways, then it becomes more likely that a merger or series of mergers will be in the public interest.

The analysis of mergers has turned out to be extremely complicated. Theoretical discussion in terms of the particular characteristics of industries is unmanageable because there are such a large number of variables. Only in a small number of more simple cases, where one or two features are of overriding importance, is it possible to reach any definite judgment as to whether or not a merger is in the public interest. Deep-seated difficulties occur at all stages in the analysis. It is, however, those which are related to the determination of the causes of mergers which are fundamental because, as has been seen, the causes are closely related to the effects which are, in turn, closely related to judgments. Where the causes are many and their relative importance unmeasurable it is likely to be difficult to compare the situation after a merger with the possible alternative developments. Where the effects varied and each lasted for different lengths of time, judgment is difficult; where the things which need to be done to promote efficiency change over time, it is complicated still further.

The case studies have indicated that mergers are unlikely to be successful unless there are considerable economies of scale, and that they are unlikely to take place unless those economies of scale are difficult to realize in the absence of mergers. This point is of some importance because it suggests that, on the whole, mergers only take place when there are likely to be results which are in the public interest. The structure of an industry must be judged as good, if the incentives to take decisions in the public interest are strong and the incentives to take decisions less in the public interest are relatively weak. Any alteration in the structure of the industry which makes it necessary for firms to place greater emphasis upon actions which are in the public interest is an improvement.

It must be concluded that the analytical problem of the results of mergers is such that in many cases a verdict of not proven must be accepted. This is a rather negative conclusion and the case studies suggest a slight bias in favour of mergers. They indicate not only that mergers are normally associated with economies of scale and that long-period price competition is seldom stifled to any important degree, but also that the alternative situation is very rarely purely competitive. The rather complacent conclusion that mergers are not often against the public interest has no general application; each case has to be studied separately.

INDEX